The Cambridge Companion to Operetta

Those whose thoughts of musical theatre are dominated by the Broadway musical will find this book a revelation. From the 1850s to the early 1930s, when urban theatres sought to mount glamorous musical entertainment, it was to operetta that they turned. It was a form of musical theatre that crossed national borders with ease and was adored by audiences around the world. This collection of essays by an array of international scholars examines the key figures in operetta in many different countries. It offers a critical and historical study of the widespread production of operetta and of the enthusiasm with which it was welcomed. Furthermore, it challenges nationalistic views of music and approaches operetta as a compositional genre. This *Cambridge Companion* contributes to a widening appreciation of the music of operetta and a deepening knowledge of the cultural importance of operetta around the world.

ANASTASIA BELINA is Senior Research Fellow at the University of Leeds. She is author and editor of *A Musician Divided* (2013), *Die tägliche Mühe ein Mensch zu sein* (2013), *Wagner in Russia, Poland and the Czech Lands* (2013, co-edited edition) and *The Business of Opera* (2015, co-edited with Derek B. Scott). Between 2014 and 2019 she researched the reception of German operetta in Warsaw as part of an ERC-funded project. She is currently working on the BBC and AHRC project Forgotten Female Composers for which she is researching the life and work of Augusta Holmès.

DEREK B. SCOTT is Professor of Critical Musicology at the University of Leeds. His books include *Sounds of the Metropolis* (2008) and *Musical Style and Social Meaning* (2010). His musical compositions include two symphonies for brass band and an operetta, *Wilberforce*. He has also worked professionally as a singer, actor and pianist in radio, TV, concert hall and theatre. In 2014, he was awarded an Advanced Grant by the European Research Council to fund a five-year project researching the twentieth-century reception of operettas from the German stage on Broadway and in the West End.

Cambridge Companions to Music

Topics

The Cambridge Companion to Ballet
Edited by Marion Kant

The Cambridge Companion to Blues and Gospel Music
Edited by Allan Moore

The Cambridge Companion to Choral Music
Edited by André de Quadros

The Cambridge Companion to the Concerto
Edited by Simon P. Keefe

The Cambridge Companion to Conducting
Edited by José Antonio Bowen

The Cambridge Companion to Eighteenth-Century Music
Edited by Anthony R. DelDonna and Pierpaolo Polzonetti

The Cambridge Companion to Electronic Music
Edited by Nick Collins and Julio D'Escriván

The Cambridge Companion to Film Music
Edited by Mervyn Cooke and Fiona Ford

The Cambridge Companion to French Music
Edited by Simon Trezise

The Cambridge Companion to Grand Opera
Edited by David Charlton

The Cambridge Companion to Hip-Hop
Edited by Justin A. Williams

The Cambridge Companion to Jazz
Edited by Mervyn Cooke and David Horn

The Cambridge Companion to Jewish Music
Edited by Joshua S. Walden

The Cambridge Companion to the Lied
Edited by James Parsons

The Cambridge Companion to Medieval Music
Edited by Mark Everist

The Cambridge Companion to Music in Digital Culture
Edited by Nicholas Cook, Monique Ingalls and David Trippett

The Cambridge Companion to the Musical, third edition
Edited by William Everett and Paul Laird

The Cambridge Companion to Opera Studies
Edited by Nicholas Till

The Cambridge Companion to Operetta
Edited by Anastasia Belina and Derek B. Scott

The Cambridge Companion to the Orchestra
Edited by Colin Lawson

The Cambridge Companion to Percussion
Edited by Russell Hartenberger

The Cambridge Companion to Pop and Rock
Edited by Simon Frith, Will Straw and John Street

Composers

Instruments

The Cambridge Companion to

OPERETTA

....

EDITED BY

Anastasia Belina
University of Leeds

Derek B. Scott
University of Leeds

CAMBRIDGE
UNIVERSITY PRESS

CAMBRIDGE
UNIVERSITY PRESS

University Printing House, Cambridge CB2 8BS, United Kingdom

One Liberty Plaza, 20th Floor, New York, NY 10006, USA

477 Williamstown Road, Port Melbourne, VIC 3207, Australia

314–321, 3rd Floor, Plot 3, Splendor Forum, Jasola District Centre,
New Delhi – 110025, India

79 Anson Road, #06–04/06, Singapore 079906

Cambridge University Press is part of the University of Cambridge.

It furthers the University's mission by disseminating knowledge in the pursuit of
education, learning, and research at the highest international levels of excellence.

www.cambridge.org
Information on this title: www.cambridge.org/9781107182165
DOI: 10.1017/9781316856024

First published 2020

Printed in the United Kingdom by TJ International Ltd. Padstow Cornwall

A catalogue record for this publication is available from the British Library.

Library of Congress Cataloging-in-Publication Data
Names: Belina, Anastasia. | Scott, Derek B.
Title: The Cambridge companion to operetta / edited by Anastasia Belina, Derek B. Scott.
Description: Cambridge, United Kingdom ; New York, NY : Cambridge University Press,
2019. | Includes bibliographical references and index.
Identifiers: LCCN 2019018392 | ISBN 9781107182165 (alk. paper)
Subjects: LCSH: Operetta.
Classification: LCC ML1900 .C3 2019 | DDC 782.1/2–dc23
LC record available at https://lccn.loc.gov/2019018392

ISBN 978-1-107-18216-5 Hardback
ISBN 978-1-316-63334-2 Paperback

Contents

Illustrations

Tables

Music Examples

Notes on Contributors

Micaela K. Baranello is Assistant Professor of Music at the University of Arkansas. Her book in progress, *The Operetta Empire*, examines operetta in Vienna from 1900 to 1930. Her publications include 'Die lustige Witwe and the Creation of the Silver Age of Viennese Operetta' (*Cambridge Opera Journal*) and articles in the *Journal of the American Musicological Society, Opera Quarterly* and *Puccini and His World*, as well as a number of features and reviews in *The New York Times*. She has received the Mellon/ACLS Fellowship and a Fulbright study grant in Austria.

Tobias Becker is a research fellow at the German Historical Institute London where he is working on the 'nostalgia wave' during the 1970s. Before joining the GHIL he worked on popular musical theatre. Publications include *Inszenierte Moderne. Populäres Theater in Berlin and London, 1880–1930* (2014) and *Popular Musical Theatre in London and Berlin*, 1890–1939 (edited with Len Platt and David Linton, 2014).

Anastasia Belina is a senior research fellow at the School of Music, University of Leeds, where she worked with Derek B. Scott on an ERC-funded project, *German Operetta in London and New York in 1907–37: Cultural Transfer and Transformation*. She is author and editor of *A Musician Divided: André Tchaikowsky in His Own Words* (2013), *Die tägliche Mühe ein Mensch zu sein* (2013), *Wagner in Russia, Poland and the Czech Lands: Musical, Literary, and Cultural Perspectives* (2013, co-edited edition) and *The Business of Opera* (2015, co-edited with Derek B. Scott). She is also an opera director and librettist, has appeared on BBC3 and presented a documentary film *Rebel of the Keys* (2015).

Bruno Bower studied at Oriel College, Oxford; Birmingham Conservatoire and King's College London. He completed his PhD at the Royal College of Music in 2016 with a thesis on critical readings of the programme notes written by George Grove for the Crystal Palace Saturday Concerts between 1865 and 1879, illuminating the ideas and ideology surrounding music in Victorian Britain. His doctoral work was supported by a Lucy Ann Jones and a Douglas and Hilda Simmonds Award, as well as by an AHRC Doctoral Studentship. He now teaches music history and analysis modules for various colleges at Cambridge University, and music appreciation evening classes in the Centre for Languages, Culture and Communication at Imperial College London. He became a devotee of Gilbert and Sullivan through regular performances as an oboist in the orchestra for numerous productions of the Savoy Operas.

Valeria De Lucca is Associate Professor of Music at the University of Southampton. She is interested in opera and musical theatre, with particular emphasis on questions of gender and patronage, singers and systems of production in early modern Europe, and on the reception and adaptation of foreign operetta in Italy at the end of the nineteenth century. She has published articles and chapters in *The Journal of Musicology, Renaissance Studies, Early Music, The Journal of Seventeenth-Century Music* and *The Oxford Handbook of Opera* (ed. by Helen Greenwald). Her forthcoming publications include the monograph *The Politics of Princely Entertainment: Music and Spectacle in the Lives of Lorenzo Onofrio and Maria Mancini Colonna (1659–1689)* (Oxford University Press) and the collection of essays *Sound, Space and the Performance of Identity in Early Modern Rome* (co-edited with Christine Jeanneret; Routledge).

Lisa Feurzeig is Professor of Music at Grand Valley State University in Michigan. Her research is centred on text–music relations in vocal music, especially German art song, the Viennese popular theatre and Wagner's operas. In her book, *Schubert's Lieder and the Philosophy of Early German Romanticism*, she argues that Schubert created musical equivalents for complex abstract ideas in settings of Schlegel and Novalis. Her critical edition with John Sienicki, *Quodlibets of the Viennese Theater*, explores practices of musical quotation and reference. Her first operetta-focussed project is a study of political meanings in the 2004 Vienna Volksoper production of Kálmán's *Herzogin von Chicago*. She is an organizer of concerts and symposia in Hermann, Missouri, tracing aspects of German-American musical culture. As a performing singer, she has emphasized early music, lieder and music since 1900.

Stefan Frey is a writer, broadcaster, lecturer, dramaturg and director. As an assistant director at the Deutsche Schauspielhaus Hamburg, LTT Tübingen and Thüringer Landestheater Rudolstadt, he directed several productions. From 2004 to 2006 he was the head of the Studio Theatre of the Institute for Theatre Studies at Munich University; since then, he has been lecturer there and at the University of Vienna. Frey is the author of numerous articles on operetta in academic and non-academic publications, radio features and books such as *Franz Lehár oder das schlechte Gewissen der leichten Musik* (Tübingen 1995), *Was sagt ihr zu diesem Erfolg. Franz Lehár und die Unterhaltungsmusik des 20. Jahrhunderts* (Frankfurt a. M. / Leipzig 1999), *Emmerich Kálmán: Unter Tränen lachen* (Berlin 2003; English translation: Culver City 2014) and *Leo Fall. Spöttischer Rebell der Operette* (Vienna 2010).

Lynn M. Hooker is Associate Professor of Music History at Purdue University's Rueff School of Visual and Performing Arts with a courtesy appointment in the Department of History. Her book *Redefining Hungarian Music from Liszt to Bartók* was published in 2013 by Oxford University Press. She has published on music and modernism, nationalism, race and popular and folk culture in (among other places) *Musical Quarterly, Anthropology of East Europe Review, Twentieth-Century Music, Ethnomusicology* and *European Meetings in Ethnomusicology*. After beginning her scholarly career working on the history of music and culture through historical documents, she began in 2000 doing systematic fieldwork in both Europe and North America in Hungarian folk and popular music scenes, focussing on the role of Romani performers. She is currently drafting a book on the transformation of the 'Gipsy music' industry in twentieth-century Hungary, based on oral history interviews and archival research.

Matthias Kauffmann is a lecturer at the Ludwig-Maximilians-University Munich. His PhD thesis, funded with a scholarship of the Studienstiftung des deutschen Volkes, focussed on popular musical theatre in the Third Reich. In collaboration with Jens Malte Fischer, he has curated an exhibition of Gustav Mahler (Theatre Museum, Munich, 2010/11) and has also worked as an assistant director with Thalia-Theatre (Hamburg), Frankfurt Opera and the Bavarian State Opera. In 2015 he began working as a dramaturg for musical theatre at Stadttheater Gießen.

John Kenrick, an internationally recognized authority on the history of musical theatre, combines a passion for entertainment history with the practical know-how earned working on stage productions at every level from amateur to Broadway. He served as personal assistant to six Tony-winning producers, working on such Broadway productions as the Pulitzer Prize-winning *Rent*. He created the educational website Musicals101.com and has taught courses on musical theatre history at New York University's Steinhardt School, Marymount College, Philadelphia's University of the Arts and The New School University. He is the author of *Musical Theatre: A History, The Complete Idiot's Guide to Amateur Theatricals* and contributed a history of Broadway to the Carolina Academic Press textbook *Theatre Law*. He has appeared on PBS, A&E's Biography, BBC TV and radio, National Public Radio and in numerous DVD documentaries.

Raymond Knapp, Distinguished Professor of Musicology and Humanities at UCLA, has authored five books and co-edited two others, including *Symphonic Metamorphoses: Subjectivity and Alienation in Mahler's Re-Cycled Songs* (2003), *The American Musical and the Formation of National Identity* (2005; winner of the George Jean Nathan Award for Dramatic Criticism), *The American Musical and the Performance of Personal Identity* (2006) and *The Oxford Handbook of the American Musical* (2011, with Mitchell Morris and Stacy Wolf). His published essays address a wide range of additional interests, including Beethoven, Wagner, Brahms, Tchaikovsky, Mahler, nationalism, musical allusion, music and identity, camp and film music. His recent book, *Making Light* (2018), considers Haydn and American popular music in the context of German idealism.

Barrie Kosky is a director in the field of opera and theatre. As a director he is working in international houses such as Bayerische Staatsoper in Munich, The Bayreuth Festival, Glyndebourne Festival Opera, The Salzburg Festival, Teatro Real Madrid, Oper Frankfurt, The Royal Opera House, Covent Garden, the English National Opera London, Opernhaus Zürich and the Opernhaus Amsterdam, as well as at houses such as Deutsches Theater Berlin and Schauspiel Frankfurt. He was the Artistic Director of the Adelaide Festival in 1996, Artistic Co-Director of Schauspielhaus Wien from 2001 to 2005, and since 2012 he has managed Komische Oper Berlin as General Manager and Artistic Director.

Ulrich Lenz studied musicology, drama and art history in Munich, Berlin and Milan. During his stay in Italy, as correspondent for the newspaper *Die Welt*, he reported regularly on cultural events in northern Italy. He began his theatre career in the season 1997–8 as an assistant dramaturg at the State Opera, Stuttgart. In succeeding years, he worked as an opera dramaturg at theatres in Linz and Mannheim. In 2006 he became chief dramaturg of the Staatsoper, Hanover, and, since 2012, he has been chief dramaturg in Barrie Kosky's leading team at the Komische Oper, Berlin.

Pentti Paavolainen is an independent scholar who worked previously for many years as a research professor at the Theatre Academy in Helsinki. His recent work consists of a three-volume biography of the theatre and opera manager, founder of the Finnish Theatre company, Kaarlo Bergbom (research funded by the Finnish Academy and private foundations). From 2004 to 2006, he was President of the Society of Theatre Research in Finland, and he has also served two terms in office as President of the Nordic Society for Theatre Research (1995–9). His contributions to edited collections have been numerous, and his articles have been published in the journals *Nordic Theatre Studies* and *Synteesi* (Synthesis). His history of theatre in Finland is accessible on the Uniarts.fi pages.

Derek B. Scott is Professor of Critical Musicology at the University of Leeds. He researches into music, culture and ideology and, among other books, is the author of *The Singing Bourgeois* (1989, R/2001), *From the Erotic to the Demonic: On Critical Musicology* (2003), *Sounds of the Metropolis: The 19th-Century Popular Music Revolution in London, New York, Paris, and Vienna* (2008) and *German Operetta on Broadway and in the West End, 1900–1940* (Cambridge University Press, 2019). He has edited or co-edited numerous books, including *The Ashgate Research Companion to Popular Musicology* (2009) and *Confronting the National in the Musical Past* (2018). He has written numerous articles in which he has been at the forefront in identifying changes of critical perspective in the socio-cultural study of music.

Jan Smaczny is well known as an authority on many aspects of Czech music. As an academic he has taught at the universities of Oxford, Birmingham and Queen's Belfast, where he is Emeritus Professor of Music. His publications include a book on Dvořák's B Minor cello concerto (Cambridge University Press, 1999) and edited collections of essays on Irish Music (*Music in Nineteenth-Century Ireland*, Four Courts Press, 2007) and Bach's B minor-Mass (*Exploring Bach's B minor Mass*, Cambridge University Press, 2013). Much of his work has been based on archival research into the operatic repertoire of the Prague Provisional and Czech National Theatres. Of particular relevance to the present project is his book, *The Daily Repertoire of the Prague Provisional Theatre* (Prague, 1994) an extensively annotated catalogue of operas and operettas performed in the theatre and 'Grand Opera in the Czech Lands' (in David Charlton ed., *The Cambridge Companion to Grand Opera*, Cambridge University Press, 2003).

Christopher Webber is an actor, stage director and writer, and a leading authority on Spanish Zarzuela. His book *The Zarzuela Companion* (Scarecrow Press, 2002, with foreword by Plácido Domingo) is the standard English-language reference work on the genre. A major contributor to the *Oxford Companion to Music* (Oxford University Press, 2002), he wrote and edited many entries on Iberian and Ibero-American genres, composers and countries. As Editor in Chief since 1997 of the internet portal *zarzuela.net*, he has published many articles and reviews on Spanish lyric theatre, and he is a regular, wide-ranging contributor to *Opera* magazine. Webber has lectured and published on zarzuela for international symposia at the Universities of Sheffield (UK), Tübingen (Germany), Oviedo and Valencia (Spain) and has directed and performed zarzuela in London's West End, as well as adapting two zarzuelas for Santa Fé Opera. He also serves on the theatre and music panels of the *Dictionary of National Biography*.

Avra Xepapadakou is a lecturer at the Department of Philology, Division of Theatre and Music Studies, University of Crete, where she teaches history of theatre and opera. Her research interests focus on nineteenth-century theatre, music and cultural life. She has published articles and papers on topics such as the relations between Italian and Ionian opera, the question of westernization/orientalism in modern Greek theatre and art music, the foreign opera troupes touring in nineteenth-century south-eastern Europe and the Orient and the invasion of operetta on the modern Greek stage. The subject of her recent book is the Ionian opera composer Pavlos (Paolo) Carrer (Athens, 2013). She is the project leader of the research project 'Archivio', concerning the theatre archive of Romeo Castellucci and the Socìetas Raffaello Sanzio. In the spring of 2015 (February–May) she conducted research at the California State University, Sacramento, and recently she was granted a research visitorship from the Balzan Musicology 2012 Programme *Towards a Global History of Music* (2015–16).

Chronology, 1855–1950

Sources include the *Zeittafel* in Bernard Grun, *Kulturgeschichte der Operette* (Munich: Langen Müller Verlag, 1961), 552–63; the chronology in Ewen, *European Light Opera*, 263–7; Bernard Grun, *The Timetables of History: A Horizontal Linkage of People and Events* (New York: Simon and Schuster, new edition 1979); Hywell Williams, *Cassell's Chronology of World History: Dates, Events and Ideas that Made History* (London: Weidenfeld & Nicolson, 2005), and Music and History http://musicandhistory.com/.

1855   Alexander II becomes Tsar of Russia. *Leaves of Grass*, Walt Whitman. *Les deux aveugles* and *Ba-ta-clan*, Offenbach.

1856   Crimean War ends. Sigmund Freud born. *Les Contemplations*, Hugo. *Le financier et le savetier*, Offenbach. Schumann dies.

1857   Siege of Delhi. *Madame Bovary*, Flaubert. *Le mariage aux lanternes*, Offenbach.

1858   Arthur Sullivan studies in Leipzig. Covent Garden opera house is built. *Orphée aux enfers*, Offenbach.

1859   Victor Herbert born. *On the Origin of Species*, Darwin. *A Tale of Two Cities,* Dickens. *Faust*, Gounod. *Geneviève de Brabant*, Offenbach.

1860   End of Second Opium War (China); Victor Emmanuel proclaimed king of Italy. *Das Pensionat*, Suppé (first Viennese operetta).

1861   Abraham Lincoln is President of the USA; outbreak of US Civil War. The emancipation of Russian serfs is completed. *Great Expectations*, Dickens. *La Chanson de Fortunio*, Offenbach.

1862   Bismarck becomes prime minister of Prussia. Austrian botanist Ludwig Ritter von Köchel catalogues Mozart's compositions. Anton Rubinstein founds St Petersburg Conservatoire. The first Monte Carlo gambling casino opens in Monaco. *Fathers and Sons*, Turgenev. *La forza del destino*, Verdi. *Bavard et bavarde*, Offenbach.

1863   Emancipation Proclamation issued by Lincoln. World's first underground railway opens in London (The London Underground). The Football Association is established in London and draws up the rules for the game. First instalment of *War and Peace* by Leo Tolstoy published. *Lischen et Frizchen*, Offenbach.

1864   Marx founds First International Workingmen's Association. *Notes from the Underground,* Dostoyevsky; *Voyage au centre de la terre,* Jules Verne. Millöcker is Kapellmeister in Graz. Ku Klux Klan

(KKK) is formed in Pulaski, Tennessee. *Alice's Adventures in Wonderland,* Lewis Carroll. *La belle Hélène,* Offenbach.

1865 End of American Civil War. *Tristan und Isolde,* Richard Wagner. *Die schöne Galathée,* Franz von Suppé.

1866 Austro-Prussian War. Cretan Revolt. Paul Lincke born. Travel agent Thomas Cook offers its first organized tours to the USA. Moscow Conservatoire is founded by Nicholas Rubinstein. *Crime and Punishment* and *The Gambler,* Dostoyevsky. *Barbe-bleue* and *La vie parisienne,* Offenbach; *Les chevaliers de la table ronde,* Hervé; *Leichte Kavallerie,* Suppé.

1867 Paris World Exposition. The USA buys Alaska from Russia for $7,200,200. *Peer Gynt,* Ibsen; *Thérèse Raquin,* Zola. *La Grande-Duchesse de Gérolstein,* Offenbach. Granados born.

1868 Shogunate abolished in Japan. Spanish Revolution. The game of badminton invented in Gloucester. *Die Meistersinger,* Wagner. *La Périchole,* Offenbach.

1869 Opening of the Suez Canal. The National Woman Suffrage Association is established in the USA. The first college for women is founded at Cambridge University (Girton College). Rickshaw invented in Japan. *The Idiot,* Dostoyevsky. The first performance of Wagner's *Das Rheingold* in Munich. *Les brigands,* Offenbach; *Le petit Faust,* Hervé. Berlioz dies.

1870 Franco-Prussian War. Franz Lehár and Oscar Straus born. *Vingt mille lieues sous les mers,* Jules Verne. Dickens dies.

1871 Paris Commune. The Royal Albert Hall opens in London. The German Second Reich. Stanley finds Livingstone in East Africa. Johann Strauss Jr visits the USA. *Aida,* Giuseppe Verdi, premiered at the newly built Cairo Opera House. *Indigo und die 40 Räuber,* Strauss.

1872 World Peace Jubilee, Boston. Japan's first railway opens, built by British engineers. James Abbott McNeill Whistler paints *Arrangement in Grey and Black No 1: Portrait of the Painter's Mother. La fille de Madame Angot,* Charles Lecocq.

1873 Crash of the Vienna Stock Exchange in May. Leo Fall born. *Une Saison en enfer,* Arthur Rimbaud; *Le tour du monde en quatre-vingts jours,* Jules Verne. *La veuve du Malabar,* Hervé.

1874 The first Remington typewriter is sold. First impressionist exhibition, Paris. *Boris Godunov,* Mussorgsky; *Die Fledermaus,* Johann Strauss. *Giroflé-Girofla,* Lecocq; *El barberillo,* Barbieri.

1875 Uprising against Ottoman rule in Bosnia and Herzegovina. The Paris Opera House, designed by Charles Garnier, is completed, where Bizet's *Carmen* is premiered. Piano Concerto No. 1 in B flat minor, Tchaikovsky. *Trial by Jury*, Gilbert and Sullivan.

1876   Japan recognizes Korea's independence from China. Bayreuth Festival opens. *The Adventures of Tom Sawyer,* Mark Twain; *Daniel Deronda,* George Eliot. Offenbach in the USA. *Fatinitza,* Suppé. Manuel de Falla born.

1877   Russo-Turkish War. Queen Victoria proclaimed Empress of India. *Anna Karenina,* Leo Tolstoy. *Swan Lake,* Tchaikovsky. *Les cloches de Corneville*, Robert Planquette.

1878   Congress of Berlin. *H.M.S. Pinafore,* Gilbert and Sullivan; *Madame Favart*, Offenbach.

1879   Zulu War. Frank Winfield Woolworth opens the store where everything costs 5 cents. Albert Einstein born. *Eugene Onegin,* Tchaikovsky. Gilbert and Sullivan in the USA. *Boccaccio,* Suppé; *Gräfin Dubarry*, Millöcker; *The Pirates of Penzance*, Gilbert and Sullivan.

1880   Disraeli resigns and Gladstone becomes prime minister for a second time. The game of table tennis is invented. Robert Stolz born. Victor Herbert is a cellist in the Strauss Orchestra. *Nana,* Zola. *L'Arbre de Noël,* Lecocq. Flaubert and Offenbach die.

1881   Alexander II is assassinated and is succeeded by his son, Alexander III. Boston Symphony Orchestra is founded. Electric lighting in the Savoy Theatre, London. *Der lustige Krieg*, Strauss. *Patience, or Bunthorne's Bride,* Gilbert and Sullivan. Mussorgsky and Nicholas Rubinstein die.

1882   Robert Koch discovers that tuberculosis is a communicable disease. *Parsifal,* Wagner. Emmerich Kálmán born. *Der Bettelstudent*, Millöcker; *Iolanthe*, Gilbert and Sullivan.

1883   Metropolitan Opera House opens. Brooklyn Bridge opens. *Eine Nacht in Venedig,* Strauss; *Mam'zelle Nitouche*, Hervé. Wagner dies.

1884   Paul Nipkow's invention of rotating scanning devices anticipates development of television technology. Ralph Benatzky born. *Princess Ida,* Gilbert and Sullivan; *Gasparone*, Millöcker.

1885   Fingerprint identification system is invented. A bicycle with two wheels of the same size is developed in France. The Boston Pops Orchestra is formed and gives the first concert of light classical music. Eduard Künneke, Jerome Kern and Alban Berg born. *Germinal,* Zola. *Der Zigeunerbaron*, Strauss; *The Mikado*, Gilbert and Sullivan.

1886   Gladstone introduces Irish Home Rule Bill. Coca Cola is invented as a headache and hangover cure. Liszt dies. *Le Baiser* (sculpture), Auguste Rodin. *La Gran Vía*, Chueca.

1887 Queen Victoria's Golden Jubilee. Esperanto is invented. *Otello*, Verdi. *Ruddigore*, Gilbert and Sullivan; *Ali-Baba*, Lecocq.

1888 Dunlop invents the pneumatic tyre. Irving Berlin born. *The Sunflowers*, Vincent Van Gogh. *The Yeomen of the Guard*, Gilbert and Sullivan.

1889 Eiffel Tower opens as entrance to the World Exposition in Paris where *Ode triomphale en l'honneur du centenaire de 1789* by Augusta Holmès is premiered by 1,200 performers. *Three Men in a Boat*, Jerome K. Jerome. *Les Bourgeois de Calais*, Rodin. *The Gondoliers*, Gilbert and Sullivan.

1890 First Japanese general election. Electric chair is introduced in New York state as a 'humane alternative' to hanging. Paul Whiteman born. *Frühlings Erwachen* (*Spring Awakening*), Frank Wedekind. *Sleeping Beauty* and *Queen of Spades*, Tchaikovsky; *Cavalleria rusticana*, Pietro Mascagni. *L'Égyptienne*, Lecocq.

1891 Formation of the Young Turk Movement. The first advertising agency is founded in New York. A telephone link is established between London and Paris. Carnegie Hall opens in New York. The first electric oven for domestic use is sold in the USA. *Hedda Gabler*, Ibsen; *The Picture of Dorian Gray*, Oscar Wilde. *Der Vogelhändler*, Zeller.

1892 Pan-Slav Conference, Kraków. Paul Abraham born. *The Adventures of Sherlock Holmes*, Sir Arthur Conan Doyle; *The Diary of a Nobody*, George and Weedon Grossmith. *The Nutcracker*, Tchaikovsky; *Werther*, Massenet.

1893 World Exposition, Chicago. Wall Street market crash is followed by a four-year depression. The first cultured pearl is produced in Japan. Ivor Novello and Cole Porter born. *The Scream*, Edvard Munch. *Hänsel und Gretel*, Engelbert Humperdinck; Symphony No. 6 in E minor (*Pathétique*), Tchaikovsky.

1894 Tsar Alexander III dies and is succeeded by his son Nicholas II. First motorcycle (Hilldebrand & Wolfmüller, Munich). *Arms and the Man*, Shaw; *The Jungle Book*, Rudyard Kipling. *Der Obersteiger*, Zeller. *La verbena de la Paloma*, Bretón.

1895 Gillette invents the safety razor. The first American pizzeria opens in New York. Oscar Wilde is sentenced to two years' hard labour for 'gross indecency' (homosexual behaviour). Brothers Lumière stage the first public screening of a motion picture in Paris. The first commercial screening of a four-minute film of a boxing match in New York. Henry Wood conducts the first of the annual Promenade Concerts ('Proms') in London. *Waldmeister*, Strauss; *The Wizard of the Nile*, Herbert. Suppé dies.

1896   Marconi invents the wireless telegraph. *Daily Mail* is founded. The Tate Gallery opens in London. *The Seagull,* Chekhov. *The Geisha,* Sidney Jones. Bruckner dies.

1897   Famine in India. Discovery of the electron. *La Bohème,* Giacomo Puccini. *The Stars and Stripes Forever,* Sousa. *The Belle of New York,* Gustave Kerker. Brahms dies. *La revoltosa,* Chapi.

1898   Construction of Paris métro begins. Stanislavsky founds Moscow Arts Theatre. George Gershwin and Vincent Youmans born. *Véronique,* André Messager; *Der Opernball,* Heuberger; *The Fortune Teller,* Herbert. Spanish–American War.

1899   Boer War. Global cholera pandemic starts. Aspirin is developed. *Uncle Vanya,* Chekhov; *Resurrection,* Leo Tolstoy. *Frau Luna,* Lincke; *Die Landstreicher,* Ziehrer. Johann Strauss and Suppé die.

1900   Paris métro opens. First Mercedes car. Kurt Weill born. Isaak Dunayevsky born. *Tosca,* Puccini. Arthur Sullivan dies.

1901   The Commonwealth of Australia established. Queen Victoria dies. Marconi transmits the first transatlantic wireless signals. First Nobel prizes are awarded. *Buddenbrooks,* Thomas Mann. *The Toreador,* Caryll. Verdi dies.

1902   Caruso's first acoustic recordings. Richard Rodgers born. *Imperialism,* J. A. Hobson. *Merrie England,* Edward German; *The Duchess of Dantzic,* Caryll.

1903   The Russian Social Democratic Labour Party splits into Menshevik and Bolshevik factions. Severe anti-Jewish pogroms begin in Russia. Emmeline Pankhurst founds the Women's Social and Political Union. First successful aeroplane flight by the Wright brothers. *The Cherry Orchard,* Chekhov. *Bruder Straubinger,* Eysler; *Babes in Toyland,* Herbert. Planquette and Whistler die.

1904   Japanese–Russian War. The Trans-Siberian Railway opens. First radio transmission of music in Graz, Austria. Picasso's 'pink period' begins with his arrival in Paris. *Madama Butterfly,* Puccini. *Die lustigen Nibelungen,* Straus. Chekhov dies.

1905   'Bloody Sunday' in Russia provokes a series of revolutionary outbursts. A treaty of separation between Sweden and Norway is signed. Einstein's theory of relativity. *Salome,* Richard Strauss. *Die lustige Witwe,* Lehár.

1906   Opening of Simplon rail tunnel between Switzerland and Italy. *Tausend und eine Nacht,* Strauss, arr. Reiterer. Cézanne dies.

1907   First mass march by suffragettes in London. Women are given the right to vote in Norway. Florenz Ziegfeld's revue *Follies of 1907* starts a new vogue for the slim figure as a model for female fashion.

Ein Walzertraum, Straus; *Der fidele Bauer*, Fall; *Die Dollarprinzessin*, Fall.

1908   Model T Ford car. Two-sided phonograph record discs are invented. *Der tapfere Soldat*, Straus; *Die geschiedene Frau*, Fall. *The Kiss*, Gustav Klimt.

1909   Freud gives lectures in the USA on psychoanalysis. The Victoria and Albert Museum opens in London. *Elektra*, R. Strauss. *Ein Herbstmanöver*, Kálmán; *Der Graf von Luxemburg*, Lehár; *The Arcadians*, Talbot and Mockton.

1910   *Traité de radioactivité*, Marie Curie. *The Firebird*, Stravinsky. *Zigeunerliebe*, Lehár; *Die keusche Susanne*, Jean Gilbert; *Naughty Marietta*, Herbert. Leo Tolstoy dies.

1911   Famine causes mass starvation in Russia. Revolution in China. 'Alexander's Ragtime Band', Berlin; *Der Rosenkavalier*, R. Strauss. *Eva*, Lehár. Mahler dies.

1912   Sinking of the Titanic. *Pierrot Lunaire*, Schoenberg. *Der Zigeunerprimas*, Kálmán; *Der liebe Augustin*, Fall; *Der lila Domino*, Cuvillier. *La generala*, Vives.

1913   Balkan War. Grand Central Station is completed in New York. *Man with a Guitar*, Picasso. *Le sacre du printemps*, Stravinsky. *Endlich allein*, Lehár; *Die Kino-Königin*, Gilbert; *Polenblut*, Nedbal; *Sweethearts*, Herbert; *La vida breve*, Falla.

1914   World War I commences. Concert of noise music in Milan given by Luigi Russolo. *Dubliners* and *A Portrait of the Artist as a Young Man*, James Joyce. *Rund um die Liebe*, Straus.

1915   Torpedo sinks the Lusitania. Absinthe is outlawed in France. In the USA, the millionth Ford car is produced. *Die Csárdásfürstin*, Kálmán; *Die Kaiserin*, Fall.

1916   Easter Rising, Dublin. *Die Rose von Stambul*, Fall; *Das Dreimäderlhaus*, Berté/Schubert; *Chu Chin Chow*, Asche and Norton.

1917   Russian Revolution. *Schwarzwaldmädel*, Leon Jessel; *The Maid of the Mountains*, Harold Fraser-Simson.

1918   End of World War I, but there is worldwide deadly influenza pandemic from January 1918 to December 1920. Leonard Bernstein born. Lecocq dies. *Wo die Lerche singt*, Lehár; *Phi-Phi*, Christiné.

1919   Spartacist Uprising, Germany. *Das Dorf ohne Glocke*, Kunneke; *Die Frau im Hermelin*, Gilbert; *Monsieur Beaucaire*, Messager; *La La Lucille*, Gershwin.

1920   League of Nations established. *Das Hollandweibchen*, Kálmán; *Die blaue Mazur*, Lehár; *Der letzte Walzer*, Straus; *Sally*, Kern.

1921   BBC founded. First regular radio programmes begin in USA. *Der Tanz ins Glück*, Stolz; *Der Vetter aus Dingsda*, Künneke; *Die Bajadere*, Kálmán; *Blossom Time*, Romberg.

1922   Creation of Irish Free State. Mussolini becomes Italian Prime Minister. *Frasquita*, Lehár; *Madame Pompadour*, Fall.

1923   Value of German mark drops severely. *Die Perlen der Cleopatra*, Straus; *Mädi*, Stolz; *Katja, die Tänzerin*, Gilbert; *Ciboulette*, Hahn; *Doña Francisquita*, Vives.

1924   Herbert and Puccini die. *Gräfin Mariza*, Kálmán; *Rose-Marie*, Rudolf Friml; *The Student Prince*, Sigmund Romberg; *Lady Be Good*, Gershwin.

1925   Fall dies. *Der Orlow*, Granichstaedten; *Paganini*, Lehár; *No, No, Nanette*, Youmans.

1926   General Strike, UK. *Muskrat Ramble*, first of Armstrong's Hot Five recordings. *Die Zirkusprinzessin*, Kálmán; *The Desert Song*, Romberg; *Oh Kay!*, Gershwin.

1927   *Der Zarewitsch*, Lehár; *Die gold'ne Meisterin*, Eysler; *A Connecticut Yankee*, Rodgers; *Funny Face*, Gershwin; *Show Boat*, Kern.

1928   Fleming discovers penicillin. Gershwin in Vienna. *Friederike*, Lehár; *Die Herzogin von Chicago*, Kálmán; *Die Dreigroschenoper*, Weill; *The New Moon*, Romberg; *Casanova*, Benatzky/Strauss.

1929   Wall Street Crash. *Das Land des Lächelns*, Lehár; *Strike up the Band*, Gershwin; *Bitter Sweet*, Noël Coward.

1930   *Viktoria und ihr Husar*, Abraham; *Im weißen Rössl*, Benatzky; *Schön ist die Welt*, Lehár; *Walzer aus Wien*, Strauss/Korngold/Bittner; *Die Drei von der Tankstelle* (film operetta), Heymann.

1931   *Die Blume von Hawai*, Abraham; *Of Thee I Sing*, Gershwin; *Die Dubarry*, Millöcker, arr. Mackeben; *Der Kongress tanzt* (film operetta), Heymann.

1932   Famine in USSR. *Ball im Savoy*, Abraham; *Glückliche Reise*, Künneke; *Wenn die kleinen Veilchen blühn*, Stolz; *Eine Frau, die weiss, was sie will*, Straus; *Gay Divorce*, Cole Porter.

1933   Hitler becomes Chancellor. *Clivia*, Dostal; *Zwei Herzen in Dreivierteltakt*, Stolz; *Let 'em Eat Cake*, Gershwin.

1934   Mosley holds Fascist mass meetings in UK. *Giuditta*, Lehár; *Anything Goes*, Porter; *Conversation Piece*, Coward.

1935   *Porgy and Bess*, Gershwin; *Drei Walzer*, Strauss/Straus; *Glamorous Night*, Novello; *Der Kuhhandel*, Weill.

1936   Spanish Civil War. BBC television service begins. *Careless Rapture*, Novello; *Johnny Johnson*, Weill; *On Your Toes*, Rodgers; *Kaiserin Josephine*, Kálmán; *La tabernera del puerto*, Sorozábal.

1937   Gershwin dies. *Polnische Hochzeit*, Beer; *Die Maske in Blau*, Raymond; *The Cradle Will Rock*, Marc Blitzstein; *Crest of the Wave*, Novello; *Babes in Arms*, Rodgers.

1938   Austrian Anschluss. *Saison in Salzburg*, Raymond; *The Boys from Syracuse*, Rodgers; *Operette*, Coward.

1939   World War II commences. *Die ungarische Hochzeit*, Dostal; *The Dancing Years*, Novello.

1940   Trotsky assassinated in Mexico. *Die Geigerin von Wien*, Steinbrecher; *Ein Liebestraum*, Lincke.

1941   Bombing of Pearl Harbor. *Quatuor pour le fin du temps*, Messiaen. *Traumland*, Künneke; *Lady in the Dark*, Weill.

1942   Mass extermination of Jews by Nazis using gas chambers. Symphony No. 7, 'Leningrad', Shostakovich. *Hochzeitsnacht im Paradies*, Schröder; *Black, el pavaso*, Sorozábal.

1943   Warsaw ghetto massacre. *Oklahoma!*, Rodgers and Hammerstein; *One Touch of Venus*, Weill.

1944   D-Day landings in Normandy. *On the Town*, Bernstein.

1945   Nuclear bombing of Hiroshima and Nagasaki. World War II ends; Nuremberg trials begin; United Nations established. Kern and Youmans die. *Perchance to Dream*, Novello; *Carousel*, Rodgers.

1946   Peace conference attended by twenty-one nations in Paris. Lincke dies. *Annie Get Your Gun*, Berlin.

1947   Partition of India into two independent states. *Brigadoon*, Lerner and Loewe; *Street Scene*, Weill.

1948   Gandhi assassinated. Lehár dies. *Kiss Me, Kate*, Porter.

1949   Communist People's Republic proclaimed in China. *South Pacific*, Rodgers and Hammerstein; *King's Rhapsody*, Novello.

1950   Protests in Johannesburg against apartheid. Weill dies. *Call Me Madam*, Berlin; *Guys and Dolls*, Loesser; *Feuerwerk*, Burkhardt.

Introduction

ANASTASIA BELINA AND DEREK B. SCOTT

No musical form has acquired such a disparate collection of admirers and detractors as operetta. Nietzsche tried writing it, Turgenev wrote libretti for four and even acted in one, Stanislavski thought it was 'artistic' and produced it, Nemirovich-Danchenko directed and produced it, Hitchcock filmed it, Adorno scorned it although he was not entirely averse to some of Leo Fall's and Oscar Straus's works, Stalin and Hitler loved it, Rachmaninov admired it, Zola wanted it eradicated, Shostakovich was fascinated by it and composed one, even Mozart composed a stage work that is deemed to be its predecessor, and box offices thrived on it. Operetta was a global success, a democratic genre that was indiscriminate about whom were its patrons.

This *Companion* does not pretend to be all-embracing in its coverage of operetta. The editors were keen to place an emphasis on the production and reception of operetta in different countries and to examine its travels as an important form of cultural transfer. That said, the coverage is not all-inclusive, and, for example, it disappoints the editors that Croatia has been neglected, despite a thriving operetta culture that included composers such as Ivan Zajc and Srecko Albini. It is important, however, to be aware that specific national traditions rarely occupy centre stage in operetta, and there is much that is cosmopolitan in its music and in its networks of transcultural exchange, which reached around the world. For instance, a variety of Australian touring companies (often sharing members) visited New Zealand, India, Hong Kong, Jakarta, Yangon, Singapore and Shanghai in the 1870s. In July 1879, Howard Vernon's Royal English Opera Company gave performances of Offenbach's *The Grand Duchess of Gerolstein* and Lecocq's *The Daughter of Madame Angot* at the Gaiety Theatre, Yokohama, Japan, and excerpts of the former were interpolated into a westernized kabuki play at the Shintomi-za theatre in Tokyo.[1]

Operetta scholarship, in all its domains – historical and analytical, editing and performance – has been growing in the past dozen years. In 2015 Bettina Brandl-Risi, Ulrich Lenz, Clemens Risi and Rainer Simon edited *Kunst der Oberfläche*, a collection of essays that came out of a symposium on operetta held at the Komische Oper in Berlin.[2] Further evidence of new academic interest in the history of operetta and popular lyric theatre is provided by *Musical Theatre in Europe 1830–1945*

(Turnhout: Brepols, 2017), edited by Michela Niccolai and Clair Rowden. It is a wide-ranging survey of diverse forms of musical theatre in Europe, but the editors hold that operetta and its derivatives took centre stage. It contains informative chapters on Offenbach's operettas, Viennese operetta, English operetta and musical comedy, and Italian operetta, and includes case studies of operetta in Croatia, Portugal and Spain.

New research is not confined to remedying the neglect that fell over silver-age operetta, it is also focussing on major figures of the nineteenth century and reassessing their output. For example, no longer are the closing years of the career of Johann Strauss Jr seen as evidence of diminishing creative energy. The release of a world premiere recording of his last operetta *Die Göttin der Vernunft* (The Goddess of Reason) in 2011 demonstrated that it is a rich and significant work.[3] What the editors of the present volume feel has been most neglected, hitherto, is the extent to which operetta became, by the second decade of the twentieth century, part of the cultural mainstream in larger cities around the world. The chapters that follow offer examples of wide-ranging operetta scholarship in the twenty-first century and expound the arguments of an international selection of academics who have taken a special interest in this genre. There already exist broad surveys of a cataloguing and descriptive nature by Mark Lubbock and Robert Letellier, which may be consulted usefully in tandem with the present book.[4] In addition, there are condensed histories of operetta, among which those by Richard Traubner and Andrew Lamb are recommended.[5]

The editors regret that there is no chapter in this volume on Yiddish operetta. Scholarly interest has grown remarkably in recent years, but the editors searched in vain to find someone to contribute on this subject. In the early twentieth century, Yiddish theatre was very popular, especially in New York, where immigrants from eastern Europe arrived in large numbers during this period. Joseph Rumshinsky's 1923 Yiddish operetta *Di goldene Kale* (The Golden Bride), edited by Michael Ochs, was published in 2017 in the American Musicological Society's MUSA series. The score was found in the Harvard Music Library, and the orchestral parts were in a manuscript collection deposited by Rumshinsky's relatives at UCLA. In December 2015 the operetta ran for a month, performed by the National Yiddish Theatre Folksbiene, at the Edmond J. Safra Hall, New York, and received two Drama Desk Award nominations for outstanding revival of a musical and outstanding director of a musical. It was revived again, Off-Broadway, in summer 2016.

The reader will notice in the pages that follow the scanty treatment of a small number of Broadway composers, whose stage works are often called operettas, or considered akin to operettas.[6] The reason for this apparent neglect is that they have already found a place in the *Cambridge Companion to the Musical* (Victor Herbert, pp. 31–4; Reginald de Koven, pp. 34–5; Jerome Kern, pp. 44–5; Rudolf Friml and Sigmund Romberg, pp. 48–56).[7] That *Companion* did not, however, feature composers of musical comedy of the late Victorian and Edwardian eras, and so the reader will find Sidney Jones, Ivan Caryll, Lionel Monckton and others in the present book. Nevertheless, some brief overlaps between these *Cambridge Companions* remain, which for the most part result from the inevitable disagreements that arise when deciding whether a particular piece is best served by being called an operetta or a musical.

Part of that confusion is created by the tendency of producers and theatre owners to choose a label that primarily suits their marketing strategy. Sometimes, other considerations come into play: Gilbert and Sullivan opted to use the description 'comic opera' because it carried stronger connotations of artistry and moral respectability than did 'operetta'. The definitional lines of operetta are blurred, and all sorts of nuanced meaning may come into play when we are confronted with terms such as *opéra bouffe*, comic opera, operetta, musical comedy and musical play, but the crucial factor that separates all these genre descriptions from the high-status term 'opera' is that they denote music of the commercial theatre. With the influential stage works of Jacques Offenbach (1819–80), this music developed its own characteristic features, making it a third type of music to be distinguished from that of the concert tradition on one side, and folk music on the other. 'Opera' remained a high-status term until the advent of rock operas in the 1960s.

Bernard Grun claims that the label 'operetta' (in its French form, *opérette*) was first used for Offenbach's *La rose de Saint-Flour*.[8] That operetta was first performed at the Salle Lacaze, Paris, on 12 June 1856, and contained three characters only, owing to the legal restrictions under which the composer was permitted to present stage works at this time. The word 'operetta' was not unknown before this, but it was usually in reference to the qualities of short duration and mundane content. Schilling's *Universal-Lexicon* of 1837 defines operetta as 'a smaller opera that either lasts a shorter time in performance, or takes its content from ordinary life, dealing with it lightly and, instead of high-status characters, containing those easily comprehensible and easily found'.[9] This definition is contradicted by the content and character of operettas of the second half of the nineteenth century, from *Orpheus in the Underworld* (1858) on. Most significantly, in Schilling's description there is no mention of musical style, and yet, within a couple of decades, operetta would begin to be marked above all by its musical readiness to be part of the burgeoning market for entertainment music. In theatres, salons and dance halls, new styles of music were developing, creating a growing schism between what was considered entertainment and what merited the designation 'serious art'. The music of operetta was to be characterized as the aesthetic opposite of 'serious music'; it was 'light music' (in the sense of lightweight or easy music). In this sense, the label 'operetta' bears no more relationship to the past than Beethoven's Pastoral Symphony does to Handel's Pastoral Symphony (even though musical pastoral conventions are found in both). One of the first attempts to write a critical history of operetta was made by Erich Urban in 1903, who argues that it has its own justification, meaning and history as a genre, and recognizes that a common thread links operetta in various European countries (including Spain) to the early stage works of Offenbach.[10]

The Théâtre des Bouffes-Parisiens, which Offenbach founded in 1855, has been described as a kind of 'experimental lab' for French operetta, and it was an influence on theatrical entertainment in cities such as Vienna, London and St Petersburg.[11] A song from scene 4 of Jacques Offenbach's early *opérette-bouffe, Le financier et le savetier* (1856) demonstrates the new third type of musical style that is neither folk nor classical. The song, titled 'Fable', has a refrain designed by both lyricist Hector Crémieux and the composer to be both simple and irritatingly memorable. However, the simplicity it possesses is not that of a rustic song or dance. Its words and its music have been carefully polished by professionals. Its very triviality is carefully constructed to be a source of fun. The style is what one might call sophisticatedly trite: the falling chromatic semitones and the play on words demonstrate this (see Example 0.1). The cobbler of this fable works in a basement; hence, the repetitions of 'cave' (basement or cellar) shouted by his neighbours appear to make sense; therefore, we feel both tricked and amused when we finally hear this word as the beginning of the question, '*qu'avez vous ?*' (what's up with you?)

Operetta, as a new form of urban entertainment, first flourished in Second Empire Paris. Siegfried Kracauer describes French society in this period as 'exclusively a town product', and argues that Paris was uniquely placed as a city in which were present 'all the elements, material and verbal, that made operetta possible'.[12] It was a time of financial speculation and dreams of sudden fortune but also of political repression – a combination that fed a desire for high-spirited entertainment, especially among those of the bourgeoisie who were enjoying increased affluence. Kracauer identifies the new bohemians of the Second Empire as those to whom Offenbach's operettas principally appealed. They constituted a less exclusive social stratum than those before the revolution of 1848. They were part of the bourgeoisie and had money to spend yet were keen to distance themselves

Example 0.1 'Fable' from *Le financier et le savetier*, lyrics by H. Crémieux, music by J. Offenbach

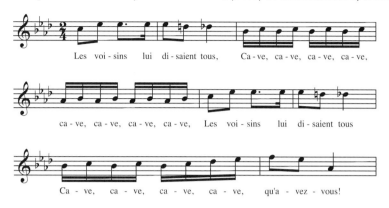

Les voi-sins lui di-saient tous, Ca-ve, ca-ve, ca-ve, ca-ve,

ca-ve, ca-ve, ca-ve, ca-ve, Les voi-sins lui di-saient tous

Ca-ve, ca-ve, ca-ve, ca-ve, qu'a-vez-vous!

from staid bourgeois manners, relishing, instead, the mockery, satire, bacchanalia and frivolity of operetta.[13]

Unlike 'serious' opera, which prefers historical and mythological subject matter, operetta has often chosen to engage with the contemporary and modern. Even an apparently mythological theme does not rule out contemporary allusion. Offenbach's *Orphée aux enfers*, for instance, contains a character named Public Opinion, after a phrase that had come to popularity in the 1850s, when this *opéra bouffe* was written. It also quotes *La Marseillaise* when the gods revolt against Jupiter. In the first two decades of the twentieth century, it was common for operettas to embrace or relate to features of modernity, such as trains, city restaurants, cinemas and so forth. They also related to social and moral issues linked to the development of a capitalist economy (as in Leo Fall's *Die Dollarprinzessin*).

Operetta thrived for a period of eighty years, from 1855 (the year Offenbach first leased a theatre in Paris) to 1935 (when many Jewish artists who were involved in all aspects of operetta production had either fled Nazi Germany or were no longer able to work under the Goebbels regime). The second half of the nineteenth century is often referred to as the golden age of operetta, but its glitter began to fade at the *fin de siècle*. The silver age of operetta is usually thought of as the thirty-year period that followed the revitalizing effect of the novel and immensely successful *Merry Widow* (first performed in Vienna in December 1905). The first flowering of operetta of the Offenbachian type in Vienna was seen in the stage works of Franz von Suppé (1819–95), who began as an emulator of Offenbach. Between 1858 and 1870, forty-six operettas by Offenbach were produced in Vienna.[14] Johann Strauss Jr (1825–99) and Carl Millöcker (1842–99) began to lend a more Viennese character to operetta, the former leaning heavily on his own social dance music. In London, W. S. Gilbert (1836–

1911) and Arthur Sullivan (1842–1900) were at first indebted to Offenbach (and his frequent librettists Henri Meilhac and Ludovic Halévy), but they were also aware of what was happening in Vienna. The kiss duet from Suppé's *Die schöne Galathée* (1863), for example, pre-dates 'This Is What I'll Never Do', the kiss duet in *The Mikado* (1885). *The Grand Duchess of Gerolstein* was produced at Covent Garden in 1867, but it was *Geneviève de Brabant* at Islington Philharmonic music hall in 1871 that started the Offenbach craze in London. It ran for more than a year and turned that music hall into 'the rendezvous of fashionable London'.[15] The USA took to Offenbach also, and he toured there in 1876. However, it was another musician from overseas, Victor Herbert, who settled in New York in 1894 and composed a series of successful operettas that put the USA on the operetta map. His stage works leaned heavily on the Viennese style, as did those of Ludwig Engländer (who had been born in Vienna). Gustave Kerker's *The Belle of New York* (1897) had a disappointing run on Broadway but was the first operetta to score a major success in Europe (London and Berlin, especially).

La fille de Madame Angot by Charles Lecocq (1832–1918) was at the Gaiety in 1873, and transferred to the Opera Comique, and it was at the latter theatre that Gilbert and Sullivan rose to fame. French operetta remained popular in England. *Les cloches de Corneville* (1877) by Robert Planquette (1848–1903) was a favourite, and Hervé (Louis Auguste Florimond Ronger, 1825–92), who had helped to pioneer the new style of *opéra bouffe* alongside Offenbach, enjoyed his greatest success in both Paris (1883) and London (1893) with *Mam'zelle Nitouche* after Offenbach's death. As late as 1904, Messager's *Véronique* (Paris, 1898) ran for 495 performances at the Apollo. The London interest in French operetta declined rapidly, however, after the production of *The Merry Widow* in 1907. Over the next thirty years, the operetta composers who dominated the stages of Europe, North America and elsewhere around the globe were Franz Lehár (1870–1948), Oscar Straus (1870–1954), Leo Fall (1873–1925), Jean Gilbert (real name, Max Winterfeld, 1879–1942) and Emmerich Kálmán (1882–1953). The appetite in the UK and USA for operetta from the German stage meant that some exceptional French *opérettes* failed to gain an airing in the West End or on Broadway. Among these neglected operettas were Reynaldo's Hahn's *Ciboulette* (1926) and *Brummel* (1931), although Sacha Guitry's play *Mozart*, to which he supplied incidental music, was heard in both cities. It is strange that no one thought the tuneful operetta about Beau Brummel would have appealed to a London audience.

By the mid-1930s, the supply of operettas from the German stage was drying up as a direct consequence of Nazi policies. The Jewish contribution to operetta had been significant from the start (Offenbach was Jewish), and the German operetta world of the 1930s was dominated by Jewish artists, composers, lyricists and impresarios. Broadway musical theatre had been making headway in Europe from the mid-1920s, and after World War II, operetta was largely confined to nostalgic revivals. The operetta director Arthur Maria Rabenalt expressed his confused feelings about the future of operetta in 1948: 'Operetta is dead! – Is operetta dead?'[16] We remain just as confused about the vitality of operetta today. The last operetta that David Ewen included in his *Book of European Light Opera*, published in 1962 was Ivor Novello's *King's Rhapsody* of 1949; he confidently announced, 'Nobody today writes operettas.'[17] It would not be accurate, however, to say that qualities associated with operetta were nowhere to be found in later twentieth-century works for the West End and Broadway stages: John Snelson describes *Phantom of the Opera* as a 'witty play with genre boundaries across temporal divides, bringing together opera, operetta, and various elements of musical theatre'.[18]

Operettas used to be part of a theatrical production system that is still associated with theatres in the West End or on Broadway. An operetta was produced, and it ran until the audience figures declined. Then another new operetta was produced. An opera house, in contrast, announces a new season in which three or four different operas may feature. Operetta is now caught between the two systems. One theatre may be offering a single operetta night after night, and another (for instance the Volksoper in Vienna) will have an operetta season containing new productions of several operettas, each being performed on a different night.

The illustrious West End entrepreneur and producer George Edwardes always trusted the theatre-going public. Cameron Mackintosh showed the same kind of trust when he decided to transfer *Les Misérables* to the Palace Theatre, after largely hostile critical reviews, because the public was demanding tickets. A change in the mid-1980s, initiated by the success of *Phantom of the Opera*, was the desire to see the same production in one city as in another, but, in the period this book deals with, productions could vary from city to city, and even their titles changed. To give two examples, Leo Fall's *Der liebe Augustin* became *Princess Caprice* in London, and Eduard Künneke's *Der Vetter aus Dingsda* became *Caroline* in New York. Another change in the 1980s was prompted by tourism. In London, tourists were accounting for 44 per cent of West End ticket sales,[19] yet many of them were far from fluent in English, so wordy scenes were going to pass over their heads.

Franchising became common in big musical productions in the later twentieth century. It meant that a product was offered under the brand of an existing company, for example, a Really Useful Group production of a Lloyd Webber musical. However, this model can be seen emerging with the London production of *White Horse Inn* at the Coliseum in 1931. It was basically the same production that had been given at the Großes Schauspielhaus, Berlin, in 1930, and it varied little when it went to New York in 1936, even if there was a new version of the book and lyrics. In all three cities, there was a huge auditorium to fill (New York's Center Theater held around 3,500), and Erik Charell and Ernst Stein were asked to oversee the spectacle in each theatre.

In many ways, musicals such as *Phantom* and *Les Misérables* resemble operettas, but not in one crucial way, that of singing style. In operetta, the singing style is predominantly operatic. Despite the occasional prioritizing of acting over singing that Gilbert and Sullivan gave to comic male roles, and despite a few exceptions in the twentieth century, such as *Die Dreigroschenoper*, operetta calls for the same kind of singer as in opera. The only difference is that the singer is also expected to act and dance skilfully. In musical theatre, the operatic voice is a style, and one of six 'voice qualities' that form part of the training system devised by voice coach Jo Estill. For her, 'opera' was something that came in inverted commas, like vocal 'twang' and 'belting'. In opera and operetta, in contrast, there was a perception that good singing could only be done one way, rather than there being an acceptance that singers might position their vocal chords in several ways so as to create different musical effects. Operetta tended to follow operatic decisions about what vocal techniques were legitimate. The falsetto voice (another of Estill's types) was, for example, used sparingly in opera, and the very designation 'falsetto' implies that it is a 'false' voice.

The second edition of the *New Grove Dictionary* of 2001 comments, 'Today operetta is scarcely to be found in the commercial theatre and, apart from a few works that have been accepted into the operatic repertory, it has become increasingly of interest to a specialist audience'.[20] The 200,000 people who visit the Seefestspiele Mörbisch each year offer a clear indication, however, that the audience for operetta is not small. It may also be argued that opera, itself, attracts a 'specialist audience'. It is puzzling why some opera companies (Opera North and English National Opera (ENO) in the UK being notable examples) are readier to perform a Broadway musical than an operetta, when the singing style demanded by an operetta is usually much closer to operatic vocal technique. Asked about operetta style by a journalist in 2007, the legendary operetta diva Marta Eggerth, aged 94, commented, 'Technically, there is no difference between opera and operetta … Either you can sing it or you cannot sing it'. The real distinguishing characteristic of operetta, she claimed, lies elsewhere, beyond the style and way of singing: 'Operetta is really a very erotic thing. Today, there is no erotic. On the beach the bikini, two little leaves over the breasts: there it is. That is not sex. Sexiness is something which is not shown right away.' The same applies to operetta: 'this not knowing but suspecting, kind of teasing one another – that makes it interesting, sexy, but funny at the same time. This is my whole principle of what makes operetta'.[21]

Noël Coward remarked on the capacity of popular tunes to 'probe the memory more swiftly than anything else'[22] – and that is no doubt why, when operetta productions waned, the genre held a strong nostalgic appeal to an ageing audience. This was especially the case in Austria and Germany. Operetta became permeated with nostalgia after World War II. Sentiment would overtake works in which frivolity, vulgarity and caricature had once predominated, such as in *Im weißen Rössl*. An attempt to get closer to Erik Charell's conception of this revue operetta was given an enthusiastic reception at the Bar jeder Vernunft, Berlin, in 1994. The cobwebs blown away, another admired production took place in Basel in 2005.

There is now a shift in the way operetta is being perceived. In Vienna, controversy greeted Birgit Meyer's production of Kálmán's *Gräfin Mariza* at the Volksoper in 2006. Meyer responded by arguing that those who rejected new interpretations were no longer attending operetta performances but that younger audiences were receptive to new ideas.[23] In 2004 the production of Kálmán's *Die Herzogin von Chicago*, directed by Dominik Wilgenbus at the Volksoper, was another example of changes in interpretation. Instead of focussing on its historical status in the Third Reich as *entartete Musik* (decadent music), it was re-envisioned as a critique of the global reach of twenty-first-century American capitalism.[24]

In 2014, Volker Klotz brought lengthy theatrical experience as critic and dramaturg to a book on the ways and means of reviving operetta.[25] In Berlin, the person who deserves a lot of credit for reimagining operetta is Barrie Kosky, Intendant of the Komische Oper. He was voted Director of the Year in 2016 by *Opernwelt* magazine, and it is certain that the recent innovative productions of operetta played a major role in that award. During the Operetta Festival held 23 January to 8 February 2015 (which included a three-day symposium on operetta), the production of Paul Abraham's *Ball im Savoy* (1932) was a sensation. Kosky showed there were new ways to treat works like this and let their spirit live. They do not need to be either treated as sentimental kitsch or be subjected to some doom-laden Regietheater interpretation (Canadian Opera Company's *Die Fledermaus* in 2012 acquired a Nazi Act 3, drained of the slightest trace of comedy). Nevertheless, despite an acknowledgement that Kosky has brought wonderful high energy, excitement and sexiness to operetta, he has been criticized for a failure to construct a 'conceptual framework making broader claims about the work's meaning or reception history'.[26] Nevertheless, Kosky did end the evening performances of *Ball im Savoy* with a striking gesture. The cast sang 'Goodnight' from Abraham's *Viktoria und ihr Husar* (1930), a song that could not fail to conjure up the painful circumstances of the Jewish composer's destroyed career and exile from Berlin. Not least among Kosky's achievements has been his ability to stimulate the interest of young people in operetta, and their presence in the Komische Oper's audience is unmistakable. This reveals how misguided and out of touch is the notion that operetta is a nostalgic genre for the elderly.

Is any of this likely to encourage writers and composers to return to operetta? To the surprise of many, a new operetta caused something of a sensation in Los Angeles in 2006. It was *The Beastly Bombing* by Julian Nitzberg (libretto) and Roger Neill (music). Nitzberg knew that operetta was exactly the theatre form he was looking for when he saw a performance of *The Pirates of Penzance*; he explained:

> I happen to hate modern show music … Operetta is the only format that could allow us to write 8 minute songs with many different parts and musical themes. Operetta allows for sophisticated patter songs and wordy, witty lyrics.[27]

Neill and Nitzberg chose uncompromising subject matter, which included white supremacists, Al Qaeda terrorists, a paedophile priest and a gay Jesus. They wanted their work to be political but not dull or didactic. What they aimed for was 'cyanide wrapped in chocolate', and operetta helped them achieve what might be described as the first successful post-9/11 comedy.

In soliciting the chapters that follow, the editors sought broad accounts of operetta in different countries but also wanted the *Companion* to reveal how operetta spread across borders, to become in the twentieth century – along with the popular songs of Tin Pan Alley – part of a global entertainment industry. That is why dance-band songs and operetta were both targets for Theodor Adorno's vituperative criticism.

The structure of the *Companion* proved a challenge, and no amount of juggling around of themes and topics furnished a division into parts as convincing or logical as the simple chronological design that was finally chosen. That said, this is not a chronological history of operetta but, rather, a study of recurring themes in the development of operetta, such as urban environments, cosmopolitanism, cultural transfer, business practices and theatrical professionalism. The three parts: 'Early Centres of Operetta',

'The Global Expansion of Operetta', and 'Operetta since 1900' work surprisingly well because operetta declined around 1895 but suddenly came back fighting in 1905 with *Die lustige Witwe*, which is generally regarded as the first of the silver-age operettas. In fact, we considered calling Parts 1 and 3, 'Golden Age' and 'Silver Age', but those terms really apply only to Austro-German operettas.

The editors hope this *Companion* provides readers with a substantial introduction to operetta that will stimulate interest in operetta's creative artists and reception history. The contributors have drawn on recent research and are all active and inspiring champions of this neglected genre. Their chapters have been written with the desire to be accessible to students and general enthusiasts, and to appeal, also, to professionals and practitioners involved with operetta, its production and promotion.

Notes

1. Harue Tsutsumi, 'Howard Vernon's Encounters with Japan in 1879 and 1885: *Wanderer's Strange Story: Western Kabuki*', 20th Congress of the International Musicological Society, Tokyo, March 2017.
2. Bettina Brandl-Risi, Ulrich Lenz, Clemens Risi and Rainer Simon (eds.), *Kunst der Oberfläche: Operette zwischen Bravour und Banalität* (Leipzig: Henschel Verlag, 2015).
3. Naxos 8.660280–81. The score was reconstructed by Christian Pollack after he found the manuscript score in the music archive of the Theater an der Wien (now located in the Österreichische Nationalbibliothek Musiksammlung).
4. Mark Lubbock, *The Complete Book of Light Opera*, with an American section by David Ewen (London: Putnam, 1962); Robert Ignatius Letellier, *Operetta: A Sourcebook*, 2 vols. (Newcastle: Cambridge Scholars Publishing, 2015). Other standard reference books, broader in coverage are given in the bibliography.
5. Richard Traubner, *Operetta: A Theatrical History* (New York: Routledge, 2003); Andrew Lamb, *150 Years of Popular Musical Theatre* (New Haven, CT: Yale University Press, 2000).
6. To choose but one example, the editors would stress that they do regard Romberg's *The Student Prince* as an operetta. Those who harbour doubts will find them quickly dispelled by listening to the performance recorded by the orchestra and chorus of West German Radio, Cologne, conducted by John Mauceri, CPO 555 058–2 (2016), 2 CDs.
7. See Orly Leah Krasner, 'Birth Pangs, Growing Pains and Sibling Rivalry: Musical Theatre in New York, 1900–1920', and William A. Everett, 'American and British Operetta in the 1920s: Romance, Nostalgia and Adventure' in Everett (ed.), *The Cambridge Companion to the Musical* (Cambridge: Cambridge University Press, 2008), 29–46 and 47–62.
8. Bernard Grun, *Kulturgeschichte der Operette* (Munich: Langen Müller Verlag, 1961), 123. It may be that *Madame Papillon* (1855) was also termed *opérette*, at least *Wikipedia* thinks so: https://en.wikipedia.org/wiki/List_of_operettas_by_Offenbach (accessed 11 Feb. 2018). The *Grove Dictionary* is unhelpful, as is the review in *Le Figaro*, 7 Oct. 1855.
9. Gustave Schilling (ed.), *Universal-Lexicon der Tonkunst*, Vol. 5 (Stuttgart: Franz Heinrich Köhler Verlag, 1837), 250.
10. Erich Urban, 'Die Wiedergeburt der Operette', *Die Musik*, 3, no. 3–4 (1903): 176–86, 269–81.
11. See Peter Hawig, 'Offenbachs Bouffes-Parisiens: Ein Knotenpunkt nicht nur des französischen Musiktheaters' in Peter Ackermann, Ralf-Olivier Schwarz and Jens Stern (eds), *Jacques Offenbach und seine Zeit* (Fernwald: Musikverlag Burkhard Muth, 2006).
12. Siegfried Kracauer, *Jacques Offenbach and the Paris of His Time*, trans. Gwenda David and Eric Mosbacher (London: Constable, 1937), 174.
13. Kracauer, *Jacques Offenbach and the Paris of His Time*, 202.

14. Bernard Grun, *Prince of Vienna: The Life, the Times and the Melodies of Oscar Straus* (London: W. H. Allen, 1955), 15.
15. B. W. Findon, 'Opera Bouffe to Musical Comedy', *The Play Pictorial*, 18, no. 108 (Aug. 1911): xviii–xxviii, at xxvi.
16. Arthur Maria Rabenalt *Operette als Aufgabe: Aufsätze zur Operettenkrise* (Berlin: Heinz Menge-Verlag, 1948), 11.
17. David Ewen, *The Book of European Light Opera* (New York: Holt, Rinehart and Winston, 1962), xiii.
18. John Snelson, *Andrew Lloyd Webber* (New Haven: Yale University Press, 2004), 41.
19. Figures quoted on *The Story of Musicals*, BBC 2 television, Sat. 3 Mar. 2012.
20. Andrew Lamb, 'Operetta, §5: The Modern Scene' in Stanley Sadie (ed.), *The New Grove Dictionary of Music and Musicians*, Vol. 18 (London: Macmillan, 2nd ed. 2001), 497–8, at 497.
21. Anne Midgette, 'Retrofitting Operetta for a 21st-Century Crowd', *The New York Times*, 9 Jan. 2007, www.nytimes.com/2007/01/09/arts/music/09oper.html?emc=eta1&_r=0 (accessed 23 Aug. 2017).
22. Noël Coward, *Present Indicative* (London: Heinemann, 1937), 398.
23. Birgit Meyer, 'Regietheater im Spannungsfeld zwischen künstlerischem Anspruch, Kulturauftrag, ökonomischen Zwängen und Kulturpolitik am Beispiel der Volksoper Wien: Ein Statement aus dem Theateralltag', *Vorträge des Salzburger Symposions 2005* (Anif/Salzburg: Müller-Speiser, 2007), 100–12, at 104.
24. See Lisa Feurzeig, 'Can Creative Interpretation Keep Operetta Alive? Kálmán's *Die Herzogin von Chicago* at the Vienna *Volksoper* in 2004', *Studia Musicologica*, 57, no. 3–4 (December 2016): 441–70.
25. Volker Klotz, *Es lebe: Die Operette: Anläufe, sie neuerlich zu erwecken* (Würzburg: Königshausen & Neumann, 2014).
26. Ryan Minor, 'Operetta Dramaturgies Today? On Barrie Kosky's *Ball im Savoy*' in Bettina Brandl-Risi, Ulrich Lenz, Clemens Risi and Rainer Simon (eds.), *Kunst der Oberfläche: Operette zwischen Bravour und Banalität* (Leipzig: Henschel Verlag, 2015), 208–10, at 208.
27. Quoted in Kevin Clarke (ed.), *Glitter and be Gay: Die authentische Operette und ihre schwulen Verehrer* (Hamburg: Männerschwarm Verlag, 2007), 21. Clarke writes a short account of this operetta, 260–5, which is the source of other information in this paragraph.

Recommended General Reading

Everett, William A., ed. *The Cambridge Companion to the Musical*. Cambridge: Cambridge University Press, 2008.
Grun, Bernard. *Die leichte Muse: Kulturgeschichte der Operette*. Munich: Langen Müller Verlag, 1961.
Lamb, Andrew. *150 Years of Popular Musical Theatre*. New Haven, CT: Yale University Press, 2000.
Niccolai, Michela and Clair Rowden, eds. *Musical Theatre in Europe 1830–1945*. Turnhout: Brepols, 2017.
Traubner, Richard. *Operetta: A Theatrical History*. New York: Routledge, 2003.

Reference Books

Anderson, James. *The Complete Dictionary of Opera and Operetta*. New York, NY: Wings, 1993.
Bordman, Gerald Martin and Richard Norton. *American Musical Theatre: A Chronicle*. New York: Oxford University Press, 4th ed. 2011 (orig. pub. 1978).
Drone, Jeanette Marie. *Index to Opera, Operetta and Musical Comedy Synopses in Collections and Periodicals*. Metuchen, NJ: Scarecrow Press, 1978.

Ewen, David. *The Book of European Light Opera.* New York: Holt, Rinehart and Winston, 1962.

Gänzl, Kurt. *Encyclopedia of the Musical Theatre.* New York: Schirmer, 1994.

Green, Stanley. *Encyclopedia of the Musical Theatre.* New York: Dodd, Mead, 1976.

Letellier, Robert Ignatius. *Operetta: A Sourcebook.* 2 vols. Newcastle: Cambridge Scholars Publishing, 2015.

Lubbock, Mark. *The Complete Book of Light Opera.* With an American section by David Ewen. London: Putnam, 1962.

Norton, Richard C. *A Chronology of American Musical Theater.* 3 vols. New York: Oxford University Press, 2002.

Oster, Louis. *Guide raisonné et déraisonnable de l'opérette et de la comédie musicale.* Paris: Fayard, 2008.

Raymond, Jack. *Show Music on Record from the 1890s to the 1980s.* New York: Frederick Ungar Publishing, 1982.

Schneidereit, Otto. *Operette A–Z: Ein Streifzug durch die Welt der Operette und des Musicals.* Berlin: Henschelverlag, 1975.

Wagner, Heinz. *Das große Operettenbuch: 120 Komponisten und 430 Werke.* Berlin: Parthas-Verl., 1997.

Wearing, J. P. *The London Stage 1890–1959: A Calendar of Productions, Performers, and Personnel.* 14 vols. Lanham, MD: Rowman and Littlefield, 2nd ed. 2013.

PART I

Early Centres of Operetta

1 French Operetta: Offenbach and Company

JOHN KENRICK

Introduction

Jacques Offenbach is the grandfather of musical theatre as we know it. *Oklahoma, A Chorus Line, Hamilton* – all are direct descendants of his operettas. He composed almost a hundred of them, the best of which became the first musicals to enjoy international popularity. And Offenbach's trademark combination of infectious melody, wry humour and sheer fun still echoes through the great stage and screen musicals of our time. He did not invent operetta, but he was the first to write operettas that earned worldwide acclaim.

In mid-nineteenth-century Paris, a city obsessed with appearances, Offenbach's appearance was anything but average. Standing barely five feet tall, he had a pencil-thin build. To offset his oversized hawk-like nose, he grew shoulder-length hair and mutton-chop whiskers. A casual observer might have thought him just another eccentric. But anyone who looked into his dark, penetrating eyes could see the passion that made him an artistic pioneer. But before we get ahead of ourselves, just what is operetta? Some sources have defined it as a comic or lighter alternative to grand opera, but that tells us what operetta is not. I respectfully offer a more comprehensive definition:

> Operetta is a versatile form of musical that integrates songs and musical sequences with dialogue to dramatize a story, retaining the vocal pyrotechnics and forms of grand opera (arias, choruses, act finales, etc.) but relying on more accessible melodies. The songs develop character and/or advance the plot, which can be comic, romantic, or a combination of both.[1]

Musical theatre requires a sizeable audience, so it must reflect the popular culture of its era. In order to understand Offenbach and the birth of French operetta, we have to consider the city and the ethos that inspired and embraced his work.

Paris and the Second Empire

Sometime in the third century BC, a Celtic tribe called the *Parisii* established a trading centre on an island in the middle of the Seine, now called the Île de la Cité. Under the Romans, the settlement expanded on both banks of the river. In 508, the Frankish kings made it their capital. By the Middle Ages, Paris was one of Europe's premier cities. It became a filthy, treacherous labyrinth of streets and alleyways, with palaces and slums within a stone's throw of each other.

More than stones flew when the first French Revolution began in the 1780s. Once Parisians discovered that mobs and barricades could topple governments, they made a habit of it. Republican regimes came and went, heads rolled off the guillotine, and Napoleon Bonaparte's empire rose and fell. When 'Citizen King' Louis Philippe was swept off his throne in 1848, a Second Republic was declared.

Political uncertainty fed a nostalgia for happier times. Louis Bonaparte (1808–73), a nephew of Napoleon and a masterful manipulator of public opinion, returned from exile and got himself elected first president of the new republic. In 1851, he staged a coup and declared himself dictator. Press opposition was silenced, and a revised constitution reduced the National Assembly to little more than a rubber stamp. Within a year Louis 'allowed' himself to be declared emperor. Because a cousin (twenty years dead) had technically inherited Napoleon I's crown for a few days, Louis dubbed himself Napoleon III.

Once in power, the ruler of the so-called Second Empire encouraged financial expansion. The Industrial Revolution did wonders for the French economy. Manufacturing, shipping and business investments flourished. But could a rejuvenated empire be content with an ageing and rebellion-prone capital city? Although a major manufacturing centre, Paris was strangled by a tangle of narrow, putrid streets.[2]

The emperor appointed Baron Georges-Eugène Haussmann, a bureaucrat with a genius for organization, to oversee the rebuilding of Paris. When public funds ran short, Haussmann quietly borrowed billions from a government-owned bank. Much of Paris was literally rebuilt on credit. As the historic web of twisting streets was demolished, over three hundred thousand impoverished Parisians were forcibly relocated to outer *arrondissements* that soon became as desperate as the old ones.[3] New boulevards, too broad to be barricaded, were lined by townhouses and posh apartment buildings designed for the expanding upper-middle class. These residential structures were restricted to six storeys, giving the boulevards a handsome uniformity. Occasional imperfections were intentionally included to prevent monotony.[4] Glass-covered arcades called *passages* led off the boulevards to provide access to shops, *boîtes* and cafés. Parisians became *boulevardiers*, regularly strolling the streets to admire the latest additions.

Haussmann sprinkled Paris with public parks, and the grounds of Louis Napoleon's Tuileries Palace were opened to the public. The imperial residence was handsomely redecorated, but all was done on the cheap.

The new imperial silverware was merely gilt. The shiny 'golden' imperial insignia shining on army uniforms were brass. No one really cared. If all that glittered was not gold, at least there was plenty of glitter – and appearances were what mattered. Masked balls at the Tuileries and elsewhere gave the impression of Paris as a never-ending carnival.[5]

Much of the glitter was provided by the emperor, his courtiers and the nobles and diplomats who made up the *beau monde* of Parisian high society. Many are attracted by shiny objects, and Second Empire Paris attracted adventurers of every stripe. Investors and charlatans crowded the bustling stock exchange in the Place de la Bourse. Fortunes were made and lost on a daily basis. Men with money attracted the attentions of a new breed of courtesans known as *grandes horizontales*. Their beauty and scandalous behaviour made these women celebrities in their own right. They were one of the most visible elements of the *demi-monde*, which historian Virginia Rounding has described as 'that half-way world between respectable high society and the low life of the common prostitute … where nothing is quite as it seems'.[6]

The *demi-monde* included artists, actors, shady business men, would-be courtesans – anyone who looked more respectable than they were. And looking respectable was easier thanks to department stores that sold affordable, mass-produced *haute couture*. Anyone who could scrape together a few sous could fit in while strolling among the rich and powerful or sitting beside them in theatres.

Journalists faced stern censorship, but those who wrote for the stage had an easier time. As long as one avoided direct attacks on the emperor or his government, there was room for creativity. Opera and theatre flourished, attracting an ongoing procession of talented hopefuls anxious to make their mark in Paris. Most were French, but some were immigrants – including the composer who would become the musical voice of the Second Empire.

Offenbach: Early Life and Career

Isaac Eberst was an itinerant Jewish musician in southern Prussia. Hoping to avoid anti-Semitic prejudice, he renamed his family after Offenbach-am-Main, a suburb of Frankfurt. By the time his seventh child, Jakob Offenbach, was born on 20 June 20 1819, Isaac was cantor of a Cologne synagogue. Jakob showed an early passion for music. Encouraged to study the violin, he insisted on switching to the cello, on which he proved to be a prodigy. He formed a trio with a brother and a sister and played in local restaurants.

Determined to give his son every opportunity, Isaac sent thirteen-year-old Jakob to Paris. The Conservatoire admitted only native French students, but Jakob's audition won him immediate admission. Within a year, the headstrong teen quit the school and joined the orchestra of the Opéra-Comique. He was befriended by chorus master Fromental Halévy, who instructed the ambitious youngster in composing for the stage. Two years later in 1837, Johann Strauss the Elder brought his Viennese orchestra to Paris, where his waltzes became the rage. Offenbach quickly published several waltzes of his own, winning his first taste of celebrity. To make his name sound less foreign, he began billing himself as 'Jacques Offenbach'.

Offenbach began turning out songs as well as dance music. He performed at the finest soirées, where he charmed some of the most influential people in France. With the *beau monde* in attendance, his cello concerts became social events. He toured England, giving a command performance for Queen Victoria at Windsor Castle. On his return to Paris, he converted to Catholicism and married Hérminie d'Alcain.

Offenbach wanted to write full-length musical stage works – but something lighter than grand opera. The Comédie-Française appointed him musical director and allowed him to provide incidental music and songs for various plays. But company policy forbade full-length musical productions. While the government considered Offenbach's application for a licence to open a theatre of his own, he wrote *Oyayaye ou La reine des îles*, a musical farce presented for a few performances at the Folies-Nouvelles. The manager there was Florimond Ronger (1825–92), a trail blazing operetta composer who protected his job as a church organist by writing and performing in stage works under the pseudonym Hervé. He wrote more than 120 operettas, but because his licence limited him to no more than two singing characters, his dramatic options were limited. Although tuneful, Hervé's works never found a large audience outside of Paris (his late work *Mam'zelle Nitouche* excepted). Hervé may have been the first French operetta composer, but, thanks to talent, timing and sheer determination, Offenbach would turn this local phenomenon into a worldwide sensation.

The Right Time

In 1851, Great Britain built a 990,000-square foot steel and plate glass 'Crystal Palace' in London to house a world's fair. Celebrating the miracles of modern English industry, it drew millions of visitors. Not to be outdone, Louis Napoleon started planning an 1855 *Exposition Universelle* of his own to showcase France's economic advancement under his reign. Offenbach realized that masses of fairgoers looking for entertainment would provide a unique opportunity. He leased a dilapidated wooden theatre on the avenue des Champs-Élysées, crammed in a few hundred seats and dubbed it the Bouffes-Parisiens.[7]

With the help of several well-connected admirers – including Henri de Villesment, founder of the newspaper *Le Figaro* – he obtained a licence to present comic plays with music. Because of the small size of the theatre, the licence limited Offenbach to one-act works with no more than three characters; a fourth non-singing character could be added for an added fee. Offenbach had a new one-act operetta ready. But audiences would expect a full evening's entertainment. To create additional material, he called in Ludovic Halévy (1834–1908), an aspiring playwright and nephew to Fromental Halévy. (Who you know mattered even then!) It was the beginning of what would prove to be a long and profitable collaboration.

The Bouffes-Parisiens opened on 5 July 1855. The programme included a prologue (*Entrez, Messieurs, Mesdames),* a pastoral (*Une nuit blanche)* and a pantomime. But the highlight was the operetta *Les deux aveugles.* Billed as a 'bouffonnerie musicale', this half-hour long one-acter involved two beggars pretending to be blind while battling for the right to panhandle on a popular bridge. Such con men were common on the streets of Paris. Étienne Pradeau and Jean-François Berthelier triumphed as the beggars.

With jaded tastes and substantial disposable income, Parisians had developed a craving for anything new and sensational. They packed the Bouffes-Parisiens nightly, and Offenbach's theatre became *the* place to be seen. Tickets were so hard to get that the composer's wife had to sit on the aisle steps. The emperor was unwilling to appear at a theatre that was not funded by his government but got around that by having a command performance at the Tuileries.

During the run, Offenbach was introduced to Berthelier's mistress, soprano Hortense Schneider (1833–1920). When she auditioned for the composer, he stopped her before she had finished her second song and hired her on the spot. She made her Bouffes debut soon afterwards and proved an immediate sensation. Although not a great beauty, her charm and stage presence were undeniable. We can only wonder if either the composer or the soprano realized that each would become a defining factor in the other's career.

When the chill winds of autumn forced the Exposition to close, *Les deux aveugles* was still playing to capacity houses. Offenbach leased a winter-friendly theatre located in the Passage Choiseul, a fashionable shopping arcade on the rue Monsigny. After costly renovations, Offenbach had a 900-seat jewel box auditorium with excellent sight lines and acoustics. He gave this venue the old name of Bouffes-Parisiens.

On 29 December 1855, the new theatre opened with *Ba-ta-clan*, a one-act 'chinoiserie musicale'. Fé-an-nich-ton and Ké-ki-ka-ko are two Parisians stranded in the royal court of China. While plotting their return home, they learn that Emperor Fè-ni-han is another stranded Parisian. To everyone's surprise, the scheming captain of the guard, Ko-ko-ri-ko (the French equivalent of 'cock-a-doodle-doo'), is yet another Parisian. This unseen character communicates via notes and sends the other three back to France so that he can become the new ruler.

This was Offenbach and Halévy's first major collaboration. The music spoofed grand opera, with quotations of Meyerbeer melodies thrown in. The libretto, in which political power was a joke, court life empty mummery and an emperor a poseur, was a sly comic reflection of the French court. But the show was so charming and the satire so genial that it would have looked clumsy if Louis Napoleon's censors had tried to shut it down. So, the emperor and his ministers joined in the applause, and *Ba-ta-clan* thrived.

The true challenge of theatrical success is to keep the hits coming. And Offenbach had to keep standards high. The intimacy of the Bouffes-Parisiens meant that the lyrics and dialogue mattered just as much as the music, and artistic flaws were hard to miss. In an 1856 article, he wrote:

> In an opera which lasts only three quarters of an hour, in which only four characters are allowed and an orchestra of at most thirty persons is employed, one must have ideas and tunes that are as genuine as hard cash. It is also worthy of note that with a small orchestra, such as incidentally sufficed for Mozart and Cimarosa, it is very difficult to cover up mistakes and ineptitudes such as an orchestra of eighty players can gloss over without difficulty.[8]

In 1856, Offenbach wrote and produced seven one-act operettas. The zany plots were always rooted in social satire. In *Le 66* (1856), a peasant thinks he holds the winning lottery ticket 66, only to find out that he's actually got number 99. Unable to meet the constant demand for new operettas, Offenbach presented comic operas by Adam, Mozart and Rossini. He also held a competition, asking composers to create music for a Halévy libretto. There were two winners – Charles Lecocq (1832–1913) and Georges Bizet. Both versions were presented at the Bouffes. But Lecocq, infuriated by the implication that anyone was his equal, held a lifelong grudge against Offenbach.

Offenbach usually did not compose until he had a completed libretto in hand. A speedy worker, he was always pushing Halévy and other playwrights to deliver. Offenbach even had a writing desk installed in his carriage so that he could compose during Paris traffic jams. Uneasy with solitude. he threw lavish parties and sketched new melodies amid chatter and gossip. His attention to musical detail was extraordinary. He purposely used tempi and melodies to strengthen the overall dramatic effect. Even so, nothing he wrote was sacrosanct. Once rehearsals began, he would ruthlessly cut and revise material. After premieres, any music that did not please the public was disposed of.

Offenbach's melodies delighted all classes, with his music equally at home in taverns and in ballrooms. Tourists took these melodies home with them, and Offenbach's songs swept through Europe. Offenbach's troupe toured the continent in 1857, bringing his works to Vienna and London, where local translations became standard fare until well into the next century.

Orpheus in the Underworld: Audiences in Heaven

The more money Offenbach made, the more he spent. He poured profits into theatre renovations and new productions. He entertained lavishly, was generous to anyone in need and was an inveterate gambler. So even though the Bouffes-Parisiens was packed at every performance, the composer and his company were soon swimming in debt.[9]

Offenbach's answer was to dream bigger. Now that Napoleon III himself was a fan, the government issued the Bouffes a new licence permitting larger casts. Halévy provided a multi-act libretto inspired by the Greek myth of Orpheus. Since Halévy had just been appointed secretary general to the Ministry for Algeria, playwright Hector-Jonathan Crémieux expanded and revised the text. Anxious to keep his new job, Halévy gave Crémieux sole credit. While Offenbach avoided bill collectors by hiding out in a series of hotels and borrowed rooms, he turned out his most ambitious score up to that point. Having long since perfected the art of dramatizing characters in intimate works, he and his collaborators made the transition to writing large-scale operetta with ease.

When *Orphée aux enfers* (Orpheus in the Underworld) opened on 21 October 1858, it boasted six principals, more than a dozen supporting characters, a full chorus,and sets by artist Gustave Doré. As in the original Greek myth, the musician Orpheus goes into the dreaded land of the dead to bring back his deceased wife Eurydice. But in this version, Orpheus is bored with his cheating spouse and only makes the trip to placate a nagging character named Public Opinion. Jupiter and the gods of Olympus are depicted as vain and capricious, a direct reflection of Louis Napoleon and his court. However, this operetta's intention was not to incite rebellion but to evoke laughter. In the world of *opéras bouffes*, nobody is perfect, and everyone can afford to laugh –even at themselves.

Jupiter is depicted as an overworked philanderer with a jealous wife and a self-indulgent mob of courtiers. The king of the gods also shared Napoleon III's obsession with public opinion. Jupiter warns the gods, 'Let us preserve appearances, for everything depends on that!' But like his imperial echo, Jupiter has a knack of getting his way. At the end of the operetta, he frees the beautiful Eurydice from Hades to appease Public Opinion. But he tricks Orpheus into making a minor mistake and as a 'punishment' sends Eurydice to Olympus to serve as an acolyte to Bacchus. Orpheus and his unwanted wife are free of each other, Public Opinion is thwarted, and Jupiter has ready access to a new mistress.

Initial response to the piece was positive, but there were rumblings of dissent. French intellectuals treated ancient mythology as a serious subject, and some took issue with Offenbach's irreverent approach. Six weeks into the run, just as ticket sales were slowing down, a major critic published an article vigorously condemning the show for 'profaning sacred antiquity'. Sensing an opportunity, Offenbach published a witty reply in a competing paper – pointing out that the same critic had spoofed mythology in his own writing. Parisians loved a juicy controversy and wanted to see what was inspiring this ruckus. Ticket sales soared. After 280 performances, the exhausted cast demanded a break, protesting that it was unnatural for a large production to run so long. In a few months, *Orphée aux enfers* was reintroduced at the Bouffes, and the composer would revive it whenever his income needed a boost.

Many of Offenbach's upbeat melodies have an infectious, giddy lilt that this author refers to as the 'Offenbach bounce'. It offers the sonic equivalent of drinking fine champagne – minus any hangover. In *Orphée,* the god Mercury's *rondo saltarelle* ('E hop! E hop!' / Look out! Look out!) sets feet tapping and inspires delight on the first hearing as well as the hundredth. And Offenbach's 'galop infernal' in the final scene became the most popular cancan music of all time. It remains the oldest musical theatre tune still in widespread use, a universally recognized melodic symbol of Paris and of French culture.

The lack of international copyright laws made Offenbach's scores irresistible to US producers, who staged his works without paying him a penny in royalties. Throughout the 1860s and 1870s, ten or more Offenbach revivals played on Broadway almost every year. These productions then made fortunes touring North America, advertised as coming 'Direct from Broadway'. The composer wasted little energy worrying about receiving royalties from the United States or other countries that ignored French copyrights. With new hits pouring out of his pen, he earned far more than most composers of his time could dream of.[10]

Offenbachiades: The Golden Years

Orphée aux enfers was the first in a decade-long series of jubilant, full-length operettas that are referred to as 'offenbachiades'. These celebratory send-ups of Second Empire politics and society were so genial and seductive that no one was quite sure whether Offenbach and his librettists were critics or publicists of their comic subjects. A few went so far as to call Offenbach *'le grand corrupteur'*.[11] By any measure, Offenbach was a leading figure in society. In 1860, he formally became a French citizen and a year later received the Legion of Honour. Then the emperor's stepbrother, the influential Duc de Morny, asked to co-author an Offenbach libretto with Halévy. *Monsieur Choufleuri* was not a major hit, but the involvement of a member of the royal family meant that Offenbach and his operettas were as in vogue as could be.

Aside from his penchant for overspending, he lived the life of a respectable gentleman. He relished fine clothes, had a fine residence in Paris and a country estate in Étretat. He made regular trips to the spa at Ems, where he 'took the waters' in a vain attempt to alleviate his chronic arthritis. When in Paris, he was almost always immersed in composing, producing and managing his productions. A rare free hour might find him strolling in the gardens of the Tuileries or conversing with colleagues at a café. When vacationing or on tour, he pestered collaborators with letters and telegrams. He was always impatiently waiting for the next libretto or just the next scene to compose for.

In 1864, Meilhac and Halévy concocted *La belle Hélène*, inspired by the legendary Helen of Troy. As Offenbach began turning out a beguiling score, he realized the title role would be perfect for Hortense Schneider. However, the actress, who had gone to another company to obtain a higher salary, had just left that company for the same reason. With no producer willing to meet her record-breaking demands, Schneider abruptly announced her retirement, sold her furniture and was packing to leave Paris.

Offenbach and Halévy showed up at her door, hats in hand. After some lively negotiation, the two men agreed to pay Schneider an unprecedented 2,000 francs a month. Her temperamental outbursts made rehearsals at the Théâtre des Variétés exasperating. More than once, Offenbach walked out swearing he would never return. But in the theatre, triumph heals all wounds. When *La belle Hélène* opened, *le Tout-Paris* embraced the show, which ran for 700 performances. Within six years, it was performed in every major theatrical city in Europe and the United States.

In this version, Helen is depicted as the ultimate Parisian courtesan. Bored with her marriage to the King of Sparta, Helen is so hungry for a change that she welcomes being kidnapped by Paris, the prince of Troy. Once again, Offenbach and his team turned an ancient legend into a genial satire, but this time their target was Parisian society's insatiable thirst for pleasure. The newest member of that team was co-librettist Henri Meilhac (1830–97), a journalist and boulevardier-turned-playwright, and a former schoolmate of Halévy. That acquaintance opened the way to a collaboration that would last for years. Together, Meilhac and Halévy co-authored the librettos for several of Offenbach's greatest hits, as well as numerous plays and eventually the libretto for Bizet's *Carmen* (1875). The two writers became so closely identified with each other that Offenbach referred to them as 'Meil-hal'.

Spoofing Courts and Crowns

By 1866, years of over-indulgence were catching up with Louis Napoleon, who now suffered painful bladder stones. The powerful Duc de Morny died at age 53 thanks to dissipated living and quack physicians. Even the French economy, built on reckless investments and a constant cycle of booms and busts, was showing signs of exhaustion. In an ominous development, Prussian chancellor Otto von Bismarck was building a federation of more than two dozen petty monarchies to form a new German Empire. With a large and well-equipped army, Germany posed a serious threat to France. In short, it was the perfect time for an operetta with a macabre sense of humour.

Barbe-bleue (1866) revisited the ghoulish French folktale of a knight who marries and murders half a dozen wives. But in this version, his chief poisoner has secretly kept them alive and . . . well serviced. All this occurs under the nose of a despotic king and his dissolute court. Eventually, Bluebeard's latest wife leads the others in humiliating and escaping forever from their murderous spouse. A century after its debut, this work found renewed popularity in East Germany, where audiences saw parallels to their own experiences under a communist dictatorship.

For *La vie parisienne* (1866), Offenbach, Meilhac and Halévy dispensed with mythical settings and set the action in contemporary Paris. The plot involved a boulevardier betting that he could seduce a titled tourist. With characters from all classes of society, this operetta gave audiences at the Théâtre du Palais-Royal the opportunity to laugh at mirror images of themselves. Reality had become improbable enough to be accurately depicted in a comic operetta.

At one point in *La vie parisienne*, a Brazilian millionaire arrives, determined to have a whale of a time in the city of lights. In a rapid-fire rondo brimming with 'Offenbach bounce', he explains that as this is his third visit to Paris, he knows exactly what to expect:

> I am Brazilian, I have gold,
> And I come from Rio de Janeiro
> Twenty times richer than before,
> Paris, I come back to you again!
> Hurray! I just landed,
> Put on your false hair, cocottes!
> To your false teeth I bring
> My whole fortune to consume!
> The pigeon comes, so pluck me bare!
> Take my dollars, my bank notes,
> My watch, my hat, my boots,
> But tell me you love me!
> I will behave exquisitely,
> But you know my nature.
> I will get pleasure in return,
> Yes, I will get my money's worth![12]

Tourists like this one were about to flood Paris as never before. With the Second Empire showing serious signs of fatigue, Louis Napoleon decided to mount another *Exposition universelle* in 1867. Determined to make it bigger and more impressive than its predecessor, it was enclosed in a vast open iron and glass arena. Along with millions of commoners, this fair drew most of the crowned heads of Europe. All were suitably impressed by the technological wonders on view at the Expo, but both royalty and the general public were far more excited to see Offenbach's newest *opéra bouffe*.

Just days after the Expo's opening, *La Grande-Duchesse de Gérolstein* (1867) premiered at the Théâtre des Variétés. Halévy and Meilhac's libretto was a hilarious satire of the chaos caused by promiscuous, self-indulgent monarchs. Thanks in large part to Schneider's seductive performance, royals chose to see *La Grande-Duchesse* as a send-up of Catherine the Great. But it was aimed at the sexual excesses of monarchs of either gender. In the operetta, the female ruler of a fictional German duchy has a weakness for men in uniform. She declares a needless war in order to find new prospects. Reviewing new recruits, she admits in the ribald 'Ah, que j'aime le militaire':

> Ah, how I love the military!
> Their cocky uniforms,
> Their moustaches and their stiff plumes.[13]

She promotes Fritz, a handsome but naive private, to the rank of general. To the dismay of her jealous courtiers, he wins a battle without firing a shot – by getting the enemy drunk. When he fails to respond to the duchess's romantic overtures, she allows her courtiers to humiliate him.

Fritz returns to his peasant fiancée, and the Grand Duchess is manoeuvred into marrying her long-time betrothed, the foppish Prince Paul. She acquiesces with the wry observation, 'When you cannot have what you love, you must love what you have.'

Almost every world leader visiting the exposition made a point of catching *La Grande-Duchesse*. Many of them also paid court to leading lady Hortense Schneider. So many stopped by her dressing room that the hallway leading to it was dubbed 'le passage des princes'.[14] To Schneider's dismay, the same nickname soon applied to her. Her generous admirers added to her celebrated collection of diamonds. Schneider kept them in a lockbox in her dressing room, guarded by eight dogs – none of which was nearly as ferocious as their owner. One afternoon, Schneider's carriage arrived at the exposition's gate. When police explained that only royalty could drive into the grounds, she replied with mock grandeur, 'Make way, I am the Grand Duchess of Gérolstein!' The gendarmes saluted and passed her through. No one took offence. After all, the boundary between reality and make-believe was growing blurrier by the day.

Disaster and Renewal

The public's appetite for 'Offenbachiades' was fading, so Offenbach shifted gears and stepped closer to the world of *opéra comique*. Meilhac and Halévy's libretto for *La Périchole* (1868) dispensed with satire, offering the tale of a beautiful Peruvian street singer who fights off the amorous obsessions of a viceroy. Hortense Schneider won acclaim as the titular peasant and kept the Variétés packed for months. In 1869, Offenbach labelled *Vert-Vert* an *opéra comique*, as he did *Fantasio* (1872), *Madame Favart* (1878) and *La fille du tambour-major* (1879).

When Offenbach and his team offered Schneider another role short on glamour, she refused – a decision she probably came to regret. *Les brigands* (1869) involved a band of common forest bandits out to fleece the Duke of Milan. They outsmart the *carabinieri*, military police who proclaim their approach with the plodding tramp of their boots ('de bottes, de bottes, de bottes!'). The *carabinieri* became the toast of Paris, re-enacting their number in full costume at balls and parties. With Bismarck threatening to put a Prussian prince on the Spanish throne, nervous Frenchmen enjoyed a chance to laugh at men in uniform.

In 1869, Offenbach turned fifty. He was the undisputed master of the operetta world. *Les brigands* was the latest in a string of hits reaching back more than a decade. His scores dominated the stages of Paris, Vienna, London and New York. His music was familiar to most of the civilized word. But *sic transit gloria mundi*. Within two years, this triumphant moment would be a bitter memory. Realizing that the French army was all flash, Bismarck sabotaged peace efforts and lured Louis Napoleon into the Franco-Prussian War.[15] Paris sent the army off to war with patriotic fervour, singing marches from *La Grande-Duchesse*. Louis Napoleon and his disorganized troops suffered a crushing defeat at Sedan in September 1870, and a Republican government sued for peace. The emperor went into exile, and that should have been the end of it. But Paris declared itself an independent commune, and the resulting siege left thousands dead and much of the city in ruins. Rebuilding began almost immediately, but the acrimony of defeat lingered.

Post-war Paris belonged to a new and expanding middle class. The *beau monde* of the imperial court, and the demi-monde that shadowed them, were gone. With almost all the other icons of the Second Empire either dead or in exile, Offenbach became a prime target. The German press attacked him for being French, the French press attacked him for being German, and both sides despised him because he was a Jew. Caricatures depicted 'the Great Corrupter' as a monkey, and for a time the major theatres of Paris would not even consider staging anything by Offenbach.

The frivolous *opéras bouffes* of the past were out of fashion, but Offenbach (as usual) needed money. He turned his energies to *opéras féeries*, operettas that stressed large casts, fantasy plots and spectacular effects. Playwright Victorien Sardou provided the libretto for *Le roi Carotte* (1872), in which an irresponsible king is replaced by a magical giant carrot with a court of dancing vegetables. *Le voyage dans la lune* (1875) was based on one of Jules Verne's outer space novels. Both enjoyed profitable runs.

In between, Charles Lecocq scored a whopping success with his score for *La fille de Madame Angot* (1873), the story of a girl seeking romance who gets tangled up in the aftermath of the 1793 'reign of terror'. The historic setting and straightforward plot meant that it is usually classified as an *opéra comique*, but to our ears today it is an operetta. Lecocq wrote several other hits, most notably *Giroflé-Girofla* (1874) and *Le petit duc* (1876). The charm and easy humour of Lecocq's operettas were appealing to middle-class audiences, and he delighted in temporarily eclipsing Offenbach.

Robert Planquette (1848–1903) was a Parisian café pianist who achieved a surprise success with his first operetta score, *Les cloches de Corneville* (1877). A romantic comedy involving mistaken identities in a French village during the reign of Louis XIV, it proved a great favourite in London (where it ran for over 700 performances) and New York as *The Chimes of Normandy*. Planquette had several other international hits, most notably *Rip Van Winkle* (1888).

Falling back on his first full-scale hit, Offenbach revived *Orphée aux enfers* as a spectacle in 1874. With over 200 in the ensemble and expanded to four acts, *Orphée* won fresh praise. Amid all the fun, Parisians found themselves once again warming to the ageing composer. That same year, a lavish revival of *La Périchole* succeeded, with Hortense Schneider back in the title role. Schneider next starred in Hervé's *La belle poule* (1875). When critics mentioned that the forty-two-year-old diva was looking 'motherly', she promptly retired. That same year, Offenbach debuted no fewer than five new scores.

Although Offenbach had composed several grand operas over the years, none had enjoyed major success. He collaborated on and off over several years with poet Jules Barbier on *Les contes d'Hoffmann* but kept setting it aside to complete new operetta scores that were not among his best efforts. The Opéra-Comique finally agreed to present *Hoffmann*, but the costly production suffered a succession of delays. Despite crippling pain, the composer supervised rehearsals until his health collapsed. Offenbach died on 5 October 5 1880 at the age of sixty-one. When rain thinned the crowd at his funeral, one friend never wavered. Hortense Schneider walked with the coffin all the way to Montmartre Cemetery. In February 1881, *Les contes d'Hoffmann* premiered, and it remains a favourite at opera houses worldwide.

By contrast, the French operettas of Offenbach and his contemporaries are now rarely performed outside of France. But these works are the artistic ancestors of musical theatre as we know it, and they are more than echoes of Second Empire Paris. A century and a half after their premieres, the best of these works remain insightful and entertaining, with scores rich in melody and filled with the 'Offenbach bounce'. And scores that have fallen out of use are ripe for rediscovery.

Notes

1. John Kenrick, *Musical Theatre: A History* (New York: Bloomsbury, 2017), 21.
2. Colin Jones, Paris: *The Biography of a City* (New York: Viking 2004), 304.
3. Jones. *Paris*, 318.
4. Stephane Kirkland, *Paris Reborn: Napoleon III, Baron Haussmann, and the Quest to Build a Modern City* (New York: St. Martin's Press, 2013), 172–3.
5. Alistair Horne, *The Seven Ages of Paris* (New York: Alfred A. Knopf, 2002), 241.
6. Virginia Rounding, *Grandes Horizontales: The Lives and Legends of Four Nineteenth-Century Courtesans* (New York: Bloomsbury, 2003), 2.
7. Peter Gammond, *Offenbach: His Life and Times* (London: Omnibus Press, 1980), 37.
8. Siegfried Kracauer, *Jacques Offenbach and the Paris of His Time* (New York: Zone Books, 2002), 85.
9. James Harding, *Jacques Offenbach: A Biography* (London: John Calder, 1980), 89.
10. See Harding, *Jacques Offenbach*, 155.
11. Jacques Rancière, *The Intellectual and His People: Staging the People.* (London: Verso, 2012), Vol. 2, 18.

12. Author's translation.
13. Author's translation.
14. Alexander Faris, *Jacques Offenbach* (London: Faber & Faber, 1980), 149.
15. Jonathan Steinberg, *Bismarck: A Life* (Oxford: Oxford University Press, 2011), 285–6, and 288.

Recommended Reading

Burchell, Samuel C. *Upstart Empire: Paris During the Brilliant Years of Louis Napoleon*. London: MacDonald, 1971.

Faris, Alexander. *Jacques Offenbach*. London: Faber & Faber, 1980.

Fenby, Jonathan. *France: A Modern History from the Revolution to the War with Terror*. New York: St. Martin's Press, 2015.

Gammond, Peter. *Offenbach: His Life and Times*. Neptune City, NJ: Paganiniana, 1981.

Harding, James. *Jacques Offenbach: A Biography*. London: John Calder, 1980.

Hussey, Andrew. *Paris: The Secret History*. New York: Bloomsbury, 2006.

Jones, Colin. *Paris: The Biography of a City*. New York: Viking 2004.

Kenrick, John. *Musical Theatre: A History*. New York: Bloomsbury, 2017.

Kirkland, Stephane. *Paris Reborn: Napoleon III, Baron Haussmann, and the Quest to Build a Modern City*. New York: St. Martin's Press, 2013.

Kracauer, Siegfried. *Jacques Offenbach and the Paris of His Time*. New York: Zone Books, 2002.

2 Viennese Golden-Age Operetta: Drinking, Dancing and Social Criticism in a Multi-Ethnic Empire

LISA FEURZEIG

The essence of Austria is not the centre, but the periphery.[1]

It is not necessary to go into the early history . . . to perceive clearly that the Habsburg rule taken as a whole lost its predominant German character . . . and assumed the multinational character of its combined domains . . . at a time when in western Europe just the opposite movement, the rise of the national state, was in full swing. From a purely political standpoint, the Habsburg lands here began to lose step with the development of the Western world, and were never to regain it.[2]

Since individual initiatives were generally excluded or of secondary importance, criticism of the system as a whole could only be articulated indirectly – for example in the aesthetic realm, as distanced through literary travesty, in parody, or in the style of ironic self-reflection.[3]

In the early 1880s, Austrian Crown Prince Rudolf became the sponsor of an ambitious project: an encyclopedia of the far-flung empire he was to rule, which eventually filled twenty-four volumes. Titled *The Austro-Hungarian Monarchy in Words and Pictures*, and published in German- and Hungarian-language editions, this work explored all regions of the monarchy, emphasizing their landscapes, folk traditions and artistic craftsmanship. It was intended to promote unity in a monarchy threatened by the increasing pressure of nationalistic forces, and Rudolf's involvement showed his belief in the value of cultural diversity. His tragic death at Mayerling in 1889 did not stop the project, which was completed in 1902.

To understand Viennese operetta, one must know the special circumstances of this empire, essentially different from other countries where the genre flourished. France and England, for example, exerted military and economic power mostly through commerce and colonization outside of Europe. Austria's power, by contrast, was rooted in its control of a European empire. Its capital, Vienna, had long been a melting pot where citizens of many regions, languages, religions and social classes coexisted and interacted.

The ramifications of this simple fact affected the daily experiences of residents of the empire and its capital city. Mobility and cultural exchange were the norm. For example, the large imperial bureaucracy frequently transferred officials from one side of the empire to the other to assure their loyalty to the whole rather than to one region or ethnic group. As historian Waltraud Heindl-Langer explains: 'Even into the late years of the monarchy, many changes of both place and agency were provided, as the memoirs of officials tell us. It was in the interest of the authorities to make the officials familiar with as many regions, groups of people, and jobs as possible.'[4]

Talented individuals often worked in other parts of the empire: both Haydn and Schubert, though born in Austria, spent significant time in Hungary, employed by different branches of the aristocratic Esterházy family. The experiences of daily life also reflected this mobility. For example, typical foods of Vienna then and now combine traditions from different places: Czech dumplings, Hungarian stews and Dalmatian fish dishes are common in Vienna, while coffee and apple strudel came to Austria from its adversary Turkey, and the famous Wiener schnitzel from Austrian-governed parts of northern Italy.

The Austro-Hungarian Compromise (*Ausgleich*) of 1867 divided the empire into eastern and western sections holding equal power. This raised Hungary's political importance at the expense of other ethnicities, such as Czechs (still in the Austrian half) and Croats and Poles (now governed by the Hungarian half). This inequity created new tensions that contributed to the dissolution of the empire after World War I. The *Ausgleich* and its move towards recognizing non-Germanic cultures within the empire affected operettas and their sociopolitical messages. Many works drew on the empire's diversity as a source of new musical material, reflecting Rudolf's message of the value of cultural variety.

Operetta in Vienna began as a response to the works of Offenbach, which were quickly exported to this significant capital. Two aspects of the city helped Vienna to make operetta its own: its complex identity, as described above, and its own theatrical tradition, which prefigured operetta in important ways.

Prehistory of Viennese Operetta: The *Volkstheater*

You will come to know the highly praised foreign lands ... and yearning will drive you back to the motherland ... Here are your talismans: a purse that fills with money every time you think of [Austria] with love and joy; magical boots that will carry you wherever you want to go; and finally, a mirror that enables you to appear as whatever you claim to be.[5]

Operetta's raging popularity in the third quarter of the nineteenth century makes it tempting to view this genre and its development as fully self-contained – but of course comic musical theatre already existed in rich variety throughout Europe before the 1850s. Dating from the early eighteenth century, Vienna's tradition of popular musical theatre was known as *Volkstheater*. The word 'Volk', meaning 'the people', implies that these works were aimed at everyone in Vienna, not only the elite.

The pioneer in this tradition was Josef Anton Stranitzky (1676–1726), leader of a marionette theatre and then a group of travelling actors. He presented open-air performances in Vienna for a few years and was finally granted a theatre building – the first in the city – in 1707. The plays he wrote for his company were parodies of the operas presented in the court theatres, thus introducing those grand works to a broader public in a new form. Known as 'Haupt- und Staatsaktionen' (actions of leaders and states), these plays told the same stories as their models, adding the character of the servant Hanswurst – played by Stranitzky himself – who served as an ironic, earthy and irreverent foil, commenting on the heroic characters he worked for and providing a lower-class perspective on their grand exploits. As Otto Rommel, venerable historian of the *Volkskomödie*, writes: 'the comedy of the Wiener Haupt- und Staatsaktionen stands in vivid, dynamic antagonism with the serious plot[s]'.[6] Rommel also comments that 'the Viennese evidently recognized themselves in Hanswurst's comedy, and influenced by their applause, it became more and more Viennese [*immer wienerischer*]'.[7] These musical plays foreshadowed operetta through their social-political critiques and recognizably Viennese character. A brief example shows Stranitzky contrasting Hanswurst's literal-minded common sense with his master's grandiosity.

> *Oronta. Ritter, was bringstu?*
> *Octavius. Krig und Todt.*
> *Hw. Quarck und Speck.*[8]

> Oronta: Knight, what bringest thou?
> Octavius: War and death.
> Hanswurst: Cheese and bacon.

Stranitzky was so closely identified with Hanswurst that no one could truly replace him in this role (though many imitators arose all over the German-speaking world). After him, a series of Vienna comic actors created their own stock characters, each with his own personality and recognizable style. The next Viennese Hanswurst, Gottfried Prehauser (1699–1769) – noted for his fine singing – transplanted Hanswurst into an urban Viennese setting and made him more refined. His comic partner and rival, versatile mimic Josef Felix von Kurz (*c.*1717–84), created the new character Bernardon, somewhat of a clever brat.

The next character in this evolving tradition was Kaspar, usually known affectionately as Kasperl or Käsperle, '[a character] so irresistible that it not only governed the Viennese of its own time for forty years, but was then transferred from adult theatre to the puppet plays of the whole German people'.[9] Even now, puppet theatres across Germany and Austria are known as *Kasperltheater*. Created by actor Johann LaRoche (1745–1806), Kasperl was the quintessential figure at the Leopoldstädter Theater built in

1781, which became the central venue of the *Volkstheater* tradition. LaRoche was noted for his exaggerated motions and skilful improvised references to Viennese goings-on; his Kasperl moved the *Volkstheater* towards the charm later emphasized in operetta.

While playwrights of the early *Volkstheater* were often actors as well – and the performers were at its centre more than particular plays – there was a middle phase when writers and actors became more separate and theatre composers were no longer anonymous. Despite his brief career – he died only two years after the first public productions of his plays – writer Philipp Hafner (1735–64) had a long shadow. His plays, complex and full of intrigue, were adapted into musical comedies in the 1790s by the highly effective team of writer Joachim Perinet (1763–1816) and composer Wenzel Müller (1767–1835), who could be compared to later teams such as Gilbert and Sullivan or Rodgers and Hammerstein. Hafner created interesting, complex stories, Perinet contributed effective song texts, and Müller composed simple, memorable tunes. Their hit shows, such as *Das Neusonntagskind* (Sunday's Child, 1793) and *Die Schwestern von Prag* (The Sisters from Prague, 1794), contained as much music as typical operettas. Müller's extended musical scenes at the ends of acts are operatic finales, not unlike those of his contemporary Mozart in length and design.

Another playwright, Ferdinand Kringsteiner (1775–1810), is of particular importance because he wrote travesties – new versions of old familiar stories – setting them in Vienna and transforming tragedies by substituting happy endings. The word *Verwienerung* (Viennifying) was coined to describe this technique, which also falls into the larger category of the *Lokalstück*, which can be applied to any play emphasizing the local landmarks and features of one particular place. A typical work, *Die Braut in der Klemme* (The Bride in the Trap, 1804), is a parody of the Bluebeard folktale that had recently been the subject of an opera by Grétry. In the cellar, the unfortunate wife finds not the bodies of her husband's murdered wives, but (spoiler alert!) his wine cellar – and he knows that she has disobeyed him because she is drunk when he gets home. Shakespeare was the target for his parody *Othello, der Mohr in Wien* (Othello, the Moor in Vienna). Such travesties prefigured Offenbach's operetta retellings of classical myths.

In the post-Napoleonic era, from about 1813 to 1825, a group of playwrights known as the 'big three' (*grosse Drei*) dominated the Vienna theatre scene. Adolf Bäuerle (1786–1859), Josef Alois Gleich (1772–1841) and Carl Meisl (1775–1853) wrote a total of nearly 500 plays. Meisl continued the travesty tradition with works such as *Orpheus und Eurydice, oder So geht es in Olymp zu* (Orpheus and Eurydice, or That's How it Goes in Olympus, 1813), with texts in *Knittelvers*, an archaic poetic metre that was used in this period to sound exaggerated and silly. Some of

Gleich's and Bäuerle's plays daringly criticized the politics of the time. Bäuerle's play *Aline, oder Wien in einem anderen Weltteil* (Aline, or Vienna on Another Continent, 1822), set in India, prefigured operetta's fascination with exotic locations.

The final flowering of the *Volkstheater* featured two playwright-actors: Ferdinand Raimund (1790–1836) and Johann Nestroy (1801–62). Both emphasized typical Viennese character types, but from very different perspectives. Raimund's plays usually feature a magical element that is used as a psychological tool to encourage the human potential for goodness, and his typical hero is someone ordinary who rises to the occasion. A perfect example of his work is the play *Der Bauer als Millionär* (The Farmer as Millionaire, 1826), in which a simple peasant is put to the test as a by-product of intrigues in the fairy world. At first, he falls for the temptations of wealth, but returns to his modest goodness after he magically grows old overnight.

Nestroy presents a more negative, realistic view of human nature; his characters are not morally admirable. He also wrote lower-class roles in Viennese dialect, bringing out the real sound of Vienna's streets. Nestroy was an important transitional figure to operetta, because he was still active as a playwright, actor and theatre manager as the first works of Offenbach reached the city.

Operetta Composers and Style Characteristics

Glücklich ist, wer vergisst, was doch nicht zu ändern ist.[10]
  (Happy is he who forgets what cannot be changed.)

While the name of Johann Strauss Jr (1825–99) remains central to Viennese nineteenth-century operetta, particularly what is still performed today, he worked among other gifted composers. The earliest Viennese operettas were composed by Franz von Suppé (1819–95). He was already a prolific composer of theatre music when he added operetta to his oeuvre beginning with the one-act *Das Pensionat* (The Boarding School) in 1860 – thus preceding Strauss's entry into the theatre by over a decade. These two men dominated the operetta scene in the 1870s and 1880s, along with their younger contemporary Karl Millöcker (1842–99). Strauss continued to compose operettas well into the 1890s.

Texts, both song lyrics and spoken dialogue, were a central element of operettas. Librettists shaped the plots and language of operetta, so their contributions cannot be ignored. Two individuals, often working as a team, created a major proportion of the libretti of golden-age operettas:

Richard Genée (1823–95) and Camillo Walzel (1829–95), who usually used the pseudonym Friedrich Zell. While there were other librettists, these two were predominant. Their partnership was a forerunner to that of Julius Brammer (1877–1943) and Alfred Grünwald (1884–1951), who collaborated on the libretti of many twentieth-century Viennese operettas.

Suppé's early operetta *Die schöne Galathée* (Beautiful Galathea, 1865) used a device traceable both to the *Volkstheater* and to Parisian operetta – the retelling of a Greek story in a more modern context. It is hard to know whether Meisl or Offenbach is the primary influence on this work, in which characters such as King Midas and Galathea (the beautiful statue brought to life) are represented as greedy and silly rather than as grand mythological archetypes. The *Volkstheater Verwienerung* is also found in some operettas, notably Strauss's *Die Fledermaus* (The Bat, 1874). Though the operetta is based on a French model, a Viennese ball replaces the original supper party, while the serving of champagne by the decadent Prince Orlofsky can be read as a veiled reference to the extravagant Count Moritz von Fries (1777–1826) and his home in the town of Bad Vöslau, known for producing the first champagne-method wines in Austria. Like the *Lokalstück* of Viennese theatre, operettas in Austria often introduced characters and references that added a distinctly Viennese flavour to otherwise generic stories.

Many operetta plots of this period emphasize cultural and ethnic differences. Some feature cultures from outside the empire, partaking in the larger European artistic movement of exoticism. For example, Suppé's *Fatinitza* (1876) is set in a Russian army camp during the Crimean War and addresses cultural difference, though mostly through stereotypes such as a Russian love for vodka and Turkish harem life. This was evidently appealing material for Viennese audiences. Other works set within the empire and emphasizing the diversity of their own countrymen may have furthered the integration and acceptance of different groups in the complex social world of Austria-Hungary.

Along with ethnic difference, class division is a frequent theme in the ironic romantic-comedy plots of operetta. Characters from different social stations often fall in love. While golden-age operettas challenge societal expectations, they usually do not overtly defy them; instead, the lovers are aided by sudden changes in their identity or fortune. For example, at the end of Millöcker's *Bettelstudent* (The Beggar Student, 1882), the title character, a poor student who loves a noblewoman, is elevated to the Polish nobility for his services to the Polish rebellion. Knowledge of the *Volkstheater* tradition can help us interpret these convenient solutions. Before 1848, when theatre texts were subject to strict censorship, it was a strong part of the Austrian theatrical tradition to raise the audience's awareness of a significant problem simply by mentioning it. A conventional ending did not undo the importance of what had been suggested earlier.

Operetta plots often mock the stiff, self-conscious elements of nineteenth-century life. In Strauss's *Zigeunerbaron* (The Gypsy Baron) there is a 'Morality Commission' charged with making sure that young people do not violate social norms in their courtships. In *Der Bettelstudent*, the whole plot turns on the overblown German sense of honour: Colonel Ollendorf is mortally offended when a woman slaps him with her fan to rebuff his unwanted kiss; he constantly complains about this by singing his tag phrase, 'ah, but I only kissed her on the shoulder'. While perhaps exaggerated for dramatic purposes, such representations captured real tendencies in central European culture: it was the sense of familiarity that made them so funny.

Viennese operettas also had musical conventions. One was an emphasis on social dances of the period. The waltz, associated with Vienna since the early nineteenth century, was frequently used in operettas, and other couple dances such as the polka were also common. This functions as a way of universalizing the situation: no matter what time or place an operetta might be depicting, it would likely bring in a waltz as a way of signifying its relevance for contemporary spectators. This device also validated the dominant culture of the empire by implying that no matter what exotic world might be portrayed on stage, deep down the central characters – especially the romantic couple – had an essentially Austrian identity and sensibility.

When operettas expanded beyond one-act structures, they usually had three acts: a first to introduce the characters; a second, often a large party in which the dramatic conflicts were intensified; and a third in which people recovered from the excesses of the party and resolved the situation. An important musical feature linked to this design was the climactic finale for each act. This tradition came from both *Volkstheater* and opera, going back to Mozart, Wenzel Müller and Rossini among others. The typical pattern of a finale is that more and more characters gather on stage, some type of unexpected plot event occurs, and the characters' various reactions create growing dramatic and musical tension. Finales usually combine vocal solos, ensembles of the key characters and choral responses to the surprise. This was an ideal opportunity for librettists to develop the plot and composers to build musical intensity, giving an exciting finish to the act, or the entire work.

A third musical feature – inherited from French operetta and in turn passed on to the twentieth-century cabaret – was the couplet: a musically simple song with many verses and a tag-line refrain. The performer was expected to add improvised verses that usually referred to topical matters such as social gossip and political scandals of the day. Audiences looked forward to couplets as moments when the operetta story was linked to their everyday world. This practice continues in Vienna to this day. Cabaret artist Kurt Tucholsky, writing in 1920, conveyed the spirit of the couplet:

> In the couplet, language must write itself. The song they are singing up there is such a flimsy wooden floor, it can't carry much weight. The words must follow one another, light and unforced, the thoughts light and clear – the couplet can definitely not bear tangled, cobbled-together ideas. It's just right for the simplest things, so it can be understood on the fly – you can say anything in a couplet, but you must say it very simply. And before you have happily unified the rhythm, rhyme, and ideas, a whole night may pass. *But nobody should be able to tell.* Only when people say 'You just shook that out of your sleeve!' – only then is the couplet a success.[11]

Franz von Suppé

The family of composer Suppé provides an interesting model of the wide-ranging geographic mixture that could come about in the Austrian Empire. His mother was from Vienna, and his father's family came from what is now Belgium – at a time when the Low Countries were part of the Habsburg domains – but had eventually settled in Italy. His grandfather and father were imperial government officials in present-day Croatia, and Franz grew up in the city of Zara (now Zadar) near the Adriatic Sea: a community that was 'more an Italian than a Dalmatian town' marked by Venetian influence.[12] After his father's death, Suppé and his mother moved to Vienna. He studied music at the Konservatorium der Tonkünstler, where his mentor was Ignaz Ritter von Seyfried (1766–1841), who had studied piano with Mozart and conducted the first performance of Beethoven's opera *Fidelio*.[13] Through his upbringing and training, the young musician encountered various musical influences and had a stronger connection with the past than one might expect of someone born well into the nineteenth century.

Suppé quickly became a man of the theatre. In a career spanning over fifty years, from 1841 till his death in 1895, he composed music for about 200 plays, two ballets and nearly thirty operas and operettas.[14] As music director and composer at various Vienna theatres, he was expected to compose the music needed for whatever new plays were being performed.

Vienna's lively theatrical scene was still deeply imprinted by the *Volkstheater*. Nestroy was widely viewed as the last great master of the *Volksstück*, and, as manager of the Carl-Theater, he was one of several theatre managers who tried to lure Offenbach from Paris to Vienna after Offenbach's operettas became influential throughout Europe. He also played the comic role of Jupiter in Offenbach's *Orpheus in der Unterwelt* (Orpheus in the Underworld) in 1860, when it was performed in Vienna just two years after its Paris premiere.[15]

During Suppé's first twenty years as a theatre composer, he wrote music for many farces (*Possen*) and also for other genres, as designated in the elaborate theatrical language of the time, including magic plays (*Zauberspiele*), portraits (*Charakter-Gemälden*), fairy tales (*Märchen*), dialect folk plays (*Lokalstücke*) and more. It is not surprising that this versatile composer soon took on the challenge of the newly popular operetta genre, beginning with one-act works such as *Das Pensionat* (1860), *Die schöne Galathée* (1865) and *Banditenstreiche* (Bandit Tricks, 1867) and eventually moving to three-act operettas including *Fatinitza* (1876) and *Boccaccio* (1879). His music was sometimes criticized for being too Italianate, sometimes for being unoriginal, but it can certainly be argued that his ability to absorb musical styles served his operettas well – as a brief discussion of scenes from *Fatinitza* and *Boccaccio* will demonstrate.

Suppé was a skilled composer of vocal ensembles and extended scenes. The opening scene of *Fatinitza*, which depicts the awakening of the army camp on a cold morning, offers a good example. After a quiet, tiptoeing opening orchestral theme, the watchman calls for Reveille, and the orchestra responds with a fanfare, symbolizing military life. The staccato instrumental theme returns as a legato solo line for the watchman, who praises the beauty of the snow as a symbol of Russia – but after a glorious arpeggiated cadenza to end the verse, he moves on to a series of octave glissandos on the word 'Brrrrr', adding a touch of humour to his patriotism. Soon afterwards, he is hit by a snowball, and the chorus of military cadets joins him in a playful musical exchange before they too take up the refrain of 'Brrrrr'. Oddly enough, this is a mixed chorus. This surprising gender combination foreshadows the cross-dressing title character, since Fatinitza is an imaginary woman played by soldier Vladimir, who is in turn played by a mezzo-soprano.

The 'Toilet Chorus' from Act II shows Suppé's understated use of exoticism. In this ensemble, the four wives of the Turkish leader put on their make-up and comment on the importance of pleasing him through their beauty. The text indicates that they accept their subordinate position as co-wives, and the musical structure, in which they sing harmoniously in pairs and then alternate solo lines, affirms this. While musical markers of the exotic are muted – some subtle chromaticism and a single augmented second in the instrumental introduction – the delicately interweaving female voices provide a clear symbol of the harem and the Turkish way of life.

Boccaccio presents a rollicking story of late-medieval Italy. The irreverent young writer Boccaccio wins the girl he loves against a background of archetypes often associated with the Middle Ages: proud craftsmen, women who flirt and scold, and lusty students. There are also scenes directly linked to specific stories in Boccaccio's famous collection the *Decameron*. In the duet 'Ein armer Bettler' Boccaccio approaches his beloved while disguised as a blind beggar. In an *Andante* section, he pleads for her pity in operatic style, supported by dramatic chord changes; she then recognizes his voice, and he quietly admits who he is. At this point, the tempo switches to *Allegretto grazioso*, and the music moves into dance style. Some of the rhythms hint at a polka, while others do not quite fit that model. Rudolf Pietsch, a scholar and performer of central European dance music, describes this passage as follows: 'It has the scent of a polka, the idea of a polka – but without the realization. That is important for the composition, because an actual polka would be too primitive.'[16] The music suggests that the couple begins to dance, though this does not actually happen, and the shift of style clearly signals that we are in late-nineteenth-century central Europe, breaking the illusion of medieval Italy and bringing the story directly into the modern empire.

Johann Strauss

Strauss, son of a prominent dance composer and conductor, followed in his father's footsteps at an early age and became known as 'The Waltz King'. He had a busy and lucrative international career as the composer-director of his own dance band when he began to write theatrical works in 1869. He eventually composed a dozen operettas, the most famous being *Die Fledermaus* (1874), *Der Zigeunerbaron* (1885) and *Eine Nacht in Venedig* (A Night in Venice, 1883). From those last two titles, it is clear that the Viennese pattern of representing different ethnic and cultural groups of the empire characterizes Strauss's work just as it did Suppé's. *Die Fledermaus*, in particular, is often seen as a symbol of the values and charm of old Vienna and the empire – though, as we shall see, it presents a gently satirical view.

The plot revolves around a prank played on a wealthy bourgeois couple by a friend. He arranges for both husband and wife, and their chambermaid as well, to attend an elegant party hosted by a decadent Russian prince. They all come to the party separately and in disguise, unaware that the others will be there. Interesting results ensue: husband Gabriel flirts shamelessly with his own wife, Rosalinde, who is masked and playing the role of a Hungarian countess. He also insults their maid, Adele, by exposing her identity in public. Each of the women has a musical showpiece: for Rosalinde, a stage version of the traditional Hungarian csárdás, a dance that moves from a dramatic slow introduction to a vivid, energetic fast section. This role was created by the famous Marie Geistinger (1836–1903), who also played many Offenbach roles in Vienna. Adele sings a coloratura piece – known as 'The Laughing Song' because of its 'ha ha ha' refrain – denying that she is a maid, for in that case how could she have such a perfect face and figure? As Gabriel, Adele and the audience are all aware that she is indeed a chambermaid, this piece gently mocks class prejudice.

This party scene also features the bored, self-indulgent Prince Orlofsky – another pants role played by a mezzo-soprano – whose motto, explained in his couplet, is 'Chacun à son gout' (To each his own). Orlofsky clearly represents difference, but there are so many possible reasons that it is impossible to pin him down: does his otherness result from being Russian? Being a prince? His ambiguous sexuality? This highly distinctive role is open to many interpretations. Orlofsky insists that all his guests enjoy themselves and urges dancing and drinking. There is a waltz centred on champagne and a wild polka.

The central moment of the Act II finale captures the remarkable mixture of irony and sentimentality that characterizes golden-age operetta. The intoxicated guests all enter into symbolic brother-and-sister relations by agreeing to use the informal word 'Du' (thou), a very significant ceremony in Germanic culture. This section of the finale opens as Falke – the character who has set up the whole situation – sings a captivating melody that mixes the harmonic stability of arpeggiation with dissonant leaps and chromatic passing tones for emotional emphasis. This is taken up, in harmony, first by the other lead characters and then by the whole chorus. The invitation to call one another 'Du' comes in the following text:

> *Brüderlein und Schwesterlein*
> *Wollen Alle wir sein,*
> *Stimmt mit mir ein!*
> *Lasst das traute Du uns schenken,*
> *Für die Ewigkeit,*
> *Immer so wie heut,*
> *Wenn wir morgen noch d'ran denken!*[17]

> Little brothers and sisters
> We all want to be,
> Join in with me!
> Let us give each other the intimate 'Du',

For eternity,
Always just like today,
If we still remember it tomorrow!

Considering all the conflicts that have been brought out just before this – the attempted adultery of a husband with his own wife (who, as the audience knows, is also considering cheating on him), the inequality of social classes and the contradictions of a society divided by factors such as cultural background and sexual preference – this sentimental moment of universal love for humanity is hard to take seriously. The text supports this, reminding us that these deliriously happy people are all drunk on champagne and unlikely to remember any of this the next day.

Yet somehow the music carries listeners along, making us want to believe in the wondrous possibilities of reconciliation. The choral text degenerates into nonsense words based on Du: 'duidu, duidu, la la la la la la', whose lush harmony imitates the Austrian folk sound, grounded in the improvised vocal singing of the Tyrol and other Alpine regions. Harmony, national pride and wishful thinking carry the night, no matter how they may be shattered in the light of morning.

Mundane reality returns in Act III as all the bleary, hungover characters meet in the local prison. Here, another operetta tradition is found: the third-act comedian. This role is usually designed for a particularly good actor and is normally a speaking part in Viennese dialect. This actor is expected to improvise new lines and to make contemporary references, as in a couplet. Usually the character represented comes from the lower class and thus can be viewed as a return of the Hanswurst tradition. (There are exceptions in later works: for example, in Emmerich Kálmán's 1928 operetta *Die Herzogin von Chicago* (The Duchess of Chicago), the third-act comedian plays a king.) In *Die Fledermaus*, this role belongs to the jailer, Frosch. He tries to make sense of the strange relationships of the people who show up at his jail, as the operetta winds its way to a resolution of all its conflicts and contradictions.

The Role of Hungary in Austrian Operetta

The multi-ethnic nature of the empire was a central preoccupation of Viennese operetta, perhaps even a generating force. Even works like Suppé's *Fatinitza* that portray cultures from outside the empire may have been inspired by the diversity within it. Over time, Hungarian life and Gipsy culture within Hungary particularly attracted the creators of operetta, especially after the *Ausgleich*. Simultaneously an outsider and an insider, Hungary was a clear symbol of the challenges facing a multi-ethnic political state.

As early as 1846, only two years into his bandleader career, Johann Strauss on tour in Pest (now Budapest) composed a *Pesther Csárdás*, op. 23.[18] Twenty years later, Suppé composed the operetta *Leichte Kavallerie* (Light Cavalry): 'an early stage of the turn towards Hungary, a reverence [Verbeugung] for its people and their feelings'.[19] Amid musical references to Hungary, the story shows how the alien Hungarian girl in a German village is eventually accepted and embraced. Rosalinde's csárdás in *Die Fledermaus* has been mentioned already as an example of Hungarian folk music represented on the operetta stage.

Strauss's exploration of Hungarian style reached its peak in 1885 with *Der Zigeunerbaron,* based on the novella *Sáffi* by Hungarian writer Mór Jókai (1825–1904). Composed less than twenty years after the *Ausgleich*, it presents a positive view of both Hungarians and Gipsies. As historian Moritz Csáky explains:

> The image of the Gipsies drawn by the *Zigeunerbaron*. . . can be seen as a direct and deliberate attempt to provide respect and recognition to this particular ethnic group, which was often forced as a despised outsider to the farthest margins of society. This image of the Gipsies also contains an indirect invitation to tolerate and respect ethnic minorities in general, and to integrate them into the multiethnic fabric of the monarchy.[20]

Saffi's 'Zigeunerlied' presents the Gipsy perspective. Its first stanza refers to the common stereotype of Gipsies as thieves: 'Man, watch out for your horse! Woman, watch out for your child! Dschingrah, dschingrah, the Gipsies are here!' In the second stanza, these phrases are repeated, but the warnings are replaced by reassurances: 'trust him with your horse/child'.[21] The typical Hungarian is represented by the endearing pig farmer Zsupán. When this character first appears onstage, he is asked to sign a document, and his reply, the song 'Ja, das Schreiben und das Lesen' (Yes, reading and writing) became particularly beloved. In this piece, Zsupán explains that book learning is of no use to him, since his entire life is dedicated to raising pigs. As Richard Specht writes, in Zsupán, Strauss created a lively character 'who is immediately embodied and made present by striking up just a few bars of his music'.[22] This role was created by the fine singer-actor Alexander Girardi (1850–1918).

While it might appear to a modern sensibility that such representations of typical Hungarians and Gipsies are grounded in stereotypes rather than reality, this bringing to life of stereotypes as memorable individuals with whom the audience could identify and sympathize was part of the process of integrating the empire – a process in which operettas played an important role. Similar to their French models, Viennese operettas poked fun at social norms while glorifying life's pleasures: drinking, dancing and sexuality. Grounded in their *Volkstheater* history, they emphasized typical characters from various parts of the empire. Their charming, fun-loving exterior often hid a deeper purpose. Through clever representations of people, communities and institutions, they encouraged self-expression, tolerance and social integration. Beneath their charm lay a basic concern for the needs of the empire and perhaps also a prophetic awareness that its precarious balance of centripetal and centrifugal forces might not endure.

Notes

1. Joseph Roth, *Die Kapuzinergruft*, quoted in Moritz Csáky, *Ideologie der Operette und Wiener Moderne: Ein kulturhistorischer Essay* (Vienna, Böhlau, 1996), 202. All translations are my own.
2. Robert A. Kann, *The Multinational Empire: Nationalism and National Reform in the Habsburg Monarchy 1848–1918*, Vol. 1 (New York: Columbia University Press, 1950), 8.
3. Csáky, *Ideologie der Operette*, 188.
4. Waltraud Heindl-Langer, *Josephinische Mandarine: Bürokratie und Beamte in Österreich. Vol. 2: 1848–1914* (Vienna: Böhlau, 2013), 171.
5. Adolf Bäuerle, *Wien, Paris, London und Constantinopel* (Vienna: publisher anon., 1823), 13–14. Albert Schatz Collection, Library of Congress, www.loc.gov/resource/musschatz.13331.0/?sp=4 (accessed 19 Mar. 2018).
6. Otto Rommel, *Die Alt-Wiener Volkskomödie: Ihre Geschichte vom Barocken Welt-Theater bis zum Tode Nestroys* (Vienna: Anton Schroll, 1952), 230.
7. Rommel, *Alt-Wiener Volkskomödie*, 229.
8. Rudolf Payer von Thurn (ed.), 'Triumph Römischer Tugend und Tapferkeit oder Gordianus der Grosse' in *Wiener Haupt- und Staatsaktionen*, Vol. 1 (Vienna, Verlag des Literarischen Vereins in Wien, 1908), 15.
9. Rommel, *Alt-Wiener Volkskomödie*, 430.
10. Johann Strauss, *Die Fledermaus*, piano score arranged by Richard Genée. Friedrich Schreiber (Vienna, no date), 43.
11. Kurt Tucholsky, 'Das Couplet', *Kritiken und Recensionen: Gesammelte Schriften (1907–1935)*, www.textlog.de/tucholsky-das-couplet.html (accessed 5 Oct. 2017).
12. See Hans-Dieter Roser, *Franz von Suppé: Werk und Leben, Neue Musikportraits III* (Vienna: Steinbauer, 2007), 13–15.
13. On Ignaz and his brother Josef (1780–1849), both linked to the Viennese theatre scene, see Christian Fastli, 'Seyfried, Familie' in *Oesterreichisches Musiklexikon Online*, www .musiklexikon.ac.at/ml?frames=no (accessed 8 May 2019).
14. See the detailed catalogue of Suppé's works in Roser, *Franz von Suppé*, 257–75.
15. See Roser, *Franz von Suppé*, 79–81.
16. Private communication.
17. Strauss, *Die Fledermaus*, 97–8.
18. Norbert Linke, *Johann Strauß (Sohn) in Selbstzeugnissen und Bilddokumenten* (Reinbek bei Hamburg, Rowohlt: 1982), 42.
19. Roser, *Franz von Suppé*, 119.
20. Csáky, *Ideologie der Operette*, 88.
21. Johann Strauss, *Der Zigeunerbaron*, piano score (Leipzig: Aug. Cranz, 1886), 46–7.
22. Richard Specht, *Johann Strauße* (Berlin: Marquardt, 1909), 65, quoted in Linke, *Johann Strauß*, 135.

Recommended Reading

Allinson, Mark. *Germany and Austria 1814–2000.* Abingdon, UK; New York: Routledge, 2014.

Crittenden, Camille. *Johann Strauß and Vienna: Operetta and the Politics of Popular Culture.* Cambridge: Cambridge University Press, 2000.

Csáky, Moritz. *Ideologie der Operette und Wiener Moderne: Ein kulturhistorischer Essay.* Vienna: Böhlau, 1996.

Linke, Norbert. *Johann Strauß (Sohn) in Selbstzeugnissen und Bilddokumenten.* Reinbek bei Hamburg: Rowohlt, 1982.

Roser, Hans-Dieter. *Franz von Suppé: Werk und Leben, Neue Musikportraits III.* Vienna: Steinbauer, 2007.

Traubner, Richard. *Operetta: A Theatrical History.* New York: Routledge, 2003.

3 London and Gilbert and Sullivan

BRUNO BOWER

There is something rather mischievous about including Gilbert and Sullivan in *The Cambridge Companion to Operetta*. In *The Cambridge Companion to Gilbert and Sullivan*, published in 2009, Meinhard Saremba stated in no uncertain terms that these shows are not operettas and that the idea of them being so is a myth. There is clearly much at stake for Saremba: 'Calling these comic operas "operettas" implies a degradation which much too often results in routine and second-rate musical standards.'[1] He supports his claim by pointing out (correctly) that neither Gilbert nor Sullivan ever referred to the productions as operettas and that the political satire was mild enough to allow Queen Victoria herself to enjoy them. He also draws parallels with comic works by Mozart and Rossini. Certainly, it is clear from the opening of the chapter that he feels that these shows could aim considerably higher: 'The crucial question is: are these works merely a sociological phenomenon that deserves nothing more than a marginal note in music histories, or are they substantial operas that can claim their place in the history of European music theatre?'[2] Saremba clearly has the latter view in mind, as his chapter is littered with references to high-status composers that he would no doubt like to see Sullivan associated with, such as Wagner, Mahler and Tippett.

Saremba's position is one that scholars working on operetta will no doubt find sympathetic. Older writings on Gilbert and Sullivan, even those which were ostensibly attempting to justify academic attention for these shows, often unintentionally perpetuate a genre hierarchy. For example, an article in *The Musical Times* by Gavin Thomas from 1992 suggests that, over the course of the collaboration, the shows progressed towards 'true music drama'.[3] If Wagnerian opera is the bar for achievement, we can be in no doubt that Thomas's general use of the word 'operettas' to describe the shows is not a compliment. By 2000, *The Musical Times* had clearly shifted its position, as reflected in an article by Nigel Burton. Here he argued that the shows represent 'comic operas', taking his cue from the work of Gervase Hughes, but in doing so implied that works that really were operettas would be unworthy of attention.[4] These articles make it clear that the wider community of Gilbert and Sullivan enthusiasts and scholars may have had good reasons to retain the title 'Savoy Operas', created by the original promoter, Richard D'Oyly Carte.

[47]

If much of the agitation over genre is motivated by status anxiety rather than by real concern for accuracy, then it should perhaps alert us to the presence of some problematic claims, not least to do with the word operetta. Gilbert and Sullivan might not have used it, but then neither did Offenbach, who tended to use the terms *opéra bouffe* or *opéra comique*. The fact that 'operetta' stuck for Offenbach's works shows that it was not the composer's intention that determined the label but rather the more general contemporary understanding of what the word meant. In 1860s and 1870s London, operetta signified a French production with racy plots and revealing costumes. Shows such as Offenbach's *La belle Hélène*, opening in London in 1866, obviously fitted that description, whereas Gilbert and Sullivan openly sought to avoid those elements in their productions. D'Oyly Carte's creation of 'Savoy Operas' as a title was therefore a marketing ploy as much as anything else, ensuring that the audience would perceive a distance between these shows and their morally dubious competitors. It had very little to do with structure or quality of the material; these aspects were treated as being of a piece with the moral concerns.

This is a very different understanding from the present-day usage of operetta, a technical term for pieces of musical theatre that use spoken dialogue rather than recitative and generally have a 'light' character. Importantly, it no longer carries the Victorian connotation of something scandalous. On this basis, there is clearly plenty of scope for thinking of these shows as operettas. Viewed purely as a guide to public perceptions, the Wikipedia page on 'Operetta' is particularly indicative, with a discussion of Gilbert and Sullivan forming roughly half of the section entitled 'Operetta in England'. In another example, Joe Deer and Rocco Dal Vera's *Acting in Musical Theatre* matter-of-factly puts the Savoy Operas in a section entitled 'Gilbert and Sullivan operetta', as distinct from 'European operetta', when providing overviews of different musical theatre styles.[5] Rather than viewing it as a negative term, musical theatre performers seem to view operetta as just another category of work with which they are expected to engage. Recent scholarly work has also begun drawing these shows into the history of the British musical, another genre altogether, but one that evidently owes much to the Savoy Operas, showing that there is room for a flexible understanding of what genre these shows represent.[6] On a final, practical note, Saremba's concern over 'second-rate' performances as inherent to operetta seems difficult to sustain when we think of recordings of, say, Elisabeth Schwarzkopf in *The Merry Widow* (1953/63), Placido Domingo in *Die Fledermaus* (1986) or Natalie Dessay in *Orphée aux enfers* (1997).

For the present chapter, it does not really matter what label we give to the collaborative efforts of William Schwenck Gilbert (1836–1911) and

Arthur Seymour Sullivan (1842–1900). Whatever one calls them, the following discussion demonstrates that they provide plenty of interest for musicologists working on operetta, and the status anxiety surrounding them is especially useful in this regard. An opening section on the history of the Savoy Operas shows that respectability was a primary motivation behind the way the shows were created and marketed, and that it formed the background to changing perceptions of the two creators ever since their deaths. More balanced reappraisals have appeared during the last fifteen years, but there are still some aspects that need critical attention, especially the continued entanglement of ethical and aesthetic concerns in scholarly writing. The second section addresses distinctive features of the content of these shows, in particular Gilbert's legal influences and stage-craft, and Sullivan's musical deadpanning. Anxiety appears again over the quotations and references in both the music and text, but this can be understood as a fundamental part of the audience experience and closely tied to the creation of class identity. Finally, a discussion of modern Gilbert and Sullivan performances and enthusiast communities serves as a springboard for considering issues of politics, particularly in the way the shows are staged, and points the way to possible left-wing interpretations.

History

There are fourteen works for which Gilbert wrote words and Sullivan wrote music, listed below (see Table 3.1).

Thespis was a Christmas entertainment commissioned for the Gaiety Theatre by the manager, John Hollingshead. It was a success within limited expectations (it was only meant to last for the Christmas season) but was thought to be too highbrow for the usual Gaiety audience, who were used to a more straightforward variety of burlesque. No further collaborative work was undertaken until Richard D'Oyly Carte brought them together to produce *Trial by Jury*, a programme filler that achieved astounding success in its own right. Carte immediately set about persuading the two to work together again, realizing that a full-length work would be a highly market-able proposition to the crowds who had flocked to see *Trial*. However, he had to fight off competition from other promoters, who had made the same observation, and it took time to acquire enough financial backing to get anything off the ground. The Comedy Opera Company was finally launched in 1877 and commissioned the work that became *The Sorcerer*. It was not quite the phenomenon that *Trial* had been but was enough of a success to persuade the backers that further full-length works should be

Table 3.1 *Gilbert and Sullivan collaborations*

Name	Date	No. of London performances (original runs)
Thespis; or, The Gods Grown Old	1871	63
Trial by Jury	1875	131
The Sorcerer	1877	175
H.M.S Pinafore; or, The Lass That Loved a Sailor	1878	571
Pirates of Penzance; or, The Slave of Duty	1879	363
Patience; or Bunthorne's Bride	1881	578
Iolanthe; or, The Peers and the Peri	1882	398
Princess Ida; or, Castle Adamant	1884	246
The Mikado; or, The Town of Titipu	1885	672
Ruddigore; or, The Witch's Curse	1887	288
The Yeomen of the Guard; or, The Merryman and His Maid	1888	423
The Gondoliers; or, The King of Barataria	1889	554
Utopia Limited; or, The Flowers of Progress	1893	245
The Grand Duke; or, The Statutory Duel	1896	123

supported. *H.M.S. Pinafore* finally proved Carte correct, eventually achieving enormous international success and providing the necessary finances to detach himself from the backers of the Comedy Opera Company and set up the D'Oyly Carte Opera Company. The proceeds from *Pirates of Penzance*, an even greater success, were then directed towards the construction of a new purpose-built theatre, the Savoy. The theatre opened in 1881 with *Patience*, which transferred there mid-run from the Opera Comique, and thereafter the Savoy served as the primary venue for the rest of Gilbert and Sullivan's joint works.

Everything about the way the shows were created, staged, performed and promoted showed an intense concern with status and respectability. Regina B. Oost and Michael Goron have shown, between them, that these ideas motivated the actions of everyone in the company.[7] Carte's marketing material was directed at an affluent middle class who thought that theatre attendance was disreputable and reassured them that they would be experiencing an entertainment of the utmost propriety. Gilbert exercised strict and complete control over the stage action and the cast with the explicit intent of preventing improvisation or gagging, and to ensure that the costumes would be appropriately modest, especially for the women. His plots upheld middle-class moral values even as they satirized them, with his constant stream of complex vocabulary, legalese and puns appealing to the well-educated. As a former Mendelssohn Scholar and a well-respected composer of symphonic works, incidental music and oratorio, Arthur Sullivan brought with him a guarantee of musical quality. The cast were carefully selected from companies that already held sound reputations, such as the German Reed Entertainments. For their own part, the cast strove to present themselves as highly skilled and morally unimpeachable to counter the idea that theatre work was degrading. All of this was wrapped up in a distinctly nationalistic package: the fact that the producer, creative team and most of the cast were British was exploited to the full, allowing the audience to enjoy the entertainment with pride in their country. Of course, it was just as important that, implicitly, as much distance as possible was put between these shows and the racy productions associated with the French, especially *opéra bouffe* and operetta.

In the end, the partnership dissolved for two reasons, both present from the beginning. The first was a creative difference: Gilbert's preference for shallow, satirical characters and a stock plot (known as the 'lozenge plot') that involved a supernatural element causing the action and then reversing it sat badly with Sullivan, who wanted more expressive scope for the music, both in terms of humane characters and realistic action. These issues were at the root of a brief row between *Princess Ida* and *The Mikado* but continued to cause problems once the partnership had resumed. The second issue was to do with money. Gilbert distrusted D'Oyly Carte's financial management right from the start of the D'Oyly Carte Company, eventually leading to a major confrontation over a minor expenses quibble in 1892, known as the 'Carpet Quarrel'. The affair permanently damaged the working relationship between composer and dramatist. They were persuaded to work together twice more, primarily in the hope of further profits for Carte and for Tom Chappell, the publisher of their music, but *Utopia Limited* received a rather mixed reception, and *The Grand Duke* was considered to be a failure (at least in comparison with the earlier successes). Without the promise of financial reward to drive further work, and with recriminations abounding on both sides, the partnership collapsed for good.

Wider perceptions of Gilbert and of Sullivan have fluctuated considerably since they ceased to work together. For most of the twentieth century, Sullivan was generally dismissed as a frivolous composer unworthy of serious attention, an appendage to Gilbert's genius. The latter was credited with much greater influence on subsequent generations of dramatists and librettists, including Ira Gershwin, Oscar Hammerstein II and Tim Rice. This image was further boosted by the fiercely loyal accounts by D'Oyly Carte cast members, no doubt engendered by the intense working relationship that Gilbert's directorial approach required.[8] However, this began to change during the 1980s and 1990s with the publication of several biographical studies which openly sought to dispel the image of Gilbert as a tough but essentially likeable character, focussing instead on his aggressive, bullying behaviour. David Eden brought in readings of Freud, concluding his assessment of Gilbert's personality by stating that: 'everything we know about him can be accommodated within the assumption that the basis of his personal and artistic psychology was sadomasochistic at the infantile level'.[9] Eden no doubt intended to be matter-of-fact rather than judgemental, but it is difficult to read this assessment as entirely neutral. As Gilbert's stock declined, Sullivan's rose. Scholars began to pick up on the lone voices who had previously promoted Sullivan, such as Thomas Dunhill and Gervase Hughes, and developed a more sympathetic view of the composer's output. The shift might have been partly aided by the emergence of Popular Music Studies, which challenged the notion that only 'high' art was worthy of serious attention. However, as noted earlier, the terms which the older scholars used to promote Sullivan were generally of the hierarchical variety: they described him as a 'genius', and his scores as 'masterpieces'. Interestingly, Sullivan's rise in status was matched by calls for Gilbert's contribution to be downgraded, as if one could only ever be promoted at the expense of the other. As Saremba put it, 'If we unscrew the firm's nameplate and replace it, for example, with "Sullivan: *Patience*, libretto by W. S. Gilbert", it would be much easier to free worn-out conventionalities.'[10] Writing in 2009, Saremba was something of an exception: on the whole, the new millennium seems to have brought with it some more balanced approaches. Ainger's dual biography and Crowther's work on Gilbert both present more rounded (not to say careful) pictures of their subject(s).[11]

One aspect of Sullivan's personality does perhaps need some critical attention: he is often portrayed as being unhappy about the way the Savoy Operas took time away from his 'serious' music. There has been little acknowledgement that this image derives from Victorian sources that would have been quite happy to suppress aspects of Sullivan's personality which did not fit the contemporary ideal of how a great composer should behave. Mozart, Beethoven and Schubert (among many others) were already being whitewashed into paragons of moral virtue, and this was the mould that Sullivan was expected to fit. In this cultural climate, we should expect no one, least of all Sullivan himself, to have admitted that he was perhaps more attached to his Savoy Operas and their attendant money and fame than to his serious works. True geniuses were supposed to view their lesser works with scorn and maintain indifference to immediate financial rewards. Nonetheless, Sullivan continued to work with Gilbert long beyond the point where a more aesthetically driven composer might have stopped. More importantly, his pride in his creations can be seen both before and after the partnership had collapsed. He conducted for revivals (at least for the first nights), including *Mikado* in 1895 and *Yeomen* in 1897, and attended gala performances, such as the twenty-first anniversary performance of *Sorcerer* in 1898. He also conducted a 'command performance' of *The Mikado* in Berlin in 1900, requested by Kaiser Wilhelm II. As president of the 1900 International Loan Exhibition of Musical Instruments at the Crystal Palace, the ten manuscripts he donated included the full scores for *Mikado* and *Cox and Box* (an early comic collaboration with F. C. Burnand from 1866).[12] These were not the actions of a man who genuinely resented his lighter works.

There is a deeper issue at work here, namely that there remains some anxiety around creative artists who do not conform to 'correct' behaviour. In principle, there is nothing about Gilbert's difficult personality or Sullivan's possible preference for light music that inherently prevents scholarly interest in their output and its context. Nevertheless, a heightened interest in Gilbert's endless legal wranglings was implicitly used to justify a drop in his status. Sullivan's evident attachment to the Savoy Operas and to the idiom they represent remains unspoken and quite possibly a source of embarrassment for those who wish to promote him. It suggests that present-day academics continue (perhaps unintentionally) to conflate ethics and aesthetics in ways that might impede more balanced reappraisals.

Content

Gilbert's scripts contained much of the character stereotypes and satire of social conventions and current affairs that we would expect from a lighter theatrical genre, but one thing that made his contribution particularly distinctive was its reliance on legal language.[13] Gilbert had studied law at King's College London, and, after detours through the civil service and the military, went to the Bar in 1861. It quickly became clear that he was not going to be successful in this line of work, and he slowly began building a parallel career on the poetry, plays and journalism that had already started to provide some steady income. However, he never truly left the world of law. In his personal life, he was known to be extremely litigious, preferring to go to court over any (perceived) slight no matter how trivial, even where an ordinary conversation might have settled the dispute. It is therefore no surprise that the law plays such an important role in his libretti. It serves as the basis for major and minor plot points (to say nothing of *Trial*, in which it forms the entire piece), and legalese peppers much of the dialogue.

Gilbert's directorial approach was as distinctive as his words. He used wooden blocks and a model theatre to work out every movement in advance of the first rehearsal. He would then proceed to rigorously drill the actors until they followed his exact plan and produced the precise vocal inflections he had in mind. Any kind of inaccuracy or improvisation was forbidden. His scenarios and costumes were intended to be realistic (albeit stereotypical), as shown by the fact that he went to Portsmouth to examine naval uniforms in preparation for *Pinafore*. The purpose of all this control and focus was aimed at generating a particular kind of humour, one that highlights the ridiculousness of the words through the ordinariness of the surroundings, and through the characters treating every absurdity as normal and expected. The effect is subtle and would quickly be destroyed by actors playing their characters as too self-aware, going off script or breaking the fourth wall. The word that best summarizes the kind of comedy that Gilbert was aiming for is 'deadpan'. The fact that the word did not exist in Gilbert's time (it was coined in the US in the late 1920s) emphasizes the originality of his approach. It explains why he had to behave so autocratically with his actors: it is a difficult effect to maintain, and they had probably never encountered this kind of humour before.

The idea that Gilbert's comedy was essentially deadpan is universally accepted; it is rarely noted that Sullivan was often striving for the same effect, though the recent work by James Brooks Kuykendall on Sullivan's 'humour in incongruity' is a welcome exception.[14] In principle, this should not come as a surprise: one of the pleasures Gilbert had in working with Sullivan was the fact that he never had to explain the jokes. Sullivan must surely have understood, then, that music could also heighten the comedy by appearing to be entirely serious. However, Sullivan's music is generally understood to be the softening, humanizing counterbalance to Gilbert's satirical bite. This is undoubtedly true in some places: the music for 'He lives' (*Iolanthe*), with its absence of parody in the text, would be impossible to perform in any manner other than heartfelt. Nonetheless, there are plenty of songs that could be performed much less sincerely than their serious surfaces imply. The pseudo-nationalistic songs are the most overt examples, including 'He is an Englishman' (*Pinafore*) or 'There is a little group of isles' (*Utopia*), but there are also more subtle examples of musical deadpanning. Yum-Yum's meditation on her own beauty in 'The sun whose rays' (*Mikado*) and Lady Jane's thoughts about her own lack thereof in 'Silvered is the raven hair' (*Patience*) are generally played as emotionally straight, and indeed more than one author has asserted this is the only correct approach. But other possibilities do exist: the music in both these songs could easily be treated as only *seemingly* sincere, reinforcing the ridiculousness of the lyrics. It requires a different style of performance and staging, but the effect is certainly achievable. The fact that this approach is rarely taken might be connected with the wish to emphasize the seriousness and corresponding respectability of Sullivan's music, as discussed above. It may as yet be too unpalatable for scholars, stage directors and conductors to admit that, most of the time, he might have been aiming for something less disruptive of Gilbert's verbal satire.

Both the words and the music made reference to a huge variety of pre-existing sources. Someone watching the original run of *Ruddigore* could spot not just a quotation from Shakespeare's *Hamlet* ('Alas, poor ghost') but also note overtones of Ophelia in Mad Margaret's characterization. There is even a specific reference to Henry Irving's 1878 production at The Lyceum, with Ellen Terry as Ophelia, built into the lyrics for Mad Margaret's opening number:

> Mad, I,
> Yes, very.
> But, why?
> Mystery!

The musical setting and the rhyme-scheme ensure that the last word will be pronounced 'Miss Terry'. Alongside that, the audience would be able to exercise their awareness of Donizetti's *Lucia di Lammermoor*, Ambroise Thomas's *Hamlet*, the sailor's hornpipe, vampire stories and a range of nautical and gothic melodramas, not to mention Gilbert's own self-referencing of *Ages Ago*, written for the German Reed Gallery of Illustration, and the source of the device of ghosts emerging from their portraits. The texture of references found in the Savoy Operas has often been a source of anxiety for the scholars working on them, with authors expressing concern that the musical quotations may be taken as signs that Sullivan was not totally original and that by inference he was therefore not a genius (Gilbert generally escapes such concerns). Even Kuykendall's otherwise nuanced exploration of Sullivan's allusions perpetuates this idea by deliberately giving less attention to quotations, which he deems to be 'superficial', in favour of 'deeper' references. Recent scholarship has begun to move beyond these narrow concerns and has found ways to put such references to productive use. Carolyn Williams's work is exemplary, both for the thoroughness with which she outlines the reference material that Gilbert and Sullivan drew on and also for the breadth of her cultural interpretations, especially on issues of gender and society.[15]

As yet, though, there has been little attempt to address a much more direct question: why did Gilbert and Sullivan include straight quotations in the first place? Allusions to overall genres of music and theatre would perhaps have been difficult to completely avoid, but literal quotations could easily have been left out, sidestepping questions of originality or plagiarism. The point of the quotations must surely have been that they were supposed to be recognized. Viewed from this angle, we can begin to see the dynamic of reference and recognition as one of the fundamental aspects of the experience for the Savoy audience. Michael Goron made passing reference to this phenomenon in his work, stating that '[Sullivan's] clever parodies of grand opera ... would have flattered the musical aware-ness of the *cognoscenti* ... ', but we could go much further than simply treating references as flattery.[16] Every time an audience member recog-nized a quotation, it helped them create an identity as being the kind of person who knows such things. To put it shortly: it did not just flatter *cognoscenti*, it created them as well. Moreover, the breadth of the reference material on offer in the Savoy Operas suggests that the in-crowd was familiar with rather more than just grand opera, as shown by the *Ruddigore* example above. These were people who knew (or at least seemed to know) both their Shakespeare and their melodrama, their grand opera and their parlour music, their ballad song and their operetta, and would have been keen to demonstrate this wide-ranging knowledge. Overall, it seems reasonable to suggest that these quotations and allusions were intensely bound up with a bourgeois cultural identity and were every bit as involved in defining a middle class as the marketing, costumes and staging.

Gilbert and Sullivan Today

When it comes to the modern world of the Savoy Operas, there are few voices more authoritative than Ian Bradley. His published work has dis-cussed most of the twentieth-century performance history in the UK and the US, especially the period following the expiration of the D'Oyly Carte Company's copyright in 1961.[17] Among other things, he has summarized the major professional and amateur productions, outlined the general character (including gender balance and predominant personalities) of the amateur community and documented the history and practices of the International Gilbert and Sullivan Festival, beginning in Buxton in 1994. He has also listed the hugely varied parodic and rewritten versions of the shows, and the references that have appeared in books, television and film. One thing that Bradley has not yet had the opportunity to list are the references in video games. These can be little nods, such as the protagonist Princess Ida in Ustwo Games's *Monument Valley*, possibly motivated by the topsy-turvy Escher-like landscapes. A more overt instance is the short excerpt of the Major General's song from *Pirates* included as a hidden bonus scene in BioWare's *Mass Effect 2*, sung by the alien doctor Mordin Solus as 'I am the very model of a scientist Salarian'. The scene prompted several fan responses, posted on YouTube, including an expanded version rewriting the entirety of the original song for a 'scientist Salarian', a version entitled 'I am the very model of a Mass Effect enthusiast', and a somewhat tangential rewriting of the Lord High Executioner's song, 'As someday it might happen' (also known as the 'Little List' song) from *Mikado*, satirizing aspects of both the *Mass Effect* series and the community around it.[18] In the internet age, these creations must surely represent only a fraction of the unexpected byways down which the Savoy Operas are passing.

Studies of the Gilbert and Sullivan community usually include some musing on the future of Savoy Opera performance. Many of the existing enthusiasts are ageing, and attention is given both within the community and in some of the studies which discuss them to the question of how to engage a new generation. Stephanie Pitts mentions several strategies in her study of the attendees at the Buxton Festival and sensibly argues that the annual youth production may be achieving more in this respect than the idea, suggested by several participants, that all it would take is better advertising.[19] Over the last fifteen years, the UK has seen a noticeable increase in productions by mainstream opera companies, with Opera North's *Ruddigore* (2012) and English National Opera's new stagings of *Gondoliers* (2006), *Pirates* (2005 and 2015) and *Iolanthe* (2018). They are often seen as safely profitable bets with the usual older crowd, rather than serious attempts to bring in a younger audience.[20] More headway on that front has perhaps been made by Sasha Regan's all-male productions, which began with *Pirates* in 2009: one reviewer of the 2017 production of *Mikado* noticed a 'refreshingly youthful' audience in attendance.[21] In the meantime, the International Festival continues to attract plenty of companies and enthusiasts, with seven university societies entering productions into the annual UniFest competition in 2018.[22] Graduates from these student groups, along with those from the many others round the country that did not enter the competition, will no doubt go on to fill the ranks of adult amateur, semi-professional and professional companies. One way or another, performances of the Savoy Operas will not be ending any time soon.

The present body of research on the Gilbert and Sullivan community provides a very solid foundation on which subsequent researchers can now build more critical studies. The following serves as a possible example. Every year, there are dozens of productions of *Mikado* put on by amateur, semi-professional and professional groups around the world. Many of these shows will follow the well-established practice of providing new words for the 'Little List' song, replacing the now unpalatable list of people that Gilbert deemed expendable with up-to-date references to politics and popular culture. A study of 'Little List' rewrites would provide an unusually candid window on to the way performing companies construct their identity, especially if the location, age group and professional status of the company are taken into account as well. It would also provide insight into the kinds of audiences these groups expect to play to. The value of such a study would lie in its ability to address an otherwise difficult subject for Gilbert and Sullivan scholars: the conservative views of many current enthusiasts. This aspect of the community is only mentioned in passing in the existing accounts by Bradley, Pitts and Shani D'Cruz.[23] A study of 'Little List' rewrites would cut through to the heart of the matter, allowing us to speak with much greater certainty about the political leanings associated with Gilbert and Sullivan performance today. Bradley may wish to debunk Jonathan Miller's statement that the shows represent 'UKIP set to music', or Germaine Greer's description of the audiences as 'racist, right-wing Olde English nerdery'; but without some proper data to show how the political terrain lies, such debunking will be difficult to achieve.[24]

This is not just a matter of sociological interest but is also essential for understanding the choices made by directors and actors in terms of how the shows are interpreted and staged. For one thing, if the community really is as conservative as it often seems, then it would explain the overall paucity of productions which exploit the potential left-wing readings of the Savoy Operas. The idea that these shows can support such interpretations at all might seem surprising to those familiar with Gilbert's social conservatism. However, Michael Goron has recently pointed out that the middle-class audience that Carte targeted required mockery of the upper classes as much as of the lower in order to define their position as being in between the two. In this context, it becomes easier to see a running thread emerging from Gilbert's texts: the rich and powerful are often shown to be above the law. The Bad Baron in *Ruddigore* never seems to be at risk of any legal repercussions for the daily crime he is cursed to commit. The Judge in *Trial* can get away with breaching his promise to marry his wealthy patron's 'elderly, ugly daughter', whereas the Defendant, Edwin, has been put on trial for the same crime and would probably be found guilty amid the transparent bias against him. Ralph's patriotic defence for trying to marry above his station ('I am an Englishman') at the end of *Pinafore* is initially ignored. However, once his high-ranking birth has been revealed, he can now marry whoever he wants, and the final chorus of 'He is an Englishman' implies that now his patriotism is one of his defining virtues.

These political points would resonate very strongly with the increasing public awareness of wealth and power inequalities and could doubtless inform some fresh interpretations. A modern-dress production of *Pirates* in which members of an inner-city street gang were all revealed at the end to be investment bankers and hedge-fund managers 'gone wrong' would perfectly capture Gilbert's point that the rich and powerful can get away with illegal activity, and even be promoted, where the poor would simply be arrested. It would render an archaic and often confusing plot immediately relevant to present-day concerns, without even needing to change much of the text. It would also regain the satirical bite that the plot must have conveyed to its original audiences, who were much closer to the time when pirates were unambiguously criminal rather than adventurous and free-spirited (even if the image was already starting to shift towards the latter at the time). For those wishing to attract younger audiences, the kind who turned out in unexpectedly large numbers to vote for the (left-wing) Labour Party during the UK's 2017 General Election, such readings could be exactly what is required to get a new generation interested in Gilbert and Sullivan.

Notes

1. Meinhard Saremba, '"We sing as one individual?" Popular Misconceptions of "Gilbert and Sullivan"' in David Eden and Meinhard Saremba (eds.), *The Cambridge Companion to Gilbert and Sullivan* (Cambridge; New York: Cambridge University Press, 2009), 55.
2. Ibid., 51.
3. Gavin Thomas, 'The Sullivan Paradox. A Fresh Look at Sullivan's Achievements: And Failures', *The Musical Times* 133, no. 1791 (May 1992): 223.
4. Nigel Burton, 'Sullivan Reassessed: See How the Fates', *The Musical Times* 141, no. 1873 (Winter 2000): 15–22.
5. Joe Deer and Rocco Dal Vera, 'Unit 16.2: Gilbert and Sullivan Operetta', in *Acting in Musical Theatre: A Comprehensive Course* (London; New York: Routledge, 2008), 320–8.
6. Carolyn Williams, 'Comic Opera: English Society in Gilbert and Sullivan', in Robert Gordon and Olaf Jubin (eds.), *The Oxford Handbook of the British Musical*, Oxford Handbooks (New York: Oxford University Press, 2016), 91–116.
7. Regina B. Oost, *Gilbert and Sullivan: Class and the Savoy Tradition, 1875–1896* (Farnham; Burlington: Ashgate, 2009); Michael Goron, *Gilbert and Sullivan's 'Respectable Capers': Class, Respectability and the Savoy Operas 1877–1909*, Palgrave Studies in British Musical Theatre (London: Palgrave Macmillan, 2016).
8. For example, see Jessie Bond, *The Life and Reminiscences of Jessie Bond, the Old Savoyard*, ed. Ethel MacGeorge (London: John Lane The Bodley Head Ltd., 1930).
9. David Eden, *Gilbert & Sullivan: The Creative Conflict* (Cranbury: Fairleigh Dickinson University Press, 1986), 82.
10. Saremba, 'We sing as one individual?', 64.
11. Michael Ainger, *Gilbert and Sullivan: A Dual Biography* (Oxford; New York: Oxford University Press, 2002); Andrew Crowther, *Gilbert of Gilbert & Sullivan: His Life and Character* (Stroud: History Press, 2011).
12. The other items included the full score of *The Golden Legend*, the anthem *Sing O Heavens* and six solo songs. *Crystal Palace International Loan Exhibition of Musical Instruments, Official Catalogue* (London: The Crystal Palace Company, 1900), 37.
13. Andrew Goodman's exploration of the legal references in the shows remains one of the best accounts of the historical context: Andrew Goodman, *Gilbert and Sullivan at Law* (Rutherford; London: Fairleigh Dickinson University Press; Associated University Presses, 1983). Other aspects of Gilbert's legal nonsense are outlined in Jon Kertzer, 'Life Plus Ninety-Nine Years: W. S. Gilbert and the Fantasy of Justice', *Mosaic: An Interdisciplinary Critical Journal* 36, no. 2 (June 2003): 1–18.
14. Part of James Brooks Kuykendall, 'Musical Contexts I: Motives and Methods in Sullivan's Allusions' in Eden and Saremba, *The Cambridge Companion to Gilbert and Sullivan*, 124–6.

15. Carolyn Williams, *Gilbert and Sullivan: Gender, Genre, Parody*, Gender and Culture (New York: Columbia University Press, 2011). See also Williams, 'Comic Opera'.

16. Goron, *Gilbert and Sullivan's 'Respectable Capers'*, 70.

17. See in particular Ian C. Bradley, *Oh Joy! Oh Rapture! The Enduring Phenomenon of Gilbert and Sullivan* (Oxford; New York: Oxford University Press, 2005).

18. The original excerpt from the game can be found here: *Mordin Sings Scientist Salarian*, www.youtube.com/watch?v=uXiU6kiq_Ms (accessed 18 Aug. 2017). Links to the others are, respectively: Abhlach Pastiche, *The Very Model of a Scientist Salarian*, www.youtube.com/watch?v=k5IA4iOLNPs (accessed 18 Aug. 2017); GrombarSmash, *I Am the Very Model of a Mass Effect Enthusiast (SPOILERS)*, www.youtube.com/watch?v=b5ZcNFZAaWk (accessed 18 Aug. 2017); Abhlach Pastiche, *A Little List*, www.youtube.com/watch?v=pRrnqrseZIs (accessed 18 Aug. 18 2017).

19. Stephanie E. Pitts, 'Champions and Aficionados: Amateur and Listener Experiences of the Savoy Operas in Performance' in D. Eden and M. Saremba (eds.), *The Cambridge Companion to Gilbert and Sullivan* (Cambridge: Cambridge University Press, 2009), 190–200, at 197.

20. See, for example: Vanessa Thorpe, 'Mike Leigh's First Opera Goes to Rescue of Struggling ENO', *The Observer*, 18 April 2015, sec. Music, www.theguardian.com/music/2015/apr/19/eno-pirates-covent-garden.

21. Mark Valencia, 'Review: The Mikado (Richmond Theatre and Tour)', *WhatsOnStage.com*, 25 May 2017, www.whatsonstage.com/london-theatre/reviews/review-the-mikado-richmond-theatre-and-tour_43688.html.

22. The Festival moved to Harrogate in 2014 and will be shared between Buxton and Harrogate in 2019.

23. Shani D'Cruze, 'Dainty Little Fairies: Women, Gender and the Savoy Operas', *Women's History Review* 9, no. 2 (2000): 346.

24. Ian C. Bradley (ed.), *The Complete Annotated Gilbert and Sullivan*, 20th anniversary edition (New York: Oxford University Press, 2016), vii.

Recommended Reading

Ainger, Michael. *Gilbert and Sullivan: A Dual Biography*. Oxford; New York: Oxford University Press, 2002.

Bradley, Ian C. *Oh Joy! Oh Rapture! The Enduring Phenomenon of Gilbert and Sullivan*. Oxford; New York: Oxford University Press, 2005.

Eden, David, and Meinhard Saremba, eds. *The Cambridge Companion to Gilbert and Sullivan*. Cambridge; New York: Cambridge University Press, 2009.

Goron, Michael. *Gilbert and Sullivan's 'Respectable Capers': Class, Respectability and the Savoy Operas 1877–1909*. Palgrave Studies in British Musical Theatre. London: Palgrave Macmillan, 2016.

Oost, Regina B. *Gilbert and Sullivan: Class and the Savoy Tradition, 1875–1896*. Farnham; Burlington: Ashgate, 2009.

Williams, Carolyn. *Gilbert and Sullivan: Gender, Genre, Parody*. Gender and Culture. New York: Columbia University Press, 2011.

4 Hungarians and Hungarianisms in Operetta and Folk Plays in the Late-Habsburg and Post-Habsburg Era

LYNN M. HOOKER

Central European operetta has always been viewed, rightly, as a primarily German-language product launched from German-speaking cities, mainly Vienna, its place of origin, and Berlin, the hub of the early twentieth-century transcultural theatre industry.[1] Within that repertoire Hungarians have usually appeared as exotic Others, often alongside Gipsies, allowing entertaining contrast between Viennese elegance and 'Hungarian fire'.[2] Yet so-called Viennese operetta was in many ways defined by composers, performers and impresarios with Hungarian connections – and musicians from Hungary, including Jews and Roma, made ample use of other stereotypical ethnic representations from the region, such as Gipsies, Jews and peasants of various ethnicities.[3] This chapter briefly explores the history of operetta in Hungary and how Hungarian contributions complicated representations of ethnicity on the stage.

From the West, Hungary may seem to be 'an underdeveloped country whose capital, compared to the cultural centers of Western Europe, is at best second-rate'.[4] But from 1869 to 1910, that capital, Budapest, was growing faster than any city in Europe; as World War I approached, it was Europe's sixth largest city, nearing one million in population. The region manufactured weaponry for the Dual Monarchy, internal combustion engines and the world's first electric-powered locomotive.[5] As it expanded, the city added numerous performing arts institutions, including the Academy of Music and the Folk Theatre, both opened in 1875; the Royal Opera House, opened in 1884, and several commercial theatres – the Víg [Comic] (opened in 1896), the Magyar [Hungarian] (1897) and the Király [Royal] (1903), plus many less prestigious entertainments, from cabarets to cafés to brothels.[6] *Fin-de-siècle* Budapest 'presented a frenetic scene of urban revelry and subversive entertainment that continued unabated from midnight until dawn'; as one Budapest magazine put it, 'we go to Vienna to sleep, and the Viennese come to Budapest to have fun'.[7]

A Brief History of Musical Theatre in Budapest: From Népszínmű to Operetta

It was not always thus. Public culture in Hungary, including theatre, was limited first by the Ottoman occupation (ended in 1699) and then by Austrian suppression following a rebellion against Habsburg rule (ended in 1711). Only at the end of the eighteenth century, with the relaxation of censorship under Joseph II, did public theatre begin to blossom.

It began in German, like much of urban culture in Hungary, including in the largest population centre, Buda-Pest. The Pest German Theatre opened in 1812, twenty-five years before the opening of the Pest Hungarian Theatre. That theatre's opening, at a time when promotion of the Hungarian language was a key rallying point of the national 'Reform Movement', was a centrepiece of patriotic sentiment. In 1840 it became the Hungarian National Theatre, with the support of the National Diet.[8]

Central to the repertoire of the Hungarian National Theatre was the *népszínmű*, or folk play. This genre drew on a variety of influences, particularly Viennese farce and *Volksstücke*; its defining playwright, Ede Szigligeti (1814–78), expanded on this framework and made it 'completely Hungarian, and truly popular'.[9] Folk plays emphasized a Hungary defined by rural stock character types – 'hussar, magistrate, and peasant, heyduck [irregular peasant soldier], Gipsy musician and landowner', among others – crystallizing 'everything that is considered a symbol of Hungary beyond [the] borders'.[10] Crucial to the appeal was the inclusion of dances and *magyar nóta*, or folk-style artsongs, understood as folksongs since they were sung by peasant figures on stage.[11]

Operetta Comes to Buda-Pest

Folk plays shared the Hungarian stage with popular works from abroad, which increasingly meant operetta. As had been the case in Vienna and London, Offenbach was key to the introduction of operetta to Hungary: *Le mariage aux lanternes* was performed in German in Buda and in Hungarian in Brassó and Kolózsvár in 1859, two years after it debuted in Paris.[12] Offenbach's own company gave performances in French at the Hungarian National Theatre in 1861, the same year that works of Suppé and Zajc first appeared in Hungary. The National Theatre featured other operettas in Hungarian translation, particularly Offenbach's works, alongside folk play, spoken theatre and opera. The popularity of both folk plays and operetta drove the development of the Folk Theatre in Budapest, opened in 1875, while opera moved to the new Hungarian Royal Opera

House in 1884. Pest's German Theatre was in decline in this period, in part because of pressure from 'protectors of Hungarian culture', and it was not rebuilt after it burned down in 1889; in its efforts to survive, however, it mounted several successful operetta performances, some including guest appearances by Viennese stars like Alexander Girardi and Marie Geistinger.[13] While the Opera House was conceived as a 'high art' institution, it also presented operettas, 'diversifying' its repertoire 'in order to attract the attention of the public'.[14]

The challenge for Hungarian music theatre, as with Hungarian music at large, was finding the balance between the local and the cosmopolitan. In the 1860s and 1870s, advocates for the development of a (government-subsidized) Folk Theatre insisted on the linkage between the local and the folk play as a specifically national genre and the superiority of this genre over operetta on nationalist grounds.[15] In its first four seasons, the Folk Theatre presented 519 folk play evenings and 484 operetta evenings; in 1898–1901, it presented 562 operetta performances compared to 302 folk play performances.[16] Despite the folk play's appeal to ideas of national character, these statistics suggest that audiences quickly came to prefer operettas.

In addition to presenting foreign works in translation, including Offenbach, Strauss and Sullivan, Hungarian authors worked to create works that could match the wit and musical sophistication of those works. This effort drew heavily on international models, as *Az eleven ördög* (The vivacious devil) illustrates. This work, based on a French comedy, was composed by a Warsaw-born Jewish composer, József Konti (1852–1905). Trained in Vienna, Konti worked for several years as Suppé's assistant before moving to Hungary at age 26 to work as a theatre conductor, Hungarianizing his name (originally Josua Kohn) and becoming the orchestra director of Budapest's Folk Theatre in 1885. *Az eleven ördög* was performed throughout Hungary hundreds of times from its 1883 premiere until 1913 – and notes in the scores, parts and reviews indicate that many of the initial performances were in German. Still the show came to be remembered as 'the first Hungarian operetta', in part because Lujza Blaha (1850–1926), the Folk Theatre's leading prima donna during this period, had a great success in the lead role.[17]

Folk vs Urban Cosmopolitan Ideal: Two Prima Donnas

The fact that operetta took hold as a 'native' Hungarian genre in a comedy about French aristocrats highlights Hungary's continuing struggle over whether to define its cultural establishment as 'traditional', as in folk plays,

or 'fashionable, bourgeois', as in operetta.[18] It also underlines the importance of performers such as Blaha, remembered as 'the nation's nightingale'. Like other successful performers, she was versatile, appearing in
works by Offenbach, Strauss and Suppé, as well as Verdi and Meyerbeer.
Yet Blaha was identified – and identified herself – as a Hungarian actress
specializing in Hungarian works.[19] As one critic wrote in 1919, 'Blaha was
not a real peasant girl … in the folk plays, but rather [she was] all the
charm, beauty, kindness, sensuality and candor that the whole Hungarian
public had tied to the ideal of folk-like Hungarianness … She herself was
the genre.'[20]

By contrast, Blaha's slightly younger contemporary, Ilka Pálmay
(1859–1945), had a thoroughly international career. By the age of
twenty, Pálmay rose from the theatres of the Hungarian provinces to
Budapest's Folk Theatre, where she performed for most of the 1880s.
In the 1890s she performed in Vienna, Prague, Berlin and London; she
created the roles of Christel, opposite Alexander Girardi, in Zeller's
Der Vögelhändler (Theater an der Wien, 1891) and Julia Jellicoe in
Gilbert and Sullivan's *The Grand Duke* (London Savoy Theatre, 1896),
and in 1905–6 she appeared onstage in New York. She continued to
perform irregularly until 1928, when she celebrated her retirement
with a performance at Hungary's National Theatre.[21] Though
Pálmay, like Blaha, performed both folk plays and operettas, she was
more cosmopolitan. Her case shows how Hungarian talent was integrated into a 'complex [system] of cultural transfers amidst the Pest–
New York–Berlin–Paris theatre and [later] film industries'.[22]

Hungarian-Gipsy Style from Vienna: Johann Strauss Jr

The role of Hungarian actors, authors and others in the theatre world,
however, was distinct from the way Hungarians were depicted on stage.
That was defined, at least in operetta, by Johann Strauss's *Der
Zigeunerbaron* (1885). This work apparently came about in part because
of the recognition of the potential appeal of Hungarianness on the
Viennese stage. In June 1883, Hungary's Folk Theatre played for three
weeks in Vienna, featuring three prima donnas – Blaha, Pálmay and the
'Gipsy prima donna' Aranka Hegyi (1855–1906) – in operettas and folk
plays; the popularity of these performances demonstrated the draw of
Hungarian topics in Vienna.[23] In November of that year, Strauss
met Mór Jókai, the most popular Hungarian writer of the age, in Vienna,
and Jókai worked with Strauss's librettist, Ignaz Schnitzer, to create a new
operetta on a Hungarian subject.[24]

The title character of *Der Zigeunerbaron,* Sándor Barinkay, is the son of an exiled Hungarian nobleman. As the operetta opens, Barinkay is return- ing to his ancestral lands, and an Austrian official, Carnero, informs those living there – Zsupán, a Hungarian pig farmer who has taken over the property, as well as a band of Gipsies who are camped there, led by Saffi, a mysterious Gipsy girl, and Czipra, her mother – that Barinkay's land and title have been reinstated. In an effort to forestall the land transfer, Zsupán offers his daughter, Arsena, as Barinkay's potential bride, but she objects that he is not a true member of the nobility (covering for the fact that she is in love with someone else). Barinkay declares he prefers Saffi after all, and they spend the night together, 'married' by forest birds, to the shock of the Austrians. After a rousing recruiting scene to end Act 2, most of the male characters join the Hungarian hussars – Barinkay to prove himself worthy of Saffi (suddenly revealed to be a Turkish princess), Zsupán by mistake; they return victorious from their military adventures in Act 3 to seal the happy ending. The presentation of Arsena as bride in Act 1, the recruiting scene in the finale to Act 2, and the entrance march in Act 3 provide opportunities for production numbers with attractive national costumes, dancing, and scenery. Strauss described his vision of the Act 3 introduction thus: 'Around 80 to 100 soldiers . . . Market women in Spanish, Hungarian, and Viennese costume [. . .] it must be an impressive scene, since this time we want to imagine an *Austrian* military and *Volk* in a *joyful* mood about a victorious conquest!'[25]

The Hungarian elements in *Zigeunerbaron* were thus part of an exotic pageant, serving to 'rouse enthusiasm . . . for the existing empire and its elegant capital'.[26] Strauss uses music to contrast East and West, as András Batta wrote: 'The csárdás represents the village . . . dominated by the long- established nobility and peasantry. The waltz is a district of the city, the cosmopolitan and industrial center.'[27] But the exotics in *Der Zigeunerbaron* consist of more than just the csárdás, and Strauss blurs the line between its various Others, be they Hungarian, Gipsy or Turkish – beginning with the title character. Barinkay's costume is described in the original libretto as 'half oriental, half Hungarian'; as he relates in his entrance aria, he has been working as a travelling acrobat, sword- swallower, animal-tamer, magician and fortune teller – professions that 'contemporary urban audiences would readily have ascribed . . . to Gipsies'.[28] On the other hand, the refrain of this aria is a waltz in major mode, the 'neutral' sound in Strauss's music. The chorus of Gipsy smiths forging weapons for the Austrian military features triangles and cymbals, conventionally heard as 'Turkish percussion'; these instruments also appear in the fast section of the 'Gipsy song' with which the heroine, Saffi, introduces herself, possibly hinting at her true Turkish identity.[29]

The slower sections, meanwhile, include many elements more usually associated with Hungarian-Gipsy style.[30]

Recalibrating Ethnic Representation in the Silver Age

Strauss's Hungarians, Turks and Gipsies blend together, all serving as a 'stimulus of fantasy' for the West.[31] Meanwhile, ethnic representations in works from composers from the eastern half of empire are often more complex. Perhaps no one at the turn of the century was better positioned to depict characters of all kinds of backgrounds than the quintessential Austro-Hungarian Franz/Ferencz Lehár. Lehár's father was a military bandmaster and dance music composer who was posted all over the empire, moving to Budapest with his family in 1880. Young Lehár grew up speaking Hungarian, so at the age of twelve, he was sent to relatives in his father's hometown to improve his German enough to study at the Prague Conservatory, chosen over the conservatories in Vienna and Budapest because it welcomed younger students.[32] After completing his studies, he became a military musician himself, posted successively in Losoncz, Trieste, Pola and Budapest.

After Lehár left the military for a post at Theater an der Wien – under the management of another migrant from Hungary, Vilmos/Wilhelm Karczag (1857–1923) – he soon produced his first two operettas, *Wiener Frauen* (Vienna Women) and *Der Rastelbinder* (The Pot-Mender), both premiered in 1902. *Der Rastelbinder* premiered in Hungarian at the Opera House in Budapest less than a year later as *A drotostót* with Lehár himself conducting.[33] (This Hungarian title is almost identical to *A két drotostót* (The Two Pot-Menders), a folk play by Győző Kempelen (1829–65) with music by Béni Egressy (1814–51), which was performed in Budapest at least into the 1890s.[34]) In the prologue, a young tinker says farewell to the girl to whom he is engaged as he leaves his Slovak (in Hungarian, *tót*) village to seek his fortune in the big city; in *Der Rastelbinder* that city is Vienna, while in *A drotostót* it is Budapest. Years later they meet in the city, where there are romantic complications as well as commentary and comic relief from a 'stereotypical yet not purely unsympathetic and demeaning' Jewish character, the onion seller Pfefferkorn.[35]

Whereas a cast of exclusively peasant characters was unusual in operetta, it was common in folk plays. Folk plays also had a long history of stereotypical ethnic characters, including (mostly) sympathetic Jewish characters, going back at least to Szigligeti's *A zsidó* (The Jew) of 1844. Moreover, Hungary was not the only place in eastern Europe where Jews were featured on the stage: by the 1870s, Polish theatre productions such as

Jew in the Barrel delighted working-class audiences, both Jewish and non-Jewish. Stereotypes of Jewish identity were used not just by anti-Semites but also by Jewish actors and theatre musicians satirizing anti-Semitism.[36]

Given the large multi-ethnic in-migration to Vienna and Budapest, Lehár could expect that audiences in both cities would respond to tropes of 'Jewishness' and to musical markers of 'Slovakness' or 'Slavonicness' – the latter attached both to folk practices and to Dvořák, his former teacher. More than signifying deeply felt Slovak identity, these were part of a palette of national topics Lehár could use to add colour to his score. His mixture of waltzes, folksong (or pseudo-folksong) and buffo writing became 'the most popular model for [operetta] composition'.[37]

Lehár turned his attention to the Hungarian-Gipsy topic in *Zigeunerliebe* (Gipsy Love), premiered in January 1910 in Vienna and November 1910 in Budapest. As he had for *A drotostót,* Lehár himself conducted these premieres, withdrawing from a previous commitment to conduct Hamburg's two-hundredth performance of *Der Graf von Luxemburg* to be in Budapest.[38] The Budapest magazine *Színházi hét* (Theatre Week) published Lehár's telegrams about this last-moment decision, underlining to its readers that no matter how successful the composer had become in Vienna and beyond, Lehár was still one of their own.

According to Jonathan Bellman, the first to analyse the Hungarian-Gipsy topic in detail in English, *Zigeunerliebe* is diminished by Lehár's incorrect use of Hungarian-Gipsy musical conventions – particularly his 'uncharacteristic' four-bar phrases – as well as the way that 'the plot reduces the complexities of the Gipsy stereotype to pap'.[39] The second act of *Zigeunerliebe* does rely heavily on stereotype: it is an elaborate dream sequence in which Zorika, a young Transylvanian Hungarian gentlewoman, impulsively runs away with Gipsy musician Józsi, 'living in a caravan telling fortunes and stealing watches' before returning to her boring Hungarian fiancé.[40] On the other hand, Zorika and Józsi's relationship could have been considered more realistic than Barinkay and Saffi's relationship in *Zigeunerbaron.* In *Zigeunerbaron,* Hungarian Barinkay's decision to be with (fellow exotic) Gipsy/Turkish princess Saffi can lead to a happy ending. Lehár's Zorika is clearly a respectable European who happens to live in Hungary, contrasted with the passionate, fickle, nomadic Gipsy Józsi, at a time when many Hungarians considered Gipsies 'primitive' or even animalistic.[41] A true match between the two was unfathomable.

The next major operetta composer to come out of Hungary was Imre/ Emmerich Kálmán (1882–1953), born in Siófok, a growing resort town on the southern shore of Lake Balaton. He studied piano and frequented the theatre there, then moved to Budapest to attend secondary school and the Academy of Music, where he shared a composition teacher with Béla

Bartók (1881–1945), Zoltán Kodály (1882–1967) and fellow operetta composers Viktor Jakobi (1883–1921) and Albert Szirmai (1880–1967). Kálmán initially concentrated on serious works and newspaper criticism but turned to light genres around 1907; his first operetta, *Tatárjárás*, a tale of romance among Hungarian military officers at a country estate, was premiered in Budapest in 1908.[42] At the first performance, his wife recalled, the directors of the Theater an der Wien, Karczag and Karl Wallner, along with composer Leo Fall, fresh from the success of his *Dollarprinzessin* (1907), approached him in his box. After a night on the town with Kálmán, Szirmai and Jakobi,[43] Fall encouraged Karczag and Wallner to bring *Tatárjárás* to Vienna, where it opened in 1909 as *Ein Herbstmanöver*. This show was successful enough, and Kálmán relocated to Vienna.

The way *Tatárjárás* was received, however, indicated that what worked in Budapest would not always suit Vienna. Critics there considered *Ein Herbstmanöver* 'insufficiently dramatic' and too 'rustic', perhaps because of the density of Hungarian-Gipsy tropes, perhaps because of the countryside setting; so Kálmán found a way to give Viennese audiences 'the "Gipsy fire" they expected of him'.[44] But he still emphasized the point of view of Hungarians, especially urban Hungarians.

A decidedly Hungarian urbanity is at the centre of Kálmán's biggest hit, *Die Csárdásfürstin* (The Csárdás Princess), premiered in Vienna in 1915 and in Budapest in 1916. In the show's first big vocal number, 'Heia, in den Bergen ist mein Heimatland' (Heia, in the mountains is my homeland), 'csárdás princess' Sylva – Szilvia in the Hungarian version – sings about her rural Transylvanian origins accompanied by a Gipsy band, foregrounding the exotic Hungarian element, but as part of her Budapest nightclub act, complete with applause from the onstage audience. After this number, Kálmán's score relies more on cosmopolitan popular styles of the time, in keeping with its urban setting. Where *Zigeunerbaron* contrasts the supercilious Viennese with rustic and lightly differentiated exotics (Hungarians, Gipsies and Turks), the Hungarians and Gipsies of Sylva's cabaret in *Csárdásfürstin* are part of a sophisticated community of Budapest entertainers and hangers-on that contrasts with the hypocrisy of the aristocratic life of Vienna (where Acts 2 and 3 take place). The plot is driven less by national difference than by sexual mores and class. Sylva and Prince Edwin are in love, but Sylva works in a not-very-respectable Budapest cabaret, and, as Count Boni Káncsianu, a regular patron of the cabaret, tells Feri von Kerekes, another habitué, 'princes marry variety girls only in operettas'.[45] The reason variety girls were not considered marriage material, of course, was an attraction for patrons flocking to Budapest nightspots from all over Europe – their 'sweet sins' and the 'love school' in which they teach, attractions Feri and Boni celebrate in a peppy march titled 'Die Mädis vom Chantant' (The girls of the cabaret) even as police doctors in real-life Budapest worked to regulate them.[46] This number and Boni's subsequent solo, 'Ganz ohne Weiber geht die Chose nicht', resemble (both musically and in subject) the praise of women in *Die lustige Witwe*'s 'Maxim's' and 'Ja, das Studium der Weiber', but now the women are Hungarian showgirls instead of Parisian ones.

Kálmán's next most successful show, *Gräfin Mariza* (Countess Mariza, 1924), is set in the countryside rather than the city, on the estate of the title character; her love interest is her estate manager, Count Tassilo Endrődy-Wittenburg, working under an assumed name to pay off his late father's exorbitant debts and earn a dowry for his younger sister. *Zigeunerbaron* uses its potpourri of characters to glorify the past of the empire and its capital, as well as the old-style Hungarian aristocracy whose 'values, habits and lifestyle . . . the Budapest press abhorred and the Viennese appreciated and found amusing'.[47] *Mariza* satirizes the contemporary challenges those aristocrats faced when called to pay for their lifestyle.

Kálmán and his librettists highlight this shift in viewpoint through ironic reference to *Zigeunerbaron*: Mariza announces her engagement to an imaginary fiancé (the better to avoid the mob of gold-digging suitors) whom she names, after the pig farmer in *Zigeunerbaron*, Baron Kálmán Zsupán. This fictitious engagement is complicated when a 'real-life' Baron Zsupán, a patriotic Hungarian who also owns many pigs, turns up at Mariza's estate for their engagement party. Also, like *Zigeunerbaron*, *Mariza* draws a range of exotic colours from its setting: it includes multiple scenes with dancing peasants, uses a Gipsy band on stage and opens with a Gipsy girl, Manja, singing about the vagaries of fate ('Glück ist ein schöner Traum'). The opposition between csárdás, the music of Hungarian peasants and Gipsies, and waltz, the music of the city, is in full force, but Mariza and Tassilo confirm their position by their mastery of both. Each has a csárdás song – Mariza's grand entrance aria and Tassilo's lament for his past – but both songs emphasize their roles as aristocratic patrons, singing 'Play, Gipsy!' They also waltz, signifying both their romance and Tassilo's nostalgia for his old life of leisure, and dance the Charleston and foxtrot.[48] Their musical catholicity stresses that these are cosmopolitan European characters with roots in a colourful place.

Which Audience?

As the Hungarian audience for operetta grew, composers and librettists could either target their works specifically for Hungary or aim for the broadest possible international audience, perhaps adding certain elements for Hungarian versions. In a popular theatre context, tailoring works to particular audiences was expected and could happen in a variety of ways. For example, at the 1882 Budapest premiere of Strauss's *Die Fledermaus,* a brief dialogue was added after Rosalinde's csárdás commenting humorously on the number's possible problems for a Hungarian public, with one character protesting that it was 'certainly no Hungarian song'.[49] What has come to be the best-known song from *A csárdáskirálynő,* 'Hajmási Péter, Hajmási Pál', did not appear in *Die Csárdásfürstin;* Kálmán added it to replace a csárdás song that had already appeared in Budapest in his *A kis király* (1912).[50] Some text changes had significance beyond just creating a singing translation in a different language. In *Mariza,* Zsupán's 'Komm mit nach Varaždin' (Come with me to Varaždin) became 'Szép város Kolózsvár' (Kolózsvár is a beautiful city), celebrating with syncopated rhythms a major Transylvanian city Hungary had lost to Romania at the end of World War I. (Croatian Varaždin was also lost, but Transylvania was invested with more national sentiment.) Still, however much Kálmán – and Lehár – might have desired a continued connection with the land of their birth, they sought a broader public than was available there. Using the formula established by Lehár, composers and librettists contrasted exotic settings and their associated styles (Hungarian or not) with contemporary styles. Three farther-flung examples by Hungarian-born Jewish composers from the interwar period are Kálmán's *Golden Dawn* (1928), set in the jungles of Africa; Sigmund Romberg's *The Desert Song* (1925), set in French colonial Morocco and Pál Ábrahám's *Die Blume von Hawaii* (1931).

This approach contrasted with that of two non-Jewish Hungarian composers, Jenő Huszka (1875–1960) and Pongrácz Kacsóh (1873–1923), who each wrote several shows that were popular only in Hungary. Huszka's second operetta, *Bob herceg* (Prince Bob, 1902), about an English prince's romantic adventures in London, had considerable international success, but Huszka chose to continue his career in the Hungarian government rather than pursuing international productions. He did not even attend the German-language premiere of *Bob* in nearby Vienna, despite the fact that Karczag, the producer and a fellow Hungarian, sent him a train ticket and reserved him a first-class hotel room.[51] His later works do not appear to have been performed in translation. Beyond snubbing his producer, Huszka flouted the rules of the 'exotic' niche that Viennese operetta allotted to Hungarians, as *Gül baba* (1905), a historical romance set at the time of the Ottomans' capture of Buda in 1541, illustrates. The plot of *Gül baba* includes the same three 'exotic' character types found in *Zigeunerbaron* – Hungarian, Turkish and Gipsy – but they are provided with distinct music in ways that might not be understood by much of the non-Hungarian operetta audience.[52] The show also depends on at least a cursory knowledge of sixteenth-century Hungarian history to be fully appreciated. Huszka's *Mária főhadnagy* (Lieutenant Mária, 1942), a tale of Hungary's 1848 revolution, similarly relies at least in part on a Hungarian audience's historical knowledge, patriotic sentiment and appreciation of the musical variations of status among Huszka's Hungarian characters.

Kacsóh's best-known show, *János vitéz* (John the Hero, 1904), is another that was clearly created with the Hungarian, not international, audience in mind, as both its music and its mostly peasant characters suggest the continuation of the folk-play tradition. In it, young shepherd János is forced to leave his village and his beloved, the orphan girl Iluska. After joining the hussars, rescuing a French princess, and defeating Turks and witches, he is reunited with Iluska by magic in the land of the fairies. Ensembles are relatively simple compared to contemporary operettas, and most characters' solos consist of *magyar nóta* (folk-style artsongs conventionally accompanied by Gipsy bands), except for the foursquare song of the French king and the waltz songs of his daughter the princess. Though its music is charming, much of the appeal of *János vitéz* comes from its source material, the 1845 epic poem of the same name by national poet Sándor Petőfi (1823–49). It was not meant to travel.

The influence of *János vitéz* and the folk play does appear, however, in a work that has travelled, Kodály's *Háry János* (1926). *Háry* is labelled a Singspiel, but the peasant characters – including a title character named János – tell a different tale. There is even a supporting princess character whom János must resist in favour of his peasant sweetheart. Like the princess in *János vitéz*, *Háry*'s princess sings a sort of waltz song, 'Ku-ku-ku-kuskám', though like most of *Háry*'s other tunes, it is based on musical material collected by Kodály in the countryside, identified as an 'artsong of foreign origin' and filed in Kodály's archive with 'Artsongs among the folk'.[53] Most of the attention paid to this work focuses on how Kodály harnessed 'the poetic power of folklore' by putting 'genuine folksong on to operatic stage'.[54] To international audiences, *Háry János* has become a colourful and 'authentic' representation of that power, chiefly as an orchestral suite. To a domestic audience of the time, there would also have been a clear connection to folk plays and *magyar nóta*, a song type that Kodály called inauthentic.

Hungarian Operetta since World War II

Operetta did not fit easily into the ideological framework of state socialism in post-World War II Hungary, filled as it is with frivolous aristocrats, sexually suggestive humour and musical styles from the imperialist West (especially jazz). But its popularity meant that it was the starting point for popular theatre in the new era, so theatres and critics puzzled over how to transform it from 'capitalist kitsch' into 'progressive model plays'.[55] Ottó Vincze's *Boci-boci tarka* (Spotted-spotted cow, 1953) shows several methods for doing so: it introduced an ideologically appropriate setting, the collective farm, and included 'authentic' folksongs (following Kodály's example), including the title children's song, as well as mass songs in its score.[56] But the most popular operettas in post-war Hungary included older works that had been made more ideologically appropriate. Budapest's Operetta Theatre took both *Boci-boci tarka* and a revised *A csárdáskirálynő* on tour to the Soviet Union in 1955–6, and Kálmán's work appears to have won the day.[57]

Though operetta was superseded by newer popular genres by the 1960s, it maintains a place in Hungary's cultural landscape to this day. In 2013, Hungarian operetta was added to the 'Collection of Hungaricums', a heritage list 'for the identification, collection and documentation of national values important for the Hungarian people'.[58] Its application for inclusion in the Collection emphasized operetta's attraction not just for Hungarian audiences but for international ones, whether they be tourists in Budapest or audiences for Hungarian operetta performances abroad. Since 1989, this repertoire appeals to local audiences' nostalgia for the pre-war past, while impresarios, musicians and connoisseurs in Europe and North America promote Hungarian operetta as the core of this light classical repertoire.

Notes

1. Derek B. Scott, 'Silver-Age Operetta: The Power of an Early 20th-Century Transcultural Entertainment Industry', presented at the symposium Popular Music and Power, held at Humboldt-Universität, Berlin, 23–5 June 2016, www.academia.edu/27081736/Silver-Age_Operetta_The_Power_of_an_Early_20th-Century_Transcultural_Entertainment_Industry (accessed 1 Mar. 2018).
2. Micaela Baranello, 'The Operetta Empire: Popular Viennese Music Theater and Austrian Identity, 1900–1930', unpublished PhD dissertation, Princeton University (2014), 358.
3. The word Roma – adjectival form 'Romani' – means 'man' in the Indic language spoken by many Roma across Europe; the word 'Gipsy' (or 'Gypsy') is based historically on the mistaken notion that these people are from Egypt and is often used stereotypically or pejoratively. However, many Roma call themselves 'Gipsy' or its local equivalent, including in Hungary. The term 'Gipsy music' is commonly used in Hungary, to refer to the genre of entertainment music performed by urban Romani musicians, mainly at restaurants and cafés. Here, I use the term 'Gipsy' primarily to refer to stereotypical representations of the ethnic group and to the musical occupation; Roma refers to members of the ethnic group more generally.
4. Judit Frigyesi, *Béla Bartók and Turn-of-the-Century Budapest* (Berkeley: University of California Press, 1998), 1.

5. Ignác Romsics, *Hungary in the Twentieth Century* (Budapest: Corvina/Osiris, 1999), 20–7. Budapest was created in 1873 by combining Buda, Pest and Óbuda; discussion of earlier history refers to Buda-Pest or to its constituent parts.

6. Ildikó Nagy, 'Polgárosuló színház a polgári Budapesten' in Miklós Lackó (ed.), *A tudománytól a tömegkultúráig: művelődéstörténeti tanulmányok, 1890–1945* (Budapest: MTA Történettudományi Intézet, 1994), 191–6; Lynn M. Hooker, *Redefining Hungarian Music from Liszt to Bartók* (New York: Oxford University Press, 2013), 26–7.

7. Mary Gluck, *The Invisible Jewish Budapest: Metropolitan Culture at the Fin de Siècle* (Madison, WI: University of Wisconsin Press, 2016), 141. The director of the Theater an der Wien confirmed this view of Vienna when he remarked that 'every piece that plays past 10 o'clock [at night] is *lost*'. Quoted by Camille Crittenden, *Johann Strauss and Vienna: Operetta and the Politics of Popular Culture* (Cambridge: Cambridge University Press, 2000), 174; emphasis in original.

8. See George Bisztray, 'Hungary, 1810–1838' in Laurence Senelick (ed.), *National Theatre in Northern and Eastern Europe, 1746–1900* (Cambridge: Cambridge University Press, 1991), 278–80; Peter Nemes, *The Once and Future Budapest* (DeKalb, IL: Northern Illinois University Press, 2005), 128; and Alice Freifeld, *Nationalism and the Crowd in Liberal Hungary, 1848–1914* (Washington, DC: Woodrow Wilson Center Press, 2000), 33.

9. József Bayer, Introduction, *Szigligeti Ede színművei*, I. (Budapest: Franklin Társulat, 1902), 18. For more on *Volksstücke*, see Feurzeig, this volume, Chap. 2.

10. András Batta, *Träume sind Schäume . . . : Die Operette in der Donaumonarchie*, trans. Maria Eisenreich (Budapest: Corvina, 1992), 11.

11. Dénes Tóth, *A magyar népszínmű zenei kialakulása* (Budapest: Zeneműkiadó, 1953), 48.

12. See Péter Bozó, 'Operetta in Hungary, 1859–1960', Magyar zene a 20. században, MTA BTK ZTI, 2014, http://real.mtak.hu/13117/1/bozo_operetta_in_hungary.pdf (accessed 27 Nov. 2017); György Székely, Kerényi Ferenc and Gajdó Tamás (eds.), *Magyar színháztörténet* II., 1873–1920 (Budapest: Magyar Könyvklub–Országos Színháztörténeti Múzeum és Intézet, 2001), 125–7, http://mek.oszk.hu/02000/02065/html/2kotet/20.html (accessed 27 Nov. 2017).

13. Székely et al., *Magyar színháztörténet* II., 1873–1920, 413–15, 420, http://mek.oszk.hu/02000/02065/html/2kotet/77.html (accessed 29 Jan. 2018); Bozó, 'Operetta in Hungary, 1859–1960'.

14. Markian Prokopovych, *In the Public Eye: The Public Opera House, the Audience and the Press, 1884–1919* (Vienna: Böhlau, 2014), 231. Though this passage addresses the staging of Lehár's *Fürstenkind* at the Opera House in 1910, Prokopovych also discusses productions of Offenbach in the 1880s (140–7) and Strauss's *Der Zigeunerbaron* in 1905 (195–220).

15. Gyöngyi Heltai, 'Népszínház a nemzetépítésben. A szakmai diskurzus kialakulása (1861–1881)', *Korall* 37 (Nov. 2009), 60–5.

16. Székely et al., *Magyar színháztörténet* II., 1873–1920, 111, 125, http://mek.oszk.hu/02000/02065/html/2kotet/20.html#22 (accessed 7 Feb. 2018).

17. Péter Bozó, 'Piszkos partitúrák, szennyes szólamok, avagy *Az eleven ördög* és a magyar operett nem teljesen szeplőtelen fogantatása', *Magyar zene* 52, no. 3 (Aug. 2014), 318, 331.

18. Quoting Sándor Hevesi, 'A régi népszínmű és a magyar nóta' in *Az igazi Shakespeare és egyéb kérdések* (Budapest: Táltos, 1919), 124; and Nagy, 'Polgárosuló színház a polgári Budapesten', 193.

19. Her husband and Suppé attempted to launch her Viennese career at the Carl-Theater, but she wrote in her diary that if they persisted 'I will leave him, because I will never be a German actress, never'. *Blaha Lujza naplója*, ed. Ilona Csillag (Budapest: Gondolat, 1987), 77.

20. In Sándor Hevesi, 'A régi népszínmű és a magyar nóta', *Az igazi Shakespeare és egyéb kérdések* (Budapest: Táltos, 1919), 125.

21. See Székely et al., *Magyar színháztörténet* II., 1873–1920, 136 http://mek.oszk.hu/02000/02065/html/2kotet/20.html#22 (accessed 13 Feb. 2018) and 'Pálmay Ilka, Életrajz', *Színészkönyvtár*, 2003, www.szineszkonyvtar.hu/contents/p-z/palmayelet.htm (accessed 13 Feb. 2018).

22. Gyöngyi Heltai, 'Roboz Imre és a Vígszínház nemzetközi kapcsolatrendszere az 1930-as években: Budapest–New York–Párizs–Berlin', *Multunk* 2018, no. 1, 137.

23. Amadé Németh, *Az Erkelek a magyar zenében* (Békéscsaba: Békés Megyei Tanács VB, 1987), 114; see also *Blaha Lujza naplója*, 199–201. For more on Hegyi, daughter of a Romani musician from Subotica, see Géza Csemer et al., *Hegyi Aranka cigány primadonna (1855–1906) emlékkönyv* (Budapest: Napház-Khamorro, 1996).

24. D. Péter Forgács, '"A czigánybáró" operett igaz története', *Új forrás* 37, no. 3 (2005), 33–43 http://epa.oszk.hu/00000/00016/00103/050313.htm (accessed 21 Feb. 2018).

25. Quoted by Crittenden, *Johann Strauss and Vienna*, 174; emphasis in original.

26. Crittenden, *Johann Strauss and Vienna*, 175.

27. Batta, *Träume sind Schäume*, 152–3.

28. Crittenden, *Johann Strauss and Vienna*, 181.

29. Lynn M. Hooker, 'Turks, Hungarians, and Gypsies: Exoticism and Auto-exoticism in Opera and Operetta', *Hungarian Studies*, 27, no. 2 (2013), 299–302.

30. Jonathan Bellman, *The Style Hongrois in the Music of Western Europe* (Boston: Northeastern University Press, 1993), Chap. 3.

31. Timothy D. Taylor, *Beyond Exoticism: Western Music and the World* (Durham, NC: Duke University Press, 2007), 90.

32. Otto Schneidereit, *Lehár*, trans. V. Ágnes Meller (Budapest: Zeneműkiadó, 1988), 19–21; Péter Hanák, 'The Cultural Role of Vienna-Budapest Operetta' in *The Garden and the Workshop: Essays on the Cultural History of Vienna and Budapest* (Princeton, NJ: Princeton University Press, 1998), 141. Lehár's parents, like many Hungarian citizens, came from families of other ethnicities who embraced Hungarian language and identity in the nineteenth century. Baranello indicates, however, the media (presumably in Vienna) described him as Slavic rather than Magyar (*The Operetta Empire*, 227).

33. See Baranello, *The Operetta Empire*, 103–4, and '"A drótostót" az Operaházban', *Huszadik század* (April 1903) www.huszadikszazad.hu/cikk/a-drotostot-az-operahazban (accessed 21 Feb. 2018).

34. See *A Városligeti Színkör, 1889–1934*, Színháztörténeti Füzetek, no. 79 (Budapest: Országos Színháztörténeti Múzeum és Intézet, 1991), 82, among others. Another set of music to go with Kempelen's play, by Géza Allaga (1841–1913), is mentioned in Péter Szuhay (ed.), *Megvetés és önbecsülés: Igaz történet üstfoltozóról, drótostótról, teknőscigányról* (Budapest: Néprajzi Múzeum, 2014), 50.

35. Baranello, *The Operetta Empire*, 105.

36. Halina Goldberg, 'The Jewish Self/The Jewish Other: Performing Identity in the "Majufes"', presented at Jewish Music Forum, University of Chicago, 26 Feb. 2009, 9–10.

37. Baranello, *The Operetta Empire*, 135.

38. 'A Király-színház nagyhete', *Színházi hét*, 1, no. 2 (6–13 Nov. 1910), 8 http://epa.oszk.hu/02300/02365/00002/pdf/EPA02365_szinhazi_het_1910_02.pdf (accessed 23 Feb. 2018).

39. Bellman, *The Style Hongrois*, 216–17.

40. Baranello, *The Operetta Empire*, 225.

41. See Hooker, *Redefining Hungarian Music*, 119–21.

42. 'The Biography of Emmerich Kálmán', *Emmerich Kalman Memorial Home* http://emlekhaz.konyvtar-siofok.hu/?p=the-biography-of-emmerich-kalman (accessed 3 Mar. 2018).

43. Vera Kálmán, *Emlékszel még . . . : Kálmán Imre élete*, trans. V. Ágnes Meller (Budapest: Zeneműkiadó, 1966), 58.

44. Baranello, *The Operetta Empire*, 232, 214.

45. András Gerő, Dorottya Hargitai and Tamás Gajdó, *A csárdáskirálynő: Egy monarchikum története* (Budapest: Pannonica Kiadó, 2006), 77.

46. Quotations from *Die Csárdásfürstin*, text by Leo Stein and Béla Jenbach, music by Emmerich Kálmán (Leipzig: Josef Weinberger, 1916), 17; see also Gluck, *The Invisible Jewish Budapest*, 141, and Judit Forrai, 'Kávéházak és kejnők', *Budapesti negyed* 12–13, no. 2–3 (1996), 110–20.

47. Markian Prokopovych, 'Celebrating Hungary? Johann Strauss's Der Zigeunerbaron and the Press in Fin-de-Siècle Vienna and Budapest', *Austrian Studies* 25 (2017), 128, 134.

48. *Gräfin Mariza*, text by Julius Brammer and Alfred Grünwald, music by Emmerich Kálmán (Vienna: Karczag, 1924).

49. Crittenden, *Johann Strauss and Vienna*, 205.

50. Gerő, et al., *A csárdáskirálynő*, 29.

51. Róbert Gál, *Délibábos Hortobágyon: Huszka Jenő élete és művei* (Budapest: Rózsavölgyi, 2010), 74, 92.

52. Hooker, 'Turks, Hungarians, and Gypsies', 302–5.

53. János Bereczky, Katalin Paksa, Mária Domokos, Imre Olsvai and Olga Szalay, *Kodály népdalfeldolgozásainak dallam- és szövegforrásai* (Budapest: Zeneműkiadó, 1984), 50.

54. Tibor Tallián, 'Háry János', *Oxford Music Online* https://doi.org/10.1093/gmo/9781561592630 .article.O005826 (accessed 2 Mar. 2018).
55. Gyöngyi Heltai, *Az operetta metamorfózisai, 1945–1956: A 'kapitalista giccs'-től a haladó 'mimusjáték'-ig* (Budapest: ELTE Eötvös Kiadó, 2012).
56. Péter Bozó, 'Műfaji hagyomány és politikai kisajátítás Vincze Ottó Boci-boci tarka című operettjében (1953)', presented at the conference in honour of Melinda Berlász's seventieth birthday, Budapest, November 2012. www.zti.hu/mza/docs/Berlasz70/ Berlasz70_BozoPeter_Mufaji_hagyomany_es_politikai_kisajatitas.pdf (accessed 3 Mar. 2018).
57. Bozó, 'Operetta in Hungary'.
58. Hungarikum Bizottság, *Hungarikumok Gyűjteménye/Collection of Hungarikums* http://hungar ikum.hu/sites/default/files/hungarikumok-lista.pdf (accessed 3 Mar. 2018).

Recommended Reading

Bozó, Péter. 'Operetta in Hungary, 1859–1960', Magyar zene a 20. században, MTA BTK ZTI, 2014, http://real.mtak.hu/13117/1/bozo_operetta_in_hungary.pdf (accessed 8 May 2019).

Gluck, Mary. *The Invisible Jewish Budapest: Metropolitan Culture at the Fin de Siècle*. Madison, WI: University of Wisconsin Press, 2016.

Hanák, Péter. *The Garden and the Workshop: Essays on the Cultural History of Vienna and Budapest*. Princeton, NJ: Princeton University Press, 1998.

Hooker, Lynn M. 'Turks, Hungarians, and Gypsies: Exoticism and Auto-exoticism in Opera and Operetta'. *Hungarian Studies*, 27, no. 2 (2013): 291–311.

Prokopovych, Markian. 'Celebrating Hungary? Johann Strauss's Der Zigeunerbaron and the Press in Fin-de-Siècle Vienna and Budapest'. *Austrian Studies*, 25 (2017): 118–35.

5 Operetta in the Czech National Revival: The Provisional Theatre Years

JAN SMACZNY

In his pioneering 1924 study of Dvořák, Karel Hoffmeister described the Prague National Theatre as 'our one artistic hearth'.[1] Hoffmeister's epigram could apply as appropriately to the Prague Provisional Theatre in relation to the crucial years of the Czech national revival.[2] When it opened its doors on 18 November 1862, the Provisional Theatre's overriding purpose was to provide a stage for opera and, within just a year of its opening, operetta, and plays exclusively in Czech. In the twenty years of its existence,[3] the theatre, modest in size and resources, saw the premieres of seven of Smetana's eight completed operas and the first six of Dvořák's eleven operas along with signal works by Šebor, J. N. Škroup, Blodek, Bendl, Skuherský, Rozkošný, Hřímalý, Fibich and Nápravník, comprising in short, the foundations of Czech national opera.

The problem for the growing Czech-speaking population of Prague, drawn to the city by burgeoning employment prospects in the early decades of the nineteenth century, was not a lack of will to build cultural institutions but the difficulties of making these aspirations concrete. Prague was still at this stage a majority German-speaking city, as it had been for nearly two hundred years, and unsurprisingly the developmental infrastructure needed for creating an establishment in which to perform operas and plays in the native language was slow to develop.

The economic circumstances of the Czech lands had been improving markedly through the early decades of the nineteenth century with investment in mining from Paris and Vienna leading to a systematic exploitation of the mineral riches of Bohemia and Moravia. The drift of the rural Czech-speaking population to find work in majority German-speaking Prague inevitably led to a shift in the capital's demography. The financial circumstances of the incomers were further advanced by the abolition of guild monopolies in 1859. The removal of trade tariffs between Hungary and the Czech lands, resulting in the importation of cheap corn, certainly created economic difficulties in the countryside, but it further intensified industrial prosperity in the towns and cities. By the 1870s Prague had become a majority Czech-speaking city with consequent pressure for native cultural institutions of which opera in Czech had to become a major feature.

In fact, opera in Czech, if not a regular feature, had been a presence in Prague's musical scene some decades before. *Die Zauberflöte*, for example, was given in Czech as *Kouzelná píštála* (the Magical Whistle) as early as 1794,[4] and translations of standard repertoire were becoming more frequent from the 1830s onward. In the years leading up to the opening of the Provisional Theatre, plays and opera in Czech were allowed in the German Theatre at Sunday matinées and occasionally on weekdays (usually Thursdays).[5] The concept of a building dedicated to performances in Czech dates back to discussions among the city's cultural leaders as early as 1844. A petition, ironically, though inevitably at this stage written in German, for a parcel of land on the banks of the Vltava was submitted by the great Czech historian František Palacký to the Bohemian Diet on 19 January 1845.[6] Notwithstanding a high-minded vision, events proceeded at a leaden pace not helped by revolution in 1848. At its most grandiose, as advocated by Palacký, the theatre was to seat two thousand five hundred and would accommodate a concert hall, restaurant, café and meeting rooms. However, when the Czechs were victorious in the 1861 municipal elections, the result was driven by conservative caution, and a rather modest 'Provisional' Theatre was proposed. Designed by Ignác Ullmann, previously responsible for the Czech Savings Bank and the Lažanský Palace, including Slavia, the coffee house, all located at the end of Národni Třída (National Boulevard), the theatre was built in six months on the site of a salt warehouse on the embankment of the Vltava just over the road from these buildings.

The opening, on 18 November 1862, was resplendent with a Festive Overture (Slavnostní ouvertura) by Hynek Vojáček and the premiere of a five-act tragedy, *King Vukašín*, by the respected young writer and member of the Provisional Theatre's board, Vítězslav Hálek. The theatre's operatic debut came two nights later with a gala presentation of Cherubini's *Les deux journées* performed in Czech under its alternative title, *Le porteur d'eau* (*Vodař* in Czech). Cherubini's opera, while popular in the nineteenth century in Prague, exposed the glaringly obvious fact that there was no body of Czech operas nor any signal native masterpiece to launch the musical repertoire of the Provisional Theatre. The first Czech offering was František Škroup's modest Singspiel *Dráteník* (*The Tinker*) of 1826, given on 8 December; while the work was held in considerable affection by audiences, not least because of the inclusion of the song 'Where is my home?' ('Kde domov můj?'), which much later became the Czech national anthem, its appearance was hardly the resonant beginning of a national school.[7]

The conventional operatic repertoire, unsurprisingly, reflected local capabilities and, inevitably, the taste of the musical directors.[8] Under the first, Jan Maýr, a conductor with a wide range of experience, the bias was towards the Italian romantic repertoire. French opera, while less frequent, was represented by a broader range of composers, including Auber, Halévy, Méhul, Meyerbeer, Boieldieu and Offenbach. Balfe's *Bohemian Girl* enjoyed a brief vogue in 1863 and 1864 with nine performances, although its title was discreetly changed in Czech translation to *Cikánka* (The Gipsy Girl). German opera was represented by Mozart, Weber, Lortzing and Flotow. The arrival of Smetana as musical director at the beginning of the 1866 to 1867 season secured the position of French grand opera; even after his withdrawal from the theatre in 1874, owing to deafness, it remained an important feature of the repertoire with Meyerbeer's *Les Huguenots* and *Robert le diable*, Auber's *La muette de Portici*, Halévy's *La Juive* and Rossini's *Guillaume Tell* leading the field. In 1882, the last year of the Provisional Theatre, thirty-one performances were of French grand opera, and only twenty-three were by the Italians Bellini, Donizetti and Verdi. Twenty-four of the performances were accounted for by Beethoven, Flotow, Gluck, Lortzing, Mozart and Tchaikovsky, and thirty-nine were of operas by Czechs. The remaining seventy-nine performances, however, were of operetta, which means – if one includes the nine performances of Anger's *Záletníci* (The Philanderers) and Hřímalý's *Zakletý princ* (The Enchanted Prince), both of which were described as operettas on their posters – approaching half the performances of this final year of the theatre's existence were given over to operetta. This was not a novel trend.[9]

Operetta entered the Provisional Theatre's repertoire during its first full year on 13 December 1863 with Offenbach's *Orphée aux enfers*, which remained a popular part of the repertoire, notably in the summer months, and was given new productions in 1868 and 1873. This was but the start of a marked trend towards operetta as an intrinsic part of the theatre's repertoire. *Orphée* was joined in 1865 by *Le mariage aux lanternes* and *La chanson de Fortunio*, and almost year on year new premieres of operettas by Offenbach were added to the repertoire. While *Orphée* remained popular, both *Les brigands* and *La princesse de Trébizonde* surpassed it in numbers of performances (see Table 5.1). Hopp, Lecocq, Planquette, Johann Strauss Jr and Zajc all proved popular in the period, but Offenbach was undoubtedly the leader in the field where operetta was concerned throughout the existence of the Provisional Theatre.

Orphée met with critical enthusiasm as the pseudonymous critic, -l-, of *Slavoj* noted: '[its] high-spirited humour will certainly win an abundance of admirers'.[10] A more philosophical tone was struck by the writer and critic Jan Neruda in August 1864, who speculated that operetta might be a much more natural genre for the enjoyment of audiences essentially more attuned to folksong and national farce. As will be seen below, the

Table 5.1 *The most frequently performed operettas in the Provisional Theatre, Prague*
The Czech rendition of titles, followed by an English translation, are given where they differ from the original; a translation is also given in the case of Czech titles. The number of performances is followed by the performance span.

Composer	Title	Perfs	Year(s)
Mořic Anger (1844–1913)	*Záletníci* (The Philanderers)	14	1882–3
Richard Genée (1823–95)	*Der Seekadet*	12	1877
	Nanon	3	1878
	Die letzten Mohikaner	9	1879
Julius Hopp (1819–85)	*Morilla* (Čarovný prsten; The Magical Ring)	14	1872–5
Vojtěch Hřimalý (1842–1908)	*Zakletý princ* (The Enchanted Prince)	34	1872–83
Emile Jonas (1827–1905)	*Javotte/Cinderella the Younger* (Javotte, Popelka bostonská; Javotte, the Boston Cinderella)	21	1873–7
Charles Lecocq (1832–1918)	*La fille de Madame Angot* (Angot, dítě pařížské tržnice; Angot, child of a Parisian market)	35	1875–9
	Giroflé-Girofla	47	1875–80
	Fleur-de-thé (Čajové kvítko; Tea flower)	5	1875–6
	Graciella	10	1877
	Le pompon (Dr Piccolo)	6	1877
	Le petit duc (Malý vévoda; The little duke)	42	1878–82
	Le grand Casimir	7	1879
	La Camargo	10	1879–80
	La jolie Persane	15	1880–1
	La petite mademoiselle (Nepřitelkyně kardinála Mazarina; The enemy of Cardinal Mazarin)	3	1880
	Le jour et la nuit	8	1882
Jacques Offenbach (1819–80)	*Orphée aux enfers*	63	1863–80
	Le marriage aux lanternes (Svatba při lucernách; The marriage by lamplight)	17	1865–74
	La chanson de Fortunio	5	1865–6
	Les Géorgiennes (Krásné Gruzinky; The lovely Georgian)	19	1866–79
	Daphnis et Chloë	4	1867
	Le violoneux (Čarovné housle; The enchanted violin)	2	1867
	Monsieur et Madame Denis	3	1867
	Les brigands	77	1871–9
	Geneviève de Brabant	5	1871
	La princesse de Trébizonde	86	1871–9
	Mesdames de la Halle (Pařížské zelenařky; Parisian greengrocers)	5	1871
	La boule de neige	24	1872–8
	La Grande-Duchesse de Gérolstein	21	1873–7
	Les braconniers	21	1874–8
	Barbe-bleue	17	1874–81
	Madame l'Archiduc	7	1875
	La belle Hélène	18	1875–8
	Le roi Carotte	10	1877
Robert Planquette (1848–1903)	*Les cloches de Corneville* (Duch na zámku kornevillském; The spirit in the castle of Corneville)	27	1879–83

Table 5.1 *(cont.)*

Composer	Title	Perfs	Year(s)
Johann Strauss Jr (1825–99)	*Cagliostro in Wien*	12	1875–8
	Die Fledermaus	36	1875–83
	Prinz Methusalem	10	1878–80
	Der lustige Krieg	24	1882–3
	Der Karneval in Rom	8	1882
Franz von Suppé (1819–95)	*Die Kartenschlägerin*	18	1865–72
	Zehn Mädchen und kein Mann (Žádný muž a tolik děvčat; So many girls and no man)	41	1867–77
	Flotte Bursche	14	1872–8
	Fatinitza	35	1876–81
	Die schöne Galathée	5	1878–82
	Boccaccio	46	1879–82
	Donna Juanita	24	1880–3
	Die Afrikareise	6	1883
Ivan Zajc (1832–1914)	*Mannschaft an Bord*	17	1868–74
	Lazzarne de Naples	10	1869–70
	Nach Mekka	12	1869–78
	Der Raub der Sabinerinnen	22	1870–80
	Die Somnambule	5	1871–2
	Die Hexe von Boissy	18	1871–80
	Mislav	3	1871
Other operettas by composer			
Rudolf Bial		6	1877
Johann Brandl		7	1876–7
August Conradi		3	1866
		9	1866–70
Francois-Auguste Gevaert		4	1874–5
Albert Grisar		2	1871
		7	1872–3
Aimé Maillart		3	1878
Victor Massé		3	1873
Carl Millöcker		2	1880
Louis Varney		5	1882

Figures are taken from J. Smaczny, *Daily Repertoire of the Provisional Theatre in Prague.*

response of the management of the Provisional Theatre in many ways reflected the thrust of Neruda's speculation and also to an extent the original intentions of those who had framed the competition rules for new repertoire in 1861 (see later in this chapter).[11]

In 1872, the midpoint of the theatre's existence, when Smetana was still its musical director, seventy of the one hundred and seventy-six performances were billed as operettas. Thirty-eight of these were by Offenbach (*La princesse de Trébizonde, Les brigands, Le mariage aux lanternes* and *La boule de neige*), and the majority of the rest were by Hopp and von Suppé. In fact, between 1870 and 1874, on the basis of these statistics, the most popular composer in the Provisional Theatre was not Smetana or even Verdi, who had made an extremely good showing in the late 1860s, but Offenbach. 1875 marked the high-tide mark for operetta, with one hundred and eighteen out of one hundred and ninety-one performances given over to the genre. It was also the year in which Lecocq eclipsed the popularity of Offenbach with forty-seven performances to the latter's thirty-seven. Nevertheless, the sheer extent of performances of operettas by Offenbach was a prime characteristic of the repertoire of the Theatre; if none of his works achieved the volume of Gounod's *Faust*, at one hundred and fifteen performances, or Smetana's *The Bartered Bride* at one hundred and sixteen, they were among the most consistently successful of all musical performances in the Provisional Theatre. Although it would be unwise to assert that the audiences for Offenbach, Johann Strauss Jr and Lecocq were the same as for Smetana and Meyerbeer, the importance of operetta in the repertoire of the Provisional Theatre cannot be ignored.

Indeed, the presence and significance of lighter genres was recognized at many levels. The manifesto in support of Smetana's musical directorship of the Provisional Theatre, signed by Dvořák and Fibich among others, sent to the Intendant František Ladislav Rieger and the Board of Directors on 17 October 1872, included the comment that 'with *Prodaná nevěsta* (The Bartered Bride) he [Smetana] laid the foundations of Czech light opera, indeed it can be said that he created the style'.[12]

Underpinning a taste for operetta was a marked predilection among audiences for dance. Evenings of ballet were common and guest dancers were invited almost as frequently as guest singers, and they certainly seemed to be as popular. The pattern was set early in the history of the Provisional Theatre with the appearance on 13 December 1862 of the Spanish Ballerina Marcellina Olivera, who gave three performances of an assortment of dances before the end of the year. In March 1863 a major attraction in Auber's *La muette de Portici* was the dancing of the part of Fenella by the theatre's prima ballerina, Marie Hentzová;[13] on the posters advertising the event during the rest of the year, Hentzová's name was printed in bigger letters than those of her singing colleagues.

A curious climax of this adulatory tendency where dance attractions were concerned came with the appearances of the one-legged Spanish ballet dancer, Juliano Donato, in August 1864.[14] Independent ballets were a rare occurrence in the repertoire, and typically Donato's appearances came between the acts of opera. He began in Flotow's *Alesandro Stradella* on 10 August and subsequently appeared at a number of performances, Rossini's *Otello*, *Orphée aux enfers*, *Lucrezia Borgia*, *La muette de Portici*, *La Juive*, *Il barbiere* and *The Bohemian Girl* in the space of a fortnight. This remarkable series of performances was less a testament to Donato's versatility than to the audiences' delight in seeing the dancer perform virtually the same routine on each occasion. Smetana, in his role as critic for the major Czech daily newspaper *Národní listy* (National Pages), was withering about the decline in operatic production which the wholesale deployment of the astonishing Donato represented.[15]

Another feature of planning by the management was the assembly of separate acts from different operas in order to display the gifts of visiting dancers or singers. While Smetana did not approve of this practice, he permitted it to happen under his direction, if not his baton, on a number of occasions.[16] Other opportunities for singing and dancing were offered in the numerous farces with musical accompaniment and spectacular eclectic productions such as *Cesta kolem světa v 80ti dnech* (Around the World in Eighty Days) premiered on 28 September 1876; it was described as a 'great narrative play' with spectacular scenes and a 'Grand ballabile' for the corps de ballet. To emphasize the exotic nature of the attraction, the larger-than-usual poster for the production was headed by images of a camel and a giraffe. Czech composers had a healthy respect for their audiences' liking for ballet, the predilection for which was at its strongest in the 1860s and 1870s. Along with Smetana's *Braniboři v Čechách* (The Brandenburgers in Boehmia), many of the serious Czech operas premiered in the Provisional Theatre included ballets, and all but one, the single-act *Tvrdé palice* (The Stubborn Lovers), of Dvořák's operas include dance.

Surveyed as a whole, the repertoire of the Provisional Theatre could best be described as polyglot and the tastes of its audiences omnivorous. Alongside the steady tread of native serious and comic opera, for which the theatre is now chiefly remembered, was a major helping of the froth and sparkle offered by operetta and musical farces – many of them by Johann Nestroy, of which the most popular in Prague were *Der böse Geist Lumpazivagabundus* and *Eulenspiegel* with music by Adolf Müller I. In his lively set of reminiscences of the Provisional Theatre, Karel Šípek recounts the cramped and awkward nature of its seating; he also gave an indication of the demographic of an audience, some of whom wore rustic garb and enjoyed attractions, such as the astonishing Donato, in the intervals of operas.[17] Looking just beyond the end of the Provisional Theatre era into that of the opening days of the National Theatre, a drawing of the National Theatre's auditorium by Bohumir Roubalík from the 'standing stalls' quite clearly shows a gathering of men and women some of whom are in national dress.[18]

To some extent, the intentions of those who were keen on developing a native repertoire for the theatre had to cater for the needs of an audience which had a strong rural profile and still identified strongly with the sights and sounds of village life as numerous backcloths to Czech comic opera attest.[19] In a similar spirit, Count Jan Harrach's competition rules for new repertoire, produced in 1861, not only encouraged the use of folksong in comic opera but expressed the hope that such practices would lead to the 'audience's lively participation'.[20] While Smetana was certainly opposed to the notion of the 'singalong' night as an aspect integral to Czech comic opera and vehemently opposed the use of the kind of 'medley of songs' it might produce,[21] he was not impervious to the potential of more demotic entertainment as a means of securing audience attention. The brilliant dances added to *The Bartered Bride* three years after its disappointing premiere in 1866 were certainly important in improving its fortunes with audiences. Similarly, the comedians that Smetana and his librettist Karel Sabina included in Act 3 seem a distinct nod in the direction of the more vaudevillian aspects of the theatre's repertoire.

Elsewhere, the Offenbach style had a clear impact on both Smetana and Dvořák in comic mode, in, for example, the competitive exchanges between Karolina and Anežka in Act 2, scene two, of Smetana's *Dvě vdovy* (The Two Widows) and the rumbustiously Parisian closing pages of the overture to Dvořák's *The Stubborn Lovers*. Prague's critics, not least Smetana when writing for *Národní listy*, had a tendency to hold their noses where operetta was concerned, but the undoubted allure of the genre, an attraction of which the management was certainly aware, across the twenty years of the Provisional Theatre's existence cannot be discounted.

Smetana himself seems to have continued to be ambivalent about Offenbach, particularly in relation to *The Bartered Bride*. During a speech at a banquet held by the Umělecká beseda (Artistic Society) in celebration of the hundredth performance of *The Bartered Bride* on 5 May 1882, Smetana referred to the work as a 'joke' (žert) adding 'I composed it, not out of vanity but out of spite, because after *The Brandenburgers* [*The Brandenburgers in Bohemia*] I was accused of being a Wagnerian and not capable of doing anything in a lighter national style. So I immediately hastened to Sabina for a libretto and I wrote *The Bartered Bride*. It was my opinion at the time that even Offenbach could not compete with it.'[22] For all its epigrammatic quality, this statement does encapsulate the problem for the development of a native Czech operetta. Notwithstanding its dances and circus scene, *The Bartered Bride* was fundamentally high-minded in intent and thus transcended Neruda's speculative aspirations for a local brand of operetta. Neither Anger in *The Philanderers* nor Hřimalý with *The Enchanted Prince* established a tradition of Czech operetta, and with *The Bartered Bride*, Smetana created an aspirational template for Czech comic opera that went well beyond the intentions of operetta, as Dvořák's comedies, notably *Jakobín* (The Jacobin) which owes a great deal to *The Bartered Bride*, show.

Operetta remained a presence in the National Theatre's repertoire from its second opening in 1883. Offenbach was by far the most popular composer joined later by Messager, Suppé and Johann Strauss Jr among others (including Gilbert and Sullivan with a staging of *The Mikado*). But numbers of performances were well below those sustained in the Provisional Theatre, and native operetta failed to gain traction, nowithstanding the occasional outing for Karel Bendl's *Indická pincezna* (Indian Princess). This is not to say that Czech composers could not flourish in operetta's mainstream outside the native tradition, as is attested by the huge success of the Viennese operettas of Oskar Nedbal and the American stage works of Rudolf Friml, both of whom were composition pupils of Dvořák.

Notes

1. 'své jediné umělecké ohnisko'; Karel Hoffmeister, *Antonín Dvořák* (Prague: J. R. Vilímek, 1924), 74.
2. The theatre's full name was the Royal Provincial Provisional Theatre in Prague (Královské zemské prozatímní divadlo v Praze).
3. The Czech National Theatre, which opened on 11 June 1881 with Smetana's *Libuše*, replaced the Provisional Theatre but owing to a fire closed on 24 June; it reopened on 18 November 1883.
4. The translation of *Die Zauberflöte* used in the Provisional Theatre was by Josef Krasoslav Chmelenský, first performed in Prague in 1825. See Jitka Ludvová and Collective, *Hudební divadlo v českých zemích: osobnosti 19. Století* [Musical theatre in the Czech lands: personalities from the 19th century] (Prague: Divadelní ústav – Academia, 2006), 225–8.
5. This was the theatre opened by Count Franz Anton Nostitz as the Nostitzsches Nationaltheater in 1783; the financing of the theatre was taken over by the Bohemian Estates in 1798, after which it was known as the Estates Theatre (Stavovské divadlo).
6. For a discussion in English of the construction of the Provisional and National Theatres see Otakar Nový, *The National Theatre: A Short History of its Construction and a Guide to the Building*, trans. Dagmar Steinová (Prague: National Theatre, 1983).
7. Further information on the history of opera in the Czech lands is to be found in John Tyrrell's magisterial study *Czech Opera* (Cambridge: Cambridge University Press, 1988).
8. The performing forces were tiny: the orchestra, based on Karel Komzák's dance band, comprised, by 1864, thirty-five players including a string complement of four each of first and second violins, two violas (the senior player was Dvořák), two cellos and two basses; see Tyrrell, *Czech Opera*, 33, and Jan Smaczny, 'Alfred: Dvořák's First Operatic Endeavor Surveyed', *Journal of the Royal Musical Association*, 115, no. 1 (1990), 80–106. The number of the chorus varied, but, according to the theatre's almanacs (published annually in Prague by Martince and Jarošky), in 1864 there were sixteen men and sixteen women, and in 1865 fifteen men and twenty-one women; the ballet company typically stood at eight.
9. For a complete annotated list of operas and operetta performed in the Provisional Theatre, see J. Smaczny, *Daily Repertoire of the Provisional Theatre Opera in Prague, Chronological List* (Prague: Miscellanea Musicologica, 1994). For general statistics on performances of conventional opera in the Provisional and National Theatres see Tyrrell, *Czech Opera*, 39; for general numbers of operas and operettas as well as musical farces, see Tyrrell, *Czech Opera*, 26.
10. Translation from Marta Ottlová, 'Offenbach's Arrival on the Czech Stage' in Milan Pospíšil, Arnold Jacobshagen, Francis Claudon and Marta Ottlová (eds.), *Le rayonnement de l'opéra-comique en Europe au XIX siècle* (Prague: Koniasch Latin Press, 2003), 267.

11. See Pospíšil et al., *Le rayonnement de l'opéra-comique*, 267–8.
12. A partial text of the manifesto is printed in O. Hostinský, *Bedřich Smetana a jeho boj o moderní českou hudbu* [Bedřich Smetana and his struggle for modern Czech music] (Prague, 1901), 272–5, and a translation of part of the text is available in B. Large, *Smetana* (London: Duckworth, 1970), 238–9.
13. Hentzová later choreographed the dances in *The Bartered Bride*. For further information concerning the dance repertoire of the Provisional Theatre, see J. Smaczny, 'A Study of the First Six Operas of Antonín Dvořák: The Foundations of an Operatic Style', unpublished DPhil thesis, Oxford University (1989), 17–19.
14. For a brief account of Donato's visits including a photograph see Josef Bartoš, *Prozatimní divadlo a jeho opera* [The Provisional Theatre and its opera] (Prague, 1938), 65–6. See also Tyrrell, *Czech Opera*, 27.
15. V. H. Jarka, *Kritické dílo Bedřicha Smetany* [The critical works of Bedřich Smetana, 1858–65] (Prague, 1948), 100–3.
16. See Smaczny, *A Study of the First Six Operas of Antonín Dvořák*, 18.
17. Karel Šípek, *Vzpomínky na Prozatímní* [Reminiscences of the Provisional (Theatre)] (Prague, 1918). See also Tyrrell, *Czech Opera*, 27–8.
18. Originally published in František Šubert's sumptuous commemorative volume *Národní divadlo v Praze* [The National Theatre in Prague] (Prague, 1881) 305; it is reproduced in David Charlton (ed.), *The Cambridge Companion to Grand Opera* (Cambridge: Cambridge University Press, 2003), 367.
19. For example, see František Czerný and Ljuba Klosová (eds.), *Dějiny Českého divadla*, Vol. 3 [The history of Czech theatre] (Prague: Academia nakladatelství Československé akademie věd, 1977), 119.
20. See Tyrrell, *Czech Opera*, 209.
21. See excerpt from the memoirs of Josef Srb-Debrnov printed in František Bartoš (ed.), *Bedřich Smetana: Letters and Reminiscences*, trans. Daphne Rusbridge (Prague: Artia, 1955), 67–8.
22. Bartoš, *Bedřich Smetana: Letters and Reminiscences*, 254–5.

Recommended Reading

Bartoš, František, ed. *Bedřich Smetana: Letters and Reminiscences*. Trans. Daphne Rusbridge. Prague: Artia, 1955.

Czerný, František, and Ljuba Klosová, eds. *Dějiny Českého divadla*. Vol. 3. / *The history of Czech theatre*. Prague: Academia nakladatelství Československé akademie věd, 1977.

Smaczny, Jan. *Daily Repertoire of the Provisional Theatre in Prague, Chronological List*. Prague: Miscellanea Muscologica, 1994.

Smaczny, Jan. 'Grand Opera among the Czechs'. In David Charlton, ed., *The Cambridge Companion to Grand Opera*. Cambridge: Cambridge University Press, 2003.

Tyrrell, John. *Czech Opera*. Cambridge: Cambridge University Press, 1988.

PART II

The Global Expansion of Operetta

6 Going Global: The International Spread of Viennese Silver-Age Operetta

STEFAN FREY

Operetta is the ironic Utopia of a permanent rule of capital. WALTER BENJAMIN

In 1909 a captain of the Belgian army, who was a real gourmet, sought out a native restaurant in Peking, 'hoping for bird's-nest soup, yellow fish brains or caterpillars au gratin'. Without knowing a word of Chinese, he ultimately found one, which seemed to meet his requirements. When he entered, 'an orchestra hidden behind a bank of palms turned up, and the captain thought that he was at last about to have something Chinese. But . . . the orchestra broke forth into – "The Merry Widow" waltz!'[1]

This episode, published two years later in a London newspaper, combines central aspects of international popular entertainment at the beginning of the twentieth century, such as modernity and globalization, the ubiquity and the hegemony of the Western culture, spread by the European colonial powers, and the loss of the 'local' as consequence. Viennese operetta – and especially Franz Lehár's *The Merry Widow* – was an important part of this development. For the first time in theatre history the reception of a play by a mass audience took place worldwide at the same time albeit in very different cultural contexts. Popular entertainment was no longer a specific topic of national traditions as it used to be. It was *The Merry Widow* and her successors who overcame those national boundaries and thus established a new international show business. In consequence a cross-cultural exchange emerged, confirming the 'birth of the modern world' at that time.

Along with Lehár, a new generation of composers arose, among others Oscar Straus, Leo Fall and Emmerich Kálmán. In contrast to their classical forerunners of the 'golden age' of Viennese operetta Franz von Suppé, Carl Millöcker and Johann Strauss, the 'silver age' was attributed to this new generation retrospectively. As different as they are in temperament, invention or taste, they are similar in the new style they created, which was far more original and successful than that of its predecessors. As part of a new theatrical mobility, Viennese operetta was, in the decade before the World War I, dominating the repertory of the Western world.

Balancing the 'local' and the 'global' was an important aspect of its achievement, and so it was not incidental that all those composers originated from the Habsburg Empire. This monarchy, consisting of different ethnicities, languages, cultures and religions, was like a microcosm in itself. And its centre Vienna, therefore, was seen as an experimental laboratory for the arts, with Sigmund Freud as godfather in the background. For light popular music, this became even more important, providing an opportunity to amalgamate different musicals styles, such as folksong, the operatic aria or national dances like the waltz, polka and csárdás.

A Production Without Country

In 1909, the same year as the Belgian captain visited Peking, 'strange things happened' also at the Knickerbocker Theatre in New York: 'A Viennese musical comedy – *The Dollar Princess* – was adapted for the American stage by an ultra-English comedian, George Grossmith, Jr.,' as *The Evening Mail* pondered, summing up: 'Accordingly Mr. Charles Frohman's latest musical importation might be termed a production without country – or with countries to spare, as you elect to look at it.' On top of that *The Dollar Princess*, though set in New York, contained no American music at all. Neither the composer, Leo Fall, who had grown up in Berlin and lived in Vienna, nor his librettists had ever been to the USA. But that didn't matter. As with everywhere else, it was the Viennese elements that captured the audience of *The Dollar Princess* at its Broadway debut. To counterbalance this 'global' impact, interpolations by domestic composers were usually added. In Fall's operetta, it was for instance the hornpipe quintet 'A Boat Sails on Wednesday' by the as-yet-unknown Jerome Kern, 'which included a burlesque of the Apache dance', that *The New York Times* found 'very amusing' – not without adding: 'Dr. Fall's score, however, was much above these trivialities.'[2]

Therefore, Frederic McKay, the critic of *The Evening Mail*, was right: *The Dollar Princess* on Broadway was 'a production without country' – or, better, an international one. The aforementioned producer, Charles Frohman, for instance travelled every season to Europe to buy the newest operettas for his theatres, mostly from George Edwardes, the great entrepreneur of London's West End and creator of the musical comedy. Along with his highly specialized teams of authors and practitioners, he had brought 'the order and efficiency of factory production to the world of entertainment'. And Edwardes was the first to discover Viennese operettas for the English stage – not only while importing them as a speciality from the continent, as happened before, but mixing Viennese operetta with English musical comedy. In the case of *The Dollar Princess*, *The*

New York Times actually complained, that it bore 'all the earmarks ... of a London musical comedy, and seems to have lost a great deal of its Austrian flavor'.[3]

National flavour was obviously no longer the item. The more cultural traditions became outdated, the stronger was the need for new forms in all fields of social and cultural life, as well as in musical theatre. The decade prior to World War I, when operetta went global, was a decade of general prosperity in all industrial countries, and 'the average ... income rose ... to a comfortable 150 percent above subsistence in 1914'. A new middle class emerged as the profiteer of this boom and welcomed the modern times, without any irony, as a new Utopia. For its social and cultural needs, musical theatre became the most popular vehicle and the theatrical 'representative form of modern capitalism', as Len Platt wrote in his book on the subject.[4] Like capitalism itself, musical theatre had a liberating and equalizing impact, not only as a commercial commodity but also as manifestation of a new era, which left behind old restraints, such as the social, cultural and geographical. Viennese operetta, especially, seemed to be suited for this development.

Modern Vienna

The Vienna of Franz Lehár and Leo Fall at the beginning of the twentieth century had long ceased to be the Vienna of Johann Strauss and Carl Millöcker; the population alone had tripled within a generation, so that, with more than two million people, it had become the sixth largest city in the world. By 1890 the number of those residents born out of town far surpassed that of the native Viennese. This great migration wrought fundamental societal changes. Those immigrants' strong aspirations for assimilation made it necessary to find a common background of cultural experience. And this was what operetta offered, being itself a theatrical and musical melting pot. Operettas at that time offered not only Viennese waltz, Czech polka, Hungarian csárdás or German marches but also American cakewalks, English foxtrots or Argentine tangos. Nationality and even class, ridiculed in most operettas, became secondary for this nascent middle class. The narrative of most silver-age operettas implies 'that social status is founded on wealth and consumption rather than on blood'.[5]

Like no other city in Europe, and quite comparable to New York, Vienna become a playground for the social mobility of dissimilar ethnic groups. Yet the vibrant intellectual currents of the epoch also congregated here like nowhere else. Thus, for a few years before World War I, the k. u. k.

(Imperial and Royal) metropolis became a test bed for European modernity. Names such as Freud, Karl Kraus, Arthur Schnitzler, Hugo von Hofmannsthal, Adolf Loos, Gustav Klimt, Egon Schiele, Arnold Schoenberg and Gustav Mahler suffice to bear witness to this. In this context, even contemporary operettas were received as modern, as a clean break with Viennese classical tradition. Within classical operetta, there was still stylistic unity; within the modern, in contrast, there was stylistic chaos. It was modern precisely in that sense – repesentative of the contradictions of an epoch of upheaval, not by accident the time of the final split between light and serious music. So Lehár, asked by an American newspaper in 1913 for an explanation for his success, answered: 'I admit my being the product of new circumstances and conditions in the musical world.'[6]

Indeed, he and Leo Fall represented those new conditions in the musical world as well as those in modern Vienna: societal and cultural mobility for instance, balancing between diversity and assimilation, between light and serious music. Both composers were sons of military bandmasters and, as such, familiar with the different languages and musical traditions of Austria-Hungary. Both started their musical studies at the age of twelve: Lehár as violinist in Prague, Fall as composer in Vienna. There they met for the first time in 1897 as musicians in the orchestra of Lehár's father. While Fall left soon for his family in Berlin and again later on for his career as conductor in the theatre, Lehár became a military bandmaster at the age of twenty, the monarchy's youngest one ever. He held this position for twelve years, until he wrote his first operetta, *Der Rastelbinder*. Before that he had composed the opera *Kukuška*, which was performed in Leipzig, Königsberg and Budapest. It was similar with Fall, who wrote his first operetta *Der Rebell* after having previously composed an opera entitled *Irrlicht*, which was performed in Mannheim and Brunswick. Neither composer ever stopped dreaming of their own success in the operatic field, even though they both found it in operetta.

It was Lehár who had triggered the new Viennese operetta boom in 1905 with *The Merry Widow*, but Fall followed in 1907 with *The Dollar Princess*. In the same year a third man joined them, Oscar Straus, who made his breakthrough with *A Waltz Dream*. These three composers built the great triumvirate of silver-age operetta; a smaller trio consisted of Edmund Eysler, Leo Ascher and Bruno Granichstaedten, all of whom initially had a more pronounced Viennese style. As a kind of a straggler, Emmerich Kálmán from Budapest arrived in 1909, once the claims had already been staked, and he had to fight for his place from scratch. Nevertheless, he knew as well as his colleagues that his only hope of international distribution was from Vienna. A world premiere had to take place there and was visited not by 'a pit of kings but of directors, agents and publishers from Berlin, London and America'.[7]

In the early twentieth century, Viennese operetta was what American musical is today: a global theatre epidemic. The difference is that back then operetta represented the latest style of popular music, and it was operetta that caused a distinction between entertainment and serious music in the first place. By 1905 – the year *The Merry Widow* and Richard Strauss's *Salome* premiered – the gulf between the two spheres was obvious. And it was exactly this gulf that was responsible for the success of operetta, because operetta offered what opera had seemingly abandoned: melody, accessibility, euphony. It was not only Vienna and, shortly afterwards, Berlin that fell for its magic; in London and New York, it turned into a veritable cult. Moreover, success in America proved particularly decisive for international success. Thus, for the operetta business 'Vienna was about the same as Hollywood is today for the film industry'.[8] For Karl Kraus, the critical editor of the famous satirical magazine *Die Fackel*, it was first and foremost 'a symptom of an economic boom'.[9]

'A New Genre!'

Kraus was not the only one who saw occidental culture threatened; contemporary critics launched a rabid campaign against modern operetta, whose modernity consisted chiefly of a combination of art and business that at the time seemed almost obscene. This kind of marketing was new. Wilhelm Karczag, who profited from and initiated that trend and who was Lehár's, Fall's and Kálmán's discoverer as well as director of the legendary Theater an der Wien, declared accordingly: 'It is a new genre! Does one want it or not? The audience seems to want it. A new time has begun for musical works of this sort, which have brought the composers artistic honour and financial security, not to mention that hundreds of theatrical enterprises have become wealthy.'[10]

So, in Vienna not only established stages like the Theater an der Wien and the Carl-Theater, but also the Raimundtheater, the Stadttheater and the Bürgertheater catered to the new genre. The Johann-Strauss-Theater was even newly constructed for this purpose in 1908. It was the heyday of operetta stages and long-running performance series. With the epoch's emphasis on progress, the managers, composers and other profit-makers in this business proclaimed the onslaught of modernity on operetta – and a consequent split from Viennese tradition. As the product of a new market, operetta was of course tailored to it. Worldwide distribution demanded a common denominator, to which many a local idiosyncrasy fell victim: 'Operetta, originally a child of Vienna ... is suddenly growing into a modern cosmopolitan – out of business sense ... Thus, the ambience is as international as possible ... England, America and France yield the big royalties. There, the pieces run till the end of the world.'[11]

That is exactly what happened. The end of the world, then on everyone's lips, indeed terminated the international dominance of Viennese operetta – in 1914. The rapid international distribution alone, which would have been unthinkable in the nineteenth century, even for Johann Strauss, shows clearly how much the dynamic of the epoch caught up with operetta. The genre, nearly ruined at the turn of the century, owed its real renaissance to 'times in motion: the flood of themes, the chaos of stylistic gestures'.[12] That chaos of stylistic devices had to be accommodated in a style flexible enough to absorb the musical-dramatic flights of fancy of the finales and many a low blow from the dance hits. The formal irony of such disparate music dramaturgy, however, became the method of modern operetta. This corresponded to the standard casting template of a serious, romantic couple and a comic one. While the former soulfully staged its conflicts in dramatic dancing scenes up to the obligatory 'tragic' éclat in the second-act finale, the latter engaged in more physical activity – to rousing hit routines that evolved from acrobatic dancing. As such, these numbers are less tailored to the needs of the stage than to the everyday life of the audience, an audience 'that has come immediately from its daily business and isn't in the mood to be transported to an unfamiliar spiritual world – thus, banality'.[13]

The incursion into everyday life marked a turning point. As is customary in latter-day popular culture, operetta no longer presented a fictional alternative world, but itself became the model for reality. In the days of *The Merry Widow* 'there were very many, otherwise normal people who talked, thought, and felt in quotes and melodies thereof'.[14] The barrier between stage and audience had thus been lifted. It was not for nothing that most modern operettas were set in the present. As if 'the naturalism of new drama had been transferred to operetta',[15] modern people appeared in modern operetta. Nevertheless, this operetta naturalism had little in common with its literary counterpart. Glorifying, not uncovering, social conditions was its aim. Whereas Offenbach demystified his operetta gods by turning them into contemporaries, the modern operetta turned contemporaries into gods of a smart secularized world – attorneys into counts, princes or at least barons. For Offenbach's proponent Karl Kraus, the figure of the modern operetta hero embodies 'the super clerk triumphant ... He is the figure that resulted from casting our lifetime wishes as operetta leads. The sales representative as the representative of the global department store of our culture.'[16]

Operetta Industry

The fact that modern operetta emerges with the first department stores is as little of a coincidence as the tendency of both to offer 'off the rack' goods. Most noticeably, this affected the subject matter, which was not labelled as 'operetta material' for nothing. Folklore became merely a decorative pretext; the new heroes, as middlemen of entertainment, danced urbanely across the international dance floor. The direct connection between the textile industry and light music could be read on every playbill, which readily gave the names of the costume suppliers. For even more important than singing perfection was the elegant display of the costumes, the skilled handling of the props, the ability to get things moving, the specific quality of the operetta hero. These actors did not without cause become the idols of ready-to-wear fashion. 'Operetta, an industry supporting thousands of people, should put up with being counted with those articles of daily use that serve the citizen to more comfortably appoint his daily life, like department stores, automobiles, sexual enlightenment – like all those inexpensive surrogates which in our day carry the illusion of erudition and luxury to the masses.'[17]

Furthermore, this industry had its rigid market laws, to which operetta creators were also subjected, although only very few of them realized it. Adorno remarked, 'Before the war, the most firmly established among them merged into composition trusts, which settled in the Salzkammergut.'[18] Above all, the success of the tried and tested tempted the librettists to cling to the recipe once discovered. The consequence was a stereotypical dramaturgy that finally reduced the modern operetta *ad absurdum*. Proven scriptwriters worked with proven composers. And not only were quite a few business ties forged in the Salzkammergut, but also 'in Vienna there was in session at that time ... a veritable operetta stock exchange, which had set up shop in the Café Museum'.[19]

When the famous Austrian writer Hermann Bahr detected in 1906 that 'the theatre sets the agenda for all fashions, also for those of the soul', he had solely Vienna and the time before 1906 in mind. He could not have suspected how right he was, when, in the same year, an operetta like *The Merry Widow* set the new benchmark, not merely for Viennese theatre, but for all global entertainment. The image of the waltzing pair Sonia and Danilo became emblematic for its time. According to Theodor W. Adorno, 'The Merry Widow Waltz' is the perfect example of the new style, and 'the exultation with which the bourgeoisie welcomed Lehár's operetta can be compared to the success of the first department stores'.[20]

Department Store Operetta

The department store and the operetta had, indeed, many features in common besides their simultaneity, and the most obvious was the textiles department. The costumes presented by the leading lady, or the girls, could be purchased right away in the department stores, with which the theatres shared the same urban space in the centre of the big cities. Thus the operetta 'sets the agenda for all fashions' in a much more literal sense than Bahr could ever have thought. Presenting the costume was at least as crucial for the operetta star as singing or acting, and, therefore, dancing was the best opportunity. The way this presentation proceeded soon became a role model for all audiences, as they imitated the habits of the performer. The most concise example of this ritual of reception, making life an imitation of operetta, was certainly the Merry Widow hat, as big as a cartwheel, worn by London's Sonia, Lily Elsie and inherited by Ethel Jackson in New York: 'a hat? no, a HAT – the sight of which sent every woman into ecstasy and the quick resolve to have one just like that at the earliest possible moment'.[21]

On one occasion, the management of the New Amsterdam Theatre decided to satisfy this 'resolve' in celebration of the 275th performance of the operetta in New York City by distributing hats 'as souvenirs to all the women occupying orchestra or balcony seats'. But they underrated both the intensity of this 'resolve' and the female power to effectuate it. Assuming 'that the fifty cent seats deserved souvenirs and ... that there would be some men in the audience', they had only 1,200 hats for 1,600 women in the house. When this emerged even before 'the curtain began to come down, everybody ... made a rush to the improvised bargain counter' where the hats should be distributed.[22] What then happened went down in the history of Broadway as the 'Hot Skirmish over Merry Widow Hats'. *The New York Times* reported, that a 'throng of women ... declared mob rule and began the attack ... One woman tackled a woman next to her with a vim that would have done credit to the world's champion female wrestler ... The older women did themselves credit ... and the ardor with which they threw themselves into the mêlée made their daughters look like the veriest mollycoddles.'[23]

The proof could not be more striking that operetta was a primary ingredient of everyday culture of modern urbanity. In addition to the hat, there were Merry Widow shoes, corsages and creams, or Merry Widow cakes, chocolates and liqueurs, as vehicles for a very contemporary lifestyle. Under the permanent rule of capital, such commodities became symbols of being up to date for a socially mobile middle class that was still nascent but existed in nearly every part of the Western world as a new condition for both consumers and audience. Their global similarities were about to be stronger than their local differences.

The Language of the Unconscious

This new middle class was the premise for the new international operetta business, and it was a phenomenon in all industrialized countries as a result of social advancement and migration to the cities. Thus the 'local' obviously lost relevance – even for Viennese operetta. Its setting is no longer outmoded Vienna but fashionable Paris, as in *The Merry Widow*, or modern New York, as in *The Dollar Princess*, again a good example in this context. First of all, the scene is located in New York City, the new centre of the Western world. Secondly, the characters of the play represent the supremacy of new money over old traditions – and money was certainly one of the big topics for modern operetta. The other one was rather old: the love between a man and a woman. *The Merry Widow* had already presented a model of how both could be ideally combined, the love between a poor man and a rich woman.

In *The Dollar Princess*, the heroine Alice is an American business woman who falls in love with her European secretary Freddy. For her, 'He needs not to make advances, / It's quite a useless thing, / He's just a doll that dances, / When Alice pulls the string.' According to the new gender roles being constructed at that time, her conflict is that of all modern operetta heroines: she does not want to be loved only for her money any more than Freddy wants to be 'just a doll that dances'. The shifting sexual identities, represented by Alice and Freddy, initially prevent the happy outcome obligatory for the genre. So, both have to make concessions. Freddy goes the American way as a self-made man and becomes, as a consequence, rich himself, while Alice now changes roles, becomes his secretary and, in order to establish equality, pretends to have lost her wealth.

Even if this happy ending seems to return to old models, the narrative of *The Dollar Princess* features many facets of the ermergent modern as ambivalent, such as the changed relationship between the sexes or the new social mobility, both liberating and irritating. Ambivalence itself became a primary quality of the theatrical performance. In operetta, it is the music that helps the characters to discover their real emotional identity, but it is the narrative that reveals the false social attitude. In *The Dollar Princess*, Alice and Freddy prove themselves modern, by showing social mobility, and they are rewarded. In the operetta's American Dream of equality, 'real' and 'false', love and money, are reconciled.

The novelty of *The Merry Widow* worked in another way, as the *New York Telegram* opined, 'There are no gags [instead there is] something very human in it ... If there is anything foreign to the average Broadway production it is this self-same "Merry Widow."'[24] This human touch, connected with musical comedy, seemed to confirm the usual reception habits of the genre. But what made the story of Sonia, the young rich widow, and the impoverished Prince Danilo so special? Unable to express themselves with words, it is the music, which helps them to communicate. While the lips remain silent, the feet begin to speak. Thus, the dance becomes the language of the unconscious in quite a Freudian manner. What is more, it was the waltz that allowed such an intimate dialogue of bodies and turned Sonia and Danilo into the mythical pair of their age.

Frederic McKay, the critic of *The Evening Mail*, hit the nail on the head:

> It seems strange, now that its discovery has been made, that it remains for the authors of 'The Merry Widow' to realize the value of a waltz of lovers as a dramatic expedient. If the Polka and the Two-step have been shoving the Waltz to one side of late, I have no doubt in the world, that the wonderfully contagious waltzes of 'The Merry Widow' will revive the glories of that strictly Viennese dance.[25]

He was right. The waltz, which seemed to have had its heyday in the nineteenth century as a grand collective pleasure, enjoyed a surprising renaissance as a dramatic expedient of psychological impact. It offered a piece of firm ground in a rapidly changing world. And it also offered a code for expressing the new social and gender relationships of the modern that was understood internationally by middle-class audiences in a very explicit way, as composer Franz Lehár knew: 'Indeed, at the time when this operetta was performed in all parts of the world a tremendous number of people got married.'[26]

The International Market

Though Vienna might have been the place of its artistic origin, the market place of operetta prior to World War I was London's West End, where nearly all international runs started. It was George Edwardes who exploited this market first for his musical comedies and then for his operettas. After a London success, touring was a major component of his entertaining empire. Simultaneously, there were different companies on tour, copying the London model in Britain, Canada, Australia, New Zealand, South-Africa and India. Going global for operetta already meant back then becoming a part of English-language theatre, 'governed by the law of commerce', as Edwardes's predecessor John Hollingshead had written very clearly: 'The English stage [...] must stand behind its counter to serve the customers.'[27]

In spite of its predominance, the British Empire was just one part of the new globalized world in the beginning twentieth century. The United States was another. In her first season in New York and Chicago *The Merry Widow* made a profit of about '$1.000.000 ... a record ... without a parallel', as *The New York Times* assessed.[28] In her second season, there were five companies out of town, and it was again George Edwardes who sold the rights. Thus, he profited from the American royalties nearly as much as the composer himself. With Charles Frohman as his new partner, he later controlled the business in the whole English-speaking world. But this again was only a part of the business; most of it was done over the rest of the globe, including Latin America, Europe and its colonies. In 1909, there had been more than '300 productions of *The Merry Widow* by various companies in practically all European languages'.[29]

Selling the national and foreign-language rights became a main issue of the business. So Chappell, Lehár's London publisher, paid for the English rights of his new working-class girl operetta *Eva* in 1911 the 'substantial amount of $40,000'.[30] A year later the newly built opera house in Tripoli opened with this operetta, at the instigation of Libya's new colonial power, performed in Italian. Because of that, Lehár's colleague Leo Fall, when he was requested by Frohman to write an 'operetta for America ... in the style of *The Dollar Princess*', instructed his London agent Ernest Mayer to answer that he 'can't write an operetta just for America, when the whole world stands open'.[31] Or, as librettist Leo Stein wrote in a letter to Fall, forgetting the benefits of the cross-cultural exchange of the recent years: 'When the English and Americans wish that we prepare our operettas inherently for their taste, then they should rather return to their own former genres.'[32] And that was what they did.

Silver Twilight in Berlin

After the onset of World War I, the English and Americans indeed returned to musical comedy, and, a decade after its end, a new genre grew out of this: the American musical. Even then, however, Viennese operetta was still an important component of the repertory, and a home-grown Viennese operetta emerged in the USA, created by emigrants from

Austria-Hungary like Rudolf Friml or Sigmund Romberg. Something similar happened in Berlin. After the war, established Viennese composers, such as Leo Fall and Oscar Straus, placed the first performances of their new works in the German capital, and their younger rivals Robert Stolz, Ralph Benatzky and Paul Abraham started their career there. The main reason was, of course, the economy: Berlin earned the money, while Vienna lost it. Another was the urban appeal of the city, which suited modern operetta better anyway. Finally, it was the higher standard of the *mise-en-scène* and the quality of the cast. The biggest stars, like Richard Tauber, Fritzi Massary or Gitta Alpar – all from former Austria-Hungary – worked in Berlin. When, eventually, even Franz Lehár premiered his works there, *The New York Times* wrote of his *Land of Smiles* in 1929, 'Berlin is now leading Vienna in operetta.'[33]

It was a time when, in Vienna, the famous Carl-Theater had to close down, as did most other Viennese operetta theatres in the years that followed. Only the Theater an der Wien with its rich tradition was left. Emmerich Kálmán alone kept faith with the place of his former triumphs and with the form of typical silver-age operetta, still dealing with poor aristocrats, rich women and *mésalliances*. While Lehár composed for his favourite singer, Richard Tauber, serious romantic operettas with unhappy endings, Oscar Straus and Benatzky wrote light musical comedies in a more satirical manner, one of them *The White Horse Inn*, the last worldwide success of Austro-German operetta in 1930. It was Paul Abraham, however, who mixed up all the different styles of Viennese operetta with American jazz in a last big bang. His *Viktoria und ihr Husar* or *Ball im Savoy* illuminated the twilight of silver-age operetta in Berlin.

In 1933, when the Nazis took over, this era ended abruptly. Most of those involved in it had to leave because they were Jewish. They returned to Vienna for another five years, then were scattered to the four winds. Only Franz Lehár stayed. His utopian dream of 'a new human race, the "Operetta race," the race of people who are always happy, always in good humour' was destroyed, when race was no longer a category for good humour. And his song 'Patiently smiling' from *The Land of Smiles* acquired a new sense: 'What I feel inside, concerns nobody.'[34]

Back to the captain of the Belgian army, who was vainly looking for Chinese music in the Peking of 1909. He would have been more successful twenty years later in Berlin, visiting a performance of Lehár's *Land of Smiles*. This operetta was certainly more Chinese than China itself. When Karl Kraus once asked a Japanese person what his compatriots thought about Austria, he retorted: '"One laughs!" What would a Chinese person have answered?'[35]

Notes

1. N. N., 'A Chinese Dinner', *Penny Illustrated Paper*, London, Saturday, 9 Dec. 1911, 749.
2. N. N., '"Dollar Princess" Mild Musical Show', *The New York Times*, 7 Sep. 1909; Frederic McKay, 'The Dollar Princess'. *The Evening Mail*, New York, 7 Sep. 1909. The *danse apache*, or gangster dance, originated at the Moulin Rouge in Paris.
3. N. N., '"Dollar Princess" Mild Musical Show', The New York Times, 7 Sep.1909; Thomas Postlewait, 'George Edwardes and Musical Comedy: The Transformation of London Theatre and Society, 1878–1914' in Tracy C. Davis and Peter Holland (eds.), *The Performing Century. Nineteenth-Century Theatre History* (Basingstoke: Palgrave Macmillan, 2007), 83. See also Marlis Schweitzer, *Transatlantic Broadway: The Infrastructural Politics of Global Performance* (Philadelphia: University of Pennsylvania Press, 2009) .
4. Len Platt, *Musical Comedy on the West End Stage, 1890–1939* (Basingstoke: Palgrave Macmillan, 2004), 4, 40; S. Jose Harris, *Private Lives, Public Spirit: A Social History of Britain 1870–1914* (Oxford: Oxford University Press, 1993), 33.
5. Erika Diane Rappaport, *Shopping for Pleasure: Women in the Making of London's West End* (Princeton, NJ: Princeton University Press, 2000), 210.
6. N. N., 'Franz Lehár: King of the Viennese Operette Domain'. An Interview with the famous composer, *Music Magazine*, Boston, 22 Feb. 1913.
7. Anon., '(Carltheater) *Das Puppenmädel* von Leo Fall' in *Wiener Zeitung* (*Wiener Abendpost*), 5 Nov. 1910.
8. Rudolf Bernauer, *Theater meines Lebens* (Berlin: Blanvalet, 1955), 210.
9. Karl Kraus, 'Eine Musik- und Theaterausstellung', *Die Fackel*, No. 239–40, 31 Dec. 1907, 40.
10. Wilhelm Karczag, 'Operette und musikalische Komödie', *Neues Wiener Journal*, 12 Apr. 1914.
11. Ernst Klein, 'Aus der Wiener Operettenwerkstatt', *Berliner Lokal-Anzeiger*, 29 Apr. 1912.
12. Gottfried Benn, 'Kunst und Drittes Reich', *Das Hauptwerk* (Wiesbaden, Munich: Limes Verlag, 1980), Vol. 2, 183.
13. Klaus Pringsheim, 'Operette', *Süddeutsche Monatshefte*, (Munich, 1912), Vol. 2, 182.
14. Ludwig Hirschfeld, 'Wiedersehen mit einer Witwe. Ein Rückblick im Operettenformat', *Neue Freie Presse*, Vienna, 23 Sep.1923.
15. Ernst Decsey, *Franz Lehár* (Berlin: Dreimasken Verlag, 1930), 48.
16. Karl Kraus, 'Grimassen über Kultur und Bühne', *Die Fackel*, No. 265–71, 19 Jan. 1909, 12.
17. Klaus Pringsheim, 'Operette', 185.
18. Theodor W. Adorno, 'Zur gesellschaftlichen Lage der Musik' [1932] in Rolf Tiedemann and Klaus Schulz (eds.), *Gesammelte Schriften 18 – Musikalische Schriften V* (Frankfurt a. M.: Suhrkamp, 1984), 772. Adorno was referring to Bad Ischl, whose Esplanade with the legendary Café Zauner became an operetta exchange, where, during the summer, librettists and composers negotiated the works of the next season.
19. Julius Bistron, *Emmerich Kálmán: Mit einer autobiographischen Skizze der Jugendjahre von Emmerich Kálmán* (Leipzig: W. Karczag, 1932), 32.
20. Theodor W. Adorno, 'Zur gesellschaftlichen Lage der Musik', 772; Hermann Bahr, 'Wien. Mit acht Vollbildern' in Leo Grienert (ed.), *Städte und Landschaften*, Vol. 6 (Stuttgart: Carl Krabbe Verlag, 1906), 74.
21. W. Macqueen-Pope and D. L. Murray, *Fortune's Favourite. The Life and Times of Franz Lehár* (London: Hutchinson, 1953), 114. See also Schweitzer, *When Broadway was the Runway: Theatre, Fashion, and American Culture* (Philadelphia: University of Pennsylvania Press, 2009), 1.
22. N. N., 'Women Riot Over Free Hats', *The New York Sun*, 14 June 1908.
23. N. N., 'Hot Skirmish Over "Merry Widow" Hats', *The New York Times*, 14 June 1908.
24. N. N., 'Pranks of "The Merry Widow". Franz Lehar's Operetta at the New Amsterdam', *New York Telegram*, 22 Oct. 1907.
25. Frederic Edward McKay, '"Merry Widow" Wins an Instant Success', *The Evening Mail*, New York, 22 Oct. 1907.
26. Franz Lehár, 'Das moderne Mädchen und die Musik', *Die Bühne*, Vienna, 1929 (Weinberger-Archiv Wien/File 365).
27. John Hollingshead, 'Theatres' in Walter Besant (ed.), *London in the Nineteenth Century* (London: Adam and Charles Black, 1909), 205.
28. Anon., '"The Merry Widow" Making a Million',*The New York Times*, 22 Dec. 1907.

29. Ibid.
30. Franz Lehár, cited in N. N., ‚Lehár mehrfacher Millionär', *New Yorker Zeitung*, 19 Dec. 1911.
31. Leo Stein, Letter to Leo Fall (in London), Vöslau, May 1910 (ÖNB F88 Leo Fall. 261); Ernest Mayer, 'The International Copyright Bureau Ltd.' Letter to Leo Fall, London, 15 Mar. 1910 (ÖNB F88 Leo Fall, 306).
32. Leo Stein, Letter to Leo Fall (in London), Vöslau, May 1910 (ÖNB F88 Leo Fall. 261).
33. Anon., 'Germans and Operetta: Signs that Berlin Is Now Leading Vienna in this Little Matter', *New York Times*, 8 Dec.1929.
34. Franz Lehár cited in C. de Vidal Hunt, '1000 Merry Widows: "Shahzada of the Operetta" Calls a Congress', 1925 (Weinberger-Archiv Wien, File 365).
35. Karl Kraus, 'Mer lächelt', *Die Fackel*, No. 820–6, October 1929, 52;

Recommended Reading

Arnbom, Marie-Theres, Kevin Clarke and Thomas Trabitsch, eds. *Die Welt der Operette. Glamour, Stars und Showbusiness*. Wien: Brandstätter, 2011.

Frey, Stefan. *Laughter Under Tears*. Emmerich Kálmán. An Operetta Biography. Culver City: Operetta Foundation, 2014.

Frey, Stefan. *Was sagt ihr zu diesem Erfolg. Franz Lehár und die Unterhaltungsmusik des 20. Jahrhunderts*. Leipzig; Frankfurt a. M.: Insel, 1999.

Platt, Len, Tobias Becker and David Linton, eds. *Popular Musical Theatre in London and Berlin: 1890–1939*. Cambridge: CambridgeUniversity Press, 2014.

Schweitzer, Marlis. *When Broadway was the Runway: Theatre, Fashion, and American Culture*. Philadelphia: University of Pennsylvania Press, 2009.

Traubner, Richard. *Operetta: A Theatrical History*. New York: Routledge, 2003.

7 Spain and Zarzuela

CHRISTOPHER WEBBER

What is Zarzuela?

I'll begin with a mischievous question, put on behalf of the many Spanish composers, writers and performers who contributed to their national treasure: 'What on earth is zarzuela doing in a book about operetta?'

They have a point. Many casual (and not-so-casual) commentators outside Spain have an image of zarzuela as Spanish-flavoured operetta with hands on hips and a rose between its teeth. It is not so. The story of zarzuela is littered with 'operetta wars', during which the local product was defended – with appropriately quixotic ardour – by critics and creators who saw foreign invaders as undermining the distinctiveness of zarzuela and its importance to national music. Here is the composer Julio Gómez, writing in 1912: 'Zarzuela just died again … In the eighteenth century Italian opera completely erased the musical traditions of our Golden Age of Spanish theatre, then our modern zarzuela withered under the assault of French *opéra bouffe* … and now *género chico*, last and least branch of our lyric theatre, is dying at the hands of another foreign genre.'[1] The particular 'foreign genre' which incensed Gómez was Viennese operetta, then enjoying a brief craze in Madrid's superbly equipped modern theatres, but echoes of his lament can be found from the 1650s down to the 1950s, when romantic zarzuela finally succumbed to the full frontal assault of the American musical. To paraphrase the great philosopher Bill Shankly, for Spain zarzuela isn't just a matter of life and death: it's more important than that.

Now for an even more mischievous question: 'What on earth *is* zarzuela?' The question is often posed, and with reason. No operatic genre has been subject to more misunderstanding in the English-speaking world.[2] Its common usage to mean any sort of popular, Spanish lyric theatre is surprisingly recent: in the early 1950s General Franco's LP marketing department tossed a wide range of musical fish – including Spanish-language adaptations of Viennese operettas – into a single bucket labelled 'zarzuela'. This was done to codify an official canon of one hundred or so state-approved works, recorded with top singers such as Teresa Berganza under conductors including Ataúlfo Argenta.

A glance at the printed scores reveals that relatively few of Spain's classics sport the word 'zarzuela' on the title page. Thus we might find a *drama lírico* or *comedia lírica* at one end of the scale, through to a *sainete* (short comic or satirical play) or *revista* (revue) at the other. Since it was built in the 1850s, Madrid's Teatro de la Zarzuela has become 'spiritual home' to a host of works its founders would never have recognized as zarzuelas at all. Academia has played its part too: the conventionally accepted timeline of the genre, stratifying the rise and fall of various sub-genres, has until lately followed faithfully lines laid down by the influential, nineteenth-century nationalist critic Antonio Peña y Goñi. In reality, Madrid's playwrights and composers – like those of Paris, London and Vienna – wrote in a wide variety of styles and were more interested in extending generic boundaries than slavishly following them.

Julio Gómez can help us out. When he talked about 'zarzuela' he simply meant 'a lyric stage work in Spanish, with spoken dialogue'. That is about as far as we can go with any confidence, and when I use the word here, that is all I mean by it. As to musical language, there are certain techniques which might be bundled together as 'zarzuela style'; but though a handful of through-written Spanish operas (such as Amadeo Vives's *Maruxa* and Pablo Sorozábal's *Adiós a la bohemia*) utilized enough of these techniques to end up in Franco's bucket along with everything else, spoken dialogue – lots of it – is pretty much a given.

That dialogue, added to some congruities of dramatic and musical structures, is the reason zarzuela has been shepherded into the operetta fold, sometimes for the convenience of non-Spanish reference works. Yet by those criteria you might just as well label *Fidelio* or *Carmen* operettas. Apart from their commercial popularity, many outstanding zarzuelas do not fit operetta templates any better: they are no more suitably housed in Klotz than in Kobbé.[3] Alert critics have recognized the mismatch. In the zarzuela section of *Gänzl's Book of the Musical Theatre*,[4] for example, Kurt Gänzl and Andrew Lamb fairly sum up the differences. For although most inhabitants of Franco's bucket have strong comedy elements, zarzuela rarely feels like 'just another' local variant of comic opera. The confusion arises partly from a misunderstanding of the word *comedia*, that deeply Spanish concept of 'the mirror of life', which encompasses the dark as well as the light. Taking one instance for many, Ruperto Chapí's 1898 three-act zarzuela *Curro Vargas* is certainly *comedia*, with popular scenes and comic characters aplenty; but it is written – at Wagnerian length – in blank verse, has musical finales as complex and musically advanced as anything in Falla's *La vida breve*,[5] centres on a psychotic anti-hero obsessed with Andalusian machismo and ends in a bloodbath worthy of *Hamlet*. As

Graham Vick's powerful 2014 Teatro de la Zarzuela production showed, Chapí can be every bit as cathartic as Shakespeare.

Zarzuela's subject matter is as broad as that of its elder sister, opera. Its long history, range and complexity – over 10,000 zarzuelas were written in the century from 1850 – make it a huge topic. Its blanket domination of Spain's theatrical life during that century, aesthetically as well as commercially, makes it an important one. Its intense involvement in the country's politics, not least during the democratic crises of the 1870s and 1920s, makes it a sensitive one. Even during the high summer of romantic zarzuela, from 1880 to 1910 when the distinctively short *género chico* ('little genre') ruled the roost, parallels between zarzuela and contemporary operetta soon broke down. Satiric and sentimental in tone as anything from Paris or Vienna, the farcical action of *género chico* swiftly became grittily realistic in mode, passionately focussed on the underclass life of one, great city – Madrid. When historical or rural settings are found here they are either political in intent, to bolster a sense of national identity (as in contemporary Slav opera), or pastoral in an Empsonian sense, reflecting on the evils of the metropolis through an idealized vision of peasant life.

Having said that, there is no doubt that zarzuela and operetta *are* related, to an extent which fully justifies a chapter in this book, at least in the lamentable absence of a *Cambridge Companion to Zarzuela*. Practically speaking, they demand the same wide skill set from performers. Theoretically speaking, in the romantic era a nagging dialectic between the two – prompted in turn by Offenbach, English musical plays, the Viennese operettas of Lehár and American jazz – produced fruitful tensions. There was even one, brief shining moment (*c*.1910–23) when genuine Spanish *opereta* ruled the roost. In our own day, the sunset of its commercial success gives zarzuela a common cause with operetta: a lethal mixture of changed theatrical taste, artistic snobbery and institutional prejudice against perceived 'sub-operatic' musical cultures, finds them both on life support.[6] Zarzuela's peculiar niche is illuminated by its relation to opera on one side and operetta on the other.

Zarzuela and Opera

As Julio Gómez said, the history of zarzuela is marked by local response to a series of invasions from abroad. It owed its very existence to seventeenth-century dynastic rivalries: the court entertainments instigated in the 1640s by King Philip IV at his hunting lodge in the *zarzas* (bramble-infested, scrubby countryside outside Madrid) were devised as a riposte to his

French 'brother' Louis XIV, to show that anything France could do, Spain could do better. As formulated by Pedro Calderón de la Barca, Spain's preeminent dramatist, the first zarzuelas were theatrically practical, too. With their mixture of mythological and peasant characters, prose and verse dialogue, operatic arias, popular songs and dance, baroque zarzuelas such as Sebastián Durón's *Salir el amor del mundo* (Love Leaves the World, 1696) are close in aesthetic to Dryden and Purcell's *King Arthur* from five years earlier.

Neither Spain nor England comfortably absorbed through-written lyric drama, and their home-bred, hybrid forms kept vernacular music theatre alive during the eighteenth century, when both courts were dominated by Italian opera. As with *The Beggar's Opera* in England, the later *sainete* and *tonadilla* in Madrid (both short, Spanish-language plays with music) flourished as alternative, popular theatre, showing a finger to the ruling class.

The culmination of this process saw the 'rebirth' of zarzuela in the 1850s, thanks to a determined group of musicians, writers and actors led by Francisco Asenjo Barbieri, a composer and musicologist who enjoys something of the status in Spain that Glinka does in Russia. At a time of huge political and social instability, Barbieri put zarzuela at the heart of Spain's struggle to forge a constitutional, democratic identity based on industrialization rather than monarchist nostalgia for the golden age of empire. Although his own music follows the Italian models of Donizetti and early Verdi, he worked hard to morph that into something recognizably Spanish. His writers used French theatre as a launchpad, most of their libretti being high-quality adaptations of *opéra comique* originals. Nonetheless a distinct national form emerged: the three-act *zarzuela grande*, geared to the liberal Parisian tastes of Spain's growing professional classes.

Barbieri's *Pan y toros* (Bread and Bulls, 1864) and *El barberillo de Lavapiés* (The Little Barber of Lavapiés, 1874) are cornerstones of the romantic zarzuela repertoire, their aristocratic plots yoking grand opera to dramatic crowd scenes exploiting popular Spanish song forms and dance rhythms – zarzuela of this period rarely if ever quotes actual folk songs. Superficially, the two could not be more different. *Pan y toros* is a broad, turbulent canvas of Madrid's revolt against French domination in the Napoleonic era and features Spain's artistic conscience – Goya himself – as a character. *El barberillo* is closer to Italian comic opera in style, its title not only a modest nod to Rossini but also a cheeky assertion of Barbieri's own name and his concern with a poor quarter of Madrid rather than aristocratic Seville. Yet both are *comedias* in the full sense, *El barberillo* in particular exhibiting a range of social settings and a national political spirit absent from such close contemporaries as *Die Fledermaus* or *H.M.S Pinafore*.[7]

The notion that there should have been a natural progression from zarzuela towards through-sung Spanish opera, perhaps on Wagnerian principles, has haunted Spain's composers and critics down the years. Yet in a fighting pamphlet simply entitled *La zarzuela* (1864) Barbieri warned that such 'progress' was both impossible and undesirable. He refused to accept that zarzuela – provided it remained true to *comedia* principles – was a mere junior slope halfway up the mountain to 'serious' national opera:

> Amongst the vulgar there is a general idea of putting little value on … a *tonadilla* or a *sainete*, because shorter dimensions seem to require less work or because their form is more simple and light. This kind of … entertainment however, requires a most fine feeling, fluent style and vivacity of imagination … a comedic inspiration born of the deepest study of the human heart.[8]

Stage beast that he was, Barbieri knew that serious art does not necessarily mean solemn art. Nor does art preclude entertainment. Yet the balance is hard to sustain. It was not long before Madrid audiences, swelled by the masses of country men and women coming to labour in the new factories and utility industries, looked for escapist alternatives to the noble, three-act *zarzuela grande* being perfected by Barbieri and Co. on *comedia* principles.

Offenbach and *Género Chico*

Julio Gómez laments 'the assault of French *opéra bouffe*' and its withering effect on the nascent zarzuela. Certainly, the advent of *Los bufos madrileños* in 1866 under the leading actor-entrepreneur Francisco Arderius brought Offenbach to the capital with a flourish, and Teatro de la Zarzuela was not slow to join the game. It wasn't long before Madrid's creatives were producing their own, spectacular shows in Offenbach's three-act, topically satirical vein such as *El joven Telémaco* (Young Telemachus, 1866, with music by José Rogel), a lively epigone of *La belle Hélène*, premiered in Paris two years earlier.

The fad came and went, yet this short, sharp French assault was to have long-term consequences. The catalyst was not Offenbach's big theatre style, but his slight, one-act *opérette*. Even as the craze for *Los bufos* was at its height, private clubs and *cafés chantants* were taking the French master's spirit, his tuneful directness and mockery, and infusing it into an underground music theatre burrowing under the radar of Isabella II's censors.[9] After Spain's liberal revolution of 1873, this polemic theatre emerged into the light, and the way was open for a new public system to flourish – the *teatro por horas* (theatre by the hour), originally pioneered by Offenbach himself in Paris, but perfected in Madrid. Audiences could purchase a cheap seat for a single slot, or for all three in the evening if they had the time and money. This necessitated a production line of hour-long, one-act *género chico* shows, and by 1880 the short form had eclipsed *zarzuela grande* in popularity – much to the discomfiture of Spain's intelligentsia. Julio Gómez's description of it as 'last and least branch of our lyric theatre' shows that even by 1912, when *género chico* was in its death throes, they had never quite come to terms with the little monster's triumph.

Género chico is the most remarkable culture in zarzuela's laboratory. When the monarchy was restored, the returning authorities viewed it as a dangerous pest, but official attempts to squash it underfoot were futile. Its ubiquity in theatre-mad 1880s Madrid proved a goldmine for contemporary writers, musicians and performers. Remarkably, its brew of operatic music, catchy songs and (later on) French cabaret-style *cuplés* (couplets) wrapped up in edgy, working-class farce packed a punch which remains potent today. Those commentators who opined that it took artistic energy away from 'serious' musical forms such as the symphony and grand opera were missing the jewel being dangled in front of their faces. Highly collaborative, *género chico* squares the circle of commercial quantity and artistic quality to a rare degree.

The master of the revels was the Madrid-born composer Federico Chueca, whose musical simplicity masks an unusually subtle, subversive dramaturgy fed by popular urban dance forms. The imported waltz (*vals*), polka and schottische (*chotis*) go to bed with local street dances such as the *seguidillas* and *pasodoble*. Country stalwarts such as the *jota* and Gipsy *zapateado* link hands with steamy colonial exotics, including the Argentine *tango* and Cuban *habanera*. From a musicological standpoint, Chueca's scores can be analysed as miniature dance suites with added words. For example the 1889 revue *El año pasado por agua* (Last Year Under Water), a humorous celebration of a record wet year for Madrid and attendant civic disasters, begins with an 'Umbrella Mazurka' for two lovers, followed by a French *vals* for the city's Statue of Neptune, a *pasacalle* street dance, a *habanera* for a sleazy servant girl, a pulsing *zortzico* for a Basque emigrant, a *chotis* for a lugubrious Inquisitor and a polka for the corrupt police and some street walkers. Seven numbers, seven dances. Dance binds Chueca's score into an effective unity.

His earlier revue *La Gran Vía* (1886) unexpectedly grabbed the attention of one of Europe's intellectual heavyweights, writing two years later to friends:

> Today I saw a zarzuela – Spanish, of genius … Important extension of the
> concept of 'operetta.' *Spanish* operetta. *La Gran Vía*, heard twice … from
> Madrid. Simply cannot be emulated … one would have to be a rogue and the
> devil of an instinctive fellow – and serious at the same time. It lasts exactly one
> hour … Spanish mischievousness … *La Gran Vía!*[10]

That's Friedrich Nietzsche, seeking at the end of his life an antithesis to
everything solemn, portentous and Wagnerian. First, he found *Carmen*.
Then, he found the real thing, roguish and serious, inimitably Spanish.
Felipe Pérez y González's text is a bold take on urban planning, in which
the performers play streets, buildings and utilities such as Gas and Petroleum.
All these had been bulldozed to construct the smart new Gran Vía, modelled
on London's Oxford Street, but which the city fathers didn't have the funds to
finish – it wasn't to be completed until Franco's time. Nietzsche saw the
revue's streetwise irreverence as an 'extension of the concept' (i.e. his understanding of the confining, formal cerebrality) of operetta, later picking out
Chueca's score for special praise: 'the strongest thing that I have heard *and
seen* – also as music: genius cannot be formulated'.

La Gran Vía's trenchantly genial score, in essence a Spanish avatar of
Brecht and Weill's *Threepenny Opera*, has been performed across Europe
and adapted for Broadway. It has been said that *género chico*'s localism, its
topical focus on one city, is a bar to wider acceptance abroad. The brazen
parochialism of *La Gran Vía* refutes that. Its concentrated sense of time
and place has enhanced its universal appeal, not the reverse, and Nietzsche
puts his aphoristic finger on the reason. The mischievous, little Spanish
musical devil of *género chico* sometimes takes licence to sing what the rest
of us hardly dare to think.

Género Chico and Opera

If Chueca's theatre brought about a radical Spanish reframing of
Offenbach to construct something far removed from French operetta
models, other masters of *género chico* took it in yet another direction,
towards the complexity of late nineteenth-century opera. Tomás Bretón's
La verbena de la Paloma (1894) is the most-performed zarzuela of all time,
which given its impressive musical scale and depth is no surprise. It is
traditionally presented in tandem with Chapí's *La revoltosa* (1897), as
zarzuela's own 'heavenly twins', an overt riposte to Italy's *Cavalleria
rusticana* and *Pagliacci*.

Chapí's half of the bill stands as a perfect exploration of zarzuela's
special territory, and of its difficulty fitting into the international operatic
(still less the operetta) repertoire. Despite a masterly text by José López

Silva and Carlos Fernández Shaw,[11] massive renown throughout the Hispanic world and a proudly independent heroine who has been a popular role model for more than 100 years – Mari-Pepa has even had clothing, cakes and fizzy drinks named after her – *La revoltosa* remains unknown elsewhere. Even a cameo appearance in Pedro Almodóvar's black comedy classic *Pepi, Luci, Bom* (1980), where the lead characters bawl out the ubiquitous love duet 'Por qué de mis ojos' while administering a kicking to a corrupt policeman – a plot strand straight out of the zarzuela – has failed to ignite foreign interest in this classic *sainete lírico*.

One can understand why. Though its action in a Madrid tenement courtyard plays for seventy minutes, *La revoltosa* contains barely half an hour of music. Its six numbers are ensembles, melodramas (speech over music, common in zarzuela) and choral dances. There is no significant solo *romanza* (aria). It requires a large mixed chorus and full orchestra, plus dancers and twelve principal actor-singers, including two of high operatic calibre. Such drawbacks easily explain its lack of appeal to international opera intendants: 'What on earth *is* this?', they ask. Certainly not opera. Nor yet operetta, indeed. *La revoltosa* sums up *género chico*'s frustrating failure to reach beyond 'the sunny, Spanish shores'.

Yet Chapí's contribution is far from incidental. His score sketches atmosphere, place and period with masterly brushstrokes; but beyond that, music articulates the comedy – a wry Spanish take on how the battle of the sexes ameliorates the squalor of urban poverty – with symphonic economy. The subject is downmarket, but the artistry isn't. The sweeping Prelude, the witty quartet for Mari-Pepa and her three (married) male admirers, and a stirring, Cuban-style *guajira* singalong lead up to that love duet, after which the action is resolved in a long and complex finale. The Madrid press reported that the first person to rise from his seat at *La revoltosa*'s Teatro de Apolo premiere to hail the work a masterpiece, was a regular visitor from Paris named Camille Saint-Saëns.

The duet in particular – the most celebrated in the entire zarzuela repertoire – packs a great deal into a mere six minutes. It has unusual nervous intensity, more to do with hostility than with love, but perfumed with subtle eroticism. The context is a show-down between Mari-Pepa and the only serious candidate for her affection, Felipe. When they are finally alone, what we initially get is not a clichéd outpouring of Spanish passion, but a nervous negotiation in which the soprano and baritone play the game without revealing any more cards than they must. The sexual charge is ramped up by Chapí's music, cunningly constructed from a handful of melodic and rhythmic scraps, constantly recycled and evolving. The drama unfolds as much in the orchestra as the initially fragmented vocal

Example 7.1 *La revoltosa*, '¿Por qué no me miras? ¿Por qué?'

Example 7.2 *La revoltosa*, '¡Ay, Felipe de mi alma!'

lines. Here for example, Mari-Pepa's teasing question is tempered by the solo oboe's reply (Example 7.1).

Elsewhere a repeated musical question mark, consciously modelled on a yearning, Tristanesque suspension, makes us wonder how this fragile, budding relationship will end. The music chooses not to let on, until the girl sweeps the boy into her arms and passion finally runs free, all the more movingly for the edgy, extended ambiguities of the foreplay. Chapí finally unleashes a long-breathed theme which does not just flirt with cliché but boldly asserts it. Its falling, chromatic line and exotic, Andalusian triplet turn immediately identify Mari-Pepa with Moorish Spain, Gipsies and sexual freedom, just as similar phrases in the mouths of Carmen, Verdi's Princess Eboli and Saint-Saëns's Delilah had done. Yet thanks to the compositional skill in preparing the way, the effect is the reverse of stereotype, but a powerful release of personal feeling (Example 7.2).

It may be another cliché to repeat that these 'heavenly twins', together with Chueca's more easy-going theatre, show zarzuela at its distinctive best. So be it. Their durability is in large part due to their ambiguity in walking the tightrope between opera and operetta, their vivid recording of a society caught on the cusp between laughter and despair.

Sex, London, Vienna and the Triumph of Operetta

By 1900 economic despair, amplified by the loss of Spain's last American colonies, was damping down the laughter. In his last great success *El bateo* (The Baptism, 1901), even Chueca was sousing his eternal optimism in bitter lemon, though he continued to hang on to the hope that the individual's capacity to forgive and forget might save his city from the abyss. *Género chico* soured in an outbreak of so-called *ínfimo* (trivial) works, marked by sexual explicitness, musical simplicity and savage critiques of church and state. It is no surprise to find that one of the most daring of these, Antonio Viérgol's *Caza de almas* (Hunter of Souls, 1908, with music by Rafael Calleja) revolves around the life of a sympathetic prostitute named Lulú: Wedekind's *Erdgeist* had evidently reached Madrid.

Viérgol's later *El poeta de la vida* (The Poet of Life, 1910) has the triple attraction of a tuneful score by Calleja, a Cuban cabaret scene with a chorus of half-naked girls, and a long diatribe on the state of the Madrid sewers. It may be difficult to see that one being revived any time soon, but a handful of *ínfimo* zarzuelas fluttered around until the Civil War, after which Franco and his spiritual advisers airbrushed them from Spanish theatrical history. Recent revivals have shown the best of them to be more than the titillating girlie shows music historians (not to mention the church) claimed. *Zarzuela ínfima* must be reassessed as Spain's tentative dipping of a toe into the waters of theatrical modernism, offering up life's gall to popular audiences without the honey of sentimental conclusions.

Madrid needed cheering up. What's more, the pious middle classes were turning up their noses at sexy socialist lectures, so little wonder the capital's entrepreneurs looked abroad for commercial novelties. Another 'invasion' – this time from London – showed them what was wanted, when in 1907 Madrid made the acquaintance of the musical play which had already taken most of Europe, Russia and America by storm – Sidney Jones's *The Geisha*. How did this come about? The previous year, the marriage of Queen Victoria's granddaughter Victoria Eugenie to the Spanish king Alfonso XIII resulted in a wave of Anglo-Spanish enthusiasm. As the conductor/composer Ernest Irving put it in his memoir *Cue*

for Music, 'if everybody in England was not studying Spanish, everybody in
Spain was learning English'.[12] Striking while the iron was hot, Irving led an
English company to Madrid's Teatro Comedia to perform *The Geisha*,
together with Paul Rubens's brand-new *Miss Hook of Holland* and about
ten other West End musical comedies. To their surprise, they found that a
touring Italian opera company had beaten them to the punch, and was
already in town playing *La Geisha* to packed houses, albeit somewhat
absurdly in the *verismo* manner. Soon enough the city had several of its
own highly popular productions running in Spanish. As one newspaper
put it, 'We saw it in English, and though we didn't understand a word, we
liked it; then we understood half of it in Italian; and finally we've heard it
properly.'[13] So much for Irving's belief that everyone was learning English,
but *The Geisha* and the other musicals really hit the spot. Few of the
numbers went on for more than about three minutes, which was very
much to Spanish taste, as were the gently teasing lyrics, the 'London Music
Hall' flavour of certain songs and the escapist sunshine of the show itself, a
lightly plotted intrigue between English naval officers and the locals in the
port of Nagasaki. Above all *The Geisha*, with its pretty Japanese costumes,
was devoid of the cynical, social satire of *zarzuela ínfima*.

Once the contact was made, Spanish impresarios took a closer look at
what else was going on in the West End, and when they found that Franz
Lehár's *The Merry Widow* was the talk of the town, they brought that
straight to Madrid too. Significantly, the glittering, star-packed 1909 production of *La viuda alegre* at Teatro Price translated Basil Hood's English
adaptation, not the Viennese original. Madrid was soon flooded with
similar offerings from Lehár, Fall and Jacobi, seasoned with piquant,
Spanish musical additions.

Which brings us to 1912, and Julio Gómez. Although there is no
doubting the psychological trauma of the Lehár 'invasion' upon him,
and other composers such as Amadeo Vives,[14] as a physical reality it
had largely petered out even before Gómez attacked it. The idea of a
'culture war' was promoted more by journalistic in-fighting and clever
marketing than by audience polarity. At the root of this backlash was
the perception that Viennese operettas were inferior goods, adulterat-
ing a *género chico* already under assault from nasty *zarzuela ínfima*.
For, in attacking Lehár, the traditionalists conveniently overlooked the
obvious fact that zarzuela was changing from the inside as much as the
outside. *Teatro por horas* was dying, and the split between artistically
high-flown zarzuela and popular revue was already under way, without
any foreign help.

Later Austro-Hungarian dreadnoughts such as Emmerich Kálmán scarcely made a ripple in the Spanish pond, and only one Viennese operetta was

granted honorary zarzuela status: indeed *Eva* (1911) proved unique among Lehár's works, in achieving more success in Madrid than anywhere else. That had everything to do with the fact that it was one of the least 'Viennese' of his operettas, in form and content: with its factory settings and working-girl heroine it had plenty in common with *género chico*, and the official Spanish adaptation amplified *Eva*'s social – even socialist – aspects.[15] Otherwise, as far as Viennese operetta was concerned, 1909–10 was the end of the beginning and the beginning of the end. As John Donne says of such brief affairs, 'love's first minute after noon, is night'.

Opereta-Zarzuela

By injecting spectacle and fantasy into the mix, the Anglo-Viennese invasion gave the best younger *zarzueleros* a strong sense of the way to reinvigorate tired formats. Operetta and zarzuela were coming together, fuelled in both cases by Puccini's brand of operatic populism, and for about a decade after 1910 composers such as Vives and Pablo Luna were out to prove that anything Lehár could do, they could do better. An unexpected economic upturn helped. Thanks to her neutrality during World War I (and her selling of arms to both sides), Spain became more affluent. New theatres were built in Madrid and Barcelona which were a technical match for anything in London or New York, let alone impoverished Vienna. There was money to burn and money to be made with spectacular, full-length *opereta-zarzuela*.

Vives's *La generala* (The General's Wife, 1912) stands as a true Spanish operetta which ticks all the boxes. It has 'exotic' foreign settings – Oxford and Cambridge – peopled with Ruritanian princes and princesses. It uses the full resources of an enlarged pit orchestra, a full chorus and a large roster of operatic soloists. It boasts lavish quantities of ballgowns, big hats and military uniforms. It is a magnificent star vehicle, featuring a glamorous leading lady with a shady Parisian past as a cabaret star, who – Marschallin-like – gives up her beloved prince to a younger woman, incidentally solving the Ruritanian political and dynastic crisis. Vives was a dazzling orchestrator, and he made sure that his bejewelled score was at the cutting edge of cosmopolitan sophistication. There are Scottish songs (Oxbridge local colour?) and military marches, but absolutely none of the 'Spanishry' at which Barbieri and his successors had been aiming.

Crucially, there is nothing of *género chico*'s social engagement either. The comedy is genteel – despite some teasing double-entendre in the score's melting duet 'Mi dulce sueño de adolescente', where the general's wife and her lovesick prince reminisce over the naughty French cabaret number which made her famous – and there are no bare calves or *ínfimo vulgarities*. Vives strives instead to play the operetta game, by evoking a silky, fantasy past in order to make the present more bearable. Madrid lapped up the synthesized narcotic Vives supplied: though elsewhere – despite the composer's artistry – this Spanish take on Viennese nostalgia hasn't rung true.[16]

Pablo Luna's Arabian Nights fantasy operetta *El asombro de Damasco* (The Wonder of Damascus, 1916) squares the circle more convincingly. Luna was a fervent anglophile, and this exhilarating score, alternating Moorish-Hispanic romance with West End musical comedy and the most profligate percussion section ever seen in a Madrid pit – was written with London tastes very much in mind. The entrance of the comic Kadi (chief of police) is greeted by a chorus recalling Sullivan's 'Behold the Lord High Executioner', but when the little man introduces himself it is in accents recalling Smith/Simplicitas in *The Arcadians*, the 1909 hit with music by Lionel Monckton and Howard Talbot (Example 7.3).

That drooping commentary figure [a] screams 'London Music Hall'. We find it not only scattered through the internationally familiar English musicals of the time but also in Ravel's *L'enfant et les sortilèges*, where it characterizes the pugilistic (and terribly English) Wedgwood Teapot. A much-changed version of *El asombro de Damasco* did finally make it to the West End in 1923 as *The First Kiss*, including fresh material which Luna then spliced into a second, very different 'oriental' Madrid operetta, *Benamor*.[17]

Eventually Vives's restless, intellectual spirit was to perfect the *opereta-zarzuela* model. By 1923 Spain was in crisis once again, and Primo de Rivera's military dictatorship ordered La Zarzuela to take up her patriotic duties, as the flag bearer for 'truly national' lyric theatre. Foreign operetta was out, but the so-called *operone* (operatic zarzuela) was officially sanctioned and funded. Some lovely, reactionary flowers bloomed, none more exquisite than Vives's three-act *Doña Francisquita*. The librettists Federico Romero and Guillermo Fernández Shaw took a 1604 *comedia* by Lope de Vega as their source, but, by transferring it to Madrid in the comparatively stable 1840s, they facilitated popular, operetta features – an amorous plot, sumptuous costuming, spectacular settings and massive musical forces – while obeying the political imperative for something celebratory and quintessentially Spanish. Vives's radiant, sunset-glow nostalgia is as manicured as anything in *La generala*: the difference is that here, he connected with his audience's own imagined past to create a rich, and authentic, synthesis. *Doña Francisquita* is a work of international stature, the apotheosis of zarzuela's engagement with operetta.

Example 7.3 *El asombro de Damasco*, 'Soy Alimón. Soy el Cadí'

Coda: After the Civil War

Costs spiralled and government promises were not kept. Yet though its commercial power diminished during the late 1920s, zarzuela kept its stranglehold on Spanish theatre until the cataclysm of the Civil War knocked the stuffing out of it. Indeed, the early 1930s were a compelling 'silver age' for the genre, dominated by the rivalry of two composers: the traditionalist Federico Moreno Torroba and the left-leaning Pablo Sorozábal. In vying to control the Madrid stage, they produced some of the most vital work in the genre. Torroba's historical epic *Luisa Fernanda* (1932) and Sorozábal's contemporary drama of coastal cocaine-smuggling *La tabernera del puerto* (The Port Taverner, 1936) have operatic scale and scope, while the latter's bright urban rom-com *La del manojo de rosas* (The Girl with the Roses, 1934) is a hugely satisfying mash-up of *género chico* and operetta formulas.

The German-trained Sorozábal – sometimes plausibly spoken of as the Spanish Kurt Weill – narrowly avoided being shot during the Civil War. Yet remarkably, despite his unquenchably combative liberalism, he flourished in the early Franco era. Like Shostakovich, a composer he much admired,[18] Sorozábal learnt how to code officially unpalatable truths into his music, while sticking to the letter of Franco's censorship laws.

The most astounding example of this sleight of hand is his ambitious, three-act *opereta Black, el payaso* (Black, the Clown, 1942), which he developed from a story by a Barcelona journalist Francisco Serrano Anguita. With its romantic Parisian and Ruritanian settings, aristocratic disguises and circus ambience, the plot self-consciously evokes Kálmán's *Die Zirkusprinzessin*. Sorozábal's sweet-and-sour score includes a Hungarian march and a real *lassú-friss* csárdás to validate its operetta passport. Warning bells might have sounded, had the censors noticed some decidedly non-operettish *Sprechgesang* and jazzy flashes of Klezmer scoring in the manuscript, and a closer look under the bonnet would have revealed a text far removed from chocolate-box, Viennese pastiche. Black is not the aristocrat everyone takes him for, but a circus star who by a series of farcical mistakes ends up running a dysfunctional, militaristic country at war with the world. While the true king abnegates his political responsibilities by masquerading as a concert pianist, the wearer of the crown is in reality, simply a clown.

Somehow Sorozábal got away with alluding to Franco as a clown with no mandate. As the show was premiered in Barcelona, perhaps it was given more latitude. Or perhaps the authorities simply felt that anything calling itself an 'operetta' on the title page was by definition harmless. Whatever the reason, the fractious composer got away with it. *Black, el payaso* is not quite genuine operetta, but a thinly masked allegory which uses its Viennese disguise to get through to Sorozábal's repressed compatriots. Shostakovich once said that true art is pessimistic; as an operetta fan himself, one wonders what he would have made of this one? At one level it is a bleak political fable offering no artistic or societal solutions. At another, gentler one, it is the last tribute from one lyric form to another: *Black, el payaso* stands as an ironic mid-twentieth-century message of solidarity, from zarzuela to operetta.

In the end, as Sorozábal might have put it, we sink or swim together. In the late 1950s he stopped writing zarzuela altogether, recognizing that its hundred-year odyssey was over. The goldmine was exhausted. By the time of his death in 1988, fascism too was gone, leaving a prejudice against zarzuela for younger audiences who considered it a fossilized tool of the old regime. Time is changing that, and the post-Franco generation of theatregoers and academics is better placed to valorize the qualities of Madrid's diverse collection of lyric theatre styles.[19] Whether it's the edgy, social mischievousness of *género chico* and revue, the romantic *comedia* of Barbieri's Spanish *opéra comique* or the warm, soothing nostalgia of *opereta-zarzuela*, there's still plenty of life in that teeming old bucket labelled 'zarzuela'.

Notes

1. J. Gómez, (1912) *Revista Musical* (Bilbao), 4, no. 1 (January 1912), 1–5 and no. 2 (February 1912), 25–9.
2. I recall BBC Radio 3's response to a leading producer's suggestion of a series on zarzuela. 'Isn't that really World Music?' came the reply. Perhaps they were confusing it with flamenco.
3. Volker Klotz's seminal *Operette: Porträt und Handbuch einer unerhörten Kunst* (Munich: Piper, 1991) devotes generous space to zarzuela and addresses the question of its relationship to operetta. *The New Kobbé's Opera Book* (ed. The Earl of Harewood and Anthony Peattie, Ebury Press, 1997) is the current edition of Gustav Kobbé's influential collection of opera synopses.

4. K. Gänzl and A. Lamb, *Gänzl's Book of the Musical Theatre* (London: The Bodley Head, 1988), 1207–8.
5. Which it influenced heavily. Despite Manuel de Falla's later rejection of zarzuela as 'frivolous', his development was bound up with it, and he made several forays into *género chico*. The story of why Falla came to reject the genre is instructive, but we should take his pronouncement with a pinch of salt.
6. I was surprised to find that some delegates at Ohio Light Opera's 2015 conference were uncomfortable with the diminutive 'operetta' and its negative associations.
7. Neither Johann Strauss Jr nor Sullivan made much impact in Madrid. *Die Fledermaus* – astonishingly – awaits professional staging there to this day.
8. F. Asenjo Barbieri, *La Zarzuela* (Madrid: Ducazcal, 1864), 18. (My translation)
9. My thanks to Enrique Mejías García, for sharing with me his work in progress, on Offenbach and the hitherto unresearched roots of *género chico*.
10. F. W. Nietzsche, *Selected Letters of Friedrich Nietzsche*, ed. and trans. Christopher Middleton (Chicago: Chicago University Press, 1969) 333–4, 348.
11. Later the librettist of Chapí's *La chavala* and Falla's strikingly similar *La vida breve*.
12. E. Irving, *Cue for Music* (Dennis Dobson, 1959), 41–6.
13. Anon., 'Novedades teatrales – "La Geisha" en Apolo', *El Imparcial* (22 October 1914), 3.
14. Vives made money composing a parody, *La viuda mucho mas alegre* (The Much More Merry Widow), which went through more editions than the original.
15. For many decades, the sole available recording of *Eva* was of the Spanish version, featuring Alfredo Kraus.
16. Notably for audiences at Vienna's Volksoper, where *La generala* was produced in 2002. Expecting roses and castanets, they were disappointed by what they considered a pallid imitation of operetta.
17. A. Lamb and C. Webber, *De Madrid a Londres – Pablo Luna's English Operetta The First Kiss* (2016) www.academia.edu/26447008 (accessed 12 Apr. 2019).
18. In 1955 he lost his job as conductor of the Madrid Symphony Orchestra for daring to programme the 'Leningrad' Symphony. The performance was of course cancelled, but Sorozábal received an effusive letter of thanks from Shostakovich himself.
19. Including many other variants, not least the one-act zarzuela (semi-detached from *género chico*) perfected in the late nineteenth-century work of Manuel Fernández Caballero and his *verismo* successor, José Serrano.

Recommended Reading

Asenjo Barbieri, Francisco. *La Zarzuela*. Madrid: Ducazcal, 1864.
Casares Rodicio, Emilio, ed. *Diccionario de la Zarzuela*. 2 vols. Madrid: ICCMU, 2002–3.
Casares Rodicio, Emilio. *Francisco Asenjo Barbieri. Vol. 1: El hombre y el creador*. Madrid: ICCMU, 1994.
Iberni, Luis G. *Ruperto Chapí*. Madrid: ICCMU, 1995.
Jassa Haro, Ignacio. 'Con un vals en la maleta: viaje y aclimatación de la opereta europea en España'. In Emilio Casares Rodicio, ed., *Cuadernos de Música Iberoamericana*. Vol. 20. Madrid: ICCMU, 2010.
Lamb, Andrew and Webber, Christopher. 'De Madrid a Londres: Pablo Luna's English Operetta, The First Kiss'. 2016. www.academia.edu/26447008 (accessed 12 Apr. 2019).
Lerena, Mario. *El teatro musical de Pablo Sorozábal (1897–1988)*. Bilbao: Universiddeldel Pais Vasco, 2018.
Mejías García, Enrique. 'Cuestión de géneros: la zarzuela española frente al desafío historiográfico'. In Tobias Brandenberger, ed., *Dimensiones y desafíos de la zarzuela*. Münster: LIT Verlag, 2014.

Versteeg, Margot. *De Fusiladores y Morcilleros (El discurso cómico del género chico, 1870–1910)*. Amsterdam: Rodopi, 2000.

Webber, Christopher. 'The alcalde, the negro and 'la bribona': 'género ínfimo' zarzuela, 1900–1910'. In Max Doppelbauer and Kathrin Sartingen, eds., *De la zarzuela al cine. Los medios de comunicación populares y su traducción de la voz marginal*. Munich: Martin Meidenbauer, 2009.

Webber, Christopher. *The Zarzuela Companion*. Maryland: Scarecrow Press, 2002.

Webber, Christopher, ed. *zarzuela.net*. www.zarzuela.net, 1997–2017.

Young, Clinton D. *Music Theater and Popular Nationalism in Spain, 1880–1930*. Baton Rouge: Louisiana State University Press, 2016.

8 Camping along the American Operetta Divide (on the Road to the Musical Play)

RAYMOND KNAPP

There are four reasonably persuasive origin stories for the American musical, depending on where precisely one chooses to locate the genre's beginnings.[1] While none are definitively 'true', all contribute something important to our understanding of the American musical's complex journey towards the fairly stable type that came to dominate Broadway between 1943 and the mid-1960s, before accommodating to yet other impulses and influences:

1. In the earliest and least probable version, hack playwright Charles M. Barras reworks the dramatic elements of *Der Freischütz* (1821) into *The Black Crook* (1866) and sells it to Niblo's Garden, where its earnest plotting, in which innocence triumphs over diabolical forces, is animated through a mostly forgotten pastiche score, a troupe of young women in tights acquired from a stranded French ballet company, and spectacular stage effects courtesy of the most up-to-date stage machinery.[2]

2. In another scenario, the success of Parisian *opérette* in London inspires William S. Gilbert and Arthur Sullivan to launch their hugely successful series of operettas (beginning in 1875),[3] spawning US American imitations that a generation later will lead to the musical comedies of George M. Cohan, whose *Little Johnny Jones* (1904) pays direct homage to its English operetta lineage.[4]

3. Still another version begins in Vienna: Franz Lehár's *Die lustige Witwe* (1905), deriving from a Parisian play by *opérette* librettist Henri Meilhac (*L'attaché d'ambassade*, 1861), becomes, in translation, *The Merry Widow* (London and New York, 1907), revitalizing a tradition of American operetta based, typically, on the romantic potential of exotic locales. This tradition reaches its greatest intensity in the 1920s, culminating in Jerome Kern's and Oscar Hammerstein II's *Show Boat* (1927), whose specific exotic locale, the Mississippi River, occasions a persuasive linkage to African American musical styles.

4. The final 'origin' scenario finds a sputtering tradition of American musical comedy being rescued by Rodgers and Hammerstein's 'musical play', an aspirationally integrated blend of folk opera and Americanized ballet, shaped within an operetta-based sensibility that, by the time of *Oklahoma!* (1943), and given the vaunted newness of their ambitious programme, could no longer openly admit to its old-fashioned, old-world lineage.

Significantly, all of these scenarios – each a separate phase in the early development of the American musical – intertwine with the varied histories and traditions of operetta,[5] which in the United States evolved two distinct profiles by the early decades of the twentieth century, a bifocality crucial to the dynamic that would continue to govern the American musical's development through the twentieth century and into our own. The first type to take root was based, as noted in No. 2 above, on a particular kind of fast-paced musical comedy, often satirical and/or cynical; its core repertory early on consisted mainly of operettas by Gilbert and Sullivan and their imitators, and it spawned the first sustained series of American musical comedies – perhaps not yet the 'American musical', but also no longer just operetta.[6] The second, deriving mainly from the Viennese strain, merged a fervently romantic sensibility with a sense of worldly sophistication understood to be European (or, more precisely, Continental). These somewhat opposed operetta sensibilities were blended in various ways within American operetta, but the balance between their contrasting elements generally skewed to one side or the other, notwithstanding their mutual derivation from the earlier Parisian operetta type, which had introduced and advanced the relevant elements for both. Indeed, one way to look at the larger historical trajectory is to see the Parisian *opérette* subdividing into London's and Vienna's distinctive types, which then recombine to form the American musical. But that can be a distracting construct, since the full emergence of the American musical had little to do with the originary Parisian form of operetta, and everything to do with the disjunctures created by that form's subdivision into two distinct varieties.

In this exploratory chapter, I will first draw on Gilbert and Sullivan's operettas to detail briefly the establishment of the first of these types and to probe its dynamic between the comic and the romantic.[7] I will then consider the flowering of the second type in the early decades of the twentieth century in the works of Victor Herbert, Rudolf Friml and Sigmund Romberg (born Siegmund Rosenberg). Finally, I will assess the relevance of both types to the American musical, which on the whole has favoured the second, especially in its 'integrated' phase, during which all elements of the drama are understood to support and develop the plot. Of particular interest here will be the evolution of a camp sensibility that developed in part from the *frisson* between the two types; I argue that camp's role in negotiating this divide places operetta forever at the centre of the American musical as a genre.

Gilbert and Sullivan; or, Why We Camp the Things We Love

You light up the world. You can't help it. (FANNY RONALDS TO ARTHUR SULLIVAN, IN *TOPSY TURVY*)[8]

Gilbert and Sullivan, whether by design or by accident, found a new solution to the perennial problem of English music, a problem that comes down to England's abiding, widespread discomfort with embracing so nebulous and frankly sensual an art form. Earlier solutions had of course been found: Handel, for example, had joined music to religious topics, as had Haydn, after first adding a healthy dollop of edifying humour to his London symphonies that yielded, post-Beethoven, to an earnest, specifically English regard for the potential spiritual uplift proffered by the symphony as a genre. But London's eager embrace of Haydn, who had laced uplift with genuine fun, left a promise and a challenge that Sullivan, responding to Gilbert's contrived situations and lyrics, was able to meet through a fairly straightforward device. With Gilbert's mocking humour as cover, and with the added protection of Victorian respectability (reinforced in reaction to the saucy Parisian *opérette* they sought to displace), Sullivan offered a full indulgence in music's expressive and sensual pleasures within a setting that insisted on not taking that aspect of the art seriously, as such. The device was as effective as the manoeuvre practised in the pictorial arts, which had long since found amply respectable cover for a brazen, prurient indulgence in feminine beauty, however transmuted into 'art' – except that, with Gilbert and Sullivan, audiences were encouraged to (publicly) laugh rather than (privately) leer. The price of that laughter, for Sullivan especially, was steep; as a composer of some ambition, and having studied at the Leipzig Conservatory, he knew that this form of operetta was unlikely to be taken seriously as art and could even mark him as less than a true artist. But whatever Sullivan's misgivings, operetta audiences came quickly to recognize and relish the high artistic value of his music, often imagining it to be somehow separate from Gilbert's comedic topsy-turvydom, the contribution of someone who – perhaps even to his credit as a serious artist –wasn't fully in on the joke, functioning as a kind of musical 'straight man'.

That Sullivan *was* in on the joke has in recent decades been well argued and documented,[9] but the popular notion that he was not still persists, resting on an entrenched habit of reception among both English and US American audiences that maintains two separate registers of reception, one for Gilbert's impertinent humour and another for Sullivan's often quite lovely music. This separation into two registers takes little notice of how pervasively they intermingle, the many instances when Sullivan's music either enforces Gilbert's verbal humour or elaborates a new layer of humour on to it. In reception, this bifurcation offers a direct parallel to the two types of operetta that would later emerge in the United States, with most audiences finding Gilbert's humour to be the animating spirit for the team's operettas and Sullivan's music – which on its own might just as easily have supported a more earnestly romantic libretto – its ornament. Yet, a more nuanced view of how Sullivan's music is deployed in his work with Gilbert, grounded in his own composerly practices, would come close to a high-camp appreciation, savouring both his extension of Gilbert's comedy and the opportunities it offered Sullivan to write exemplary, if sometimes exaggerated, variants of familiar musical idioms, topics and genres.

Thus, for example, Ralph's introductory number in *H.M.S. Pinafore* (1878), 'The nightingale', seems absurdly precious coming from an 'able seaman', yet is, in itself, entirely delightful, as a solo madrigal with male chorus offering warm, harmonized echoes as punctuation.[10] Because the number is so well realized musically, it is able to sustain its comically incongruous conceit throughout and even moment by moment, and can do so whether it is performed 'straight' or with comic exaggeration of its excessive refinement. This kind of ludicrous yet luminously lovely musical number became a staple of their collaborations; examples include, from their early operettas, 'Hail poetry', sung by the pirates in *The Pirates of Penzance* (1879), 'I hear the soft note of the echoing voice' and 'Love is a plaintive song' in *Patience* (1881), and in the contrast between British pastoral and pomp, each sumptuously realized, in *Iolanthe* (1882, e.g., in 'Good-morrow, good mother' and 'Loudly let the trumpet bray'). For *The Mikado* (1885), with its application of a melismatic 'Oriental' idiom, and *The Yeomen of the Guard* (1888), with its aspirations towards something like high drama, this dimension becomes core, with too many specific numbers to list beyond singling out, from the former, 'The sun whose rays are all ablaze', 'Alone and yet alive' and 'On a tree by a river', and, from the latter, 'I have a song to sing, O!' and 'Strange adventure'. Yet, despite this element, for most audiences, the tone of the more overtly comic numbers dominates, reflecting both Gilbert's own sensibilities and his lawyerly background, which emerges most characteristically in their trademark patter songs.

In order for an operetta to hold these two receptive modes in balance, it will rely most often on an alternating emphasis on each, but within Gilbert and Sullivan's reconstitution of the genre, it will also, if not quite so often, allow musical enchantments to hold sway while simultaneously encouraging us to laugh at – or, perhaps more accurately, laugh with or alongside – our susceptibility to such enchantments. Although Gilbert and Sullivan belong to the prehistory of camp sensibilities, the frequency with which

Sullivan's music encourages this 'double image' response creates a close alignment with high camp, which similarly entails a knowing, perhaps even mocking sensitivity to the artificial trappings of aesthetic experience, without denying the value of that experience and while maintaining a crucial affection for the camp object. This alignment of Sullivan's contributions with camp sensibilities is not happenstance, since musical theatre provided one of the crucial incubators for camp, whereas high camp tastes are nowhere more effective than when seeming absurdity combines with a serious core of exquisite music.

That Sullivan thus placed his music within an environment where its beauties would mainly operate as something like camp, lends credence to the notion – especially for those less attuned or sympathetic to camp tastes – that he was oblivious to that aspect of the collaboration. Yet, we know he was not and so must imagine that he did so deliberately, confident that his carefully, even lovingly rendered contributions would establish their own place, whether following or running against the grain of Gilbert's sometimes caustic verbal wit. And so they have, providing a model of sorts for how hardy such devotion to art could be under the protection of high-camp receptive environments. The hardiness here depends on the affectionate spirit that governs high-camp appreciations, whereas the protection derives from camp's deflection of attention away from the thing we most love, in this case allowing the music's aesthetic value to register under cover of comedy, rather than having to stand more nakedly on its own. Borrowing Yum-Yum's conceit in *The Mikado*'s 'The sun whose rays': in writing music for Gilbert's libretti, Sullivan overtly foregoes playing the role of the bold sun, yet nevertheless positions his music to illuminate the otherwise drab moon of Gilbert's sometimes tired conceits. If, truth to tell, they light up well, their borrowed light is a generous gift from Sullivan.[11] Mike Leigh's *Topsy Turvy* makes a similar point, if obliquely, by hinting at the aria's melody in the soft underscore for Fanny's declaration (quoted in the epigraph for this section) and then cutting directly to Yum-Yum and her aria, which closes the film.

Upward Mobility and the Struggle to Keep Comedy in Its Place

By the turn of the twentieth century, composers of US American musical comedies deriving from Gilbert and Sullivan's operettas did not reach, or even generally aspire to, Sullivan's musical heights. This may have been because they adhered to the widespread conviction that the governing tone of the team's operettas was comic but may also stem from the nature of particular successes from the previous generation of US American operetta composers, headed by John Philip Sousa, who is now known more for his marches than for his operettas. For example, *El Capitan* (1896), Sousa's most successful operetta (and the basis for the repertory march by the same name), offers a topsy-turvy plot, a romantic foreign setting (Peru) and a musical palette that, while effective and 'home-grown', was no equal to the diversity of Sullivan's scores. As composers of this type of comic operetta continued to work within US American idioms in the new century, their turn towards popular musical tastes was often offset by a more serious dramatic core – necessary, perhaps, to help sustain a full evening's entertainment, even if the resulting mix could easily devolve into unintentional camp. Thus, Cohan's *Little Johnny Jones* adopts a brash comic tone while presenting its earnest story of a US American jockey who goes to London to ride in the Derby (inspired by the real-life story of Ted Sloan), whose cocky demeanour is deflated when he loses and then has to clear his name against false accusations that he lost deliberately, before he can return to the United States to rescue his fiancée from the clutches of the man who framed him. Though by most accounts the show's comedy was successful in its day (if depending too often on now offensive ethnic and national stereotypes), the more serious numbers seem less successful, especially with the turn to philosophizing at the end, in 'Life's a Funny Proposition'. More happily, 'Yankee Doodle Boy' effectively conveys Johnny's cheeky Irish American swagger, 'Captain of a Ten Day Boat' deftly pays homage to *H.M.S. Pinafore* and 'Give My Regards to Broadway' plays effectively, if shamelessly, to its New York audience, with music that has endured as well as Sullivan's. On the whole, however, despite vital connections to operetta, Cohan's music marks a striking departure from its main English-language operetta models, just as the placement of the comic tone within a serious story similarly departs from Gilbert's topsy-turvydom, putting aside the partial exception of *Yeomen of the Guard*.

Meanwhile, French *opérette* and Viennese operetta, even though conceived in a spirit of rebellion against the seriousness that had taken hold of opera in nineteenth-century Europe, had never let go of the high musical styles and standards associated with prevailing operatic styles, especially in the works of Jacques Offenbach and Johann Strauss Jr, who established and constituted for a time the mainstream for these two traditions. The high style itself, sometimes carried over as parody but often more sincerely representing serious elements in the drama, was part of a mix that included a preponderance of comic numbers and helped allow the more beguiling musical entertainments of operetta to compete with more serious operatic fare. Moreover, within the context of popular musical theatre more broadly, operetta's musical adjacency to opera placed it in a relatively elevated position, by default. In this respect, especially, the emergence of such figures as Cohan in the United States represented a signal line of departure – specifically, in the direction of musical comedy and away from operetta as such – since Cohan's aspirational gestures, even when they include a strong musical component, veer in that realm away from opera and towards the popular.

But coincident with Cohan's rise, operetta composers from Europe fed a resurgent US American taste for something musically more elevated, whose European roots could be embraced as a hedge against the encroach-ment of a (by some lights) coarsening 'popular' style. Thus, while Cohan and others looked to the United States itself for inspiration and validation, operetta in this period generally looked to Europe, even when its topics were, eventually, often grounded in the New World. In the years immedi-ately following *The Merry Widow*, other Viennese operetta imports found significant New World success in English translation, including Oscar Straus's *A Waltz Dream* (NYC 1908, with a plot reminiscent of *The Merry Widow*) and *The Chocolate Soldier* (NYC 1909, based on Shaw's *Arms and the Man*), along with Leo Fall's *The Dollar Princess* (NYC 1909, with its libretto rewritten from its London adaptation and with additional music by Jerome Kern) and several subsequent Lehár operettas, including *The Count of Luxembourg* (NYC 1912), which, like the much more suc-cessful *The Merry Widow*, was set in Paris and featured an 'inappropriate' romantic coupling set against an atmosphere of old-world cynicism, for-tunes lost and remade, complications based on hidden identities, and a pre-determined happy ending. Inevitably, a home-grown variety of operetta also soon achieved great success, largely supplanting such imports but maintaining a vital link to the tradition not only in terms of style and tone but also through significant composerly ties to Europe. Indeed, an American operetta composer's European heritage – whether in the form of Herbert's Irish origins and early careers in Germany and Austria, Friml's Czech background or Romberg's Hungarian birth and Viennese training – carried both musical and symbolic weight.

There were, to be sure, partial exceptions to the line of development launched by *The Merry Widow*. German-born Gustave Kerker, for exam-ple, wrote musical comedies more evocative of Offenbach, in effect main-taining a kind of middle-ground between the London and Viennese types; his *The Belle of New York* (1897), which enjoyed a huge success in London after a modest run in New York, situates its earnest plot, in which goodness wins out, amid copious absurdities and much titillation. But a more central line of development is evidenced by Ivan Caryll, a Belgian composer with conservatory training in both Liège and Paris, who worked in London before moving to the United States in 1911. Caryll first achieved considerable success in musical comedy (in the English music-hall style); at one point, in 1903, he had five shows running simultaneously in the West End, including the long-running *The Toreador* (1901). *The Pink Lady* (1911), his second New York show and a major success, responds to its Parisian derivation and setting with a romantic, waltz-based score redolent of the Viennese operetta type and governed by what has been touted as a more 'integrated' approach to the deployment of songs within a story than is usually evident during this period. But the central early work in establishing a distinctive US American extension of the Viennese tradition was Herbert's *Naughty Marietta* (1910).

Herbert, with a strong penchant for romantic melody, was (like Sullivan) always a multi-faceted composer of some ambition, early on writing both serious concert music and musical comedy and dabbling in operetta even before *The Merry Widow*. Thus, his musical comedy *The Wizard of the Nile* (1895) enjoyed extensive international success, whereas *Mlle. Modiste* (1905) and *The Red Mill* (1906), which were closer to operetta in style (but also, in the latter case, including ragtime, and labelled a 'musical play' decades before *Oklahoma!*),[12] had longer runs in New York than *Wizard*, with *The Red Mill* also achieving some international renown. In between came his children's operetta *Babes in Toyland* (1903), which, like *Naughty Marietta*, would have both immediate success and a sustained afterlife.

What has made *Naughty Marietta* more important to the history of American operetta is Herbert's ability, despite a sometimes-confusing libretto (by Rida Johnson Young), to meld operetta sensibilities securely to a US American subject. Even the libretto's failings, especially its non-sensical representation of actual historical situations, play a role in this fusion. Indeed, the version of late-eighteenth-century New Orleans in which *Naughty Marietta* takes place, which includes familiar elements and themes from history but never existed as such, substitutes for oper-etta's imaginary European countries (Ruritania, Barataria, Marsovia and the like). It becomes, like them, a location borrowed for its suggestion of romance and political ferment, and used with little heed paid to historical plausibility. Within this exotic milieu, the vibrancy of a global crossroads, located between the pirate-infested Caribbean and the teeming frontier, provided the backdrop for a melting pot that could stand in for the nascent United States more broadly: a stowaway Italian Contessa (Marietta) who has escaped an arranged marriage by joining and then deserting a group of 'casquette girls' (girls recruited, mainly from orphanages and convents, to become brides in Louisiana), a troop of unaffiliated American mercenaries (including a mixed group of Americans, Irishmen, Canadians and Indians) led by Captain Dick, a corrupt acting government headed by Lieutenant

Governor Grandet and son Étienne, a band of Italian puppeteers, street
vendors, a notorious French pirate with a telltale tattooed arm (Bras
Piqué), a quadroon slave (Adah), a comically ambitious 'Yiddish' manser-
vant (Simon) and a variety of situations dependent on secret identities and
misunderstood motives that conspire alternately to forestall and bring
about the inevitable union of Captain Dick and Marietta.

The ways that *Naughty Marietta* is and is not 'American' are of particular interest here. New Orleans itself, while on the frontier, is dominated
by European colonists (mainly French, although, historically, the Spanish
controlled New Orleans between 1763 and 1803); when Captain Dick and
his troop arrive, they are the outsiders. But the plot is throughout sympathetic to 'America' and 'American' values. The American Captain Dick
Warrington provides the show's strong moral centre although he plays his
cards close to the vest – not unlike his near-namesake, Washington.
Contessa d'Altena, an aristocrat, becomes Marietta, a commoner, in
order to seek freedom in the New World. When Étienne puts his quadroon
lover up for auction, hoping to marry the Contessa, Captain Dick buys
her – not for himself, as the jealous Marietta suspects, but to set her free.
Perhaps the inclusion of Adah as one of the four major players is the most
telling aspect of the story; as the traditional 'tragic mulatta' figure, she is
given one of the most beguiling numbers in the show, whereas her plight
highlights the dehumanizing cruelty of slavery and gives the American
Captain Dick the role of emancipator (however disingenuously, given that
so many of the founding fathers were themselves slave owners, including
Washington).

The memorable score for *Naughty Marietta* reflects its diversity of
characters, opening with a teeming street scene as the first of three numbers that establish New Orleans as a place of exotic intrigue (the other two
are in Act 2: 'New Orleans Jeunesse Dorée' and 'Loves of New Orleans')
and offering characteristic music from all the major ethnic groups represented in the show: a French song for the casquette girls ('Taisez-Vous'), an
'Italian Street Song' for Marietta, a romantic 'ethnic' song for Adah
(''Neath the Southern Moon'), and a march for the American-led infantry
('Tramp, Tramp, Tramp'). But this panoply of styles does more than set its
melting-pot cast, since it also offers, on specifically proto-camp terms, an
important hinge between the serious story and its way of telling that story,
alternating between serious and comic, but with the former often exaggerated and 'over-the-top'. The overt comedy centres mainly around the
comic triangle of Simon, Lizette (an unclaimed casquette girl fixated on
Simon) and the inept Lieutenant Governor, around the sparring between
Captain Dick and Marietta, and around Marietta's role-playing. The latter
begins as a ruse, born of desperation, but soon acquires the considerable

Figure 8.1 Emma Trentini disguised as a Gipsy boy in 'Italian Street Song'. Photograph courtesy of Miles Kreuger and the Institute of the American Musical

(and fun) charge of successfully staged deception, as the runaway Contessa d'Altena, first pretending to be her maid Marietta, is then at turns an escaped casquette girl and a boy working for her 'father' Rudolfo, as a puppeteer. With all this role-playing built into the story already, her performance easily devolves into what would a few decades later be instantly recognizable as camp, especially given the proclivities of the first Marietta, Emma Trentini (Figure 8.1), notorious for playing shamelessly to her enthusiastic fans. Marietta sings the virtuosic 'Italian Street Song' dressed as a boy, with the sexual charge of the pants role enhanced by her all-male backup chorus singing such lyrics as 'Mandolinas gay, / Dancing as they play'.[13] Within this atmosphere, the camp dimension of the incessant repetitions of her unfinished dream song (which becomes, with Captain Dick's completion, 'Ah, Sweet Mystery of Life') and the Viennese-styled waltz 'Live for Today', sung with four different operative perspectives by Marietta, Adah, Captain Dick and Étienne, becomes more pronounced and conditions us to hear other numbers from a camp perspective, as well. Thus, for example, 'New Orleans Jeunesse Dorée' recalls too vividly *The Merry Widow*'s 'Maxim's' to be taken entirely straight. Yet, despite such strong shifts towards camp, the serious story and consistently impressive music (though, to be sure, no match for Sullivan's) keep the show grounded, with the gravitas of Adah's story, in particular, anchoring its serious dramatic core.

If *Naughty Marietta* represents an arrival of sorts for American operetta, Herbert himself did not play a hand in the genre's further development. Famously, his falling out with Trentini led to Friml's first operetta success, *The Firefly* (1912), but probably more decisive is the fact that the commercial viability of operetta quickly faded as compared to musical comedy and various types of revue. *The Firefly* reproduced some of the contours of *Naughty Marietta* – set in the New World (contemporary New York and Bermuda) and featuring Trentini's disguising herself as a young boy and being 'adopted' by her mentor – but its promise of an immediate extension of this type of operetta was, seemingly and in retrospect, forestalled by World War I, notwithstanding that Friml achieved even more success with three other outings during the war years, now largely forgotten: *High Jinks* (1913), *Katinka* (1915) and *You're in Love* (1917). His *Sometime* (1918) was even more successful, but his lasting fame stems from the trio of later major successes, which marked him, along with Romberg, as one of the greatest composers of operetta for an American stage: *Rose-Marie* (1924), *The Vagabond King* (1925) and *The Three Musketeers* (1928). Of these, the first, labelled a 'musical play', has proven most important, not only for its role in revitalizing operetta but also for its North American setting and for the rhetoric with which Oscar Hammerstein II, its librettist, referred to the show and its traditions in an essay published the following year, where he cites operetta as the most enduring type of popular musical theatre, defined – in language anticipatory of his and Rodgers post-*Oklahoma!* rhetoric – as 'the musical play with music and plot welded together in skillful cohesion'.[14]

As has often been noted, Romberg's career unfolded in parallel with Friml's, starting with classical training in Europe and a somewhat knockabout Broadway career in the mid-1910s and early 1920s (in Romberg's case as a composer mainly for revue and musical comedy but including as well the operettas *Maytime* (1917) and *Blossom Time* (1921), the latter based on melodies by Franz Schubert),[15] before he emerged, alongside Friml, as the composer of a string of major operetta successes: *The Student Prince* (1924), *The Desert Song* (1926) and *The New Moon* (1928). Both Friml's and Romberg's operetta mega-successes between 1924 and 1928 (before the bottom fell out of both the operetta and the financial markets), use exotic locales, with one from each composer taking place in North America. But what is perhaps most remarkable about the two series is their resolute earnestness, which has several consequences. For one, it heightened the differential between musical comedy and operetta; Gershwins's hit *Lady, Be Good!* (also 1924), with its distinctive jazz idiom and tap-dancing by Fred and Adele Astaire (e.g., in 'Fascinating Rhythm'), offers a convenient point of comparison for *Rose-Marie* and *The Student Prince*, the one with its murder plot and half-breed heroine, the other with its story of love forsaken, and each romantically super-charged. For another, it lined up earnestness with musical elevation and insisted on the alignment of story and music; in the same essay in which Hammerstein, in reference to *Rose-Marie*, aligns the term 'musical play' with operetta (quoted above), he makes an implicit comparison to *Lady, Be Good!*: 'Here was a musical show with a melodramatic plot and a cast of players who were called upon to actually sing the music – *sing*, mind you – not just talk through the lyrics and then go into their dance.'[16]

These consequences – crucial for subsequent developments – intertwine with the camp dimension of operetta in important ways. Whereas *Naughty Marietta* wears its proto-camp on its sleeve, inviting audiences both to take its story seriously and to have fun with it, operetta-based camp by the 1920s had retreated to the closet, in line with the submersion of this sensibility into gay subcultures, where it would largely remain until Susan Sontag outed it in the 1960s.[17] If we must imagine less visible camp engagements with operetta continuing throughout, their closeted nature allowed later audiences – for film adaptations in the 1930s and 1950s (and in the latter period, for televised versions), along with the occasional theatrical revival – to engage with them on several levels, ranging from taking them seriously to regarding them with gentle or not-so-gentle mockery for a style regarded as hopelessly old-fashioned (thus, as *unintentional camp*).

Operetta, Camp and the Re-emergence of the Musical Play

That *Show Boat* – the first American musical to secure a place in both the performing repertory and the critical canon – is first of all an operetta, provides one of the cornerstones for Gerald Bordman's over-arching argument in *American Operetta*, which reconfigures much of the history of the American musical as but one line of development within an extended history of American operetta.[18] But understanding *Show Boat* as something essentially new is at least equally compelling, since it might

also usefully be understood as a kind of fusion of two traditions that were
in 1927 drifting further apart from each other. In 1926, two years after the
watershed year of 1924, when *Rose-Marie*, *The Student Prince* and *Lady, Be
Good!* all opened within three months of each other, the three-act 'native
opera' *Deep River*, with music by Frank Harling, attracted considerable
notice – partly due to its mixed-race casting – despite the brevity of its run
(thirty-two performances).

As opera, *Deep River* aimed to be taken seriously both for its frank
treatment of a fraught American topic – slavery – and for an authenticity
based in ethnographic research into both New Orleans in the 1830s and
voodoo. Yet, because of its Broadway venue, it has also been understood as
more akin to operetta, representing the more severe extremity of the
genre's newly earnest profile (there is, for example, no comic subplot).
Among those who paid the show some attention were *Show Boat*'s creative
team, Jerome Kern and Oscar Hammerstein II, who, sympathetic to *Deep
River*'s ambitions, probably speculated that more success might be had in
this direction if dramatic severity were mitigated through an influx of
musical comedy. Such in any case was their approach in writing *Show
Boat* for the following season, even extending at one point to plans for
revue-like segments, eventually dropped.[19]

If *Show Boat* mixed elements of musical comedy back into operetta's
generic profile, the uneasy differentiation between the two genres persisted – reinforced by the success of operetta on screen in the 1930s,
which played to both earnest and camp tastes – but, in the end (with
operetta meanwhile fading as a viable option for Broadway), established
operetta as essentially outmoded. But only as such, and so named.
Elements of operetta, along with other tokens of a more serious approach
to musical comedy, continued to find their way to the Broadway stage, and
it would not be long before *Oklahoma!* demonstrated the continued
viability of the genre in its mixed *Show Boat* form, as long as that mixed
form was called a 'musical play' and no one was reminded that
Hammerstein himself had once considered that designation interchange-
able with 'operetta'.

Even if, over time, the 'musical play' has become more simply the
'musical', Hammerstein's phrase continues to matter, and centrally, since
it generates a crucial feature of both operetta and the continually evolving
form it helped stabilize. It is above all the seriousness and centrality of the
drama – the play – that both elevates the musical as a genre and reinforces
its camp dimension, its 'crackle of difference', activated whenever characters shift from speech into song.[20] This has been true from the beginning – whichever origin story we choose to believe – and has remained so
over time, even as the main point of entry for camp tastes has morphed,

from the perceived disparity between Sullivan's music and Gilbert's verbal nonsense, to Trentini's shameless pandering to her fans, to the over-the-top, melodramatic acting and singing of 1920s operetta, to the remixed genres of the 'musical play', to the seemingly constant remixing of the serious and the comic in musicals of more recent vintage. Moreover, whatever Hammerstein intended with his designation 'musical play', the shadow meaning of its long-abandoned second word continues to haunt the genre, allowing the musical to continue to play – that is, to *camp* – along the American operetta divide.

Notes

1. I wish to thank Derek Scott, Mitchell Morris, Holley Replogle-Wong and my daughters, Zelda and Rachel Knapp, for their valuable advice and consultation while writing this essay.
2. For a succinct account of *The Black Crook*, see Larry Stempel's *Showtime: A History of the Broadway Musical Theater* (New York: W. W. Norton, 2010), 42–50.
3. This dating does not count *Thespis* (1871), since its music is mostly lost and since it stands somewhat apart from their 'successful series of operettas'.
4. See Raymond Knapp, *The American Musical and the Formation of National Identity* (Princeton, NJ: Princeton University Press, 2005), 34–46 and 104–9.
5. This connection is more oblique with the first scenario. *Der Freischütz* was early on adapted as *Robin des bois* (1824), part of an entrenched *féerie* tradition in Paris that would soon intertwine with the early history of *opérette* and, more directly, provide the ballet dancers and inspiration for the musical and stage effects that helped make *The Black Crook* a success in New York. Thus, *The Black Crook*'s German inspiration gave way, in the event, to a more immediate *opérette*-inflected French influence, albeit without losing its earnest Germanic core.
6. In *American Operetta: From H.M.S. Pinafore to Sweeney Todd* (New York: Oxford University Press, 1981), Gerald Bordman distinguishes this type from operetta by calling it 'comic opera', one of several designations used across this period. I have not used this term here, partly because it is too easily confused with other traditions, such as operetta more narrowly conceived or *opera buffa*, but mainly because it is part of the book's somewhat problematic conceit, as suggested by the inclusion of *Sweeney Todd* in its subtitle, that the mature American musical should rightly be understood as, essentially, operetta. This view, included with modification as my scenario No. 4 at the beginning of this essay, provides an illuminating perspective on the genre, but is far from being its whole truth.
7. I address the general issue of Gilbert and Sullivan's role in the American musical, but with a much different set of emphases, in '"How great thy charm, thy sway how excellent!": Tracing Gilbert and Sullivan's Legacy in the American Musical' in David Eden and Meinhard Saremba (eds.), *The Cambridge Companion to Gilbert and Sullivan* (Cambridge: Cambridge University Press, 2009), 201–15.
8. *Topsy Turvy* (1999), written and directed by Mike Leigh. Produced by Goldwyn Films, Newmarket Capital Group, The Greenlight Fund and Thin Man Films.
9. Among many discussions of the acuity of Sullivan's musical wit, see Gervase Hughes's *The Music of Arthur Sullivan* (London: Macmillan, 1960), Robert Fink's 'Rhythm and Text Setting in The Mikado', *19th-Century Music*, 14 (1990): 31–47, and James Brooks Kuykendall's 'Motives and Methods in Sullivan's allusions' in *The Cambridge Companion to Gilbert and Sullivan*, 122–35. At school in Leipzig, Sullivan was already known for his spot-on improvised parodies of Rossini; see chapter 6 in Part II of Clara Kathleen Rogers's *Memories of a Musical Career* (Boston: Little, Brown, and Company, 1919).
10. As I argue in *National Identity*, apart from the immediate contextual absurdity of this number, the choice of genre points to Ralph's birthright as a gentleman, denied him by Buttercup's having switched Ralph and the Captain when they were babies (41).
11. In Gilbert's lyric to the aria, Yum-Yum compares herself to the Sun in the first verse and to the Moon in the second; the latter reads, in part, 'She borrows light / That, through the night, /

Mankind may all acclaim her! / And, truth to tell, / She lights up well, / So I, for one, don't blame her.' Ian Bradley (ed.), *The Complete Annotated Gilbert and Sullivan*, 20th anniversary edition (New York: Oxford University Press, 2016), 677.

12. The term 'musical play' apparently originated with *The Geisha* (Sidney Jones, Owen Hall and Harry Greenbank, London and New York, 1896), described as 'A Japanese Musical Play'. From the beginning, the term bespoke higher artistic aspirations than routine musical comedy.

13. I argue the inherent camp of the number and the likelihood of 'gay' being understood as 'homosexual' by at least some of the 1910 audience, in *The American Musical and the Performance of Personal Identity* (Princeton and Oxford: Princeton University Press, 2006), 32–3, 40–1 and 382–3.

14. Quoted in Bordman, *American Operetta*, 112.

15. Both *Maytime* and *Blossom Time* were derived, much reworked, from the German stage, from Walter Kollo's *Wie einst im Mai* (1913) and Heinrich Berté's *Das Dreimäderlhaus* (1916), respectively.

16. Quoted in Bordman, *American Operetta*, 113–14.

17. Susan Sontag's 'Notes on Camp', first published in *Partisan Review* in 1964, has been reprinted often, for example in her *Against Interpretation [and Other Essays]* (New York: Dell, 1966), 275–92.

18. Indeed, Bordman sees *Show Boat* as an arrival rather than a departure, claiming that '*Show Boat* was actually the first totally American operetta' in *American Operetta*, 135. Regarding repertories and canons of the American musical, see my 'Canons of the American Musical' in Cormac Newark and William Weber (eds.), *The Oxford Handbook of the Operatic Canon* (New York: Oxford University Press, forthcoming).

19. See Part I of Todd Decker's *Show Boat: Performing Race in an American Musical* (New York: Oxford University Press, 2013) for an account of the show's origins, and its relationship to *Deep River* in particular, including an account of striking dramatic, staging and musical connections between 'Ol' Man River' and 'De Old Clay Road' from *Deep River* (44–7).

20. Cf., from my *Haydn, Musical Camp, and the Long Shadow of German Idealism* (Duke University Press, 2018), 216: 'Indeed, it is an open question whether it is music or camp that provides the "crackle of difference" that Scott McMillin identifies as the musical's characteristic dramatic device', and, from my *National Identity*, 'the musical becomes camp the moment it actually becomes musical' (13). Regarding McMillin's 'crackle of difference', see his *The Musical as Drama* (Princeton: Princeton University Press, 2006), 2.

Recommended Reading

Bordman, Gerald. *American Operetta: From H.M.S. Pinafore to Sweeney Todd.* New York: Oxford University Press, 1981.

Decker, Todd. *Show Boat: Performing Race in an American Musical.* New York: Oxford University Press, 2013.

Eden, David and Saremba, Meinhard, eds. *The Cambridge Companion to Gilbert and Sullivan.* Cambridge: Cambridge University Press, 2009.

Fink, Robert. 'Rhythm and Text Setting in *The Mikado*'. *19th-Century Music*, 14 (1990): 31–47.

Knapp, Raymond. *The American Musical and the Formation of National Identity.* Princeton, NJ: Princeton University Press, 2005.

Stempel, Larry. *Showtime: A History of the Broadway Musical Theater.* New York: W. W. Norton, 2010.

9 Operetta in Russia and the USSR

ANASTASIA BELINA

This chapter will give a brief overview of the history of operetta in Russia, starting with performances and reception of German and French operettas from the eighteenth to the twentieth century and surveying home-grown Soviet operetta – a subject that is still waiting to be fully explored by researchers and writers on music.

'Everyone flocks to see this disgusting thing'

Operetta was big business in tsarist Russia, and later in the Soviet Union.[1] The first theatre built after a European model appeared during the reign of Peter the Great in 1723, when visiting German and French theatre troupes gave performances of comedies.[2] Until 1882, there was a state monopoly on theatres in Russia, but when it was abolished, private theatres and entertainment enterprises flourished. There was a proliferation of theatres, and, although drama, tragedy and opera were popular, operetta had its own huge audience, hungry for laughter and light-hearted fun. Imperial Russia in the second half of the nineteenth century was just as mad about operetta as the rest of Europe. The tastes of the bourgeoisie and nobility were very much European; they read European newspapers and magazines and knew about all the latest developments in European culture. Russian theatre artists were often in contact with their western European counterparts, and the public always appreciated foreign plays and the work of foreigners as much as that of Russians.[3] Artists and composers from Europe were traditionally made welcome in Russia. It was no different for Johann Strauss (1825–99), who paid several visits to the country between 1856 and 1886. Ironically, in 1930, together with Shostakovich's *The Nose* and Third Symphony, a waltz by Strauss was also banned.[4]

Ever since Offenbach's *Orphée aux enfers* was staged at the Mikhailovsky Theatre by a French court theatre troupe in 1859, the composer and his works became all the rage, although Russian equivalents of *opéra comique* and vaudeville already existed. Some notable examples include performances at the Aleksandinsky Theatre in St Petersburg of P. Karatïgin's *Pervoye iyulya v Petergofe* (First of July in Peterhoff) in 1839, P. Grigoriev's *Makar Grigorievich Gubin* and D. Lensky's *Lev Gurïch*

Sinichkin in 1840, Grigoriev's *Tsiryul'nik na Peskakh i parikmakher s Nevskogo* (Barber from Peski and Hairdresser from Nevsky) in 1848 and N. Kulikov's *Bednaya devushka* (Poor Maiden) in 1850.[5]

During the reign of Tsar Nikolai I, there was an entertainment centre called 'Establishment of Artificial Mineral Waters', where concerts of light music were given from 1834 until 1876. Its owner was the entrepreneur Ivan Isler, who found this enterprise so lucrative that he decided to build a summer theatre in the late 1850s, where he presented excerpts from operettas in the evening programmes. This proved hugely popular, and others followed suit by opening their own summer theatres and *cafés chantants*; among these were the famous *Villa Borghese,* operating in 1855–65, and *Eldorado,* 1867–1913, which was even described by Saltykov-Shchedrin in his 1883 satirical novel *Sovremennaya idiliya* (A Contemporary Idyll).[6]

In 1870 a new Theatre Bouffe opened in St Petersburg, where world-famous operetta stars were engaged to present excerpts from operettas and one-act operettas. The first appearance in St Petersburg of the French operetta diva Hortense Schneider (1833–1920) was so eagerly awaited that tickets were sold out a month early, and two weeks before the performances all flower shops were emptied.[7] She would perform *La Grande-Duchesse de Gérolstein* on 10 December 1871, with the whole of the city's *beau monde* in attendance. Her visit paved the way for many Parisian operetta stars' visits throughout the 1870s.

Operetta audiences were already diverse in the early nineteenth century, and, as the urban population grew with the emancipation of the serfs in 1861, support for operetta increased.[8] But not everyone shared positive feelings about operetta, which had suffered from being downgraded to a less artistically valuable, vulgar and, later in the Soviet Union, even 'pornographic' genre. A number of Russian writers, for example, voiced their dislike of operetta: Tolstoy's Vronsky, in *Anna Karenina,* compared an unsatisfactory situation he felt himself to be in with an operetta plot,[9] and several of Chekhov's short stories reference operetta. In fact, Chekhov's early plays were influenced by operetta: he was thirteen when he saw *La belle Hélène* and was impressed by its approach to satire.[10] A famous actor, Alexander Sumbatov-Iuzhin wrote a play *A Celebrity's Husband,* where an operetta diva is persuaded to become an opera singer instead.[11]

The last director of the Imperial Theatres, Vladimir Telyakovsky, left a number of diary entries showing his utter disgust with the genre which, much to his dismay, he could not eradicate from the theatres. He even used the derogatory term *operetka,* or little operetta, and often mused at the fact that the whole imperial family supported it. Telyakovsky's diary gives a good insight into operettas given in the Imperial Theatres, their stars and their patrons, as well as the level of performances and quality of productions.

Even the famous Russian bass Shalyapin was not immune to the charms of operetta. He agreed to appear in Planquette's *Les cloches de Corneville*, a hugely popular operetta in Russia at the time, and, although he grumbled at first about having to do it, he grew to like it so much that he even asked Telyakovsky if more performances could be arranged. The performance on 31 January 1904 brought a 'phenomenal sum of 15000' roubles but, for Telyakovsky, it was only due to Shalyapin, who sang wonderfully, but too good 'for operetka' that contained much vulgarity and lacked elegance.[12] Later, this operetta was given in the USSR in a new version by V. Inber and V. Zak at the theatre of Stanislavsky and Nemirovich-Danchenko. The new version was made because it was believed that the original text was of poor literary quality and that the story needed 'new heroes, new motifs, and new situations'. So, the Soviet writers introduced 'a group of persecuted, poor, but pure and morally unblemished actors' instead of the original characters: marquises, ladies and missing heirs.[13]

But some cultural figures did not see anything strange in working with operetta. Stanislavsky, for example, successfully directed Sullivan's *Mikado* in 1887 in Moscow, and when he teamed up with Nemirovich-Danchenko, he produced Suppé's *Donna Juanita*, the most popular operetta of the Viennese school on Russian stages at the time. Both Stanislavsky and Nemirovich-Danchenko actively promoted operetta, whether European or Soviet. Another famous Russian theatre producer Theodore Komisarjevsky collaborated on the production of Suppé's *Die schöne Galathea*, Pergolesi's *La serva padrona*, and a number of one-act musical plays in 'The Gay Theatre' with N. Evreinov.[14]

It is a little-known fact that one of Russia's greatest novelists Ivan Turgenev (1818–83) wrote librettos in French for operettas set to music by Pauline Viardot. The most popular of these, *Le dernier sorcier*, orchestrated by Eduard Lassen (possibly with assistance by Liszt) was performed in Weimar in 1869 and in Karlsruhe and Baden-Baden in 1870.[15] Even Alexander Borodin and César Cui, the members of the Mighty Handful, tried their hand at the composition of several lighter works.[16]

From the second half of the nineteenth century, the works by German and French composers dominated Russian operetta stages, with the most popular composers being Suppé, Offenbach, Planquette, Hervé and Lecocq. Most of their operettas were performed in St Petersburg's Aleksandrinsky Theatre, but they were also shown in private and summer theatres, many of which remained active even for a few years after the Revolution.[17]

Figure 9.1 Entrance to the Theatre Bouffe, 1909

One pre-Revolutionary summer theatre called Theatre Bouffe deserves a special mention for its popularity and quality of performances. It was established by the entrepreneur P. Tumpakov in 1901, who engaged excellent singers, chorus and orchestra. One of the stars in his theatre was Wiktoria Kawecka, the 'nightingale of Warsaw', who was one of the most popular operetta divas in Poland at the time.[18] Among operettas given in the Theatre Bouffe were Planquette's *Les cloches de Corneville,* Offenbach's *La belle Hélène,* Hervé's *Mam'zelle Nitouche,* Suppé's *Boccaccio,* Audran's *La mascotte* and many others. But the theatre's most enduring legacy lies in the fact that it hosted the Russian premieres of Lehár's *Der Graf von Luxemburg* and *Die lustige Witwe.*[19]

As can be gathered from even a brief survey of the entertainment scene in pre-Revolutionary Russia, urban popular culture was cosmopolitan. It was also daring: a Moscow Farce Theatre presented *Sarah Wants a Negro* and *Don't Walk about in the Nude.*[20] Sex, 'foreignism' and all references to decadence and bourgeois culture were banned after the Revolution.

Operetta in 1917–1929

Operetta did not immediately find favour in post-Revolutionary Russia because it was seen as a remnant of decadent and bourgeois entertainment. At first, performances of European operettas were given with newly adapted storylines, changed characters, places and situations, and new ways of moralizing and preaching of the Soviet doctrine were forced into the familiar stories. Some were lauded for their 'democratic elements in the libretto' as, for example, Millöcker's *Der Bettelstudent,* with a new libretto by N. Erdman and M. Ulitsky, which showed 'the struggle of freedom-loving Polish people for its liberation'.[21] It is ironic, given the fact that historically Russia was only too eager to appropriate Polish territories without any regard for the feelings of their inhabitants. Even *Die Fledermaus* had to find more resonance with the new order, and its libretto was adapted by the writers B. Mass and M. Chervinsky to make it 'more contemporary, imbue it with real literary gravitas, and to emphasize its social meaning'.[22]

In the autumn of 1919, the Operetta Theatre opened in Moscow, where it presented Kálmán's *Der Kleine König* as *Revolyursionerka* (The Revolutionary Woman). Despite a heavily reworked libretto, inspired by the abdication of King Manuel of Portugal in 1910, it was received sceptically by the authorities, who 'doubted whether such frothy entertainment was appropriate for the times, since every open theatre meant an extravagant consumption of heat and electricity in a period of extreme scarcity'.[23]

One of the most, if not the most, popular operettas in Russia was (and remains so today) Kálmán's *Die Csárdásfürstin,* or *Silva* (1915). Of course, for its performances in 1917, revolutionary spirit had to be reflected in the new libretto: the writers Mikhailov and Tolmachev made Silva a native of the island of Kotlin near Kronstadt (Gulf of Finland). A descendant of Baltic sailors, she achieved success only thanks to her talent and determination: she had to be a positive role model for young Soviet women.[24]

During the period of Lenin's New Economic Policy (NEP), 1921–9, which saw a temporary return to old attitudes and approaches to entrepreneurship and business, European operetta was as popular and as lucrative as it was before the Revolution. There was even a tour of 'Negro-Operetta': an American jazz band, led by Sam Wooding, engaged by an NEP entrepreneur for a show 'The Chocolate Kiddies' in Moscow in 1926. Shostakovich gushed about seeing the show in a letter to a friend: 'Their jazz band is a real discovery of America for a musician.' It seems that he equally liked the good-looking women who danced in the performances.[25] Only three years later, this kind of entertainment would be unthinkable: with the end of NEP came tighter controls and eventually strictly prescriptive socialist realism.

Laughter Therapy for the Masses

With the new class of citizens in the new country, new content to fill established and popular forms was no longer enough: fresh forms and ideals were needed. For Bolsheviks, culture had a purpose: it had to be for the masses, and it had to be strictly controlled in order to be effective as a propaganda tool. The first attempts to revolutionize culture for Soviet citizens brought no desired results: they were not interested in 'factory concerts with machine sonatas or "ballets" whose dancers were dressed as flying lizards'.[26] Contrary to the hopes of the new Soviet elite, theatre did not prove to be popular, either, during the first few years after the Revolution, because the new proletarian class did not find the complex artistic language of the artform easy to understand.[27]

Even before socialist realism became the only official way forward for creative artists in the Soviet Union, the members of the Russian Association of Proletarian Musicians (RAPM) were preoccupied with 'ensuring that workers were being properly supplied with suitable music and not dancing to foxtrots and tangos'. Multiple meetings were held where the future of Soviet music and 'foxtrotism' were discussed. At one such meeting in 1930, there was a proposal to exclude those composers who wrote 'foxtrot and gipsy music' from the Union of Composers. One of the 'foxtrotters' replied that no one could possibly know what the policy on foxtrot will be tomorrow, to everyone's laughter. Another went even further, by arguing that many of the RAPM composers were not immune to the charms of the popular dances and operetta 'pornography': one 'accidentally' arranged some foxtrots, and the other set a Soviet text to music that was 'nothing more than a cancan'.[28]

It quickly became obvious that, if culture were to be used for political propaganda, it still had to be entertaining. The people continued to enjoy popular and light songs and dances. This is why operetta proved a good fit: it was popular, its music was memorable, it was entertaining and easily adaptable. In fact, it was a perfectly suitable chalice into which the ideals of socialist realism would be poured from the end of the 1930s until Stalin's death in 1953. Socialist realism became a single style that upheld clear ideological context and strictly controlled all spheres of life in the country. It promoted revolutionary struggle for freedom, elimination of class enemies, heroism, triumph of duty, patriotism, purity of character, morality and dedication to building a new life.

Soviet operetta had to be funny, light, entertaining and promote the themes of social mobility through the Soviet system but at the same time ask serious questions and moralize. In other words, fun was allowed, but it was strictly prescribed: it had to be ordered and moral. Its tunes had to be melodious and memorable, and its songs had to be based on traditional folk elements. The characters had to appeal to the masses and be strong, self-controlled and idealistic but also fun-loving and brave.

Several genres of Soviet operetta developed: heroic, dramatic, *kolkhoz* and song operetta, to name a few. Song operetta, for example, focussed on folk-like or folksong-inspired song as a major building block of the entire structure, and *kolkhoz* operetta romanticized life in a collective farm (*kolkhoz*), colouring it with the positive, optimistic hues of socialist realism. Heroic women drivers of tractors and combine harvesters in these operettas were based on real-life women and their stories that represented examples of Soviet upward social mobility. One such woman, Praskovya Angelina (1913–59), was the highest achiever in her tractor team. When she decided to marry, her team was thrown into a state of panic about loss of productivity. This and other similar stories gave birth to a multitude of plays, novels, operettas and films.[29]

Soviet operettas often focussed on stories from the Revolution and World War II. Many operettas simply featured optimistic young people who achieve their goals in the face of adversity; mostly, these goals included working in Siberia, building new cities or gaining education. There was a drive to promote traditionally male-dominated jobs to women: combine harvesting, engineering, navigating at sea, building and so on. All featured at least one couple in love who overcome their difficulties and end up together; one or two unsavoury characters who are either spies or informants; characters who start on erroneous paths only to be shown the righteous Soviet way and heroic, strong, stable characters who inspire others to follow the happy Soviet life.

No one did more to develop Soviet operetta than Isaak Dunayevsky (1900–55). He composed the first Soviet operetta, *Zhenikhi* (The Suitors, 1927), set in a provincial town during the NEP period, where a host of greedy suitors were chasing a rich widow. Dunayevsky had a real gift for melody, which was a highly prized commodity in the country where socialist realism was the guiding star. His works reflected the official spirit of the time: optimism, enthusiasm, Soviet pride, friendship, bravery, patriotism, the joys of collective farming, support for the Red Army and fighting the Germans in World War II. He wrote a number of quintessential Soviet songs that are still well known in today's Russia. Having held a series of high-level administrative posts, Dunayevsky received a number of prestigious Soviet prizes and awards. Among his operettas are *Nozhi* (Knives, 1928), which showed the positive characteristics of Soviet youth; *Polyarnye strasti* (Polar Passions, 1929), whose heroine is a young Inuit girl, who runs away from her kulak father to go to Moscow to study at a university. Other works promote Soviet optimism even in their titles: *Zolotaya dolina* (Golden Valley, 1937); *Dorogi k schast'yu* (Roads to Happiness, 1941) and *Vol'niy veter* (The Free Wind, 1947). His last two operettas were *Sïn klouna* (Clown's Son, 1950) and *Belaya akatsiya* (White Acacia, 1955). He also composed songs, film scores, music for theatre and ballets.

From 1929 to 1941 Dunayevsky was the music director of a variety theatre, the Leningrad Music Hall, where he worked with another would-be iconic figure in Russian entertainment, the singer Leonid Utyosov (1895–1982) and his instrumental ensemble. Together, they Sovietized American jazz, which was attacked in 1928 by Gorky who identified it with homosexuality, drugs and decadent eroticism. Utyosov's jazz orchestra massively contributed to bringing back the previously outlawed dances, among them the infamous foxtrot and the Boston waltz. When Dunayevsky created the film score for *Vesyolïye rebyata* (Jolly Fellows, 1934), where Utyosov had a prominent role, both were catapulted to country-wide success.

Although acknowledged as one of the founding fathers of Soviet operetta along with Dunayevsky, little can be found about Nikolay Strelnikov (1888–1939) in existing literature. One of his first works, *Chyornïy amulet* (The Black Amulet, 1928), was an ill-fated attempt to politicize operetta. It was an anti-capitalist story about 'a plutocrat in a donkey mask who hands out wads of money to half-naked women'. But the moral of the story was lost on the audiences who rather enjoyed the 'flesh more than the sarcasm – and the critics panned it'.[30] He did better with his next operetta, *Kholopka* (Servant, 1929). Although *Kholopka* was criticized for its archaic language and its jazzy rhythms, it remained popular because of its story, which depicted serfdom, oppression and inequality. Strelnikov did not manage to avoid criticism with his next operetta, *Sertdse poeta* (Poet's Heart, 1934), where his music was derided for its jazz influences.

Boris Aleksandrov (1905–94) deserves a mention because he was praised for being the first to put 'real' people – partisans, women, children, soldiers of the Red Army – in his successful operetta *Svad'ba v Malinovke* (Wedding in Malinovka, 1937). Now a Soviet classic, it was lauded for replacing 'decaying and decadent' Viennese characters with 'bold, colourful, realistic characters' in a story about an attempted forced wedding of a Bolshevik woman, with a grand finale featuring a hydroelectric power and radio station.[31] In 1967 it was turned into an even more successful film, once again praised for its good balance of entertainment and moralizing. In fact, Soviet operetta influenced the development of Soviet film, especially the genre of musical comedy. Many of these early musical comedies became classics, such as the *Vesyolïye rebyata* (1934) and *Volga-Volga* (1938), which was reputedly Stalin's favourite film.

Operettas set in satellite socialist republics were also written, such as Rauf Gadzhiev's *Perekryostok* (The Crossroads), set in 1919–20 in Baku. It has an eclectic collection of characters: a graduate from Petersburg University; young and old inhabitants of the city; a couple in love; a singer in a *café chantant*; an English translator, Brown; Abdulla, who suddenly comes into a lot of money, and a hairdresser, Gaston. His real name is Gurgen, but he demands to be addressed as Gaston because it 'sounds like Europe' and Gurgen 'sounds like village'. He is obsessed with Europe, and his salon is called Atrada (Pleasure), but he comes to see the errors of his ways and turns patriotic, renaming his salon Krasnaya Atrada (Red Pleasure) and demanding to be called Gurgen, because Gaston 'sounds like Europe, and Europe is not on'.

But behind this mask of optimism and belief in a bright future operetta was concealing something more sinister:

> The horrors of collectivization, the great famine, the recurring waves of purge and killings, the vast network of slave and death camps were not only totally absent from popular culture; their possibility was culturally denied by visions of rural prosperity, urban harmony and a success, and a new dawn of freedom. A web of fantasy and a giant political coverup deflected dissatisfaction of the masses against alleged enemies of the people. Fantasists ascribed all achievements to the great leader and all failings to saboteurs, traitors, and spies. Agricultural shortfalls were hidden behind paintings, operettas, and movies about *kolkhoz* feasts with tables groaning under food and wine.[32]

Laughter therapy for the masses did the trick, at least until Stalin held the country in his steel grip, and never did it prove to be more needed than during the World War II years, when it was a welcome distraction for the citizens of the war-torn USSR. European and Soviet operettas shared the stage.

Perhaps these performances had the most effect in blockaded Leningrad, where they helped those who managed to make it to the theatre to forget about their hunger and stop thinking about death, which ravaged the city with increasing viciousness every day. Often, these performances were given during air raids, and the audiences were told to stay close to the walls. Normally, the secondary arias and duets were cut out, but the splendour of staging and costumes remained. Theatres were unheated, and the actors were so thin that some had to hide their dystrophy underneath thick padded winter coats, on top of which they then wore their costumes. Leningrad audiences heard Strauss's *Die Fledermaus*; Friml's *The Firefly* (given as *Sailor's Love*); Kálmán's *Silva, La bayadère, Gräfin Maritza* – 'all Viennese elegance and evening dress and gipsy romance'; Leo Fall's *Die Dollarprinzessin* and a number of others, including those by Soviet composers.[33]

But operetta singers, like many other citizens of the city, were dying of hunger and disease or being killed during air raids. Adjustments were made to deal with the shrinking theatre group: cuts were made, and various instruments were left out from the scores. Still, the Theatre of Musical Comedy (Muzkom) was doing good business in Leningrad. There was huge demand for tickets, and those who could not buy them on the black market, stood for hours in the queue from as early as 6 a.m. The performances were at 10.30 a.m. and 4 p.m. Those who went to the later ones, found that it helped them forget about hunger.[34]

Elsewhere in the USSR, during World War II, Soviet operetta theatres staged patriotic operettas: Aleksandrov's *Devushka iz Barceloni* (A Girl from Bacelona, 1942), Shcherbachev's *Tabachniy kapitan* (Tobacco Captain, 1942) and Vitlin's *Raskinulos' morye shiroko* (The Wide Sea, 1942; adapted by G. Sviridov in 1943). A new Theatre of Small Operetta was formed in Kronstadt to perform aboard the ships, and actors, singers and musicians were sent to the front to perform light music to the soldiers. These performances often included numbers from both European and home-grown operettas.

This 'therapy' was even used in the Gulag system and the cities near the labour camps both during and after the war. By the 1940s, the cities that stood at the centre of the larger camp complexes – Magadan, Vorkuta, Norilsk, Ukhta – were large, bustling places, with shops, theatres and parks.[35] Evgeniya Ginzburg wrote in her memoir *Within the Whirlwind* that when she returned to the city of Magadan, built by the prisoners in the 1940s, she saw a poster, announcing that in the House of Culture there was to be a performance of *Die Dollarprinzessin*.[36] Soviet commentators took swipes at operettic sufferings, at the sadness of suddenly impoverished nobility or the rich, revelling in asking: what is the big deal?[37]

After the war, Soviet operetta continued its optimistic march. One of the leading operetta composers in the USSR was Yuri Milyutin (1903–68), who wrote operettas about the lives of ordinary people, depicted with direct and memorable musical language firmly rooted in folksong. Like Dunayevsky, he received a number of coveted Soviet awards for his work. Among his operettas are *Zhizn' aktyora* (An Actor's Life, 1940), *Devichiy perepolokh* (A Girls' Alarm, 1944), *Bespokoynoye schast'ye* (Uneasy Happiness, 1947); *Trembita* (1949), *Pervaya lyubov'* (First Love, 1950), *Lyubushka* (1952), *Potseluy Chaniti* (Chanita's Kiss, 1956), *Fonari-fonariki* (Lanterns, Lamps, 1958), *Tsirk zazhigayet ogni* (The Circus Lights Go On, 1960), *Anyutini glazki* (Forget-Me-Not, 1964), *Obruchal'niye kol'tsa* (The Engagement Rings, 1968) and *Tikhaya semeyka* (A Quiet Little Family, 1968). His *Tsirk zazhigayet ogni* is about a character who left his homeland and only realized what a terrible mistake he had made when it was too late – a suitable topic for promotion of the joys of living in the Soviet Union.

Perhaps the best testament to the validity of operetta in the Soviet Union is the fact that one of the most influential musical figures (but not the most talented) also tried his hand in the genre. A divisive figure, Tikhon Khrennikov (1913–2007) studied composition with Vissarion Shebalin and piano with Heinrich Neuhaus. Having found favour with the Communist Party for his optimistic and accessible music, combined with a clear and lyrical style, he was catapulted to power: in 1948 he was appointed Secretary of the Union of Composers. Suddenly in the most powerful musical office and in charge of ensuring that the rules of socialist realism remained the primary guidance of Soviet composers, he had to reprimand and punish those who did not comply. Shostakovich, Prokofiev and Myaskovsky did not escape his judgement. Highly decorated with Soviet prizes, in 1974 he was elected as a deputy to the Supreme Soviet of the USSR. Khrennikov held his post for forty-three years and would have held it longer, had it not been for the collapse of the USSR in 1991. Recently, more evidence has begun to emerge about Khrennikov's milder side and his attempts to save and protect his fellow composers thanks to his high position. His output includes a number of comic operas and two operettas which are closer to European operetta than one might expect. *Sto chertey i odna devushka* (A Hundred Devils and One Girl, 1963) and *Belaya noch'* (White Night, 1967) show 'little development in their anachronistic formula of sentimental waltzes and other standard dance and song forms, their varied repetition of a limited amount of original material and their repertory of stock comic clichés'.[38]

Dmitry Shostakovich (1906–75) and Dmitry Kabalevsky (1904–87) also dabbled in operetta but managed only three completed works between them. If at first Shostakovich looked down on operetta, he learnt to like it when his close friend Ivan Sollertinsky opened his eyes to its charms, stating: 'Before that I thought it strange for a serious musician to like the music of Johann Strauss or Offenbach. Sollertinsky helped me to get rid of this snobbish approach to art. And now I like music of all genres, as long as it is real music.'[39]

The period between 1928 and 1936 saw a proliferation of Shostakovich's waltzes, polkas and galops, with a distinctly Offenbachian flavour and showing the influence of Lehár, Johann Strauss and other operetta composers. If one listens carefully, one may hear in the theme of 'invasion' in Shostakovich's 'Leningrad' Symphony the opening rhythms of 'Da geh' ich zu Maxim' from *Die lustige Witwe*, which may have also been a private family reference: Shostakovich and his son Maxim often listened to operettas at home.

A number of unfinished or unrealized operetta ideas include *Bol'shaya molniya* (The Great Lightning, 1932); *Nergo*, the contract for which he was allegedly forced to drop and *Dvenadtsat' stul'yev* (The Twelve Chairs), after Il'f and Petrov's eponymous satirical novel set during the NEP.[40] He was also presented with libretti which he discarded and which later became successful operettas by Sviridov, *Ogon'ki* (Lights), and Shcherbachev, *Tabachnïy kapitan* (Tobacco Captain).[41]

Shostakovich's one and only completed operetta is *Moskva, Cheryomushki*, premiered in 1959. A fun, sparkling, humorous work with a wonderful score, it delivers a great night at the theatre. However, it did not always find resonance with Soviet commentators: one of them chided it for failing to find the 'real meaning' and for focussing on elements that are 'not important for Soviet people, especially in the period of building enthusiasm'.[42] Even Kurt Gänzl's *The Encyclopedia of the Musical Theatre* does not mention it, and Richard Traubner in his *Operetta: A Theatrical History* mentions Shostakovich's name in passing on the last page, without naming his operetta.

Like Shostakovich, Dmitry Kabalevsky (1904–87) tried his luck with operetta. A student of Catoire and Myaskovsky at the Moscow Conservatory, he became a key figure in the Union of Soviet Composers and did much to promote music education for children. His two operettas are *Vesna poyot* (Spring Sings, 1957) and *Syostrï* (Sisters, 1967). *Vesna poyot* remains his more popular work, featuring young Moscow architects who are passionate about building palaces of culture in Siberia, an informant called Ptichkin (a little bird), two successful and two failed love stories, a journalist, an ultra-stylish daughter of a corrupt bureaucrat and a woman who tries to look younger than her years 'with an extensive biography'. It is surprising that a composer who had done so much for music education did not write an operetta for children, especially when it was so highly prized.

Towards the mid-1960s, operetta had proved itself to be a useful component in the socialist realism artistic arsenal. When, in the 1970s, the Party issued a special decree which encouraged artistic figures to pay heightened attention to the aesthetic education of the young generation, a number of works like that already existed. Composers who had already achieved success with operettas for adults wrote a number of children's works, which include S. Tulikov's *Barankin, bud' chelovekom* (Barankin, Be a Decent Man, 1964), S. Zaslavsky's fairy-tale operetta *Ne bey devchonok* (Don't Beat the Girls, 1975), A. Eshpay's *Malïsh i Karlson* (The Junior and Karlson, 1968) after a story by Astrid Lindgren, S. Banevich's *Priklyucheniya Toma Soyera* (Adventures of Tom Sawyer, 1971), G. Portnov's *Druz'ya v pereplete* (Friends in Trouble, 1966) among many others. All these composers focussed on well-known stories and characters. There was also a call for operetta for teenagers, which would look towards revolutionary themes, but only very few, if any, works were written, and these are not known today.[43]

Operetta remained popular in the Soviet Union and its range was impressive. Richard Traubner wrote in 1983 that if 'one spent two weeks in Moscow, one might catch Suppé's *Donna Juanita*, Offenbach's *La Périchole*, Friml's *Rose-Marie*, Kálmán's *Csárdásfürstin*, and Loewe's *My Fair Lady*, along with *The White Acacia* and a few more current things'.[44] Today, both European and Soviet-and-Russian operettas remain in the repertory, and even a brief glance at the Moscow Operetta Theatre seasons reveals a rich array of operettas and musicals, Russian, European and American.

Notes

1. The quotation heading this section is taken from Valdimir Telyakovsky, *Dnevniki direktora Imperatorskikh teatrov 1903–1906* [Diaries of the Director of the Imperial Theatres] (St Petersburg: Artist. Rezhissyor. Teatr, 2006), 678.
2. Felix Lourie, *Peterburg: Istoriya i kul'tyra v tablitsakh. 1703–1917, XVIII–XX veka* [Petersburg: History and Culture in Tables. 1703–1917, 18th–20th centuries] (St Petersburg: Zolotoy Vek and Diamant, 2000), 23.
3. Theodore Komisarjevsky, *Myself and the Theatre* (London: William Heinemann Limited, 1929), 28.
4. Marina Frolova-Walker and Jonathan Walker. *Music and Soviet Power 1917–1932* (Woodbridge: The Boydell Press, 2012), 268–9.
5. Lourie, *Peterburg*, 79, 85.
6. Ibid., 89, 97.
7. See Kurt Gänzl's 'Schneider, Hortense [Catherine]' in *The Encyclopedia of the Musical Theatre* (New York: Schirmer Books, 1994), 1278–9. See also Moisey Yankovsky, *Operetta: Vozniknoveniye i razvitie zhanra na Zapade i v SSSR* [Operetta: development of the genre in the West and in the USSR] (Leningrad and Moscow: Iskusstvo, 1937), 216–17.
8. Murray Frame. 'The Early Reception of Operetta in Russian, 1860s–1870s', *European History Quarterly*, 42 no. 1 (2012): 29–49, at 36.
9. This remark was also included in the film *Anna Karenina* (2012) by Tom Stoppard and Joe Wright.
10. See Rosamund Bartlett's blog entry 'Early Chekhov', www.nationaltheatre.org.uk/blog/early-chekhov (accessed 3 Sept. 2018).
11. Frame, 'The Early Reception of Operetta in Russian', 43.
12. Telyakovsky, *Dnevniki direktora*, 149–52.
13. Lidiya Zhukova, *V mire operetti* [In the world of operetta] (Moscow: Znaniye, 1976), 17.
14. Komisarjevsky, *Myself and the Theatre*, 91.
15. April Fitzlyon, 'Turgenev, Ivan Sergeyevich' in *Grove Music Online*, www .oxfordmusiconline.com/grovemusic/abstract/10.1093/gmo/9781561592630.001.0001/omo-9781561592630-e-0000002600?rskey=T4ctT3&result=1 (accessed 3 Sept. 2018).
16. The Mighty Handful was a group of Russian composers who were united by one idea: to create authentically Russian music by using folksong and folklore as a basis for their compositions. Richard Traubner, *Operetta: A Theatrical History* (New York: Routledge, 2003), 432.
17. One of these artistic cabarets, *Prival komediantov* (Refuge of comedians) (1916–19), was founded by V. Meyerhold and his colleagues. See Lourie, *Peterburg*,137.
18. For more on Wiktoria Kawecka, see Chapter 15 on operetta in Warsaw in the present *Companion*.
19. A colourful description of this Theatre Bouffe can be found in a book written by two St Petersburg dwellers, who recorded their memories of life in the city before the arrival of Communist regime: Dmitri Zasosov and Vladimir Pïzin, *Iz zhizni Peterburga 1890–1910-h godov. Zapiski ochevidtsev* [From Petersburg's life of 1890s–1910s. Notes of the witnesses] (Leningrad: Lenizdat, 1991).

20. Richard Stites, *Russian Popular Culture: Entertainment and Society since 1900* (Cambridge: Cambridge University Press, 1992), 21.
21. Zhukova, *V mire operettï*, 21–2.
22. Ibid., 28.
23. Frolova-Walker and Walker, *Music and Soviet Power*, 25.
24. For more information on the history of this operetta in Russia, see Zoltàn Imre, 'Operetta Beyond Borders: The Different Versions of *Die Csárdásfürstin* in Europe and the United States (1915–1921)', *Studies in Musical Theatre*, 7, no. 2 (2013): 175–205.
25. Sergey Sapozhnikov, *Moy Shostakovich: Ocherki iz publitsisticheskoy syuitï 'Na pereput'ye mne yavilis'* [My Shostakovich: Essays from a journalistic suite 'I saw on the crossroads'] (Moscow: Artisticheskoye obshchestvo 'Assamblei iskusstv', 2006), 81.
26. Stites, *Russian Popular Culture*, 39.
27. Tatiana Chistova, 'Tendentsii razvitiya operettï v sovetskoy kul'ture' [Tendencies of development in Soviet operetta], unpublished PhD dissertation, Moscow City Pedagogical University, 2012, http://cheloveknauka.com/tendentsii-razvitiya-operetty-v-sovetskoy-kulture (accessed 28 Aug. 2018).
28. Frolova-Walker and Walker, *Music and Soviet Power*, 262–3, 287–9.
29. Stites, *Russian Popular Culture*, 71.
30. Ibid., 81.
31. Zhukova, *V mire operettï*, 42.
32. Stites, *Russian Popular Culture*, 95.
33. Brian Moynahan, *Leningrad: Siege and Symphony* (London: Quercus, 2013), 148.
34. Ibid., 387.
35. Anne Applebaum, *Gulag: A History* (London: Penguin Books, 2004), 249.
36. Ibid., 201.
37. Zhukova, *V mire operettï*, 34.
38. Valentina Rubcova, 'Khrennikov, Tikhon Nikolayevich' in *Grove Music Online*, https://doi.org/10.1093/gmo/9781561592630.article.14980 (accessed 3 Sept. 2018) .
39. M. Yakovlev (ed.), *Dmitry Shostakovich a vremeni i o sebe: 1926–1975* [Dmitry Shostakovich about his time and himself: 1926–1975] (Moscow: Sovetskiy kompozitor, 1980), 195.
40. Ibid., 75.
41. Dmitry Shostakovich, *Pis'ma k Sollertinskomu* [Letters to Sollertinsky] (St Petersburg: Kompozitor, 2006), 226–7, Letter to Sollertinsky dated 4 January 1942.
42. Zhukova, *V mire operettï*, 68–9.
43. Ibid., 99–100.
44. Traubner, *Operetta*, 433.

Recommended Reading

Frame, Murray. 'The Early Reception of Operetta in Russian, 1860s–1870s', *European History Quarterly*, 42, no. 1 (2012): 29–49.
Stites, Richard. *Russian Popular Culture: Entertainment and Society since 1900.* Cambridge: Cambridge University Press, 1992.

10 Operetta in the Nordic Countries (1850–1970)

PENTTI PAAVOLAINEN

During the long nineteenth century, the Nordic countries witnessed economic growth, industrialization and the prominent expansion of the middle classes. In a series of treaties drawn up by the Congress of Vienna to bring to an end the hostilities across Europe caused by the Napoleonic and French Revolutionary Wars, the Nordic countries agreed to various territorial redistributions. For example, Denmark, agreed in the Treaty of Kiel (1814) to cede Norway (which had been its northern half since the Middle Ages) to Sweden. Norway then entered a personal union with Sweden under the Swedish Crown (1814–1905) until its independence in 1905. This provided some form of compensation to Sweden, which had also lost its eastern half, the Grand Duchy of Finland. Finland was occupied from 1809 to 1917 by Russia, when a war for independence – simultaneously a civil war – broke out. Finland became a parliamentary republic after that. The three other Nordic states (Denmark, Norway and Sweden) belong to the oldest existing monarchies in Europe.

Increased affluence brought a growing need for entertainment and explains the popularity and the increase in production of operettas from the 1850s onwards. Just as the nineteenth-century melodramatic repertoire can be studied as a mirror reflecting the developments in 'real' society, the same applies to operettas and their erotic, ethnic and emotional landscapes. Like all popular theatrical genres, French and German operettas can be understood – on a deep level – as expressions of audiences' dreams, fears and wishes, articulated and unarticulated. Consider, for instance, the exoticism of distant provinces, imaginary counties and nostalgic tales of more exciting lives and true love across class barriers. These images appealed to the urbanized population, who in Scandinavia still had their roots in the provinces but were aspiring to rise through the social hierarchy, as was possible in the fast-growing towns.

The differences in the operetta landscapes of those four states – Denmark, Norway, Sweden and Finland – can best be observed in the structure and ownership of the theatre venues of their respective capitals, Copenhagen (København), Christiania (spelt Kristiania 1877–97 and becoming Oslo in 1925), Stockholm and Helsinki (in Swedish, Helsingfors). Another explanation lies in the interdependence between venues or institutions and their languages. The dominant languages, cultural identities, vernacular languages and nation-building politics will be the focus of the following overview, which concentrates on the four capital cities.[1]

Copenhagen and Its Private Theatres Welcome Operetta

For its theatrical nutrition, Copenhagen has been leaning towards Paris ever since Ludwig Holberg (1684–1754) and his theatre on Grønnegade (1722–7) were greatly inspired by Molière. With the exception of a short theatrical closure (1738–46), the spirit of enlightenment reigned continually through the eighteenth and the early nineteenth centuries and paved the way for the 'golden age' of Danish Culture (1830–60). In 1748, The Royal Theatre house was first built outside the old city ramparts at Kongens Nytorv, the King's New Square.

Post-Napoleonic Paris with its French vaudevilles also inspired Johann Ludvig Heiberg (1791–1860) to create Danish vaudevilles. Well received in the Royal Theatre, they were long running. But Heiberg also propagated vaudevilles; by demanding a high position among literary genres for this combination of comedy and lyrics, he united two Aristotelian genres, poetry and drama. This elevated position enabled Heiberg also to deal with modern urban topics and to establish the central figure, the 'bedsteborgaren', the good-humoured city-dweller. His wife, the admired actress Johanne Louise Heiberg (1812–90), contributed by starring in them. Later, she wrote and composed a vaudeville of her own *En Søndag paa Amager* (A Sunday on the Amager Island, 1848), which became one of the longest runners in the Danish and Norwegian repertoires. Otherwise, Copenhagen was indulged by the French 'light operas' of D. F. E. Auber and F.-A. Boieldieu, constantly performed side-by-side with French vaudevilles even in the Royal Theatre. The best playwrights provided the Danish translations.

The growing audiences created the need to establish a less highbrow stage for popular comedy. The first private theatre was the Casino Theatre (1848) south of the Amalienborg Palace, an upper-bourgeois residential area. The Casino (demolished in 1939) survived its first decade with French comedies, housing pantomimes and ballets during the winter season, when the Tivoli was closed. Ten years later, in 1857, two more theatres were established. One, which bore several names, was in the western outskirts in Fredriksberg in an area of parkland. This Morskabsteater (Amusement Theatre) was finally taken over by the famous actress Betty Nansen, after whom it was named (1917–43) and later renamed (1980–).

The most important theatre for operetta became the Folketeatret (People's Theatre), located at Nørregade in the northern and petit-bourgeois part of the old city, which is still in existence today. Its founder Hans Wilhelm Lange (1815–73) wanted to attract more middle- and lower-class audiences in the spirit of extending social access. The Folketeatret was the equivalent of many European suburban theatres, which were the first to include operettas in their repertoires. The scope of the Folketeatret's repertory resembled, however, that of other Danish theatres, made up principally of Parisian comedies, but occasionally including something by the most popular dramatists of the Wiener Volkstheater, F. J. Raimund and J. N. E. A. Nestroy.

The success of Jacques Offenbach and his satirical operettas was repeated in Copenhagen through the Folketeatret. It started in 1859 with *Ved Lygteskin* (Le mariage aux lanternes). *Orpheus i Underverdenen* (Orphée aux enfers) opened on 11 October 1860 and made a run of ten seasons, and, although performances were not given every night, it was performed there practically every year until 1870. The Folketeatret created an audience expectation for operettas, and the theatre became the strongest competitor to the Casino. Even when the Casino tried to open three days later with *Orpheus i Underverdenen,* it had to close after nine performances. Their abridged German version could not compete with the original. The next new title had to wait until 24 November 1865, when *Den skjønne Helene* (La belle Hélène) opened in the Folketeatret, an immediate success that lasted the next four years (1865–9). The coming decades saw several revivals in other private theatres, but the Folketeatret still gained the chance to open with *Pariserliv* (La vie parisienne) in 1876.

In 1864, a war between Prussia and Denmark led to the loss of the Holstein and the northern Schleswig provinces to the expanding Prussia. This resulted in bitter feelings towards the German cultural sphere and re-enforced Denmarks' orientation towards French culture. The war may also be one of the factors that explains the six-year delay of the staging of *Die Fledermaus* in Copenhagen. First performed in Vienna in 1874, it was not until May 1880 that the *Flagermusen* (Die Fledermaus) was taken up by the Folketeatret, where there were a mere nineteen performances. Later, in 1896–7, it was the Casino that performed *Flagermusen*, with greater success. As one of the few revivals of *Flagermusen* in Copenhagen, it is worth noting how the Royal Theatre in 1930 presented it in a 'modernized version' by Erich Wolfgang Korngold and Max Reinhardt. In the 1970s, only the Kongelige Teater took up *Flagermusen* regularly; the work entered its operatic repertoire and showcased the theatre's high standard of singing.

The Casino was responsible for the first foray into British operetta, *The Mikado* by Gilbert and Sullivan. The interval after the London première (1885) was short, as this Japonaiserie appeared in Copenhagen only two years later (1887). *Mikadoen* ran for a couple of years and was revived in 1892 by both the Casino and the Folketeatret in competing performances.

The emergence of private theatres in Copenhagen seemed unexhausted: the Dagmarteatret opened in 1883 with Johann Strauss's *Den lystige Krig* (Der lustige Krieg), followed in 1884 by Carl Millöcker's *Tiggerstudent* (Der Bettelstudent). The rest of Strauss's works arrived only sporadically, just like the selection of Franz von Suppé's works. The Nørrebros Teatret (Northbridge theatre) opened in 1886 and two years later presented Sullivan's *H.M.S. Pinafore* with the title *Den gode Fregat Pinafore*. In the same year, this operetta was performed by the Dagmarteatret with an all-Danish title *Fregatten Jylland* (Frigate Jutland). Somewhat surprisingly, the other works by the London operetta kings were not seen in this maritime city, which relied instead on the revivals of French and German works.

The rights to Franz Lehár's *Die lustige Witwe* (Vienna, 1905) were immediately bought for the Casino, where, as *Den glade enke*, it had a run of a year and a half in 1906-7. During the great Lehár epidemic, Danish performers also toured Scandinavian cities, which in turn had their own competing *Widow*s. The work had many revivals, one in 1923 at the Scala Teatret. Emmerich Kálmán's reception in Copenhagen happened in the usual way: *Efteraarsmanøvrer* (Ein Herbstmanöver, 1909) came from Berlin to the Casino for the spring of 1910, when Kálmán himself stood as conductor. However, Kálmán's great wartime success, *Czardasfyrstinden* (Die Csárdásfürstin, 1915) went, instead, to the Scala Teatret in February 1917. This was an old and frequently renovated venue adjacent to the Tivoli. The Scala Teatret went on to host Kálmán's works during the 1920s: *Bajaderen* (Die Bajadere), *Grevinde Maritza* (Gräfin Mariza) and *Cirkusprinsessen* (Die Zirkusprinzessin). The interdependence of Kálmán and the Scala Teatret is comparable to Offenbach and the Folketeatret during the 1860s. It was profitable for all concerned: the composer's agent knew he would have a well-oriented audience and the audience knew what to expect. Paul Abraham's *Bal paa Savoy* (Ball im Savoy) had only a short run in the Ny Teatret, 1934–5, which remained one large venue close to the railway station. The Fønix Teatret (later the Fredriksbergs Teater and Aveny Teater) produced Abraham's *Victoria og hendes Husar* (Viktoria und ihr Husar) and then operettas by Ralph Benatzky and Oscar Straus. Fønix housed Benatzky's *Im weissen Rössl,* played with the same Danish title as the original comedy *Sommer i Tyrol,* which was well known in Copenhagen.

The frequency of operetta productions in Copenhagen fell away by the 1930s, allowing only the best ones to survive. Not even the Schlager operettas could save the situation. What did survive, however, were the Danish vaudevilles and some of the evergreen French music theatre of the previous century – a unique feature of Copenhagen. A particular episode can be observed during the five years of German occupation of Denmark (9 April 1940 – 5 May 1945). The Nørrebros Teatret survived by showing a complete round of German favourite operettas and several nostalgic German plays from the nineteenth century.[2] The reopening of the Nørrebros Teatret after the war in January 1946 was marked by waving the old French colours – with *Skønne Helene*.

In the 1950s and 1960s, operettas finally gave way to musicals. Yet, when a London West End-style musical stage, Det Ny Teatret, reopened in 1994 it also tried its luck with two perennials: *Flagermuse* (1994) and *Den glade enke* (1997). An interesting new phenomenon is the Operette-kompagniet Polyhymnia, which has taken on the responsibility for keeping this demanding genre alive by producing one classical operetta each year in the old Court Theatre (Hofteatret, at the Theatre Museum in Christiansborg). Their list of annual productions since 1997 has included a broad spectrum of the basic repertoire for the pleasure of operetta fans old and new.[3]

Christiania, the 'Little Copenhagen' Turns into a Nationalistic Oslo

Although Norway belonged to Sweden (1814–1905), its cultural life remained very much Danish until the 1830s, when Norwegian nationalist movements started to emerge in literature and art, making a stand against all Danish cultural domination as well as against what was perceived to be an emergent Swedish hegemony. The Norwegian-language movement led by academics was backed up by the rural and religious populations, living in the isolated valleys and fjords of mostly the western provinces. The three cities of the Atlantic coast, Trondheim, Bergen and Stavanger grew rapidly in their commerce and, thus, strengthened the identity of the western Norwegian bourgeoisie. Beside the 'Bokmål' (the 'book-tongue' or Eastern Norwegian) standards based on the eastern dialects and the Danish language, another standard was developed: the Nynorsk (new Norse), based on the western and rural dialects.

The Christiania Theatre (1827–99) found its permanent location in 1837 by the Bankplassen, a square in the oldest part of the city. Until the

1850s, its members were hired from Denmark and the repertoire echoed that of Copenhagen, as can be seen in a study by Børre Qvamme (2000).[4] French *opéras comiques* and vaudevilles by Auber and Boieldieu were played from 1830s to the end of the century. Danish vaudevilles and Heiberg's lyric drama *Elverhøj* came up regularly after that. Mrs Heiberg's *En Søndag på Amager* was performed over 120 times between 1848–94 in Christiania. The opening productions of *Orpheus i Underverdenen* (1864) and *Den skjønne Helene* (1866) in the Christiania Teatern arrived after only a slight delay.

By the 1870s, Christiania was also suffering from an operetta epidemic, which was cured by the opening of some new venues in the city for the active Danish and Swedish companies, as well as for some domestic initiatives. First among the private theatres was an old social entertainment locale and its stage at Møllergate, which between 1867 and 1883 was the main venue for the lighter musical repertoire (after 1876 it was called the Christiania Folketeatret). During the succeeding years it constantly played new operettas by Offenbach and his French competitors. *Fatinitza* by Suppé was of special interest in northern Europe, as its first act depicted a snowball war among soldiers in the Bulgarian mountains, before entering into a Turkish harem for the second act. The Folketeatret was active until 1885.

Christiania could not live without a Tivoli park of its own on the western side of the present city centre and near the modern city hall. Here, the Klingenberg Teater started as a summer venue but was gradually equipped for winter seasons, too. Its reputation was boosted by the Swede Knut Tivander, who drew audiences during his dynamic management (1876–8). He brought to Christiania Strauss's *Flaggermusen* (performed in Swedish as *Läderlappen),* which arrived only three years after it appeared in Vienna in the summer of 1877 and before it reached Copenhagen. Tivander himself sang Eisenstein, but it is remarkable that in this production Doctor Falke was the young handsome Swede, Albert Ranft, the future impresario.

The Tivoli Theatre, as the Klingenberg was renamed, would alternate operas and operettas, according to the nature of the company who hired it. In 1888, an English company played *The Mikado*, but, lacking a chorus, the result was a halfway effort. Sullivan was recognized as a master of his genre, however. Compensation came in 1890 when the private Vasateatern from Stockholm produced a successful version of *Mikadoen*. The main building of the Tivoli Theatre was gradually worn out until it was demolished in 1936.

For serious opera, Kristiania (with its new spelling since 1877) was dependent on the appointed manager of the Christiania Theatre. Ludvig

Josephson's period in 1873–7 was full of ambition for both drama and opera, but a permanent ensemble could not be maintained. The hiring of musical talent resulted in the increase of the lighter musical repertory, especially after 1885, when Bjørn Bjørnson was the theatre manager (1885–96), but operettas were also played. Strauss's *Flagermusen* came in for a revival run before and after New Year's Eve 1895/6, and it was performed more than fifty times over the next two years.

The Christiania Theatre was elevated to the status of Nationalteatret in 1899 and provided with a sumptuous new house close to the royal castle. Soon its finances became problematic, but a true helper was found, Lehár's *Den glade enke*, which opened on Boxing Day (Andre dagen jul) 1906. In the twentieth century, there were six productions of *Den glade enke* in 1908, 1938, 1955, 1956 and 1987 each played in seven or eight tours.

A more downmarket venue for operettas in Kristiania from 1897 onwards was Centralteatret. A beer hall and a dancing locale (Alhambra) were turned into theatre by Alma and Johan Fahlström, wherein the husband was the actor and the wife the actual manager. Later, they managed another locale, Eldorado on Torvgate, which was called Fahlstrøms Teater from 1903 to 1911. Centralteatret was bought by Harald Otto in 1902, who had been to Chicago and learnt how to run a successful entertainment business. He was the manager and the successful owner until his death in 1928, when his son took over until 1959. Centralteatret introduced *Czardasfyrstinnen* on 30 April 1917, with Naima Wifstrand cast in the leading role of Sylva Varescu. She was a major star from Stockholm, who had also enjoyed success in Kristiania. Interestingly, perfomances of Kálmán's major works arrived much later in the Nationalteatret, with *Czardasfyrstinnen* in 1934 and *Grevinne Maritza* in 1939.

The city, renamed Oslo in 1925, was clearly slow in getting a national opera institution started. Qvamme[5] attributes this to the Norwegian mindset: primarily, the commitment to economic austerity. The nationalist climate was also very much dominated by influential religious and puritan (English and American) sectarian movements, according to which anything but churchgoing was considered sin. All luxury was unnecessary, and any light entertainment should be condemned. This attitude was adopted by the leftist academics and the radical workers' movements of the 1920s. Operetta became anathema for political and cultural extremists and practically faded away from the city. No operettas were performed in the new theatre founded in 1913, which confined itself to the Nynorsk language. The repertory of Det Norske Teatret consisted of domestic and translated plays on mainly agrarian topics. They included music in the 'folktune' idiom. Only after World War II, were the more popular American musicals translated and performed in Nynorsk, such as *Teaterbåten* (Showboat) in 1950, *Annie Get Your Gun* in 1956 and *Oklahoma!* in 1960. This constitutes the introduction of musicals to Norway.

The municipal Oslo Nye Teatret in 1959 combined several previous institutions and had several venues at its disposal. It had to take responsibility for musical theatre, including revivals of the most canonized operettas. Den Norske Opera had its residence at the Youngplatsen from 1959 until the construction of the most modern opera house by the seaside and the formal establishment of the Norske Opera and Ballet in 2008 – now located very close to the oldest theatrical venues of the capital. In 2013, *Flaggermusen* had its most recent production in the new opera house.

Christianian urban culture, despite its very lively and businesslike operetta landscape until World War I, was long overshadowed by the rural, religious and social-democratic (read: didactic and moralistic) climate of opinion in Norway. By 2000, the genre was gradually recovering as part of the European urban heritage.

Stockholm's Theatre Landscapes in the Era of Operettas

The advent of permanent theatre to Sweden can justly be attributed to Gustav III (1746–92) and his personal passion for opera and drama in particular.[6] Many *opéras comiques* were adapted to take place in Sweden. The Royal Opera (Kungliga operan) was built opposite the Royal Palace on the northern side of Stockholm's strait, the Strömmen. Between 1825 and 1863, the dramatic theatre had to share the opera house with the musicians.

The monopoly of royal theatres was broken in 1846, when a new house was erected on the eastern side of the Kungsträdgården (Royal Gardens), called Mindre Teatern (Smaller Theatre). It was run mostly by Edvard Stjernström until 1863, when King Karl XV bought it in order to provide a house for the royal dramatic theatre. So it became the Old Dramaten, active from 1863 to 1907, and was abandoned only when the present Dramaten was built in 1907.

The first production of *Orfeus i underjorden* in Stockholm was staged by Pierre Joseph Deland and his troupe on 13 September 1860 at the Djurgårdsteatern, located in the Royal Game Park (Djurgården). This was a summer theatre used since the 1820s and 1830s as the Stockholm stage for touring provincial companies. Deland presented the German version of *Orfeus*, translated into Swedish, and he himself played the prince of Arkadia. As Pierre Deland headed for Finland, there was opportunity for another production in Stockholm, taken by Edvard

Stjernström in his elegant Mindre Teatern at the Kungsträdgården. Stjernström put on *Orfeus i undervärlden* in the French original version (28 December 1860). *Orfeus* could thus continue its run in Stockholm throughout the season. The next April Stjernström staged also *Ba-ta-clan*, the 'musical chinoiserie' by Offenbach. When Deland returned in the spring he was able to continue with his production of *Orfeus*, which was considered funnier than Stjernström's.

The southern side of the city, the artisans' and workers' district of Södermalm, got its first private theatre in 1852. Södra Teatern (Southern Theatre) was immediately occupied by light comedies, music and vaudevilles, and later became the venue for the popular music-hall variant, the Swedish Revue [Revy], with songs and sketches. In its commitment to the popular genres, it is no wonder that it was actually the Södran that became the real Offenbach theatre of Stockholm.[7] Some of von Suppé's and Millöckers's works were played at the Södran, but strangely, no more of the Viennese repertory came there nor any of the *fin-de-siècle* operettas; domestic musical entertainment and the Revue programme took over.

The social division of the city was reflected in the rivalry between the Mindre Teatern/Dramaten and the Södran. *Sköna Helena* had a second opening in the north-side Dramaten in 1865, where the bourgeoisie could see it on their own side of the city. Knut Almlöf, having been Deland's first Jupiter, was now Menelaus. During the next decade, the Mindre Teatern/Dramaten remained the forum for 'respectable people' to enjoy operettas. The success of *Die Fledermaus* was crucial: *Läderlappen* was premiered there as early as 2 December 1875. The performance was welcomed and acquired a constant position in the repertory; it was later repeated, at first in almost all the important private theatre venues, and then in the opera houses of Stockholm.

Albert Ranft (1858–1938) was a rather exceptional feature in the Scandinavian theatre, an actor-director who for almost three decades managed between ten and fifteen theatres. He sang in Kurt Tivander's troupe as Falke in the first *Läderlappen* in Christiania in 1877. Formerly a capable actor in serious and contemporary dramas, Ranft took up stage direction, which he wanted to accomplish in a well-planned and rational way. Having inherited money, Ranft started his independent entrepreneurship and hired several venues in the country, filling them with his companies. Later, in Stockholm, he was astute in shaping his venues for different genres.

The private Vasateatern (1886), named after the 'national' royal dynasty and close to the railway station, had from the beginning a strong profile for musical theatre. In 1895 Ranft hired the Vasateatern and mixed its repertoire of operettas with contemporary drama that challenged even the Dramaten itself. Ranft remained a devotee of serious theatre, although the demand for entertaining theatre was growing exponentially. The operetta would fully take over the Vasateatern again in 1898 with Sidney Jones's *The Geisha* (Geishan). For the folkish comedies, Ranft hired the Södra Teatern (1900–26), which was suited to such fare, being in the workers' district, and even the old Djurgårdsteatern (1882–1916). In Gothenburg he held on to the local Stora Teatern (1899–1917).

Albert Ranft's largest venue was the Svenska Teatern (1898–1925) in Blasieholmsgatan, which he bought in 1898, and where he revived some Offenbach operettas: *Sköna Helena* in 1900 and *Storhertiginnan von Gérolstein* in 1903. After that, the house concentrated on spoken drama with Olof Molander's famous stagings of Strindberg's new historical dramas, even *The Dream Play* in 1907. The Svenska Teatern was the 'crown jewel' in Ranft's business, competing with the Dramaten, The Royal Dramatic Theatre.

For operettas, Ranft needed an elegant new venue, and so the Oscarsteatern was built in 1906 at the Kungsgatan, named after Oscar II, who even lent his name to the Swedish belle époque, the Oscarian time. Never could there have been a better first success for new musical theatre than Lehár's *Den glada änkan* in 1907, which then spread its radiance over the coming years and over Ranft's businesses: the Oscarsteatern took 1,300 spectators every night and held the leading position for new operettas: *Czardasfurstinnan* opened there in 1916.

All of Ranft's theatres presented revivals of the most popular operettas, and even the Royal Opera was under his leadership in 1908–10. Yet Ranft was unjustly accused by sectarian priests for the moral decline of the audiences. He defended himself by publishing extensive catalogues of his repertoires: they were a rich selection of what was available in new European drama. Ranft's catastrophe came with the fire at the Svenska Teatern in 1925 but gradually also through the coming of cinema, the changing structures of society and new tastes in entertainment. Sadly, Ranft, this former emperor, had to go back to touring in the countryside to pay his debts and earn a living. Until World War II, the Oscarsteatern still played operettas and comedies. After the war, American musicals gradually found their home there. But the top ten classical operettas regularly starred the best from Dramaten, such as the actor Jarl Kulle as Danilo or as Henry Higgins in *My Fair Lady*.

Two influential systems expanded the operettas to provincial cities. One was the Folkets park institution; these 'people's parks' were founded in every town, mostly by the workers' movement. They had a summer stage available, which offered amusement for the large lower-middle-class and working-class audiences. The other Swedish speciality was the Riksteatern

(National Touring Company, established in 1933), which provided the countryside with theatre, just when the old companies began to need subsidies. Operettas formed part of the Riksteatern's regular tours, and the Södra Teatern was its venue in the capital. The operetta was kept alive and included works almost forgotten: *Lilla helgonet* (Mam'zelle Nitouche) in 1968, *Kusinen från Batavia* (Der Vetter aus Dingsda) in 1983 and *Den sköna Galatea* (Die schöne Galathée) in 1984.

Stockholm's strong theatre industry kept operetta alive into the 1960s. In the city of Malmö, operettas also remained in the repertoire during the 1960s. The Göteborg Stora Teatern concentrated on serious opera and ballet, until Folke Abenius during the 1970s wanted to pay homage to operetta. It was done simply by taking it seriously, as Walther Felsenstein had done during his time with the Komische Oper, Berlin. Abenius's interesting revival of *Czardasfurstinnan* in 1976 was a landmark. Post-1968 Sweden loved to debate everything in the press, and now came the question whether these old products of the class society should be shown at all. In Göteborg this successful revival paradoxically paved the way for the building of the new opera house (1994).[8]

Folkoperan (People's Opera) in Stockholm is a private institution that presents operas in contemporary and intellectually stimulating productions. They have had operettas intermittently, such as *Den sköna Galatea* in 1978, *Läderlappen* in 1992, *Orfeus i underjorden* in 2004 and, in 2008, *Den glada änkan*, with a modified feminist libretto by Suzanne Osten, described as a 'passion murder of patriarchy'. After the left-leaning years of the 1970s and 1980s, a postmodern understanding of historical genres was developed and with it came some operetta revivals during the 1990s and 2000s.

Helsinki: Operettas, Languages and Social Classes

In the 1860s, Helsinki was the growing capital of the Grand Duchy of Finland (1809–1917) within the Russian Empire. Its wooden theatre (Esplanade Theatre 1827-60) had received touring companies from the west, playing in Swedish – the first language of the Finnish nobility and bourgeoisie – and, from the east and south, German opera and drama troupes on their way around the shores of the Baltic Sea, heading to or coming from St Petersburg, the imperial capital. Turku (Åbo) in the west and Viipuri (Viborg) in the east were the halfway cities, with proper theatre houses enabling longer seasons.

Nya Theatern (New Theatre, later Svenska Teatern / Swedish Theatre) was erected in 1860 and first hired by Pierre Joseph Deland, who opened with his brand-new production of *Orfeus i underjorden,* seen already in Stockholm. On the way, while in Turku he put on *Orfeus,* which is thus recorded as the first operetta performance in Finland. So *Orfeus* was presented in Stockholm and Helsinki in the same Deland production. In the same season, he produced other frequent runners, like Hervé's *Lilla helgonet* (Mam'zelle Nitouche) and, soon after, the *Nürnbergerdockan* (La poupée de Nuremberg, 1852) by Adolphe Adam. The next Offenbach performance, *Sköna Helena,* came in 1865, given by Otto Lindmark's troupe. The venue was the Arkadia, the previous wooden theatre 'upgraded' and relocated just outside the town boundary. The audiences had now developed a real appetite for operetta – and the first moral reproaches followed. The Swedish Theatre then continued with a range of Offenbach, Auber, Boieldieu and Massé during the following decades. In November 1876, the première of *Läderlappen* was whistled and jeered at, and so were the two subsequent performances. A group of 'morally indignant university students' accused the theatre of using the state subsidies to provide morally inferior entertainment to the elite.[9] The performances were ended, and the students were given their penalties of six- to ten-months suspension, but *Die Fledermaus* had to wait fourteen years for its return to Helsinki in 1890.

This demonstration was a ploy designed to further the students' zealous desire to support the Finnish Theatre and Opera Company (1872–1902), which found itself in huge debt and was partly therefore tied to performing in the shabby Arkadia-theatre. This Finnish-language company was founded by the Fennoman party, which wanted to increase the use of vernacular Finnish and elevate it to a language of culture. The leader of the Finnish Theatre Company Kaarlo Bergbom (1843–1906) was a supporter of historical drama and romantic operas, and for him the Offenbachian satire was a horror; operettas never came to his theatre. This idealistic edifice with its commitment to the Finnish-speaking lower classes led him to accept only folk-oriented musical comedies. Even when it was elevated to the National Theatre of Finland (in 1902) it never hosted any operettas. Operettas in Helsinki were enjoyed only in the Swedish language.

Helsinki was also home to Russian garrisons with officers and their families who needed a lot of entertainment, offered first in the Arkadia-theatre, where several Russian-language operetta productions were given, such as the most popular Offenbach operettas, *Orfej v adu* and *Prekrasnaâ Elena,* among others, during the late 1860s. These were performed by Russian groups who had regular seasons in Helsinki, especially at the time of the Orthodox Fast. In 1880, a special Russian theatre house, the Alexandrovski Teatr (Alexander Theatre), was completed and filled, first, by Italian operas, then by Russian theatrical works and, in the 1890s, by Russian nationalist operas.

The demand for entertainment brought in competing operetta companies, mostly from Scandinavia, who used the now two available private venues: the stage in the park by the Helsinki southern sea pool, Brunnshusteatern (Kaivohuoneen teatteri (Theatre of the House of the Wellspring)), and the Apolloteatern (Apolloteatteri), located in the centre on the Esplanade opposite Hotel Kämp. Brunnshusteatern was hired by numerous Swedish companies performing operettas regularly for Finns and also for those Russian citizens for whom Helsinki was a summer spa. In 1899 an Austrian company had considerably increased the range of titles played in Helsinki, mostly, as might be expected, by introducing less familiar works by Strauss, Suppé and Zeller. In 1904, a group from the Vasateatern arrived, so Helsinki became an outpost of Albert Ranft's empire, who had come to know Finland during his time as an actor in 1891–2.

Apolloteatern by the Esplanade park also acquired its performers mostly from Stockholm, some Ranftian some not; others were Danish, but the spoken Danish language was too difficult to follow for audiences to whom Swedish was no problem. Apollo was the only theatre to play *The Mikado*, so Gilbert and Sullivan were rare guests in Helsinki. The English fleet was probably not so popular owing to its former military activity bombarding the Finnish coast at the time of the Crimean War (1854–5). The years around 1900–14 were the liveliest in Nordic touring activity. World War I brought difficulties, as non-Russian citizens could not remain in the country.

In 1907, there were three productions of *The Merry Widow* in Helsinki. The Danish company from the Fredriksbergs Morskabsteater put on guest performances in the Swedish Theatre, singing *Den glade enke* in May 1907 twenty times; record sales too were related to the success of the run of performances. But no sooner had the Danes left than in came Jenny Tscherninin-Larsson with her provisional Swedish ensemble. Their *Änkan* in the Alexandersteatern 'could not match the well-oiled Danish group'.[10] The third *Widow* came to the Brunnshsusteatern with August Bodén from Ranft's companies and Naima Wifstrand, the number two star, in the grand opening of *Den glada änkan* at the Oscarsteater in Stockholm.

The time had come to establish the Swedish Domestic Theatre Company (Svenska Inhemska Teatern), which hired the old Arkadia building, first presented *Lilla helgonet* and then, in 1908, *Den glada änkan*. These were the first domestic productions in Swedish and introduced the Finnish baritone Adolf Niska (1884–1960), who later made a triumphant career in Stockholm. Swedish-language activities in Helsinki were now provided by a second Swedish company, the Folkteatern company, until the Swedish spoken in Finland and by domestic actors was accepted in 1916 on the main stage of Helsinki's Svenska Teatern. The closest link with Stockholm was thus broken. In Turku, operettas were soon available in both Finnish and Swedish.

The first operetta in the Finnish language was *Pikku pyhimys* (Mam'zelle Nitouche), produced on 24 April 1904 by the permanent theatre in Viipuri (Suomalainen Maaseututeatteri, Finnish Theatre for the Provinces). Aino Haverinen thus became the capital of eastern Finland's first prima donna, and she went on to conquer all the operetta repertoire. She even headed a short-lived touring group Suomalainen Operetti (Finnish Operetta, 1912–19) first in Turku then in Viipuri.[11] This city was considered to produce its operettas most elegantly. During the 1930s there were usually two operetta premieres each year, plus revivals, providing advancement for the professional musicians and dancers of the city. This was interrupted in 1940, when Viipuri (in Russian Vyborg) and its province were annexed to the Soviet Union.

Operettas in Finnish found their best home at the Kansan Näyttämö (People's Stage) founded in 1907 in Helsinki. The venue was the Student Union House in the city centre, only one block north of the Swedish Theatre. In order to afford their serious modern repertory, they regularly confined themselves to operettas, for which there was a rapidly growing Finnish-speaking audience moving in from the countryside.

Ten years after the advent of the *Merry Widow* (1907), another triple season was experienced: *Die Csárdásfürstin* came in the spring of 1917 with three parallel productions and titles. The first was called *Varietéfurstinnan* at the Apolloteatern; it then appeared as *Zigenarfurstinnan* at the Svenska Teatern and then in Finnish as *Mustalaisruhtinatar* on the Kansan Näyttämö. This second Finnish-language theatre in Helsinki was later named the Kansanteatteri (People's Theatre) and played all the regular operettas, which in the 1920s starred Eine Laine and Sven Hildén, the leading couple, box-office magnets.

An important feature was the Workers' Theatres throughout Finland which presented operettas. This was different to the Norwegian workers' culture. From the 1910s to the 1940s, working-class audiences supported their own companies for entertainment. As the population was very divided after the tragic 1918 Civil War, it was more comfortable for the two classes to gather at their own theatrical and social venues, although they saw mostly the same repertoire, including operettas. Especially after World War II, given the keen hunger for culture, comfort and beauty, the two audiences started to mix, and operetta lovers could take their pick according to the quality of the performances, as happened in Tampere.

Seeing operetta in Helsinki could cross the language barrier, as it had been customary for the educated spectators to see their operettas presented 'more elegantly', as was the case at the Svenska Teatern. The same happened with American musicals: in the early 1960s, these could still be consumed in Swedish by Finnish spectators. In 1967 the Kansanteatteri, now renamed as the Helsingin Kaupunginteatteri (Helsinki City Theatre), was provided with a large, glamorous building and thus became the most important stage for large-scale musicals, as it was to remain.

As operetta faded in the early 1960s, the actress Hilkka Kinnunen founded her own private enterprise, Operettiteatteri, taking the main roles herself, in order to keep this somewhat outdated genre alive. She maintained her old working-class audiences, until the end of the 1980s, not least because of her choice of venues.

Until the end of the 1970s, even the top five canonic operettas had fallen out of the repertoire. The National Opera had regularly played operettas until the early 1970s but since then has offered a production only every five to ten years, mostly playing *Lepakko* (Die Fledermaus). There are also small private companies that bravely engage music students and young singers to build up their experience and to meet the continuing demand for operetta.

Conclusion

The cultural history of the four Nordic countries must be studied without nationalist blinkers. The interchange of people in the sphere of musical theatre has been constant, due to the subtle and normal form of 'cultural colonization', according to which a stronger metropole exerts its influence over a developing one. This can be seen in the two chains we have followed: Paris–Copenhagen–Oslo; and Berlin–Stockholm–Helsinki. All countries with a small population and their own distinct language are torn between embracing the 'big world' and building barriers to protect or to promote the 'vernacular' and what is understood as national – or chosen to be so.

More observations could be made on the variations of the political processes in the four countries, in which operetta has found its cultural niche somewhat differently according to the general acceptance of bourgeois entertainment culture as well as the public spaces and venues conquered by its festive appearances.

The 'cosmopolitanism' represented by operetta was also connected to the upper classes. The growing urban population presented the temptation for some political parties to attract their support by defending rural and 'national' values. But in some cases, operetta became working-class entertainment. As we have seen, these and other features in the social function of operetta were dependent on the dynamics of the infrastructures: capital vs regional, dominant vs vernacular language, urban vs rural, subsidized institutions vs commercial enterprises, competition between individual theatre businesses vs a corporate system of theatre venues, and bourgeois professional theatre practice vs working-class partly amateur theatre practice.

Another set of variations were determined by the cultural spheres in Europe: Denmark had an old connection with Paris but recurring problems with their closest neighbour, Prussia. In Sweden, there were fewer tensions with Berlin, while Helsinki reflected echoes from its triangle of close metropolises, Stockholm, Berlin and St Petersburg, the one-time train station to Europe for the Finns. In all these countries, the nationalistic historical narrative has too easily marginalized alternative narratives of the interdependence of neighbouring cultures, the mutual private travelling of the artists and their troupes to the other capitals and regional cities.

By the end of the 1800s, Helsinki had not developped any real commercial theatre landscape as had Copenhagen, in particular Stockholm and to some extent Oslo. As the emancipation of the vernacular languages carried with it a moral statement, either religious or class-based as in the case of Norway or moralistic and *Volksbildung* (educational) argument as in Finland, the new vernacular theatre institutions wanted to distinguish themselves by refusing to conform to the culturally dominant operetta culture. Once the vernacular floodgates had opened in the socially dynamic city of Viipuri in 1904, operettas performed in the Finnish language immediately began to spread across the country.

In the 1930s, when Copenhagen and Oslo had practically stopped staging operetta, it was still going strong in Stockholm and continued to do so until the late 1950s or 1960s. In Finland, operetta's heyday lasted from the 1920s to the 1950s and even into the early 1970s.

Although German and French operettas yielded to American musicals as the dominant music theatre genre during the 1960s, selected top classics like *Die Fledermaus*, *Die lustige Witwe* and *Die Csárdásfürstin* were regularly revived. The domestic production of different genres of 'Singspiel', 'Folklustspel med musik' and other nationally oriented genres emerged in all the Nordic countries though their lifespans varied . The Danes with their old vaudevilles in the repertoire are an interesting exception from the others. For several decades around 1900 and even until the 1950s, Stockholm could rightly be given the title of the 'operetta capital of Scandinavia'.

In Sweden, and elsewhere for the 1968 generation, operettas represented a vapid and outmoded genre, and the theatres were under pressure to stop playing them. Economic realities, however, forced them to continue – although operettas faded away somewhat with the ageing of their audiences. In all four countries, some devoted groups preserve the practice of this special, subtle and demanding musical and theatrical genre.

Notes

1. The following catalogues and databases have been used. Copenhagen: http://danskforfatterlek sikon.dk (accessed 15 Apr. 2019). Oslo: Öyvind Anker, Fullstendig registrant over forestellinger, forfattare, oversettere og komponister. Sesongregister (Oslo: Gyldendal Norsk Forlag, 1956); Børre Qvamme, *Musikkliv I Christiania. Fra Arilds tid til Arild Sandvold* (Oslo: Solum Forlag, 2000); Børre Qvamme, *Opera og operette i Kristiania* (Oslo: Solum Forlag, 2004). Stockholm: much can be found in the wikipedia.se under each theatre, based on the comprehensive lists of repertoires, which were collected in the 1970s. Finland: http://ilona.tinfo.fi (accessed 15 Apr. 2019).
2. This list is almost complete: *Grevinde Maritza, Czardasfyrstinden, Valsedrømme, Dollarprinsessen, Zigøjnerbaronen, Cirkusprinsessen, Greven af Luxemburg, Fuglekræmmeren, Tre Valse, Victoria og hendes Husar* and a Danish sailor play *Styrman Karlsens Flammer*.
3. *Valsedrømme, En Nat i Venedig, Greven af Luxemburg, H.M.S. Pinafore, Tiggerstudentern, Fuglekræmmeren, Den glade enke, Wienerblod, Mød mig på Cassiopeia, Pariserliv, Mikadoen, Flagermusen, Frøken Nitouche, Sommer i Tyrol, Landmandsliv, Piraterne fra Penzance, Den skønne Helene, Grevinde Mariza.*
4. Børre Qvamme, *Musikkliv i Christiania: fra Arilds tid til Arild Sandvold* (Oslo: Solum Forlag, 2000).
5. Qvamme, *Opera og operette*, 332.
6. Before Gustav III's reign, the arts had already experienced a flowering moment in Queen Christina's court ballets around 1650. After the time of regular visits of Dutch and German companies to the court of Stockholm, Swedish became the language of touring companies in the 1750s.
7. Södran played new Offenbach operettas annually: *Herrarna Dunans resa* (1862), *Sköna Helena* (1865), *Gérolstein* and *Le 66* (1867), *Pariserliv* (1868), *Primadonnan* (1869), *Frihetsbröderna* (Les brigands, 1870), *Prinsessan af Trapezunt* (1871), *Riddar Blåskägg* (Barbe-bleue, 1873).
8. See Sven Åke Heed, 'Operett och musikal' in Tomas Forser & Sven Åke Heed (eds.), *Ny svensk teaterhistoria. Vol. 3: 1900-talets teater.* (Stockholm: Gidlunds förlag, 2007), 277–82.
9. Sven Hirn, *Operett i Finland 1860–1918* (Helsinki: Svenska Litteratursällskapet i Finland. SLS, 1992), 30–2; Pentti Paavolainen, 'Two Operas or One – or None: Crucial Moments in the Competition of Operatic Audiences in Helsinki in the 1870s' in Anne Sivuoja, Owe Ander, Ulla-Britta Broman-Kananen and Jens Hesselager (eds.), *Opera on the Move in the Nordic Countries during the Long 19th Century.* Docmus Research Publications 4 (Helsinki: Sibelius-Academy, 2012), 145. Cf. also Wolff, *Opéra-comique* (2018).
10. Hirn, *Operett i Finland*, 88–89.
11. In Finland, a special form of unfortunate taxation (excise duty) was decreed between 1915 and 1981. 'Huvivero' ('nöjeskatt'; amusement tax) varied between 10 and 25 per cent of the ticket prices and was levied on movies, dances, variety shows, theatre etc. The tax was high, especially in the 1920s, and created a vicious circle for theatres, which, in order to pay the taxes they owed, needed to offer the public more of the light repertoire. Ironically, this meant that taxation was increased as a consequence. The purpose was to fund social welfare projects, but in some cases the tax was higher than the public subsidies.

Recommended Reading

Anker, Öyvind. Fullstendig registrant over forestellinger, forfattare, oversettere og komponister. Sesongregister. / The Repertoire of Christiania Theatre 1827–1899.

A Complete Record of Performances, Authors, Translators and Composers. Index to Seasons. Oslo: Gyldendal Norsk Forlag, 1956.

Forser, Tomas and Sven Åke Heed, eds. *Ny svensk teaterhistoria. Vol. 2: 1800-talets teater.* Stockholm: Gidlunds förlag, 2007.

Forser, Tomas and Sven Åke Heed, eds. *Ny svensk teaterhistoria. Vol. 3: 1900-talets teater.* Stockholm: Gidlunds förlag, 2007.

Heed, Sven Åke. 'Operett och musikal'. In Tomas Forser and Sven Åke Heed, eds., *Ny svensk teaterhistoria. 3. 1900-talets teater.* Stockholm: Gidlunds förlag. 2007, 258–84.

Hirn, Sven. *Operett i Finland 1860–1918.* Svenska Litteratursällskapet i Finland. Helsinki: SLS, 1992.

Hoogland, Rikhard, ed. *I avantgardets skugga. Brytpunkter och kontinuitet i svensk teater kring 1900.* LIR skrifter. [gupea.ub.gu.se] 2019.

Kvam, Kela, Janne Risum and Jytte Wiingaard, eds. *Dansk teaterhistorie.* 2 vols. Copenhagen: Gyldendal, 1992–3.

Lagerroth, Ulla-Britta and Ingeborg Nordin Hennel, eds. *Ny svensk teaterhistoria. Vol. 2: 1800-talets teater.* Stockholm: Gidlunds förlag, 2007.

Letellier, Robert Ignatius. *Operetta: A Sourcebook.* Vol. 1. Newcastle upon Tyne: Cambridge Scholars Publishing, 2015.

McConachie, Bruce. *Melodramatic Formations: American Theatre and Society, 1820–1870.* Studies in Theatre, History and Culture. Iowa City: University of Iowa Press, 1992.

Myggan Ericson, Uno, ed. *Myggans Nöjeslexikon: ett uppslagsverk om underhållning.* Stockholm: Bokförlaget Bra Böcker, 1992.

Niska, Adolf. *Mitt livs mazurka med Thalia. Äventyr i olika länder.* Stockholm: Albert Bonniers Förlag, 1931.

Norlander, Emil. 1918. *Det glada Stockholm. Från tingel-tangeln till den moderna kabareten.* Tionde Don Basuno-boken. Stockholm: Åhlén & Åkerlunds förlag a.b.

Nyblom, Teddy. *Operetten på Oscars. Från Albert Ranft till Anders Sandrew. 1906–1956.* Stockholm: Fridmans bokförlag, 1956.

Paavolainen, Pentti. 'Two Operas or One – or None. Crucial Moments in the Competition of Operatic Audiences in Helsinki in the 1870s'. In Anne Sivuoja, Owe Ander, Ulla-Britta Broman-Kananen and Jens Hesselager, eds., *Opera on the Move in the Nordic Countries during the Long 19th Century.* Docmus Research Publications 4. Helsinki: Sibelius-Academy, 2012.

Qvamme, Børre. *Musikkliv I Christiania. Fra Arilds tid til Arild Sandvold.* Oslo: Solum Forlag, 2000.

Qvamme, Børre. *Opera og operette i Kristiania.* Oslo: Solum Forlag, 2004.

Ranft, Albert. *Min Repertoir 1892–1921.* Stockholm: P. A. Norstedt & Söners Förlag, 1921.

Rosenqvist, Claes. 'En ny tids teaterkung'. In Ulla-Britta Lagerroth and Ingeborg Nordin Hennel, eds., *Ny svensk teaterhistoria. Vol. 2: 1800-talets teater.* Stockholm: Gidlunds förlag, 2007, 338–52.

Wolff, Charlotta. 'Opéra-comique, Cultural Polities and Identity in Scandinavia 1760–1800', *Scandinavian Journal of History*, 43, no. 3 (2018): 387–409.

11 Operetta in Greece

AVRA XEPAPADAKOU

Introduction

This chapter aims to present the history and the main features of operetta in Greece from the mid-nineteenth century until today. The introduction, dissemination and success of this musical genre, both in Greece and in Europe, is inherently connected to the development of an urban audience and the establishment of organized evening entertainment. Given that it is a genre cultivated exclusively in urban centres, its evolutionary path will be followed within the special historical and cultural framework of a new European state, which is recovering and struggling to reconnect with the Western world after 400 years of Ottoman occupation. As is the case with all related cultural phenomena in Greece, operetta too belongs to the area of the history of European theatre and European music; consequently, its trajectory in Greece needs first to be connected with the development of Greek urban life and the continuous trend for westernization and Europeanization characterizing nineteenth-century Greece. Secondly, in order to better approach the genre and follow its evolution, a brief sketch of its historical, social and cultural background is required.

Socio-historical Reality in Greece before the Appearance of Operetta

The Greek state was founded in 1830 and covered a very small territory at the southern tip of the Balkan peninsula. Its first period (1830–64), termed 'Ottonian' after the name of the first King of Greece, the Bavarian prince Otto, witnessed the foundation of the first state structures, originally in the city of Nauplion, and then in Athens, where the capital of the new state was subsequently transferred. During this period, the urban class was still unformed, and the dominant social group consists of Bavarian officials, rich expatriates, old landowners and military leaders of the successful revolution against the Ottoman Empire.

From the very first days of the establishment of modern Greece in 1830, catching up with lost time and getting into alignment with European cultural ways were tasks considered more than necessary. As a consequence, all eyes were turned to the West and a new, bourgeois lifestyle was adopted. Until the end of the century, rapid progress took place in Athens, the new capital of the independent Greek state, in the spread of western European habits, always within the general framework of conscious and hurried westernization.[1]

From the 1840s until the end of the 1860s, Italian opera reigned in the nightlife of the major Greek urban centres. Italian troupes established themselves in Athenian theatres, as well as in the tried and true 'hotspots' of the Ionian Islands, populated by Greeks but not yet annexed to the Greek state. These troupes received state funding on a regular basis and enjoyed a very wide audience. It is hard to imagine the impression of the first performances of European opera on ears accustomed, until then, only to monophonic Byzantine choral music, folk songs and oriental *amane* songs. Italian opera was even more scandalizing on a visual level, since it brought for the first time women performers on stage, and on a content level, with its focus on sensuality, erotic passion, romantic death and other extreme emotional situations.[2]

The second period (1865–1900), the reign of the next (this time Danish) king, George I, brought about major social reforms and a rapid urbanization of Greek society. The country's borders expanded with the annexation of new lands (Ionian Islands, Thessaly, Epirus); the social make-up of the population changed with the incorporation of the extremely advanced Ionian society; and local cultural life knew a new development, thanks to the rise of native artistic creation, which included a large spectrum of musical and theatrical compositions, containing, as a high point, the operas by Ionian composers. Meanwhile, three booming trade centres, the city-ports of Piraeus, Patras and Hermoupolis in Syros brought an increase to the country's urban population. This population was the audience which thronged the new theatres, built in Athens, the Ionian Islands and the three-above-mentioned new dynamic cultural markets.

In the same period, the total rule of Italian opera was threatened by the first French operetta and vaudeville companies who knocked hesitantly on the door of the Athens Winter Theatre in 1868, only to completely conquer, by the beginning of the next decade, the capital's theatrical market and draw the immature nouveau-bourgeois society, including King George I, into a Bacchic trance in the rhythm of *cordax*, i.e., the cancan. Along with their intriguing repertoire, the French artists who arrived in the Greek capital brought with them outlandish theatrical morals, and therefore created a novel sensation in the Athenian audience – but also provoked a storm of reactions from the socially and aesthetically inexperienced Athenian public.[3] Also in the same period, a new local genre of music theatre was born, termed 'comic idyll', while the distinction of cultural life between urban genres (opera, operetta, vaudeville, *café chantant, variété*, prose theatre) and folk/popular ones (open-air spectacles, shadow-theatre, *café-aman*) became stronger.

Already, by the start of the 1870s, the new king clearly showed his preference for *la culture française*. For the first time, sources of the period made mention of French comedies and vaudevilles performed in the palace. At the same time, the *café chantant* was promoted as the latest thing in bourgeois fashion. The first *café chantant* in the city opened in 1871, on the banks of the river Ilissos. It achieved success and deeply influenced the city's theatre life, as it signalled the beginning of organized music entertainment in Athenian cafés and opened the way for the first Athenian open-air theatres.[4] There, French and German beauties drove the audience crazy with their airs and graces, as well as with their light, coquettish and scandalizing repertoire.

The official advent of the operetta, with a royal seal to boot, must be placed in the autumn of the same year (1871). Since the summer, in view of the visit of King George's Danish family in the coming October, the government and major private sponsors had been collaborating to collect sufficient funds in a hurry and had sent two Greek impresarios to Paris in order to form a French operetta group. As soon as the French company started to perform, staging *La vie parisienne*, 'a drama of well-known plot and performance, serious, decent, educative on many levels, enforcing the most noble sentiments of human heart',[5] the first grumbles began against the 'vaudevillian mania which had taken over our youth and part of our society'.[6] Hervé's, Lecocq's and Offenbach's operettas, along with naughty French vaudeville plays provoked virulent reactions of the conservative press, which railed against the indecent spectacles, the bedroom tales, infidelities and divorces, the frenzied dances and the scandalous verbal obscenities.

A major scandal was created by the two great hits of the Bouffes-Parisiens, *Orphée aux enfers* and *La belle Hélène*, which were viewed as tasteless parodies of antiquity. What primarily offended some of the Athenians of the 1870s was not the affront to propriety and to bourgeois morality. It was the blasphemy against classical antiquity, a taboo period for the Greeks of the nineteenth century, for whom the antique marble pillars were the main support of their newly built but still feeble national identity. Nevertheless, most of the art-loving Athenian public, irrespective of gender and age (including the high-born guests of the palace), instead of being revolted by the 'moral poison of Greek civilization', rushed to secure their theatre boxes in order to enjoy Zeus, dressed up as an insect, buzzing the 'Fly Duet' and the whole pantheon squealing in delirium during the 'Gallop of Hell'.[7]

The triumphant course of French operetta continued over the next few years, spreading to the theatrical scenes of smaller cities, like those of Patras, Hermoupolis and Zakynthos. The most popular play by far was *La fille de Madame Angot* by Charles Lecocq. The popularity of the genre grew even more, when, in 1883, Armenian operetta troupes visited Athens to perform the oriental, Turkish-language operetta *Leblebici Horhor Aga* (Horhor Aga the Chickpea Seller) by Tigran Tsouhadjian, a play which caused a great impression on the Greek audience, thanks to 'the great originality of its oriental characters', and the 'peculiar' and 'strange' harmony of its music, which distantly evoked European melodies intermingled with 'intoxicating and sensual oriental melodies'.[8] In total, more than fifty French troupes visited Greece between 1872 and 1899, performing more than 300 different plays.[9] The most important troupes are those of Lavergne, Alaïzat, Moreau and Lassalle-Charlet.[10] French and Viennese operettas performed by foreign touring companies were all sung in their original languages; they were translated into Greek only when performed by Greek troupes.

The First Greek Operetta and Related Genres

The addiction to light musical theatre soon bore fruit, as a series of new musical theatrical genres were born out of this systematic contact during the period of the *fin de siècle*: singing comedy, comic idyll, revue and local Greek operetta. However, there is an early native genre which should be considered as a forerunner of Greek operetta: the Ionian comic idyll. It appeared as early as 1832 and constituted a mixed genre of Ionian musical singing comedy, mainly a comedy of manners, but occasionally also verging on political satire, which flourished in the islands of Cephallonia and Zakynthos. It is set to music often borrowed from well-known operatic melodies but may also include original pieces. Ionian comic idylls seem to have been performed throughout the nineteenth century both in Ionian theatres and as open-air spectacles, by amateur troupes.[11]

In any case, the Ionian tradition of the comic idyll lies at the root of the first conscious attempt to compose a Greek operetta, by the Zakynthian composer Paulos Carrer, and his compatriot idyll-writer Ioannis Tsakasianos. Carrer, was the most productive and most important Greek opera composer of the mid-nineteenth century and a sensitive receiver of new trends in the international field of musical theatre. He must have sensed the decline of Italian opera and the rise of French musical theatre on the Greek stage, and he was probably the first who felt the necessity to create a local operetta production. The thought of trying his hand at a new genre must have occurred to him around the end of the 1870s, when he had the opportunity to see French operetta close up. His first taste of it took place through Italian mediation, when, in 1879, he watched, at the Apollo Municipal Theatre of Patras, a performance of the popular *La fille de Madame Angot* by an Italian troupe in Italian translation. The 'clandestine', as it was termed due to its Italian guise, introduction of 'this prancing and intoxicated genre was received with unadulterated and drunken enthusiasm' by the public of Patras.[12]

His idea of a Greek operetta solidified when he met the naïve *satire de moeurs* rhymed plays, with a strong *couleur locale*, published from 1884 onwards by the Zakynthian poet Ioannis Tsakasianos, which featured the local character of Sparrow. The *Sparrow* poems of Tsakasianos, which represented everyday life in Zakynthos in vivid colours and with satiric intent, provided Carrer with the fitting subject matter for his first operetta, entitled *Count Sparrow* or, *Swoons and tantrums*, on which he worked for two years, from 1886 until 1888. Carrer's words, when asking Tsakasianos to write him a libretto, in a letter dated July 1886 are characteristic: 'I shall propose to you, if you are interested, to inaugurate with me the genre of Greek operetta – a kind of *Madame Angot* . . . Write for me a libretto for the *Sparrow* of Zakythos.'[13]

The action of the 'one-act melodrama (operetta) in two parts' takes place in Zakynthos. Its plot is more reminiscent of a comic idyll of manners than of a saucy operetta. It is the love story of two young people belonging to different social classes who eventually come together despite all those opposing their union. The libretto is mostly in rhymed verse, except for a few short dialogue sections in prose. The separate singing numbers, namely the arias, duets, ensembles and male and female choruses, are composed in simple metres and are full of repetitions of stanzas and refrains. *Count Sparrow* is divided in two parts and consists of twelve short scenes. Its language is vernacular, with several dialectal elements.

Having expressed doubts about the quality of the libretto, in terms of both structure and content, Carrer set the first act to music and planned the second and third acts but never completed his composition. The only surviving part of the play is one of the musical pieces, the duet of the young lovers Tonis and Marina, which was published in the illustrated magazine *To Asty* in December 1888 (Figure 11.1). Since then, the fortune of this one act of *Count Sparrow* set to music is unknown. The 'first Greek operetta' has been left, in Carrer's own words 'to sleep the big sleep in the library'. Let us hope that it will one day awaken, upon its discovery in some Ionian archive.[14]

Figure 11.1 The duet 'My star-born love' from the operetta *Count Sparrow* by Pavlos Carrer as published in *To Asty*, 18 December 1888

In any case, at the same time, during 1887–9, musical theatre – sometimes in the form of singing comedy, as in the caustic *General Secretary* by Elias Kapetanakis (1893), and sometimes in the form of comic idyll of manners (though not operetta), as in, for example, *The Millers*, of unknown authorship (1888), the *Fortunes of Maroula* by

Demetrios Koromilas (1889) and *The Solution of the Oriental Question* by Demetrios Kokkos (1889) – underwent a period of triumphant success.[15] These plays have Greek plots but follow the familiar recipe of rearranging the music of popular European tunes in combination with folk-music motifs, by composers such as the Bavarian Andrea Seiller. The comic idyll enjoyed a monopoly on Greek stage production for about twenty years and constituted the training ground for the cultivation of the two most popular genres of musical theatre in Greece, operetta and revue.

At this point, a passing mention should be made of a Greek composer of light musical theatre who achieved considerable success on the London stage during the *fin de siècle*. This is Corfiot Napoleon Lambelet, who, after a relatively successful career as a composer, conductor and music teacher in Athens and in Alexandria, emigrated to London in 1898 and met with resounding success on the British musical stage with plays such as *Yashmak: A Story of the East* (1897), *The Transit of Venus* (1898) and *Valentine* (1918).[16]

The Advent of the Twentieth Century

The first four decades of the twentieth century up to the outbreak of World War II are marked by two major movements: urbanization and emigration, especially towards the USA. The victorious Balkan wars, and World War I expanded Greek territory even more, and added new urban centres, namely the vigorous multi-cultural Thessaloniki, while the Goudi Coup strengthened a new social power, the working class. The Asia Minor disaster, and the integration of 1.5 million refugees from the cosmopolitan cities of the western Asia Minor coast (Ionia) in Greek society is the most important event of the period, and had a tremendous impact on Greek social structure.

The rich cultural harvest of this period includes Athenian revue and operetta, two musical theatre genres that enjoyed great fortune. This period also sees the cultivation, in many forms, of urban popular song, the expansion of which is linked to the development of the record industry and is connected to the dominance of musical theatre on the Greek stage. Finally, the social osmosis with the Asia Minor refugees, with their urban background and oriental music tradition redefined the dividing lines between Western and oriental and had a determining impact on artistic production and cultural life in Greece. As will be demonstrated later, operetta would function as a meeting point between the different aesthetic trends of the period.

At the dawn of the twentieth century, the reigning queens of Athenian evening entertainment were operetta and revue. The high point of Athenian revue is to be placed in the period 1907–21, while operetta takes over from 1920 until the mid-1930s. The two genres share many common features but also present several differences. Revue has an episodic structure, with 'numbered acts', and aims to comment on and satirize current events,[17] while operetta possesses a stronger dramatic unity and a more developed plot. Although revue may be considered more 'popular' and operetta more 'urban', they are in fact two communicating vessels, which allow the free movement of composers, orchestras, soloists, dancers, producers and troupe leaders from one to the other. In general, one may describe the evolution of light theatre in twentieth-century Greece as initially a transition from the comedy of manners to cosmopolitanism, and subsequently to popular entertainment. So, one may observe, during the first phase of evolution of the genre, from the beginnings to the 1920s, the protagonists of comic idyll abandoning their traditional folk costumes to adopt elegant Western attire and European dances in order to enter the salons of the European elite and the royal courts. The silly country girls with their naïve cunning transform into modern women who dance the Charleston at dancing clubs, flirt, smoke and vote.

The first decades can be considered as the Viennese phase of Greek operetta, which thrilled Athenian audiences and represented the 'imperial dream' of the inhabitants of a small country on the fringes of Europe. At the same time, Greek troupes attempted for the first time to stage European operettas, starting with *Mlle Nitouche* by Hervé, which was performed by the troupe of Antonis Nikas in 1908, with a thirty-member orchestra and the collaboration of well-known revue composer Theophrastos Sakellaridis, who was destined to become one of the most distinguished Greek operetta composers.[18] Soon after, Evangelos Pantopoulos, a successful comic actor and troupe leader, well remembered by the Athenian public thanks to his smash-hit performance as a miller in love in the comic idyll of the same name (*The Millers*), contended for and earned the right to stage the first performance of *The Merry Widow* in 1909, while also staging a number of Greek operettas with a strong popular element, such as *Pharaoh Pasha and his Harem* by Dimitris Aravantinos (1906) and *The Devils* (1909).[19] From 1908 onwards, several Greek operetta troupes were formed, competing with each other and with foreign troupes touring in Greece. Among the most memorable and active ones, one may mention the troupe 'Operetta Papaioannou', which toured in Greece and abroad for more than twenty years (Figure 11.2).

The first Greek operetta with pretensions of quality was staged in May 1909 by the Nikas troupe. It is entitled *Land-ho* or *Thalatta, thalatta*

Figure 11.2 A scene from the Greek version (entitled *Gingolette*) of the Viennese operetta *Libellentanz* by Franz Lehár printed on the cover of the musical score. This publication is related to the production by the celebrated troupe 'Operetta Papaioannou'. Source: The Demakopoulos Music Collection, Tsakopoulos Library, California State University-Sacramento.

and was set to music by Theophrastos Sakellaridis, with a libretto by Stephanos Granitsas and Polybios Dimitrakopoulos. Thanks to its plot, which is set in the Greek Navy, the play has a strong sociopolitical message, as it expresses an indirect criticism of favouritism in the armed forces. This play caused displeasure to the authorities and was cancelled, only to be staged again in a censored version. But the first truly great hit was the operetta *In the Barracks*, performed on 9 May 1914, which crowned Theophrastos Sakellaridis as the king of operetta, a title that he would have to share, after a few years, with his colleague Nikos Hadjiapostolou. The play *In the Barracks* was directly linked to the political situation and the Greek victories in the Balkan wars, as well as to World War I. The plot (a young woman disguises herself as a soldier and enlists, so as to remain in the barracks in Athens, near her sweetheart) was the cause for both national and artistic enthusiasm.[20]

Two more operettas, written by the internationally acclaimed composer Spyros Samaras were connected to historical and political events of the period. The first, entitled *The Princess of Sasson* (1915) had to do with the small island of Sasson near Corfu, ceded by Albania to Greece in 1914, while the second, *The Cretan Girl* (1916), was connected to the foundation of the Cretan State and the Union of Crete with Greece in 1913. The works of Samaras combine European and Greek musical idioms and belong, in comparison to the other operettas of the time, to a higher artistic register.[21]

Just before the end of World War I, on 18 July 1918, one of the two most popular Greek operettas ever was staged: *The Godson*, by Theophrastos Sakellaridis (Figure 11.3). From its opening night, the play caused a sensation with its unconventional representation of military officers: one of the characters, a full colonel, flirted on stage wearing his military uniform. The play was censored by the authorities, the police intervened and the producers were forced to revise it by removing the offending passages.[22] Its libretto was based on a French farce, but it was 'immersed' in Greek reality, and was characterized by clever dialogues, memorable lines, hilarious characters, catchy music and an indomitable national spirit. Thanks to these qualities, the *Godson* remains until today the most-performed Greek operetta.[23]

This first phase of evolution ended with the mass production of plays and performances of Greek operetta during the interwar period. Within the atmosphere of European belle-époque euphoria, insouciance and wild revelry between the two wars, operetta in Greece now experienced the zenith of its popularity, while original Greek operetta plays dominated the stage and public taste. Fermented by the political events of the two wars, which had taken place in the previous period, the comedy of manners made a comeback, now in the guise of urban working-class culture of the big cities. The popular element was now prominent in the plays, interlaced (often literally, since many plays end in a cross-class marriage) with the world of the bourgeoisie and the upper classes.

The most representative play of the period is undoubtedly *The Apaches of Athens* by Nikos Hadjiapostolou, performed at the Alhambra Theatre on

Θεόφραστου Σακελλαρίδη
Ο ΒΑΦΤΙΣΤΙΚΟΣ

ΕΘΝΙΚΗ ΛΥΡΙΚΗ ΣΚΗΝΗ

Figure 11.3 *The Godson* by Theofrastos Sakellaridis. Cover page of the printed programme for the production of the Greek National Opera, 1995–6. Source: private collection of the author.

19 August 1921. Boasting 'one hundred and fifty nights in a row' of continuous performance and almost mythical box-office turnout, it achieved the greatest theatrical success of the interwar period and caused the envy of all theatre producers in Greece, who vainly tried to repeat its

magic recipe.[24] What was the secret of such success? Probably the appear-ance on the urban operetta stage of a company of original, true-to-life, low-class characters of Athens: the Prince, Karoumbas and Karkaletsos. With their direct, unpretentious idiomatic language, their unaffected behaviour, their sterling character, their code of honour and their true feelings, which the nouveau riche and the high-society people lack, the play's heroes, namely the low-class streetwise toughs, the urchins, the spivs, the princes of the street, speak to the heart of the people and bring the operetta genre closer to the masses. The simplistic dual schema of the *Apaches'* 'honest poverty–dishonest wealth' revitalized the genre and the composer reached the top.[25]

It is not easy to calculate the number of plays written and performed during this period in Athens and Thessaloniki, nor the number of active troupes. It is equally difficult to categorize most of the plays as operettas or revues. There is even a new hybrid genre, the operetta-revue, which incorporates the element of critique of current affairs. But an estimation of about a thousand new original works, performances and troupes is not far from reality: a veritable operetta mania. Apart from the unbeatable duo of Sakellaridis and Hadjiapostolou, other successful creators include Giannis Konstantinidis/Kostas Giannidis – a composer who signed his work using two different pen names and two personalities, one for art music and one for light music – with the cabaret-operetta *Der Liebesbazillus* (Berlin, 1927);[26] Stathis Mastoras, later destined to become a martyr of the nation, with *Our Girl Ririka* (1934); and a number of women composers, such as Eleni Lambiri and Carolina Mastrakini.

Even major historical events such as the Asia Minor disaster did not put a stop to the rise of the operetta, which continued to dominate the stage, with expensive productions generously offering an escape from sordid reality. At the end of the decade, the economic crisis of 1929 and the American market crash would turn the public's interest towards the USA and towards the American cinema musical, which breathed new life into the operetta genre. The success story of Greek light musical theatre was interrupted only by the establishment of the junta regime of 4 August 1936, which inaugurated a period of political intervention and persecution. Many artists sought to escape to theatrical stages abroad, in diaspora cities like Constantinople or Alexandria.

The foundation of the National Opera (1939) marked the return of Athens to the tradition of Viennese operetta, which was unanimously viewed by the critics of the period as too heavy and outdated. *Die Fledermaus* by Strauss, which inaugurated the first artistic period of the new organization (5 March 1940) was perhaps the only foreign play by a Greek troupe during the interwar period. With the declaration of war just a few months later (28 October 1940), the genre seemed to disappear entirely, with wartime revue taking over. Until the end of the twentieth century, the National Opera cultivated operetta, not by producing new plays but by repeating old successes of the French and the Viennese school, as well the two greatest Greek operetta hits, *The Godson* and *The Apaches of Athens*, which was also translated as *The Gays of Athens*.[27]

Apart from revue, which maintained a dynamic presence on the Greek stage, the audience's need for musical theatrical entertainment is thereafter covered by the cinema of the 1950s, 1960s and 1970s. This includes the filming of operetta performances and the cinema adaptation of well-known operettas, but also a new genre, the Greek cinema musical, which captured the audience thanks to the fresh faces of a host of young actors, its colourful sets dominated by the Aegean Islands and the 'bouzoukia' stages; its flashy costumes with sequins, feathers, tulles and very little fabric indeed; its daring choreography; the slender bodies of its female protagonists and the remarkable voice and brio of the ex-operetta singer Rena Vlachopoulou.[28] In the next decades, operettas were only very rarely staged by mainstream commercial troupes and protagonists; a notable exception was *The Merry Widow*, starring the 'national star' Aliki Vougiouklaki in 1980, and its TV serialization in 1991.[29]

The Cultural Contribution of Operetta

The above historical overview aimed to show that operetta was a genre which brought with it a renovation of the Modern Greek theatrical stage and life, invigorating it with a new repertoire and forming a new theatrical tradition. The key features of operetta, such as its directness, familiarity, easily consumed and memorable lines, rendered it almost addictive for more than forty years. In an attempt to discuss more deeply its meaning and contribution to Greek culture, one comes up against a multiform core consisting of a series of binary oppositions.

East and West
The new original operetta creations provided the frame for Greece's two-fold cultural identity: Western and oriental. Although the incorporation of the oriental and the exotic element in Greek music and Greek lyric theatre dates to the second half of the nineteenth century, with works such as the opera *Frossini* by Pavlos Carrer (1868) and the great favourite of Armenian origin, *Horhor Aga*, this tendency runs strong in the Greek operetta production of the 1920s. Works like *Halima* by Theophrastos Sakellaridis (1926) are based on the rearrangement of Western music in

a minor key and with oriental tunes. The contact with melodies from Asia Minor and Smyrna via the refugees from Asia Minor enhances this aesthetic, which takes the form of an idealized oriental romanticism.

Art and Pop

At the same time, operetta succeeded in functioning as a social melting pot between 'high' and 'popular' musical creation. It was the source of a great number of very widely known songs which were sung for decades as bourgeois and popular hits. So, the Greek repertoire includes works with varying degrees of art-type or pop-like music. There are waltzes, polkas, mazurkas, csárdás, jazz, music-hall hits, Latin songs, Italian cantatas, pop songs, folk dances, even oriental music and rembetika songs … Theophrastos Sakellaridis admitted that he kept 'musical stenographic minutes' of any melody he heard, so that he might later adapt it in his compositions, and included as his sources of inspiration even tarantella, *café chantant* music and tunes from the Gipsy encampments and the open-air popular spectacles performed in the western fringes of the capital. Many composers, librettists and soloists deserve the characterization of 'Janus', as they follow careers both in the 'high/art' and in the 'low/light' or even the 'popular' repertory.

Up and Down

Cross-class marriages, popular elements, low-class characters and apaches abound in Greek operetta. The satire against nouveau-riche attitudes, xenomania, and the fake aristocratic manners of the Athenians, is very strong. The stereotypical bipolar antithesis 'rich and poor' has an added dimension of 'modernity vs Greekness'. So, comedy of manners and cosmopolitanism are merged in one and the same performance, satisfying the tastes of all audiences. The moral-didactic element is also frequent: the girl that has gone astray, the honour of the poor but virtuous girl vs the corrupted nouveau-riche women of the urban classes. The emblematic play of this tendency, *The Apaches of Athens* (1921), brings with it an air of subversion: it is no longer the bourgeois characters who dominate the plot but three low-class characters, something which would be inconceivable in European operetta. The Greek operetta milieu includes not only upper-class salons but also night-clubs and cabarets of ill-repute, lowly front yards of poor people's houses and servants' quarters. It also sets on stage 'common' women with a sinful past and a golden heart, like the heroines of *The Girl of the Neighbourhood* (1922) or *The Woman of the Streets* (1923) by Hadjiapostolou (see Figure 11.4), or the public's favourite, the night-dancer Plou-Plou or Blou-Blou, who appeared in several plays, such as *The Daughter of the Storm* and *Christina* (1928) by Sakellaridis and *Blou-Blou* (1933) by Hadjiapostolou.

Figure 11.4 The cover of the musical score of the Greek operetta *The Woman of the Streets* by Nikos Hadjiapostolou

Modern Tunes and Dances

Another important aspect of Greek operetta was its contribution as an incentive for the development of the art of dancing, especially modern dance, in Greece. New rhythms were imported from America and Europe, such as the one-step, foxtrot, shimmy, Charleston and black-bottom. Dancing masters from abroad were employed to provide teaching for the supporting dance acts. The operetta and revue led to the establishment in

Greece of the new profession of choreographer, whose first representative in Greek light theatre was the German Elsa Enkel.[30] Young Greek artists chose to study in western Europe in order to specialize in the art of dancing; among them were Paraskevas Oikonomou and Angelos Grimanis, who soon took over as choreographers from their European colleagues. In the 1930s new dances were added to the operetta repertoire, such as the Argentinian tango and Cuban rumba.

Lifestyle

The enormous artistic production of the interwar period popularized not only songs but a whole aesthetic and more: dances, dress codes, manners, lifestyle. A strong asset of operetta, from its first appearance, was its patently European air, with its opulent costumes and spectacular sets, exactly like those of the theatres abroad. Operetta was the means of informing the public concerning new dance trends, light music-hall music, clubs and dancing, fashion and European or American lifestyle in general. At the same time, the cinema exercised a strong influence: sometimes operetta performances were filmed and watched as cinema spectacles, and sometimes films included full orchestras (the so-called *filmoperettas*), while frequently the plots of Hollywood films were adapted as operettas. In any case, the cinema effected an approach between operetta and the American musical.[31]

Actors and Singers

Operetta was the formative ground for a number of major actors who made a name for themselves not only in the field of musical theatre but also in the new artistic field of cinema. The protagonists of Greek operetta were mostly self-taught actors of comic idyll or agile actors of prose theatre with good voices; real classical soloists who had engaged in musical studies were rare. Among the biggest names, one should mention Rosalia Nika, Melpomeni Kolyva (Figure 11.5), Yiannis Papaioannou, Elsa Enkel, Soso Kandyli, Aphrodite Laoutari and Yiorgos Dramalis. Later, operetta and revue protagonists found their way into the cinema, as was the case with Rena Vlachopoulou, Zozo Sapountzaki and Sperantza Vrana among others.

Sociopolitical Messages

On a different note, Greek operetta proved itself several times as the carrier of forceful sociopolitical messages, especially during periods of political tension (World Wars I and II, the Goudi coup, the Asia Minor Disaster). Many plays made reference to contemporary political realities. The composers presented an idealized view of war and especially the bravery and

Figure 11.5 The operetta protagonist Melpomeni Kolyva, *c*.1910. Source: The archive of Stathis Arfanis

military exploits of the Greek army as an achievement of the lower classes, while the representatives of the upper classes were invariably represented as namby-pamby and effeminate, devoid of any trace of dignity or national pride, only concerned with purchasing an exemption from military service.

Finally, Greek operetta production numbers a long list of original stage creations, some of which are still quite popular. The two composers who stood out among the rest thanks to the quality and the popularity of their works, Theophrastos Sakellaridis and Nikos Hadjiapostolou, still retain the leading role in the Greek scene of the twenty-first century. These are two very prolific composers, who produced about two original operettas per year, from the mid-1910s until World War II. Sakellaridis, especially, was an extremely versatile composer who wrote music for operas, operettas, revues and for the cinema. Even important composers of art music, such as Pavlos Carrer, Spyros Samaras, Dionysios Lavrangas and Napoleon Lambelet fell victim to the charm and direct appeal of operetta and composed original operetta works. It is obvious that the enormous productivity and commercial success of the operetta in the interwar years was not a short pyrotechnic boom but the result of a long tradition in lyrical and light musical theatre in Greece.

To conclude, operetta underwent many transitional phases throughout its century-long history in Greece (from the mid-nineteenth to the mid-twentieth century) until it gained the leading role in Greek theatre and the preference of the Greek public. It initially stormed in with French verve and coyness; it then acquired a veneer of Viennese grace and superficiality, until it was eventually Hellenized, claiming its right to both urban and popular form and to the double aesthetic character of its new homeland, and ended up becoming the quintessence of urban evening entertainment, extravaganza, sophistication and fashion. Later, the devastating events of the mid-twentieth century, namely the outbreak of World War II, and the dark years of the German Occupation and of the Civil War, led to its decline. During the second half of the twentieth century, operetta was in effect a period genre, considered old-fashioned and rather quaint, almost completely overshadowed by theatrical and cinema musicals. However, from 2000 onwards, there developed a tendency for rediscovering forgotten plays and performing them anew, with modern directors and contemporary staging. At the same time, tribute performances are staged, such as the nostalgic compilation *Remember Those Years* (2007–8),[32] inaugurating a new phase of revival of Greek operetta, warmly embraced by the public and even younger audiences.

Notes

1. A. Xepapadakou & A. Charkiolakis, *Interspersed by Musical Entertainment: Music in Greek Salons of the Nineteenth Century* (Athens: Hellenic Music Centre, 2017), 4.
2. N. I. Laskaris, *Historia tou neohellenikou theatrou* [History of Modern Greek Theatre], Vol. 1 (Athens: M. Vassiliou, 1938–9), 206, 310–23.
3. A. Xepapadakou, 'Idolatry and Sacrilege: Offenbach's Operetta in Nineteenth-century Athens', *Studies in Musical Theatre*, 8, no. 2 (2014): 132.
4. E. Fessa-Emmanouil, *I architektoniki tou neohellenikou theatrou* [The Architecture of Modern Greek Theatre], Vol. 1 (Athens: E. Fessa-Emmanouil, 1994), 104.
5. Anon., *Aion*, 9 Dec. 1871, 3.
6. Anon., *Merimna*, 5 Nov. 1871, 3–4.
7. Anon., *Alithia*, 21 Oct. 1871, 3.
8. Smyrnios, 'Leblebidji Hor-hor Agha', *Mi chanese* [Let's keep in touch], 15 May 1883, 6–7.

9. G. Leotsakos, *Spyros Samaras* (Athens: Mouseio Benaki, 2013), 187–230.

10. For more on the itinerant French music theatre troupes travelling around the eastern Mediterranean and the Orient, see Avra Xepapadakou, 'European Itinerant Opera and Operetta Companies Touring in the Near and Middle East' in Reinhard Strohm (ed.), *The Music Road, Coherence and Diversity in Music from the Mediterranean to India* (Oxford: Oxford University Press, 2019), 316–31.

11. Ch. Stamatopoulou-Vasilakou, 'Heptanisiakes komodies met'asmaton kai komeidylia: I symvoli tous sto eptanisiako mousiko theatro tou dekatou enatou aiona' [Ionian musical comedies and comic idylls: their contribution to the Ionian music theatre of the 19th century] in *Eptanisiaki opera kai mousiko theatro eos to 1953* [Ionian opera and music theatre until 1953. Conference Proceedings] (Athens: University of Athens, Dept. of Theatre Studies, 2011), 172–3.

12. Anon., *Ephemeris*, 16 Jan. 1879, 4.

13. I. Tsakasianos, *Theatrika erga. Apo to komeidyllio sto melodrama* [Theatre plays. From comic idyll to music theatre 1876–1898], ed. Gerorgia Kokla-Papadatou (Zante: Public Historical Library of Zante, 2008), 330–2.

14. For details, see A. Xepapadakou, *Pavlos Carrer* (Athens: Fagottobooks, 2013), 189–96.

15. Th. Hadjipantazis, *To Komeidyllion* [The Comic Idyll] (Athens: Hermes, 1981), 179, 182.

16. M. Seiragakis, *Napoleon Lambelet. Enas anestios kosmopolitis* [Napoleon Lambelet. A homeless Cosmopolitan] (Athens: Hellenic Music Centre, 2014).

17. Further details on revue in Greece may be found in K. Georgakaki, *I ephemeri goiteia tis epitheorisis (1894–2014)* [The Ephemeral Charm of Revue] (Athens: Trapeza Peiraios, 2014).

18. M. Seiragakis, *To elafro mousiko theatro sti mesopolemiki Athina* [The Light Music Theatre in Interwar Athens], 2 vols. (Athens: Kastaniotis, 2009), Vol. 1, 67.

19. Ibid., 22.

20. Ch. Koutroumanou, 'I hellenikes operes kai operetes stin Ethniki Lyriki Skene' [Greek Operas and Operettas at the Greek National Opera], unpublished undergraduate dissertation, University of Crete (2015), 114–19.

21. I. Tselikas, 'I Kritikopoula tou Spyrou Samara' [The Cretan Girl of Spyros Samaras] in *The Cretan Girl* (Athens: Greek National Opera, 2011), 21–8.

22. Anon., *O Vaftistikos* [The Godson] (Athens: Greek National Opera, 1994).

23. Koutroumanou, *I hellenikes operes*, 39–52.

24. G. Sideris, 'Ex aformis enos eortasmou. I Apachides ton Athinon' [On the Occasion of a Celebration. The *Apaches of Athens*], *Paraskenia*, 22 Apr. 1939.

25. A real incident demonstrating the sense of identification of the lower-class audience with the characters of the play is the following: during one of the performances a furious spectator jumped on stage and attacked the protagonist playing the role of the Prince and stabbed him three times with a knife claiming he had stolen his life and his lifestory. Cf. Anon., *'I aimatovameni Apachides'* [The bloodstained Apaches], *The Apaches of Athens* (Athens: Greek National Opera, 2000).

26. L. Liavas, 'O exairetos kyrios Giannidis/Konstantinidis sto theatro Acropol' [The Exquisite Mr. Giannidis/Konstantinidis at Acropol Theatre] in *The Virus of Love* (Athens: Greek National Opera, 2009), 11–15, and G. Sakallieros, *Giannis Konstantinidis (1903–84). Zoe, ergo kai synthetiko yfos* [Giannis Konstantidis. Life, Works and Style of Composition] (Thessaloniki: University Studio Press, 2010).

27. M. A. Raptis, *Epitomi historia tou Hellinikou Melodramatos kai tis Ethnikis Lyrikis Skinis 1888–1988* [A Concise History of Greek Melodrama and Greek National Opera] (Athens: Ktimatiki Trapeza, 1989). See also Koutroumanou, *I hellenikes operes*, 14.

28. L. Papadimitriou, *To helleniko kinimatographico Musical* [Greek Musical on Film] (Athens: Papazisi, 2009).

29. The fifteen-episode series *A Very Merry Widow* was produced by Antenna channel, 1990–1, dir. by Takis Vougiouklakis.

30. M. Seiragakis, *To elafro mousiko theatro*, Vol. 2, 504–9. See also A. Vasileiou, 'I fternes pou miloun. I proti gnorimia is athinaikis mousikis skenes me tous americanicous chorous' [The talking heels. The First Acquaintance of the Athenian Music Stage with the American Dances], *Parabasis*, 6 (2005): 43–56.

31. M. Seiragakis, *To elafro mousiko theatro*, Vol. 2, 449–53.

32. Koutroumanou, *I hellenikes operes*, 343–54.

Recommended Reading

Laskaris, Nikolaos I. *Historia tou neohellenikou theatrou / History of Modern Greek Theatre*, Vol. 1. Athens: M. Vassiliou, 1938–9.

Tsakasianos, Ioannis. *Theatrika erga. Apo to komeidyllio sto melodrama / Theatre Plays. From Comic Idyll to Music Theatre 1876–1898*, ed. Georgia Kokla-Papadatou. Zante: Public Historical Library of Zante, 2008.

Raptis, Michalis A. *Epitomi historia tou Hellinikou Melodramatos kai tis Ethnikis Lyrikis Skinis 1888–1988 / A Concise History of Greek Melodrama and Greek National Opera*. Athens: Ktimatiki Trapeza, 1989.

Seiragakis, Manolis. *To elafro mousiko theatro sti mesopolemiki Athina / The Light Music Theatre in Interwar Athens*, 2 vols. Athens: Kastaniotis, 2009.

Xepapadakou, Avra. 'Idolatry and Sacrilege: Offenbach's Operetta in Nineteenth-century Athens', *Studies in Musical Theatre*, 8, no. 2 (2014): 129–41.

Xepapadakou, Avra. 'European Itinerant Opera and Operetta Companies Touring in the Near and Middle East'. In Reinhard Strohm, ed., *The Music Road, Coherence and Diversity in Music from the Mediterranean to India*. Oxford: Oxford University Press, 2019, 316–31.

PART III

Operetta since 1900

12 The Operetta Factory: Production Systems of Silver-Age Vienna

MICAELA K. BARANELLO

The 1911 satirical novel *Operettenkönige* begins with theft: an operetta melody is stolen. Sung in all earnestness by a young composer to his lover – an actress of questionable moral character for whom the omniscient narrator spares no scorn – it is stolen by an eavesdropping competitor who hides beneath the composer's window. It started its life as a token of genuine affection, but as soon as it escapes into the Viennese air it becomes a valuable commodity, generic enough to be planted anywhere but specific enough to possess its own exchange value.[1]

Such is the paradox of operetta production: defined by its critics as formulaic and promiscuous but by its creators and audiences as possessed of a unique romanticism and the mark of genius. Viennese operetta, more than its French or English counterparts, was marked by a tension between the demands of high and popular art. Despite its genuinely commercial nature, composers and librettists frequently seized on the discourse of high art as a way to elevate their own critical prestige. This usually backfired, but the production process itself is marked by a pull between the individual creator and the ruthlessness of commerce.

This chapter offers a practical introduction to the production of operetta in twentieth-century Vienna. By the turn of the century, the city's operetta world had developed into an industry with its own economy and division of labour. This is apparent from a host of sources ranging from newspaper and magazine stories to the memoirs and letters of librettists and composers. Though the documentation of the creation of any individual work can range from sparse to nonexistent, together these sources form a relatively consistent and complete picture of the composition and performance of an average operetta. In most respects the operetta industry operated in a regularized manner – there is even a cartoon depicting Lehár as the boss of an 'operetta factory'. The wall appears to be a theatre box office, with each ticket labelled after a different Lehár operetta. The latest is *Eva*, which dates the caricature to around 1911–13.[2] But the reception of operetta was more comprehensively preserved than its production process, for which sources of information remain scarce. Financial records in particular are lacking, and while general economic practices can be pieced together, it is usually not possible to track the box-office takings of any particular work.[3]

This chapter is intended to demystify a process often obscured by myth and scorn as well as to illuminate the many constituents involved in operetta production and some of their (often conflicting) interests. I begin by surveying the people involved in writing an operetta; then turn to the conventions of the silver-age operetta text itself; then the theatres, publication and economics of the operetta world and, finally, survey the reception and audiences who bore witness to the industry's products.

Librettos and Librettists

Viennese cafés were the nerve centres of production. An undated engraving by Sigmund von Skiwirczynski depicts no fewer than twenty-four operetta luminaries positioned around a few tables in the Café Museum, labelled 'The Fixed Stars of Viennese Operetta, Surrounded by Their Satellites'.[4] During the silver age, the fixed stars of librettos included Victor Léon, Leo Stein, Alfred Grünwald, Julius Brammer, Robert Bodanzky, Alfred Maria Willner, Fritz Löhner-Beda and Heinz Reichert. Many operetta librettos were written in such cafés, where ideas and information were traded and collaborations made and broken. Librettists were typical café-goers: bourgeois, educated and almost all Jewish.[5] When embarking upon an operetta, most librettists worked in pairs, one taking primary responsibility for the plot structure and spoken dialogue (*Prosa*) and the other writing the verse song texts, and both critiquing each other every step of the way – a process that ensured a degree of quality control but also homogenization. Dialogue librettists often began their careers as playwrights, and song-text librettists as poets or songwriters, but the division was not absolute. Some librettos were the production of a single author (most often Victor Léon, the most influential, prolific and experimental of all Viennese operetta librettists), and some are credited to three or more.

Relatively few operetta librettos were original subjects though as plots became more formulaic over the course of the twentieth century newly invented librettos became more common. The most popular source was, by far, middlebrow theatre, particularly French boulevard theatre such as that of Meilhac and Sardou. This genre was in fact the equivalent of operetta in spoken theatre: it was targeted at a similar audience and sometimes even played in the same theatres.[6] These plays' tidy plots, conventional character types and decisive endings (usually finishing with marriage) became the template for many operettas. Librettists also based operettas on short stories or novels or fitted historical figures or events into an operetta format.

Sometimes the source was credited, but often, in the interest of preserving more of the royalties for the new librettists, it was not; librettists hoped their sources would be obscure enough not to be noticed. Such ghosting was well known enough to be frequently joked about in theatrical circles. Shadow sources ranged from yet more French plays to a novel by a 'Spanish writer who has been dead for more than thirty years'.[7] Were the librettists to be caught stealing, they could be met with legal action by the original authors or their estate. The 'foreign basic idea'[8] that was credited with the plot of *Die lustige Witwe* was recognized immediately by critics as Meilhac's familiar play *L'attaché d'ambassade,* though Meilhac's estate sued the librettists only after the operetta became a massive hit and there were prodigious sums to be had.

Composers

Operetta resists the auteur framework, but composers, nonetheless, are usually identified as the single most important figure in an operetta's composition and production. (Librettos were usually written first and then marketed to a composer.) Most nineteenth-century operetta composers had little formal compositional training, their backgrounds usually being in groups such as salon orchestras and military bands. In the silver age, however, most composers came to operetta after conservatory study as art music composers and thus possessed larger compositional toolboxes. After completing their training, almost all of their biographies continue in fits and starts and odd musical jobs that typify most early careers in composition. Many operetta composers also tried their hand at writing opera, with varied results. Along the way, they discovered a knack for writing in a popular style and turned to it full time.

The first operetta composer to have a background in art music composition was Richard Heuberger, best known to scholars as second-stringer to Eduard Hanslick at the *Neue Freie Presse* and as the director of the Singakademie and Wiener Männergesang-Verein.[9] After training as an engineer, Heuberger studied composition with Robert Fuchs in Graz. Of his many operettas, his only major success was *Der Opernball* in 1898, one of the most important works of the transitional period between the golden and silver ages. Unlike Heuberger, Franz Lehár and Leo Fall were both military bandmasters in the Austro-Hungarian armed forces as well as orchestral composers; Fall, Oscar Straus and Emmerich Kálmán all came to operetta after first experimenting with cabaret songs (Straus and Fall in Berlin, Kálmán in Budapest). But all had studied at conservatories and written some 'serious' music before delving into operetta.

It should be noted that the post-conservatory experiences that led these composers to operetta – conducting in provincial theatres, orchestrating light music, working in military bands and playing for cabarets – were hardly unique, and in fact identical to the background of many of the era's composers of art music. Mahler conducted numerous operettas in his early career, as did Webern.[10] Alexander Zemlinsky worked as an orchestrator and also served as *Kapellmeister* at the Carl-Theater for two seasons; Zemlinsky's orchestration of Heuberger's *Der Opernball* amounted in some places to co-authorship, as Karl Kraus even noted publicly.[11] (Although Kraus implied that Heuberger required assistance due to a lack of technical skill, the evidence suggests that poor time management was an equal if not greater factor.)[12] Even Arnold Schoenberg worked for the *Über-Brettl* cabaret in Berlin and orchestrated operetta (inspiring his *Brettl-Lieder*).[13]

Whereas both Schoenberg and Mahler seem to have looked back at their periods in light music with fondness, other composers saw it as a period of indentured servitude before their true talents were recognized. Webern, for example, associated operetta with toil in the provinces, referring to operetta as 'Dreck' (muck).[14] While it should not be surprising that assistant conductors and orchestrators were not allowed space to demonstrate their creativity or that working conditions in provincial theatres were often bad, these poor experiences are vital background for the same composers' later condemnations of operetta.

Orchestration

As noted above, many operetta composers did not orchestrate their own work, though Franz Lehár, Emmerich Kálmán and Leo Fall, three of the most notable composers of the silver age, did. Some abstained due to, as Kraus implied, a lack of musical education, others due to lack of interest (operetta orchestration was often routine) or lack of time (as in the case of *Der Opernball*). Kálmán, Lehár and Fall all managed to do so and were abetted in their later careers by the luxury of time. Additionally, their fame was grounded in their handicraft and original voices – in which their command of the orchestra played an important role.

The issue of orchestration was a sensitive one for operetta insiders, a delicate topic in the operetta industry's collective quest to be taken seriously as artists. In July 1926, an article in *Die Stunde* asked, 'Who orchestrates Viennese operettas?' The anonymous writer reports that a prominent unnamed Viennese music critic would, at the next assembly of the Association of Playwrights and Composers, demand that the names of anonymous orchestrators be listed in theatre programmes.[15] This was motivated, the article detailed, less by a desire to give credit to the unnamed than to expose the many prominent operetta composers who were not capable of orchestrating their own music 'because they cannot master the art of instrumentation' ('weil sie die Kunst der Instrumentations nicht beherrschen') and to laud the real masters who could – Lehár, Kálmán and Fall, described as the 'matadors of Viennese operetta'. The article goes so far as to name Vienna's most popular orchestrators: conductor Oskar Stalla, Nico Dostal (later a successful composer himself) and 'der Musiker Kopsiva'.[16] No specific clients are named, though Stalla is described as having contracts with four prominent composers for the next season. It is unclear if the promised confrontation ever came to pass.

Templates

The basic recipe for a silver-age operetta was largely established by the success of *Die lustige Witwe* in 1905, as were the smaller-scale genre conventions. Some of these conventions existed well before *Witwe*, the most important earlier watershed moment being Johann Strauss Jr's *Der Zigeunerbaron* (1885). However, in the twentieth century their deployment became more predictable.

A silver-age operetta generally centred on two couples. The 'first couple', played by the leading man (a low tenor or high baritone) and leading woman (soprano) are usually somewhat older and experienced in life and given music that was relatively demanding in vocal terms. The younger couple, a soubrette and a lighter 'bon vivant' or buffo tenor, are usually younger characters with less demanding singing parts, given more comic business and are often asked to do a great deal of dancing. (*Die lustige Witwe* is exceptional in this regard.) While the singers of these roles were often younger as well, some performers spent their entire careers in second-couple roles. The supporting roles generally include several *Komiker*, purely comic characters both male and female, some singing and some only speaking. There were even specific divisions of *Komiker* and *Komikerin*, such as the *komischer Alter* or *komische Alte*, the funny elderly person (such as Njegus in *Die lustige Witwe* and Mariza's and servant Tschekko in *Gräfin Mariza*).[17]

Plot structure was also honed to perfection. Operettas were organized into three acts, opening with an overture or prelude followed by an introductory scene in a public setting in which a supporting character introduces the situation. The leading man and woman both sing entrance songs, and the secondary couple receives some material as well. The first act closes with a large finale, usually on an upbeat note with an acknowledgement of love between each couple. The second act opens with a large dance number including local colour, replicating *Die lustige Witwe's Vilja-Lied*, and subsequently features ornate twists and turns in the plot.

In the tradition of the 'well-made play', these plot confusions often involve props or 'devices' such as letters, keys, miniature portraits, fans or lockets. There are usually one or two duets for the leading couple, and the act ends with the silver age's most grandiose achievement: the infamous Act 2 finale. This is the operetta's most ambitious musical structure and contains a melodramatic twist to end the act on a note of tragedy and pathos.[18] Third acts often read as afterthoughts, vestigial structures that quickly tie up the plot. Their existence was frequently credited to a theatre's imperative to sell refreshments during a second intermission, though eliminating the second intermission would also threaten the second-act finale.[19] To maintain some interest, a new character known as the '*dritter Akt Komiker*' is occasionally introduced, who tells topical jokes that have little or nothing to do with the rest of the plot, a throwback to the jailer Frosch in *Die Fledermaus*. A few lively musical numbers, often including dance, and a quick resolution of the plot finish up the operetta. There is no major Act 3 finale, merely a brisk reprise of an earlier number as a 'Schlussgesang' (closing song). See, for example, Kálmán's *Die Csárdásfürstin* (1915) or Franz Lehár's *Eva* (1911).[20]

These constructions were entirely self-conscious, and audiences and critics were as aware of them as composers and librettists. Operetta critics often attacked the dependence on 'Schablone' (stencils), but it seemed that this predictability was what audiences wanted. The authors' skill was demonstrated in the use and development of these conventions. Were the waltz themes memorable? Was the instrumentation refined? How exciting was the twist in the second-act finale? Audiences expected certain thrills out of the operetta, and the authors were judged based on their ability to deliver the known features in a novel or satisfying way. Dramatic and musical patterns and habits that were for critics a mark of inartistic, mass production were, to operetta fans, beloved conventions of the genre.

Theatres and Productions

The Viennese theatres where operettas were produced were licensed private commercial enterprises, designated 'k.u.k. [imperial] Privattheater'. Vienna had a seemingly insatiable appetite for performances, and, until the economic crises of the 1920s and the spread of sound film, more and more theatres were built. Theatres rarely closed down entirely, but they frequently changed artistic direction.[21] While names often remained the same, programming constantly changed with fashions, ownership and artistic direction. For example, the Raimundtheater opened as a German nationalist Adam Müller-Guttenbrunn enterprise in 1893, became a spoken-word theatre in 1896, a home for visiting operetta troupes in 1900 and, finally, in 1908, was taken over by the management of the Theater an der Wien.

The closer a theatre was to the city centre, the wealthier an audience it could attract, the more media coverage it would receive in major newspapers and the higher ticket prices it could command. For operetta, the most prestigious stages were the Carl-Theater (whose name was not standardized and often appears as Carltheater) and Theater an der Wien, located in the *Vorstadt* but not far from the glittering centre. The Johann-Strauss-Theater, situated very near the Theater an der Wien, joined this elite rank when it opened in 1908. Further afield in the suburbs were the Theater in der Josefstadt, the Lustspieltheater and the Neue Wiener Bühne, playing similar, sometimes more mixed programmes with somewhat lower prices – and lower production values.[22]

The seating capacity of theatres varied; the Theater an der Wien was the largest at 1,859 spectators (reduced from its nineteenth-century capacity due to a renovation that replaced the roof and eliminated the top level), while the Carl-Theater and Johann-Strauss-Theater both accommodated around 1,200. The orchestra rosters of the three most important theatres hovered around forty-two members in 1910, while the less prestigious theatres averaged around thirty-five; however, it seems unlikely that all the members were playing on any given night. By the lean year of 1929, the Theater an der Wien's roster had dropped to eighteen musicians and the chorus to a mere ten.[23] Theatres also kept complete musical personnel on payroll including conductors, assistant conductors (often aspiring or semi-successful composers), accompanists and copyists.

Theatres maintained their own workshops for the construction of sets, costumes and props (with the occasional dramatic backdrop outsourced to one of the city's scenic painters) and kept large stocks of items which were recycled for less prestigious premieres. Whether a work received the investment of new sets and costumes or not was taken as an indication of faith from the management in the work's chances for survival.[24] Operettas were even featured in fashion spreads in the ladies' section of newspapers, where women could take cues on the latest styles from what glamorous stars like Betty Fischer or Louise Kartousch wore onstage.[25]

Economics and Publication

At some point in the composition process of a new operetta, the composer and librettists signed a contract with a theatre. In a typical contract, the royalties were divided evenly between composer and librettists, with the composer receiving half the authors' portion and the two librettists splitting the other half. Contracts often included provisions for profits from sheet-music sales and later contracts included recordings, the rights for performances outside Vienna and film adaptations. Wilhelm Karczag and the Theater an der Wien in particular strove to create a vertically integrated operetta industry. Karczag (and his successor, Hubert Marischka) ran his own publishing house, Karczag-Verlag, which printed the scores of many (though not all) of the operettas his theatre premiered. The firm also received a cut from recordings. Sometimes Marischka even negotiated a share of the proceeds for himself.[26]

Although this enabled the theatre to reap a healthy profit from success-ful works, it eventually developed into a risky model. In the 1920s, when expectations for visual opulence rose, the theatre made extremely high investments in new productions. The upfront costs could not be recouped by ticket sales in Vienna alone and required revenue from other cities, sheet music and recordings. The catch was that only a work that gained the reputation of Viennese success would bring in this additional cash. A work that flopped or was only a moderate success in Vienna could result in catastrophic losses. Ultimately, this proved ruinous.

Publication was an important step for lasting success in operetta. Successful composers had standing contracts with publishers and pub-lished all of their work; new composers sometimes waited until they achieved fame. When an operetta was published, it became available to the general public in a variety of forms, including piano-vocal scores, piano solo arrangements with the text printed above the music but without a separate vocal line (*Klavierauszug zu zwei Händen mit unterlegtem*

Text) and piano four hands with text. As well as the complete operetta, publishers also issued editions of excerpts, such as individual hit songs and short medleys of the most popular numbers. Potpourri arrangements for salon orchestra were also an important means of dissemination beyond the theatre.

After an operetta's premiere, the final version of the text was printed as a *Regie- und Soufflierbuch* (direction and prompt book) or *Vollständiges Soufflierbuch mit sämtlichen Regiebemerkungen* (full prompt book with complete production notes). These librettos were not offered for sale to the public, as their copyright stated explicitly, but were rather available only on loan or rental to other theatres producing the works. (The public could purchase a shorter libretto containing only the song texts.) This controlled the operetta's circulation, so the publisher could better collect royalties.[27] The text contains detailed notes on the original production's design and staging, which theoretically were to be replicated by provincial theatres to the greatest extent possible. Choreographies were sometimes published separately. The original staging was considered an integral part of the work, akin to the words or music, and the director responsible for the staging is noted prominently on the cover. But it is clear that for foreign stages directors adapted works for local taste and resources and that this versatility was important to its international appeal. For example, Stefan Frey surveys the international success of *Die lustige Witwe,* including the implications of changing casts, localized humour and eventual sound recordings and film.[28] Printed librettos and staging manuals should not be considered definitive records of any production.[29]

Censorship

Strict censorship was legally mandated for all licensed Viennese theatres until 1919. An operetta's spoken dialogue was first prepared in a typescript that was submitted to the police censor in duplicate for approval around a month before the premiere. The censor read the libretto, underlined any objectionable sections in red pencil on both copies and wrote a short summary and report on all the problems. One copy was returned to the theatre, the other was – thankfully for future scholarship – retained in the police's archive. The libretto was then approved for performance on the condition that the librettists adopt the censor's alterations. The law explicitly included visuals, music and gestures as well as spoken text.

Typically for the empire, the primary goal of the censor was to maintain public order and the appearance of harmony. The office had been established by an order issued during the Metternich era, on 25 Novembe 1850.

Theatres were prohibited from 'That which, in historical context, violates the need for public peace and order, that which insults public decency, shame, morality, or religion'.[30] The censor forbade several specific categories of activity: directing the actors to perform any illegal action; displaying a lack of loyalty or respect for the state or the imperial house; disparaging patriotism, mocking or displaying hatred of any nationality, religion or social class; insulting public decency, godliness or morality; any display of real Catholic vestments or imperial uniforms; and libel against any living people.[31] While this may seem sweeping, few scripts show many signs of the red pencil. Librettists were familiar with what was allowed and what was not and rarely seem to have pushed the envelope. This did not mean, however, that the censor's rules did not play a large role in the subjects chosen.

The office of the police censor was eliminated following the empire's dissolution. In an interview with the theatre magazine *Komödie*, mayor of Vienna Jakob Reumann described the censor as 'the remnant of the old police state', now outdated, and said that he believed that 'the good taste of the public' would serve as sufficient regulation for stage production.[32] Whether there was actual freedom of expression, however, was questionable: an article in *Die Stunde* from 1926 entitled 'The censor is dead! Long live the censor!' pointed out that while the formal censorship process had ceased, the police still wielded the power to shut down any production deemed out of order and that any statement against the state or offence against public decency would prompt immediate action. (The anonymous author gives no specific examples.[33]) But operettas depicting real monarchs became common – such as *Im weißen Rössl, Madame Pompadour* and *Kaiserin Josephine* – ironically, nostalgic reminders of an era when they would have been disallowed onstage.

Critics and Criticism

Reviews were published in newspapers the day following premieres and were found in the theatre and arts section. Many of the critics responsible for these reviews were enmeshed in operetta society: several wrote librettos themselves and others penned biographies of composers, and conflicts of interest were common.[34] While some reviews were anonymous, in most papers, critics were identified by their pseudonym (usually a few consonants from their surname).

Vienna had a notoriously large number of newspapers during this period.[35] The most prolific coverage of operetta could be found in the

Table 12.1 *Major Viennese operetta newspaper critics*

Newspaper	Pen Name	Name	Years Active
Neue Freie Presse	—	(reviews unsigned)	1900s–1910s
	L. Hfd	Ludwig Hirschfeld	1920s–1930s
Neues Wiener Journal	bs.	Leopold Jacobson	1900–c.1910
	a.e.	Alexander Engel	c.1908–1920s
	-ron	Julius Bistron	1920s
Neues Wiener Tagblatt	-rp	Ludwig Karpath	1901–c.1920?
	E.D.	Ernst Decsey	1920–1930s
	Dr. E.D.		
Fremden-Blatt	st.	Julius Stern	c.1900–1919
Österreichische Volks-Zeitung	A.L.	Alexander Landsberg	1900s–1910s
	St.	Julius Stern	1919–1920s
Deutsches Volksblatt	Sch-r.	Karl Schreiber	until 1922
Arbeiter-Zeitung	D.B.	David Josef Bach	1900s–1910s
Reichspost	(none)	Otto Howorka	1910s–1930s

Neues Wiener Journal, considered the most gossipy and female-targeted of the major broadsheets. A paper's theatre coverage occasionally betrayed the publication's overall political orientation, though most critics did not often espouse a prominent political agenda beyond bland centrist Liberalism. The more ideologically extreme papers are more easily labelled, such as the German nationalist *Reichspost* and the socialist *Arbeiter-Zeitung* (whose critic David Josef Bach is one of the most consistently interesting).

The most influential critics of the first decade-and-a-half of the twentieth century were Ludwig Karpath of the *Neue Wiener Tagblatt* and Leopold Jacobson of the *Neues Wiener Journal,* whose names and opinions were frequently cited by composers and librettists. In the 1920s, Julius Bistron and Ernst Decsey become more prominent. Table 12.1 lists the major critics of operetta from 1900 to 1930.

Most reviews follow the same format. Operettas are first judged by their ability to fulfil the basic goals to amuse and divert (critics often mention whether the audience seemed to be enjoying themselves). Other basic requirements include the libretto's pacing and plot twists, the composer's ability to write a waltz, very often the quality of the orchestration (ironic since many operetta composers did not do this themselves) and the charisma, singing and dancing abilities of the actors. In longer reviews, critics endeavour to place the operetta in the context of its creators' previous works. Composers receive the most attention. They are assumed to have particular strengths, weaknesses and identities, their mastery of the Viennese idiom is usually remarked upon and, if the composer in question was not native Viennese (as the majority of the major silver-age composers were not), his attempts to convince in what was considered a quintessentially Viennese language are assessed for their success.

Critical and public opinion often converged. Some works, however, were critical successes but popular flops; the opposite (critical flops and popular successes) was not common until the growth of the much-maligned revue operetta in the 1920s. For those critical of operetta as a whole – writers from more literary or serious musical circles who were generally not reviewing it on a daily basis – this collusion of criticism and market was one sign that marked operetta as non-art. Ultimately, it was the popular vote that determined how long an operetta would remain on the schedule.

Audiences

It is difficult to determine exactly the precise demographics of operetta audiences, but some details can be gleaned from contemporary accounts. While theatres did offer subscription tickets, the fixed box society of major opera houses did not exist in operetta theatres, nor did the quasi-patron power of those box holders. Some hints as to demographics can be picked up from the magazine *Komödie*, subtitled 'Wochenrevue für Bühne und Film'. In 1921, *Komödie* published a list of readers who had won a contest. Eighty-four readers in all are listed as winners, with their names and addresses supplied. Out of this number, the largest number, 57 per cent, lived in the suburban Vorstadt, between the Ringstrasse and the Gürtel; 37 per cent lived outside the Gürtel and the remaining 6 per cent lived inside the Ringstrasse in the Innere Stadt. This reinforces the oft-stated assumption that the most devoted operetta audience was the middle class and lower middle class.[36]

Due to the city's demographic changes in the late nineteenth century, the distribution of operetta audiences changed as well. In 1902, on the threshold of the silver age, Max Graf recorded a transformation of operetta taste over the past few decades, powered primarily by the streetcar.[37] While nineteenth-century Vienna had been a patchwork of neighbourhoods, public transportation now tied the city together, and its population was more likely to claim an identity as Viennese or as an immigrant rather than allegiance to their home district. In Graf's view, this had a chilling effect on operetta. While the audience had greatly expanded from a small circle of connoisseurs to a mass form, quality had decreased. What once was individual and specific – 'the wit of Offenbach, the grace of Johann Strauss, the melodic cleverness of Millöcker' – had, according to Graf, become mass-produced and generic, lowered to the folk music of a Viennese Heuriger.

Many operetta artists maintained that it was those in the gallery who made or killed an operetta, not the voices of the critics or even those who purchased the more expensive seats. Proportionately, this seems possible, since there were many more cheap seats than there were expensive ones. The silver age's tendency towards *Serienerfolgen* – hit operettas that ran for years at a single theatre – certainly encouraged writing for large audiences. *Serienerfolgen* also required a theatre to draw a largely new group of audience members every single night, akin to a modern Broadway megamusical.[38]

Conclusion

As in the field of opera research, the multimedia nature of operetta can make its study a confusing experience. Due to operetta's popularity and liminal role in the Germanic musical establishment, these sources are plentiful but are frequently scattered between departments in major libraries, often split between music and theatre collections. Several important archival collections, notably papers of librettist Alfred Grünwald and the photographic collection of librettist Victor Léon, are located in the United States (at the New York Public Library's Billy Rose Theatre Collection and Harvard University's Houghton Library, respectively). Sometimes these texts tell conflicting stories, surviving from various stages in the artistic process or concerning an ephemeral performance whose exact character will always remain a mystery. But the very plenitude of this written record and its occasional contradictions can provide a dynamic, lively view of a largely forgotten art form, one which is only beginning to be mined by scholars.

Notes

1. Franz von Hohenegg, *Operettenkönige: Ein Wiener Theaterroman* (Berlin: Lane, 1911). The pseudonymous author has not been identified, though the issue is considered in Barbara Denscher, *Der Operettenlibrettist Victor Léon: Ein Werkbiographie* (Bielefeld: Transcript, 2017), 386–7. www.transcript-verlag.de/978-3-8376-3976-6/der-operettenlibrettist -victor-leon (accessed 22 Apr. 2019).
2. This image is also reproduced on the cover of Martin Lichtfuss, *Operette im Ausverkauf: Studien zum Libretto des Musikalischen Unterhaltungstheaters im Österreich der Zwischenkriegszeit* (Vienna: Böhlau, 1989).
3. Insights into operetta economics can be gleaned from the scattered contracts left in archives. Information is most comprehensive for the post-World War I period, including a complete financial report on the Theater an der Wien's operations written around 1935, after operetta was already in severe decline (found in the Österreichisches Theatermuseum's Hubert Marischka archive) as well as, despite being German rather than Austrian, Hugo Poller's detailed 1926 economics dissertation, 'Die ökonomische Bewirtschaftung eines Operettentheaters' (Würzburg, 1920), Staatsbibliothek zu Berlin (MS 20/1052).
4. The figures include composers, librettists, impresarios and a few critics and actors and are indeed clustered in groups that often collaborated. As reproduced in Otto Brusatti and Wilhelm Deutschmann, *FleZiWiCsá & Co.: Die Wiener Operette: 91. Sonderausstellung des*

202 Micaela K. Baranello

Historischen Museums der Stadt Wien, Karlsplatz, gemeinsam mit der Wiener Stadt- und Landesbibliothek, 20. Dezember 1984 bis 10. Februar 1985 (Wien: Eigenverlag der Museen der Stadt Wien, 1984), 41.

5. A vivid, albeit rather more upper-class account, which favours high culture over operetta, can be found in Stefan Zweig, *The World of Yesterday* (University of Nebraska Press, 1964).

6. This debt is considered in Stefan Schmidl, 'À la viennoise: Sardou et l'opérette viennoise' in Isabelle Mondrot (ed.), *Victorien Sardou: Le théâtre et les arts* (Rennes: Presses univeristaires de Rennes, 2010), 182–93.

7. Ludwig Hirschfeld, 'Wie eine Operette entsteht', *Komödie*, 26 May 1923.
   Another example comes from a theatre joke book:

   'Tell me, why does X write on all his librettos "From the French"?'
   'So it doesn't come out that they're all from the English.'

   (—Sagen Sie, warum schreibt der X. auf alle seine Libretti, 'Aus dem Französischen'?
   —Damit man nicht daraufkommt, daß sie alles aus dem Englischen sind.)

   Alexander Engel, Vorhang auf! 250 Witze und Anekdoten
   vom Theater (Vienna: M. Perles, 1910), 94.

8. '*nach einer fremden Grundidee*' appears on the score's title page.

9. Peter Grunsky, *Richard Heuberger: Der Operettenprofessor* (Vienna: Böhlau, 2002).

10. Timothy Freeze, 'Gustav Mahler's Third Symphony: Program, Reception, and Evocations of the Popular', unpublished PhD dissertation, University of Michigan (2010), 140–7.

11. Kraus wrote in 1901, 'who, other than Mr. [Max] Kalbeck [who had praised *Der Opernball*'s orchestration in a review] knows that the beguiling orchestral colours of *Der Opernball* were provided not by the composer but by Alexander von Zemlinsky, who orchestrated the greater part of the operetta?' By publishing this in *Die Fackel*, Kraus assured that many more people found out. Antony Beaumont credits Zemlinsky with the orchestration of Act 1, possibly large sections of Act 3, and likely the composition of the overture. Translation from Antony Beaumont, *Zemlinsky* (London: Faber, 2000), 30.

12. Ibid. There is some dispute about whether Arnold Schoenberg also had a hand in the orchestration of Act 3. Although Webern and Ottilie Schoenberg claimed that he did, Schoenberg scholar Ernest Hilmar claims the manuscript score bears no traces of Schoenberg at all, citing the assistance of Helmut Heuberger for this verification. It may be timely for this manuscript to receive a second look. Ernst Hilmar (ed.), *Arnold Schönberg [13. Sept. 1874–13. Juli 1951.]: Gedenkausstellung 1974* (Vienna: Universal Edition, 1974).

13. His contract can be seen in Hans Heinz Stuckenschmidt, *Schoenberg: His Life, World, and Work* (London: John Calder, 1977), 537–8. Hilmar identifies Schoenberg as an orchestrator for Robert Fischhof, Victor Holländer and Bogumil Zepler, as well as possibly working for Heuberger, Leo Fall (who claimed to orchestrate his own works) and Edmund Eysler.

14. As a conductor in Bad Ischl, Teplitz, Danzig and Stettin, Webern often conducted operetta. From Bad Ischl he wrote to his cousin Diez: 'Meine Tätigkeit ist schrecklich! . . . Aus der Welt mit solchen Dreck! Welche Wohltat wäre der Menschheit getan, vernichtete man sämtliche Operetten-, Possen- und Volkstheater. Dann fällt niemanden meh rein, daß er um jeden Preis ein derartigen "Kunstwerk" zustandebringen muß! Wenn man, so wie ich, den ganzen Tag mit diesem Zeugs zu tun hat, könnte man wahnsinnig warden!' Friedrich Wildgans, *Anton Webern: Eine Studie* (Tübingen: Wunderlich, 1967), 47.

15. 'Wer instrumentiert die Wiener Operetten?', *Die Stunde*, 3 July 1926, 7.

16. 'Kopsiva' is presumably a typographical error for Franz Kopriva, a prolific credited arranger of operetta and therefore likely also an orchestrator.

17. The *Fach* system is thoroughly explored by Eugen Brixel, 'Die Ära Wilhelm Karczag im Theater an der Wien', unpublished PhD dissertation, University of Vienna (1966), as well as more recently in Heike Quissek, *Das deutschsprachige Operettenlibretto: Figuren, Stoffe, Dramaturgie* (Stuttgart: Verlag J. B. Metzler, 2012).

18. Adorno identifies this tragic second-act finale as the key manifestation of late Viennese operetta's claim to dramatic consequence. Theodor Adorno, 'Arabesken zur Operette' [1932] in Rolf Tiedemann and Klaus Schultz (eds.), *Gesammelte Schriften,* Vol. 19, Musikalische Schriften VI (Frankfurt: Suhrkamp, 2003), 516–19.

19. Christian Marten, *Die Operette als Spiegel der Gesellschaft: Franz Lehárs 'Die lustige Witwe':* *Versuch einer sozialen Theorie der Operette* (Frankfurt: Peter Lang, 1988).
20. Martin Lichtfuss lays these conventions out in a chart in Lichtfuss, *Operette im Ausverkauf*, 85–7.
21. Until the 1920s, the only thing that could really stop a theatre was a fire, as happened at the Ringtheater in 1881. See W. E. Yates, *Theatre in Vienna: A Critical History, 1776–1995*, Cambridge Studies in German (Cambridge: Cambridge University Press, 1996), 155.
22. This landscape is described and perceptively analysed by Marion Linhardt, *Residenzstadt und Metropole: Zu einer kulturellen Topographie des Wiener Unterhaltungstheaters (1858–1918)* (Berlin: De Gruyter, 2012; orig. pub. Tübingen: Niemeyer, 2006).
23. Operetta orchestration was standardized with double woodwind (second flute doubling piccolo), two trumpets, four horns and three trombones. The differences were in the sizes of the string sections. A breakdown for the Raimundtheater can be found in *Deutsches Bühnen-Jahrbuch*, 1910 edition, 674–5. Listings of orchestral and choral personnel can be found in the *Deutsches Bühnen-Jahrbuch*. The Theater an der Wien, Johann-Strauss-Theater and Carl-Theater employed forces of near-identical size; smaller theatres such as the Raimundtheater featured smaller orchestras and choruses. Deutscher Bühnenverein, *Deutsches Bühnen-jahrbuch; Theatergeschichtliches Jahr- und Adressenbuch* (Berlin: F. A. Günther, 1890), <http://catalog.hathitrust.org/Record/000551053>. The 1935 roster can be found in the Hubert Marischka Archive (unnumbered), box 'Theater an der Wien. Pläne', Österreichisches Theatermuseum.
24. Notoriously, *Die lustige Witwe*, which went on to be the most successful operetta of the twentieth century, premiered with no new costumes or sets at all. After its success was apparent, the production was completely re-outfitted. In the 1910s and 1920s, when exotic and dramatically specific settings became more common and stagings more opulent, costumes and sets were most often made to order.
25. These reports were developed into a genre by Mizzi Neumann in the *Neues Wiener Journal*. See, for example, Mizzi Neumann, 'Die lustige Viererzug in "Clo-Clo". Lehar-Premiere am Bürgertheater', *Neues Wiener Journal*, 9 March 1924; Mizzi Neumann, 'Unsere Eliteveranstaltungen. Zu Marischkas großer Erfolg', *Neues Wiener Journal*, 2 March 1924; Ella Bermer, '"Giuditta". Zur gestrigen Sensationspremiere in der Staatsoper', *Neues Wiener Journal*, 21 January 1934, sec. Unsere Mode.
26. A few contracts can be found in the Nachlass Marischka, ÖTM and the Alfred Grünwald Papers (*T-Mss 1998–30, NYPL). An excellent set of contracts for many works over the course of over a decade, including many international agreements, can be found in the Leo Fall Collection, F88 Leo Fall 281–5, ÖNB MS (Austrian National Library Music Collection) .
27. As documented in the Marischka papers, publishers spent considerable time and resources tracking down and suing provincial productions that had 'bootlegged' the operetta and were performing without paying the publisher (perhaps after having covertly copied another theatre's materials).
28. Stefan Frey, *Was sagt ihr zu diesem Erfolg: Franz Lehár und die Unterhaltungsmusik des 20. Jahrhunderts* (Frankfurt: Insel, 1999), 78–103.
29. The status of printed librettos is examined in more detail in Albert Gier, 'Alles fließt. Probleme der Edition von Operettenlibretti' in Thomas Betzweiser, Norbert Dubowy and Andreas Münzmay (eds.), *Perspektiven der Edition Musikdramatischer Texte* (Berlin: Walter De Gruyter, 2017), 163–82.
30. 'Was nach den jeweiligen Zeitverhältnissen gegen die Rücksichten für die öffentliche Ruhe und Ordnung verstößt, was den öffentlichen Anstand, die Schamhaftigkeit, die Moral oder die Religion beleidigt', l. [pseud.], 'Der neue Zensor: Gespräch mit Bürgermeister Reumann', *Komödie*, 2, no. 1 (1 January 1921): 3.
31. The rules are outlined in Yates, *Theatre in Vienna*, 42–8; Norbert Nischkauer, 'Bemerkungen zum Thema Johann Strauß und die Zensur', *Die Fledermaus*, 4 (1992): 10–16.
32. l. [pseud.], 'Der neue Zensor: Gespräch mit Bürgermeister Reumann'.
33. 'Die Zensur is tot, es lebe die Zensur!', *Die Stunde*, 27 March 1926.
34. This includes Ludwig Hirschfeld and Leopold Jacobson, both librettists, as well as Ernst Decsey, author of several libretti, plays and a partially musicalized *Volksstück* about Bruckner, *Der Musikant Gottes*.
35. The most detailed study of Viennese newspapers of this period is Kurt Paupié, *Handbuch der österreichischen Pressegeschichte 2: Die zentralen pressepolitischen Einrichtungen des Staates, 1848–1959* (Vienna: W. Braumüller, 1966).

36. 'Die Fünf mit der Maske', *Komödie: Wochenrevue für Bühne und Film*, 19 February 1921.
37. Max Graf, 'Von den Wiener Operettenbühnen', *Neues Wiener Journal*, 24 October 1905.
38. Linhardt, *Residenzstadt und Metropole*, 106.

Recommended Reading

Frey, Stefan. *Was sagt ihr zu diesem Erfolg: Franz Lehár und die Unterhaltungsmusik des 20. Jahrhunderts*. Frankfurt: Insel, 1999.

Linhardt, Marion. *Residenzstadt und Metropole: Zu einer kulturellen Topographie des Wiener Unterhaltungstheaters (1858–1918)*. Berlin: De Gruyter, 2012 (orig. pub. Tübingen: Niemeyer, 2006).

Quissek, Heike. *Das deutschsprachige Operettenlibretto: Figuren, Stoffe, Dramaturgie*. Stuttgart: Verlag J. B. Metzler, 2012.

Yates, W. E. *Theatre in Vienna: A Critical History, 1776–1995*. Cambridge: Cambridge University Press, 1996.

13 Berlin Operetta

Paris has Jacques Offenbach, Vienna Johann Strauss and Franz Lehár, London Gilbert and Sullivan but which Berlin operetta composer has made an enduring international name for himself? Theatrically Berlin is associated either with high cultural, artistically experimental stage productions of the Reinhardt-Piscator school or, thanks to *The Blue Angel* and *Cabaret*, with cabaret. Berlin is much less associated with operetta and this despite producing some domestically as well as internationally very successful examples of the genre – why is this?

There is more than one reason. Firstly, Berlin entered the popular musical stage comparatively late in the last year of the nineteenth century, when Paris, Vienna and London had already successfully established themselves as capitals of popular musical theatre. Secondly, Berlin's time in the limelight was comparatively short-lived. After 1933 the majority of its most talented composers, writers, actors, directors and managers either left the country or found themselves barred from the stage, if not faced with the threat of deportation and death because they were Jewish. Simultaneously, Berlin was cut off from artistic developments and markets in other countries. Finally, Berlin operetta, though popularly successful, lacked intellectual support. German critics either ignored or panned operetta as trite, vulgar, worthless mass entertainment. Long before Theodor Adorno took on the American culture industry, he cut his teeth excoriating Weimar era operetta.

Such judgements partly determined how operetta was seen after World War II and to some extent is still seen today. In contrast particularly to Britain and the United States, the Berlin operetta heritage was, apart from some die-hard enthusiasts, not preserved and celebrated. This might also partly have to do with operetta's association with stuffy Victorianism and, worse still, National Socialism (Hitler was a known operetta lover). A younger generation dismissed the German tradition in popular entertainment as old-fashioned, bourgeois and fascist, embracing American rock and roll and, if they cared at all for musical theatre, Broadway musicals. While some operettas, especially those by Offenbach and Strauss, were performed by opera houses and became a mainstay of provincial theatres, no self-respecting intendant would have dreamed of touching Berlin operetta. This has changed since the 2010s, when Berlin-based directors like Barrie Kosky at the Komische Oper or Herbert Fritsch at the Volksbühne began to revive the lost tradition of local popular musical theatre, drawing attention to its subversive potential. However, as this essay will show, there is still a lot to rediscover. It starts off by looking at the early history of Berlin operetta before focussing on the period between 1900 and 1933. It concentrates on the most important works, theatres, composers, writers and managers and the international traffic in operettas.

* * *

Around the middle of the nineteenth century, Berlin, the capital of Prussia, was by far the largest German city with just over 400,000 inhabitants. However, it was only after the Franco-German war of 1870–1, when Berlin became the capital of a unified Germany that it began to grow both in population and in political and cultural importance. When World War I broke out, it was the third largest European city after London and Paris. Its rapid growth gave the city a new and modern appearance, especially compared with older European cities. Mark Twain compared it to Chicago. This growth was largely due to immigration from rural parts of Germany, particularly from eastern territories such as Silesia. As many of the newcomers were Jews the make-up of the city changed and became much more cosmopolitan.

Fast-growing Berlin was a city in search of an identity. In this process, media took on a particular importance. The popular press demonstrated how to find one's bearings in the new – and, for many people from the countryside, certainly also frightening – environment, contributing to what one sociologist has called 'inner urbanization'.[1] The theatre fulfilled a similar function. Inventing Berlin characters, using Berlin dialect and representing Berlin problems on the stage, it held up a mirror to old residents and newcomers alike and helped them to come to terms with the changing city and their roles in it. It was on the stage that Berlin first claimed to be a metropolis on a par with the other capitals of the world. When the writer David Kalisch gave one of his farces the subtitle 'Berlin becomes a world city', it was meant as a joke.[2] Soon, however, it became a rallying call for Berlin's ambition to be on an equal footing with Paris and London.

Obviously, Berlin was not as politically and economically important as London, the heart of a global empire, and it was certainly not as beautiful as Paris (even many Berliners decried its ugliness). Neither could it look back on as long a history as these cities. But in the fields of entertainment and nightlife it claimed to surpass both – a bold claim given Paris's status in

that regard. Population growth, the gradual rise of wages and the increasing leisure time produced an ever-growing demand for entertainment,
which led, in a comparatively short span of time, to the opening of many
new theatres, variety theatres, music halls and countless cabarets, pubs and
summer gardens. Depending on location, size and ticket prices, these
venues were showing local as well as international entertainments,
among them many operettas. Offenbach was as popular in Berlin as anywhere in Europe, and both he and Johann Strauss conducted their works in
Berlin. In 1886 an English touring company brought *The Mikado* to Berlin.
Despite performing in English, this visit was a big success, prompting some
journalists to question why German writers and composers were unable to
produce similar entertainments.

It would take another decade for Berlin operetta to emerge and two
decades until it would reach other countries. Paul Lincke is often seen
as the father of Berlin operetta and is practically the only composer of
Berlin operettas born in Berlin. He started out as a musician, playing
the violin and bassoon. He then moved into light music, composing as
well as conducting the orchestra of the Apollo-Theater, one of Berlin's
foremost variety theatres. As a conductor, Lincke was a dandified
showman, always appearing in his trademark black coat-tails, top hat
and white gloves. Surprisingly, for someone so strongly associated with
Berlin, he moved to Paris for two years, where he conducted the
orchestra of the Folies-Bergère, Europe's foremost variety theatre.
After his return to Berlin in 1899, Lincke had his first big success –
and, indeed, the biggest of his career – with the operetta *Frau Luna*.
Originally a one-act piece and part of a variety bill, Lincke would
expand and adapt the score throughout his life.

Frau Luna successfully brought together a mixture of influences,
namely operetta of the French and Viennese school and Berlin burlesque.
What the cancan had been for Offenbach and the waltz for Strauss, the
march became for Lincke. His most famous was 'Das ist die Berliner Luft'
(This is the Berlin air) by which, to quote the historian Peter Gay, Lincke
'did not have meteorology in mind but an incontestable mental alertness'.[3]
Lincke wrote for Berlin audiences, and Berlin was the topic of his operettas.
Frau Luna featured typical Berlin characters speaking in Berlin dialect,
such as the engineer Fritz Steppke, who invents a balloon and flies to the
moon with his friends, where they get up to all kinds of mischief. It was
adapted in Paris (as *Madame de la Lune* in 1904) and in London (as *Castles
in the Air* in 1911) but – probably because of its Berlinness – did not find
much success in either city.

Trying to capitalize on his success, Lincke quickly turned out a string of
operettas, most of which followed the same plot of the bumbling comic

young Berlin man blundering into some exotic locale. More important than the plot was that most of them had at least one or two hit songs eagerly picked up by dance orchestras and barrel organists, who turned them into bona fide folksongs one could hear at every street corner of Berlin. In due course, Lincke became rich and founded his own publishing house, but with success his productivity decreased until he wrote hardly anything new.

While *Frau Luna* is still remembered and regularly performed today, the same cannot be said for the operettas of Lincke's contemporary Victor Hollaender, who is chiefly remembered as the father of the better-known writer and composer Friedrich Hollaender. From a Jewish family in Silesia, Hollaender came to Berlin to study music. Afterwards he worked as a conductor in Germany, Europe and the United States and wrote music for the stage. In 1899 he settled in Berlin, where he became the house composer of the Metropol-Theater.

The Metropol was the first Berlin theatre to stage annual revues, a genre imported from Paris which satirized social, political and cultural events of the past year. The Metropol revues quickly became the toast of Berlin and attracted visitors from all over Germany. They also launched the career of Fritzi Massary. The daughter of a Jewish merchant from Vienna, she became one of the biggest German theatre stars and *the* German operetta diva both before and after World War I.

For a while Hollaender was one of the most popular German composers, earning enough money to build a mansion in the expensive Grunewald district on the outskirts of Berlin. Some of his songs were international hits, such as his 'Schaukellied', written for a revue in 1905. It became popular in Britain as 'Swing Song' and as 'Swing Me High, Swing Me Low' in the United States, where Florenz Ziegfeld incorporated it into his *Follies of 1910*.[4] His operettas, however, were less successful and after World War I he found it increasingly difficult to keep pace with changing musical tastes.

Even before the war, Lincke and Hollaender began to be sidelined by a new generation of Berlin composers, namely Walter Kollo and Jean Gilbert. Like so many of his peers, Kollo began by working and writing for the thriving cabaret scene, soon moving into the theatre. His first success was *Große Rosinen* (Big Raisins) in 1911, followed by the even bigger success of *Wie einst im Mai* (Like One Time in May) in 1913, which told the story of two Berlin families over four generations. Kollo continued very much in Lincke's vein, writing operettas about Berlin for Berliners.

Kollo's biggest rival was Jean Gilbert, the most prolific of all Berlin operetta composers. Born as Max Winterfeld in Hamburg in 1879 into a Jewish family, Gilbert was hardly eighteen years old when he started to conduct at provincial theatres and began to compose. His first success, *Die polnische Wirtschaft* (literally Polish Business but really 'monkey business') of 1910, ran for 580 consecutive performances, an enormous number for Berlin at that time. The next year's *Die keusche Susanne* (Chaste Susan) was even more successful. Based – as so many Berlin operettas were – on a French farce, it mocked the moral reformers of the day. Gilbert may, as his critics alleged, not have been a first-rate composer, but he certainly knew what the audience liked, and he was more than ready to give it to them, turning out two or more operettas per year, touring with his orchestra and producing an endless outpour of gramophone recordings.

In the years preceding World War I, Kollo and Gilbert wrote at least one successful operetta each year – once even about the same subject: the rise of the film industry. Kollo's operetta *Filmzauber*, premiering in 1912 at the Berliner Theater, told the story of a dodgy film director, whose ill-fated attempt at shooting a biopic about Napoleon produces comic confusion. It was followed by Gilbert's *Die Kino-Königin* (The Cinema Star), in which a businessman campaigning against the dangers of the cinema is secretly filmed wooing a diva only to become an involuntary film star himself.[5] Much has been made of the competition between the popular stage and the cinema at the time as well as retrospectively. Yet, while happy to mock the film industry, operetta composers did not hesitate to work for the new medium. Walter Kollo wrote the score for a dozen films, while Jean Gilbert was under contract by a film studio as *Die Kino-Königin* came out. Indeed, operetta had a remarkable impact on the early German film industry. Already during the silent film era many operettas were turned into films.

For operetta, and especially for Berlin operetta, to tackle a contemporary subject like the cinema was not unusual. On the contrary, pre-war operetta delighted in taking up topical phenomena, fashions and fads. With the beginning craze for North as well as South American dances, European composers felt compelled to utilize the new rhythms. Jean Gilbert, for instance, used the tango in an operetta titled *Die Tangoprinzessin* (The Tango Princess). Yet, despite Lincke's penchant for the march, Berlin operetta capitalized on the waltz as much as Viennese operetta.

Gilbert's works were more cosmopolitan than those of the Berlin-centric Kollo. *Die keusche Susanne* was set in Paris, *Die Kino-Königin* in Philadelphia. This might have helped them to be adapted abroad. However, operettas by both these composers increasingly found their way on to the stages of other European cities, thanks not least to the enormous global success of Franz Lehár's *The Merry Widow* in 1907. Suddenly, every theatre manager in Europe and even outside Europe became aware of the selling power of German operetta. Whether they originated in Vienna or Berlin often did not make much of a difference.

Gilbert's *Die keusche Susanne*, for instance, played in Vienna and in Madrid (*La casta Susanna*) in 1911, in Warsaw (*Cnotliwa Zuzanna*) in 1911, in London (*The Girl on the Film*) and in Budapest (*Az ártatlan Zsuzsi*) in 1912, in Paris (*La chaste Suzanne*) in 1913, in Sydney in 1914 and in New York (*Modest Suzanne*) and in Naples (*La casta Susanna*) in 1915. In the summer of 1914, four West End theatres were showing operettas by Kollo and Gilbert. As composers realized that there was money in international sales, they reacted by writing less locally specific, more universal operettas.

Composers benefited from the overall growth of the theatre industry across Europe. The growing number of theatres led to a growing demand for new content that the domestic market was often unable to satisfy. Theatre managers therefore increasingly looked abroad for new shows, especially as theatre became more and more costly. A show that had succeeded elsewhere raised hopes that it would be successful once more. Managers, publishers and agents eagerly observed what was going on abroad and stayed in constant contact with their colleagues in other countries. The internationalization of the theatre industry, then, was driven by its development into a big – potentially extremely profitable, potentially hazardous – business. Nothing illustrates better how international it had become than the situation operetta theatres found themselves in when World War I broke out. Many had to withdraw current shows because they had been written by composers from now enemy nations and were no longer welcome. Often these shows were replaced by well-established classics or by improvised patriotic shows, which leant more towards revue than operetta.

In Berlin, both Kollo and Gilbert wrote jingoistic shows calculated to raise the morale. This in turn made their operettas even less acceptable in London and Paris. With habitual celerity, Jean Gilbert, quickly exchanging his French-sounding pseudonym for his original German name, turned out the music for two war plays in 1914: *Kamrad Männe* (War Comrade Männe) and *Woran wir denken* (What We Think Of). Like most war plays, *Kamrad Männe* took its cue from the mobilization of the army. Its first act took place before, the second during and the third right after the declaration of war, showing how Germans from all classes and regions – and especially Germans and Austrians – stood together. Popular theatre actively contributed to the war effort or at least did its best to make it appear that way to make people forget how international and cosmopolitan it had been before the war.

Like *Kamrad Männe*, Walter Kollo's *Immer feste druff!* (Beat Them Hard!) invoked the solidarity of all German people. It ran for over 800 performances, from October 1914 all through the war till the abdication of the

German emperor. This was unusual because audiences quickly got tired of propaganda as the war dragged on and began to favour escapist, sentimental plays that enabled people to forget the war for two or three hours. The two biggest wartime hits, *Die Csárdásfürstin* and *Das Dreimäderlhaus*, couldn't be further removed from the reality of war. Originating in Vienna, they were performed over 900 times in Berlin.[6]

The war years were very good years for the Berlin popular stage. Both people at home and soldiers on leave flocked to the theatre for entertainment and distraction. The slump came with looming defeat and the spread of Spanish influenza in 1918. People were scared to go to the theatre, and the box office turned sour; its fortunes improved only in the economically relative stable twenties.

After the war, Berlin became the capital of the now democratic Germany. Much like the country, its capital was rapidly changing. With the Greater Berlin Act of 1920, the city incorporated a lot of suburbs – some of them cities in their own right – and rapidly grew to more than four million inhabitants. It was now one of the largest cities in the world, almost the size of Paris. The hedonism that followed post-war austerity expressed itself on the stage in the form of grand, spectacular revues. Thanks to the abolition of theatre censorship in 1918, they could freely revel in an abundance of naked flesh never seen before or since on the Berlin stage. But apart from this, in their bombastic scale and their even more fragmented plots, they continued a pre-war tradition.

This was true for Weimar culture in general, which was not as new and original as may appear retrospectively. It often drew on forms and genres of the imperial period, and some traditions from that period not immediately associated with Weimar culture continued in the post-war period. Weimar theatre, for instance, was not all spectacular shows, avant-gardist agitprop or candid cabaret. To take an example, the fad for revues did not last very long. With the onset of the economic depression in the late twenties, shows flaunting extravagant opulence no longer seemed appropriate. All this time operetta remained a mainstay of Berlin theatres and reached a new peak in both output and popularity.

Berlin now even outstripped Vienna as operetta capital. This had partly to do with Vienna's loss of political and cultural importance and partly with Berlin's new status. With its enormous audience, its dynamic theatre industry, its star actors, its theatre publishers and its links to other capital cities, Berlin became the foremost theatre city in the German-speaking world. It is therefore not surprising that many Viennese composers decided to bring out their new pieces in Berlin. Franz Lehár's later works, for instance, such as *Friederike* (Frederica, 1928) and *Das Land des Lächelns* (The Land of Smiles, 1929), premiered at the Metropol-

Theater. The main part in both operettas went to the tenor Richard Tauber, who had started out as an opera tenor before becoming the most famous male operetta star of interwar Europe. He also appeared in the London adaptation of *The Land of Smiles* in 1931. Subsequently, he became a regular guest on the British stage, emigrating to London in 1938.

Oddly, Tauber never appeared together with the other big operetta star Fritzi Massary. Her career, substantial even before the war, now reached a new height. Oscar Straus practically wrote exclusively for her, beginning with *Der letzte Walzer* (The Last Waltz) in 1920 and culminating in *Eine Frau, die weiß, was sie will* (A Woman Who Knows What She Wants) in 1932, in which she played what could be called a disguised self-portrait: an ageing operetta diva with an illegitimate daughter. In between, Massary starred in Leo Fall's *Madame Pompadour*.

While Lehár, Straus and Fall as well as Kollo and Gilbert continued to be active in the interwar period, a new generation of composers emerged with Hugo Hirsch and Eduard Künneke leading the way. Hugo Hirsch, like many other operetta composers of Jewish descent, burst on to the Berlin scene in the 1920s. His operetta *Der Fürst von Pappenheim* (The Prince of Pappenheim, 1923), partly set in a department store, partly at a seaside resort, delighted audiences in Berlin and elsewhere. In the following year, four Berlin theatres premiered operettas by Hirsch.

After studying music in Berlin, Eduard Künneke worked as a music teacher and conductor writing music on the side. His first operetta, *Wenn Liebe erwacht* (Love's Awakening), came out in 1920. It was followed by *Der Vetter aus Dingsda* (The Cousin from Nowhere) in 1921, Künneke's biggest success. Despite its well-tried mistaken-identities plot, *Der Vetter aus Dingsda* seemed fresh because it broke with the sumptuous wartime operettas by reducing the ensemble and the sets, by doing away with the chorus and by incorporating new musical styles like the Boston, the tango and the foxtrot.

World War I had severed the network between the theatre industries of the warring nations. Soon, however, managers set out to revive it. In 1920 the British impresario Albert de Courville, eager to import German operettas, wrote to *The Times*:

> are we still at war with Germany or not? America evidently thinks not. I am told that Lehár is going over and Reinhardt has been invited. Are we in the theatrical world free to buy plays from the late enemy in the same way as we buy razors? Are we at liberty to reawaken public interest in a class of show highly delectable before the war?[7]

De Courville's answer to this question was, of course, an emphatic yes. As anti-German resentment began to fade, he and his colleagues imported the latest successes as well as the wartime hits British audiences had missed out on due to the boycott of German culture. In 1921 *Wenn Liebe erwacht* ran in London as *Love's Awakening*, followed, in 1922, by Gilbert's *Die Frau im Hermelin* (*The Lady of the Rose*) and Straus's *Der letzte Walzer* (*The Last Waltz*), in 1923, by *Der Vetter aus Dingsda* (*The Cousin from Nowhere*) and Fall's *Madame Pompadour*, in 1924 by *Der Fürst von Pappenheim* (*Toni*), in 1925, by Straus's *Die Perlen der Kleopatra* (*Cleopatra*) and Gilbert's *Katja die Tänzerin* (*Katja the Dancer*), in 1926, by Gilbert's *Yvonne* (specifically written for the West End), and in 1927, *Mädi* (*The Blue Train*) by Robert Stolz (1880–1975). Most of these plays were also adapted in Paris, New York and other cities.

Undeniably, Berlin had returned to the centre of international popular musical theatre. Not all of these plays fulfilled the expectations their continental success had aroused, though. Consequently, in the late 1920s, slightly fewer Berlin operettas crossed over to Britain and the United States. The fate of Eduard Künneke was in many ways representative. Thanks to the success of *The Cousin from Nowhere*, managers abroad hired him to write for their theatres, something few composers before him had experienced. He wrote *The Love Song* (1925) –effectively a medley of Offenbach songs – and *Mayflowers* (1925) for Broadway and *Riki-Tiki* (1926) for the West End. Unfortunately for Künneke, neither of these efforts resonated with audiences, and so he returned to Berlin.

Though the 1920s saw a lot of new operettas by well-known as well as younger composers, they were mainly associated with spectacular revues. If pre-war Metropol revues had been praised for their lavishness, the revues of the twenties were bigger in every sense: with the most numbers, the most expensive stars and settings, the latest dance rhythms and the longest chorus lines. It was one long glorious summer between post-war inflation and the Depression of 1929. No one did more to push the genre to its limits than Erik Charell. Charell had started out as a dancer and actor in Max Reinhardt's ensemble. After Reinhardt's plans to bring the classics to the masses had faltered, Reinhardt asked Charell to take over the management of the Großes Schauspielhaus, which with 3,500 seats was Berlin's biggest theatre. Charell did not baulk at the challenge. He believed he knew what the masses wanted. He began to stage revues aspiring to be larger, more inventive and spectacular than those of his competitors. He also began, in 1926, to overhaul hits from the pre-war era such as *The Mikado*, *Wie einst im Mai*, *Madame Pompadour* and *Die lustige Witwe* by giving them the revue treatment, creating what came to be called revue-operetta. While some Berlin critics enthused over his *Mikado*, the Berlin-based British critic C. Hooper Trask was incensed: 'Outside of the necessary modernisation of topical allusions, hacks of the Austrian operetta factory should be made to keep their paws where they belong', he chastised Charell.[8]

The Mikado was followed by *Casanova* in 1928, *Die drei Musketiere* (The Three Musketeers) in 1929 und *Im weißen Rössl* (White Horse Inn) in 1930 –success, success and yet more success. To stage *Im weißen Rössl* must have sounded like a risky idea, based as it was on a farce from the 1890s about the adventures of some Berlin tourists in the Austrian Salzkammergut. Its success speaks much for Charell's artistry as a director and his feel for popular tastes. However, Charell did not take any chances, bringing together some of the best writers Berlin had to offer at that time, such as the universally talented Ralph Benatzky, a composer, lyricist, writer and poet, who had already collaborated with Charell on his previous productions. *Im weißen Rössl* had everything: a well-tried plot and topical jokes; sentimental songs and topical dance tunes; the old emperor Franz Joseph I of Austria, who embodied the retrospectively idyllic pre-war Europe, and a modern jazz band. But especially it had settings no one had ever seen before, settings that grew from the stage into the auditorium. Even the exterior of the theatre became part of the show, as the Großes Schauspielhaus was made to look like an Alpine inn.

While Charell modernized well-known operettas, new operetta composers began to appear on the scene. The most talented of them was the Hungarian Paul Abraham. Abraham had begun by writing chamber music, but this only got him a job as a bank clerk. It was his *Viktoria und ihr Husar* (Viktoria and Her Hussar) that saved him from a fate behind the counter and brought him to Berlin via Vienna. The first piece he wrote for the Berlin stage was *Die Blume von Hawaii* (The Flower of Hawaii) about the Hawaiian princess Layla, who had been deposed from the throne by the US Army. In the end, Layla decides against a plot to reinstate her, renounces the Hawaiian throne and moves to the French Riviera. This plot was somewhat reminiscent of Germany's own recent history: former emperor Wilhelm II, who had been disposed in 1918, now lived in the Netherlands, where he passed his time chopping wood.

Die Blume von Hawaii was a big success, as was Abraham's following operetta, *Der Ball im Savoy*, about a couple suspecting each other of infidelity in the comfortable surroundings of the French Riviera. Abraham was an inventive composer. While effortlessly turning out sprightly waltzes, he was also open to new influences, making use of new American dances – the tango and the pasodoble being favourites – and instruments like the saxophone, almost unheard of in operetta before. He also profited from working with two experienced librettists, Alfred Grünwald and Fritz Löhner-Beda.

It is a matter of debate whether an overview on Berlin operetta should also include Bertolt Brecht and Kurt Weill's *Die Dreigroschenoper* (The Threepenny Opera). The title identifies it as an opera, but the

Dreigroschenoper was much closer to operetta, not least because it was not through-composed but a play with songs. Weill himself admitted that he and Brecht wanted to break into the commercial theatre industry to reach a wider audience. The communist director Erwin Piscator had led the way in the mid-twenties by appropriating revue in the hope of revolutionizing the masses and spreading communist ideas. Now Brecht and Weill followed his example with operetta.

The *Dreigroschenoper*, based on John Gay's *The Beggar's Opera* and set in Victorian London, but really about Weimar Berlin, was an overnight success and some of its numbers became instant *Schlager*, hit songs. Four months after its premiere in Berlin, it ran in nineteen German cities. In the summer of 1929, there were allegedly 200 productions together accounting for more than 4,000 performances. Politically, however, it was less successful. The bourgeoisie it lampooned either did not get or ignored its political message. In 1933, Mack the Knife (aka Adolf Hitler) became chancellor, the *Dreigroschenoper* was cancelled and its authors fled the country.

The *Dreigroschenoper* reached the London stage only in 1956, and then it was not very successful. Brecht's clichéd fantasy version of Soho must have struck British audiences as very strange indeed. In contrast, many of the successful Berlin operettas of the late twenties and early thirties were almost instantly adapted abroad: Lehár's *Friederike* (Frederica) in London in 1930, *Das Land des Lächelns* (The Land of Smiles) in London in 1931 and Paris in 1932, Straus's *Eine Frau, die weiß, was sie will* in London (as *Mother of Pearl*) in 1933 and Abraham's *Ball im Savoy* (*Ball at the Savoy*) in London in 1933.

The popular success of Charell's *Im weißen Rössl* also caught the attention of the British manager Oswald Stoll. Stoll was looking for a show to revive the fortunes of the Coliseum Theatre, the floundering flagship of his entertainment concern. With 2,500 seats, it was the biggest variety theatre in London at that time. He hired Charell, hoping that he would repeat his Berlin success in London. Charell remained true to his original concept. As in Berlin, he relied on overwhelming the audience with sheer excess. Again, the complete interior of the theatre was turned into a version of the Alpine uplands. The production featured 160 actors, three orchestras, live animals and a real rainstorm resulting in staggering production costs. However, Stoll's investment paid off: within twenty-four hours the box office reported bookings worth £50,000. The reviewers were suitably impressed. 'Indeed, London can never before have seen a musical play produced on such a scale', reported the *Daily Telegraph*, 'or beheld such mass movements by crowds perfectly drilled and co-ordinated, and such a succession of quickly moving scenes rich in varied (and often gorgeous) colour.'[9] The *Morning Post* called it the 'success of the century!'[10] In view of the German origin of the production, the partly German cast and the Austrian setting, the *Sunday Referee* found it important to emphasize the 'all-British chorus' and the 'all-British work-men' – one of many examples of the complicated relationship between the cosmopolitan and the national.[11] The theatre's readiness to look for inspiration and content abroad could and often did provoke raised eyebrows if not open opposition.

In any case, Charell found himself in great demand. Stoll immediately rehired him to produce a show in 1932, which became *Casanova*. At the same time, Charell oversaw the production of the Paris adaptation of *Im weißen Rössl, L'Auberge du Cheval-Blanc*, which ran for four years. An American production followed in 1936 in New York, where Charell had fled from the Nazis. That Charell looked after all these productions personally was new. Up to then, theatre managers used to buy the rights to a play and score, taking care of the production themselves. However, in the case of *White Horse Inn*, plot and music were less important than Charell's ground-breaking *mise-en-scène*. This left theatre managers no alternative other than to hire the director himself and his team. Charell thereby could be said to have pioneered the method by which a play is sold as a complete package as would become common in popular musical theatre later in the twentieth century.

For a German director to work abroad was extremely tempting in the 1930s both to escape the menacing political atmosphere in Berlin and to earn foreign currency. The Great Depression hit the German economy especially hard and led to steeply rising unemployment. For many people, going to the theatre was a luxury they could no longer afford. This again plunged the theatre industry into crisis, and many Berlin theatres closed. Those that remained open were either state-owned or part of one of just three theatre trusts. When the biggest of them, the Rotter Trust, comprising around thirty theatres in Germany, went bankrupt in January 1933, it meant further closures.

There can be little doubt, though, that the Berlin theatre industry would have revived after the end of the economic crisis as it did in other European capitals. However, by that time, Hitler had been appointed chancellor and the Nazis were in power. They ruthlessly exploited the fact that the owners of the Rotter Trust were Jewish. Claiming Jews had destroyed the German theatre, they systematically removed Jewish managers. Increasingly, Jewish artists had to fear for their lives. Many left the country, fleeing to Austria, Czechoslovakia, France and Britain, and from there often to the United States. Among them were Oscar Straus, Jean Gilbert, Hugo Hirsch, Paul Abraham, Robert Stolz, Ralph Benatzky, Erik Charell, Bert Brecht, Kurt

Weill, Fritzi Massary, Richard Tauber and many more. Not all who left were Jewish, some, like Brecht, were wanted because they were communists, others, like Marlene Dietrich, simply hated the Nazis. Those who did not get out in time were persecuted or killed, like Fritz Löhner-Beda, who was murdered in Auschwitz in 1942.

The mass exodus of Jewish talent, that had shaped Berlin theatre since the beginning of the nineteenth century, necessarily made it much poorer, but it also meant that non-Jewish writers and composers profited from the situation. Because operettas by Jewish composers were forbidden, they now found it much easier to get their works performed. Paul Lincke, Walter Kollo and Eduard Künneke, who had been sidelined by other composers, all witnessed something of a comeback during the Nazi period. Some new talents emerged. In December 1933 Berlin saw the premiere of *Clivia* by Nico Dostal, who until then had mainly worked as a conductor and arranger for more successful composers. *Clivia* was his first operetta and became an instant hit. The operetta was named after its heroine, a famous American actress who has come to the made-up South American republic of Boliguay to star in an American film. The whole project is thrown into jeopardy when the government is toppled by guerrillas and can only be saved if Clivia agrees to marry a Boliguayan gaucho.

Meanwhile back in reality, the German government had been toppled and the Germans had become married to the Nazis. For people who were not Jewish and not interested in politics, everyday life at first did not seem to change that much. Despite their attacks on Weimar culture, the Nazi regime did not replace cosmopolitan operetta theatres with pseudo-Aryan open-air *Thingspiele*. *Clivia* did not differ that much from the operettas before 1933, and it did not promote a political message. Apart from a sometimes less, sometimes more overt anti-Semitism this would remain so throughout the Nazi period. The regime saw operetta as a distraction not as a tool of propaganda. But, of course, it purged operetta of any trace of openness, subversiveness and cosmopolitanism. Foreign shows were no longer welcome in Berlin and neither did Berlin shows travel outside of Germany. Much more than World War I, World War II disrupted the network between the major theatrical hubs in Europe and abroad.

After the war, Berlin was divided into two cities, both of which did little to rescue the heritage of Berlin operetta. The nationalization of theatres that had begun in the Weimar Republic continued during the Nazi period until almost all theatres in Germany were in government hands. In both German countries, this development was not reversed. Even after 1945, theatres remained publicly funded and state-controlled, with appointed intendants. The commercial-theatre industry, once making up 90 per cent of Berlin's theatres, never revived. The publicly funded theatre saw its mission as to provide highbrow, educational fare. Operetta by contrast had been wedded to the commercial theatre from its beginning. The absence of such a commercial sector partly explains why operetta did not return. Offenbach's and Strauss's operettas, now elevated into perennial classics, were sometimes picked up by opera houses to improve attendance figures. Berlin operetta, on the other hand, was largely forgotten, the only exception was Lincke's *Frau Luna*, a perennial favourite with provincial theatres in the vicinity of Berlin.

With no new operettas coming out, the genre ossified. Compared to the Broadway musicals now performed across Germany, it looked more and more old-fashioned. It can be no surprise, then, that Berlin never regained the position in the world of popular musical theatre it had occupied before 1933. Like the city itself, its theatre became provincial. *Im weißen Rössl* was the last Berlin operetta to be staged in London, Paris and New York. Henceforth, popular musical theatre history was made in the West End and on Broadway, not on Friedrichstraße or Kurfürstendamm.

Notes

1. Gottfried Korff, 'Mentalität und Kommunikation in der Großstadt. Berliner Notizen zur "inneren" Urbanisierung' in Theodor Kohlmann, Hermann Bausinger (eds.), *Großstadt. Aspekte empirischer Kulturforschung* (Berlin: Staatliche Museen Preussicher Kulturbesitz, 1985), 343–61; Peter Fritzsche, *Reading Berlin 1900* (Cambridge, MA: Harvard University Press, 1996).
2. David Kalisch, *Haussegen, oder Berlin wird Weltstadt! Vaudeville in einem Act nach Brazier* (Berlin, [1866]).
3. Peter Gay, *My German Question: Growing up in Nazi Berlin* (New Haven, London 1998), 14.
4. Tobias Becker, 'Die Anfänge der Schlagerindustrie: Intermedialität und wirtschaftliche Verflechtung vor dem Ersten Weltkrieg', *Lied und Populäre Kultur* 58 (2013): 11–40.
5. Tobias Becker, 'The *Arcadians* and *Filmzauber*: Adaptation and the Popular Musical Text' in Len Platt, Tobias Becker and David Linton (eds.), *Popular Musical Theatre in London and Berlin* (Basingstoke: Palgrave Macmillan, 2004), 81–101.
6. On the theatre during the First World War see Martin Baumeister, *Kriegstheater. Großstadt, Front und Massenkultur 1914–1918* (Essen: Klartext, 2005); Eva Krivanec, *Kriegsbühnen: Theater im Ersten Weltkrieg. Berlin, Lissabon, Paris und Wien* (Bielefeld: transcript, 2011).
7. *The Times*, 8 April 1920, 8.
8. C. Hooper Trask, 'The Berlin Stage', *The Stage Year Book 1928* (London: Carson and Cummerford), 152. On Charell's revue-operettas see Marita Berg, '"Det Jeschäft ist richtig!" Die Revueoperetten von Erik Charell' in Ulrich Tadday (ed.), *Im weißen Rössl. Zwischen Kunst und Kommerz* (Munich: Edition Text + Kritik, 2006), 59–79; Kevin Clarke, 'Im Rausch der Genüsse. Erik Charell und die entfesselte Revueoperette im Berlin der 1920er Jahre' in Kevin Clarke (ed.), *Glitter and Be Gay. Die authentische Operette und ihre schwulen Verehrer* (Hamburg: Männerschwarm Verlag, 2007), 108–39.
9. 'A Spectacular Triumph', *Daily Telegraph*, 9 April 1931.
10. 'The White Horse Inn', *Morning Post*, 9 April 1931.
11. 'A Magnificent Spectacle', *Sunday Referee*, 5 April 1931.

Recommended Reading

Bartmuss, Hartmut. *Hugo Hirsch: 'Wer wird denn weinen . . .'* Berlin: Hentrich & Hentrich, 2012.

Becker, Tobias. *Inszenierte Moderne. Populäres Theater in Berlin und London, 1880–1930.* Munich: De Gruyter Oldenbourg 2014.

Becker, Tobias. 'Die Anfänge der Schlagerindustrie: Intermedialität und wirtschaftliche Verflechtung vor dem Ersten Weltkrieg', *Lied und Populäre Kultur*, 58 (2013): 11–40.

Gänzl, Kurt. *The Encyclopedia of the Musical Theatre.* 2 vols. Oxford: Blackwell Reference, 1994.

Grosch, Nils, ed. *Aspekte des modernen Musiktheaters in der Weimarer Republik, Aspekte des modernen Musiktheaters in der Weimarer Republik.* Münster: Waxmann, 2004.

Jansen, Wolfgang. *Glanzrevuen der Zwanziger Jahre.* Berlin: Hentrich, 1987.

Jarchow, Ute. *Analysen zur Berliner Operette: Die Operetten Walter Kollos (1878–1940) im Kontext der Entwicklung der Berliner Operette.* München: AVM, 2013.

Jelavich, Peter. *Berlin Cabaret.* Cambridge, MA: Harvard University Press, 1993.

Karl, Viola. *Eduard Künneke (1885–1953): Komponistenportrait und Werkverzeichnis.* Berlin: Ries & Erler, 1995.

Katz, Pamela. *The Partnership: Brecht, Weill, Three Women, and Germany on the Brink.* New York: Doubleday, 2015.

Klotz, Volker. *Operette: Porträt und Handbuch einer unerhörten Kunst.* Kassel: Bärenreiter, rev. ed. 2004 (orig. pub. Munich: Piper, 1991).

Lamb, Andrew. *150 Years of Popular Musical Theatre.* New Haven, CT: Yale University Press, 2000.

Lange, Kerstin. *Tango in Paris und Berlin: Eine transnationale Geschichte der Metropolenkultur um 1900.* Göttingen: Vandenhoeck & Ruprecht, 2015.

Lareau, Alan. *Victor Hollaender: Revue meines Lebens: Erinnerungen an einen Berliner Unterhaltungskomponisten um 1900.* Berlin: Hentrich & Hentrich, 2014.

Morat, Daniel, Tobias Becker, Kerstin Lange, Johanna Niedbalski, Anne Gnausch and Paul Nolte. *Weltstadtvergnügen: Berlin 1880–1930.* Göttingen: Vandenhoeck & Ruprecht, 2016.

Otte, Marline. *Jewish Identities in German Popular Entertainment, 1890–1933.* Cambridge: Cambridge University Press, 2006.

Platt, Len, Tobias Becker and David Linton, eds. *Popular Musical Theatre in London and Berlin, 1890–1939.* Cambridge: Cambridge University Press, 2014.

Sebestyén, György. *Paul Ábrahám: Aus dem Leben eines Operettenkomponisten.* Vienna: Verlag der Österreichischen Staatsdruckerei, 1987.

Traubner, Richard. *Operetta: A Theatrical History.* New York: Routledge, 2003.

14 Operetta in Italy

VALERIA DE LUCCA

The question of the origins and generic characteristics of operetta has always been contentious, but it assumed particularly heated tones in Italy, a country that prided itself on having invented most forms of musical theatre. After all, it is undeniable that the very word 'operetta' comes from the Italian 'opera'. The relationship between operetta and Italian opera – not only *buffa* but also *seria* – was central to the critical discourses about Italian music and culture between the 1860s and the 1920s, becoming closely intertwined with the debate about the position of musical theatre between entertainment and art. More broadly, the critical response to operetta in Italy reveals concerns and anxiety on the new role the middle classes were acquiring as taste makers, especially with regard to emerging concepts of social decorum and propriety. Inevitably, discussions of operetta took also strong nationalistic undertones in a country that was struggling to find a unifying national identity and that recognized operetta as a foreign import, one that could contaminate opera or illegitimately undermine its primacy on the Italian stage.

Regardless of its complex origins, operetta as we know it today was in Italy first and foremost an imported foreign genre. Starting in the 1860s, it was the French works of Offenbach, Hervé and Lecocq and later the so-called 'Viennese' imports of Suppé, Strauss Jr and Lehár that conquered the Italian stages, at first with little response from Italian composers that could undermine the foreign monopoly on operetta. These years, after all, encompassed not only Verdi's most resounding triumphs but also the consolidation of a canon that included a number of serious and comic operas by Rossini, Donizetti and Bellini. As Bruno Traversetti remarked, '[Italian] *melodramma* . . . is the only tradition that is common to the entire Italian social universe during the "bourgeois period": a model that is so voracious and comprehensive that it leaves almost no emotional residues that can be used with dignity.'[1]

If for a long time Italian composers refused to acknowledge the increasing success of French and Viennese operettas, critics and audiences were drawn to the popular foreign genre that was attracting unprecedented crowds to theatres all over the country, across large cities and small towns. While some more conservative critics looked at operetta with suspiciousness and from the superior standpoint of the time-honoured Italian operatic tradition, an increasingly voracious audience welcomed operetta as a breath of fresh air. Arguably, the success and widespread popularity of foreign operetta in Italy reached its climax at the turn of the century, particularly with the extraordinary success of *La vedova allegra*, which premiered in Milan in 1907. The Italian adaptation of Lehár's *Die lustige Witwe* took Milan and subsequently the entire peninsula by storm, stirring new interest and encouraging more Italian composers to engage with a genre that was now acquiring higher status and increasing popularity even among critics.

Production and Reception of Operetta in Nineteenth-Century Italy

From the 1860s, French touring companies, such as the much celebrated Grégoire brothers, as well as Italian troupes began to adapt, produce and perform French operettas – in French as well as in Italian – in Italy. That Italian critics found these early imports difficult to define in regard to their generic characteristics and perceived quality is immediately clear if we consider the terminology they used to discuss them. When Lecocq's *opéra bouffe Les cent vierges* premiered in Paris in 1872, an Italian critic for the *Gazzetta musicale di Milano* called it 'an opera buffa', whereas when the same work opened at the Teatro Manzoni in Milan in 1874 it was called a 'vaudeville'. Another extremely successful *opéra comique* by Lecocq, *La fille de Madame Angot*, was dismissed as 'a French buffoonerie', a 'parody that came from France ... the most French if not the most ungraceful of all'.[2] However, when Lecocq's *opéra comique Les prés Saint-Gervais* was performed in London in 1874, an Italian critic wrote that this was 'overall, an operetta that belongs more to the elegant genre of the *opéra comique*'.[3] While the presence of dialogue was clearly a strong defining element, it seems clear also that the perceived quality of the work could contribute to a definition. Only a few selected French imports could aspire, in fact, to be compared to Italian genres. Offenbach's *Madame l'archiduc*, for example, is praised by a critic for the *Gazzetta musicale di Milano* as 'a jewel', its music really worthy of an *opera buffa*.[4]

Examining the rise of operetta in Italy, Carlotta Sorba argued that 'Italian versions of French operettas developed immediately both their own more comic side as well as a greater emphasis on word and mime compared to music, thus distancing themselves from the Italian operatic tradition, with which it was particularly difficult to compete'.[5] The distinct nature of French operetta in Italy was reflected in the system of production.

Venues for *spettacoli d'arti varie*, variety shows, began to be purpose-built during the 1870s, attracting large crowds of paying audiences, who sought varied and light-hearted forms of entertainment at low prices. The Teatro dal Verme, which would see the Italian premiere of *La vedova allegra* in 1907, could host also clown and circus acts, acrobatic and equestrian displays and magic shows, and later the French import 'cabaret' as well as operetta, *opera buffa* and 'main stream' opera. La Scala, on the other hand, the temple where the increasingly codified operatic canon was consecrated, remained impermeable to the charms of operetta. And the same differentiation of venues according to repertory can be observed in other Italian cities.

The audiences of operetta in Italy during the 1860s and 1870s are often described as rowdy and loud, responding to silly gags with 'guffaws'. Even a bolt of lightning that hit the stage during one of the performances of *La figlia di Madame Angot* at the Teatro dal Verme was received with laughter, prompting a critic to comment that 'the audience, used to the school of the daughter of Madame Angot, does not have respect for anything anymore and started laughing even at lightning. This is definitely the century of parody.' The same critic seems amused and surprised to learn that at the Teatro dal Verme, 'the *clients*' (not *il pubblico* but *gli avventori*, italics in the source!) could not only smoke but also drink beer during the shows. Operetta, after all, was considered pure entertainment and could not aspire to be considered art. Therefore, the audience was encouraged to attend operettas only if 'they wanted to be amused for a couple of hours'.[6]

The audience's misbehaviour was apparently caused by what some critics considered as an extremely lascivious kind of theatre that relied on easy, vulgar and often sexual, innuendos. Again describing Lecocq's *Les cent vierges* in Paris in 1872, a critic for the *Gazzetta musicale di Milano* argues that 'honest women don't dare go to the theatre anymore' since the French librettos of these days had become so obscene that they caused them to blush.[7] When *Le cento vergini* finally arrived in Milan in 1874, another critic confirmed: 'it was said that it was immoral: let us actually say it is lewd, which is something else. It does not corrupt anything, but at times it can become nauseating.'[8] It was not only the lasciviousness of the story but also the apparently nonsensical nature of many operettas that offended the critics' good taste, as a critic observed about Offenbach's *Le corsaire noir*:

> This whole *pasticcio* is too much for one night. Incoherence merrily follows incoherence; inverisimilitude follows inverismilitude; scenes and tableaux follow more scenes and more tableaux without a logical link between them; fantasy and reality, history and fairy tale alternate without any connection between each other and without creating a harmonious whole that would fit the action.

As for the music, if in some cases critics were generally positive about two or three key numbers, usually dances like cancan, csárdás and waltzes, some operettas received harsh reviews, as for example Offenbach's afore-mentioned *Le corsaire noir* in the *Gazzetta di Milano* in 1872:

> Shame on a society, who would take as its daily musical nourishment what Offenbach is producing! Shame on an audience that would take pleasure in this nonsense, which could better suit a tavern, but is absolutely not worthy of a theatre that aims to be a temple dedicated to the arts![9]

Part of the reason for the uncompromising criticism had to do with the quality of the translations, very often deemed inadequate to convey the true verve of the original, as well as of the performances, which were described as having a very 'distinct flavour' compared to those of *opera seria*: 'the chorus sang out of tune, Chambéry, great artist, went off board with his gags in utter bad taste ... Signora Faivre did very well, and has a more robust voice that is more in tune than what we are used to hear in French theatre.'[10] According to many critics, the only redeeming feature of many French operettas was that they were increasingly staged by Italian companies who could afford performers 'born and bred in the Milanese musical entourage', therefore delivering a more reliable result. According to Sorba, it is in this context that we have to understand Friedrich Nietzsche's well-known comments on the lack of elegance of French operettas when they were performed in Italy:

> Moral: not Italy, old friend! Here where I can see the leading light-opera company in Italy, I say to myself, at the sight of each movement of the pretty, all-too-pretty little women, that they make a living caricature of every light opera. They have no *esprit* in their little legs not to speak of their little heads ... Offenbach is just as sombre (I mean thoroughly vulgar) in Italy as in Leipzig.[11]

Thus, operetta in Italy prompted very contrasting reactions: while audiences of the final few decades of the nineteenth century voraciously consumed the adaptations of French operettas and the increasing number of Viennese operettas that followed, taking great pleasure in the light, overly licentious and seemingly nonsensical plots, some critics condemned the genre as an attack on propriety and moral decorum.

But there were also those who took a different stand, such as the Italian intellectuals known as *Scapigliati* (literally 'dishevelled').[12] The movement, inspired by the ideals of German Romanticism and the French *vie bohème*, sought a renovation and rejuvenation of Italian culture starting from a refusal of tradition and rules that represented in their eyes the old and tired culture of the pre-Risorgimento upper classes. Antonio Ghislanzoni, intellectual, music critic, author of librettos and member of the *Scapigliatura*, writing in the *Gazzetta musicale di Milano* about Offenbach's *La bella Elena* in 1866, remarked on the conservatism of Italian audiences as well as of poets and composers, suggesting that operetta could in fact become the vehicle for a profound social renovation, if only Italians were open to the possibilities offered by this genre:

> I even happened to notice in our theatres that, after having laughed their hearts out during the performance of a comedy or a farce, the audience, as the curtain goes down, feels obliged to get revenge on the author and the actors who made them laugh, booing without mercy. These are contradictions that one notices every day – and in truth, they do not make our public spirit shine. Alas! If we were less pedantic, who could prevent us, too, from being called the funniest nation of Europe? Do you believe that this genre of the *opera-parodia* or even better *opera buffona*, could not be created in Italy as elsewhere, if we too had theatres consecrated to this, and if the audience did not intervene with the purpose of philosophising and judging at all costs what the Parisians make an effort to enjoy and laugh at? After all, this *genre* of 'opera-parodia' was an Italian creation of the first half of the last century, and our Scaramuccias taught it to the wigged courts of the 'Louis' who had the good sense to host and replicate it. But to do gracious parodies and jaunty and elegant music one needs poets with *esprit* and *maestri* gifted with verve and culture. Here, those who are called literati and *maestri* would feel they are degrading themselves treating such light subjects.[13]

Crossing the Generic Boundary: Critics' Responses to 'Silver-Age' Operetta

As French and Viennese operettas became increasingly successful in Italy, audiences, theatres, impresarios and a number of companies began to specialize in productions of the genre. In what many saw as an attempt to compete with opera and cross the generic boundaries that separated the two, foreign operetta productions became progressively more lavish and expensive to produce, causing a critic in 1909 to complain that prices were now as high in the venues for operetta as those to attend operas at La Scala: 'This [Teatro dal Verme] cannot be called a theatre for the people since daily *commendator* Sidoli promises *soirées élite* or at least *high life* ... to the poor mob there is nothing left now but ... La Scala, at least on the evenings at reduced prices ... This is more than ever the world upside-down.'[14] This trend reached a climax with the arrival of so-called 'silver-age operetta' and in particular with the premiere of the Italian adaptation of Lehár's *Die lustige Witwe* in Milan in 1907. The undisputed success and immediate popularity of *La vedova allegra* – which received over 500 performances on its first run – sparked lively discussions among critics on the nature of operetta. Writing soon after the premiere of *La vedova allegra*, critic Marco Ramperti expressed his concerns: 'This art form is nearing its end ... It has become comic opera, choreographic review, musical comedy, *féerie*, anything but operetta. Actors' spontaneity is extinct like authors' originality. Terrasse is the successor of Audran and Lecocq. Dall'Argine is all the riot in Italy. Lehár is acclaimed in the land of Strauss.'[15] When Ramperti published the long article that included this extract in the *Gazzetta teatrale italiana*, operetta in Italy was certainly not dead. The article was published in June 1907 and *La vedova allegra* had opened just a few weeks before at the Teatro dal Verme in Milan, taking the city by storm. Indeed, after a slow start and a somewhat lukewarm critical reception, *La vedova allegra* was to become one of the most successful operettas ever performed in Italy, reviving enthusiasm for the genre, creating expectation for more Viennese operettas and infusing energy in a new generation of Italian composers. Around the same time, the adaptations of works from the previous decades were still going strong, with Sidney Jones's *The Geisha* and Franz von Suppé's *Donna Juanita* attracting large crowds.

To be sure, Ramperti did not argue that operetta was approaching the end of its journey in Italy. In fact, operetta – both foreign and Italian – was to maintain its levels of popularity well into the 1910s and 1920s. Instead, the article reveals a profound anxiety about the transformation that operetta was undergoing at that moment, particularly the transition from 'golden-age' to 'silver-age' operetta, as critics already defined it at the time. Operetta was, according to Ramperti, going through an identity crisis because it had lost two fundamental characteristics that kept it always fresh and light-hearted: actors' spontaneity and authors' originality. In his argument, the names of Lecocq, Audran and Strauss represent the golden age and appear in sharp contrast to those of Claude Terrasse, Lehár and the Italian Luigi Dall'Argine, whose 1904 'grandiose operetta-féerie' *Dall'ago al milione* garnered great audience approval.

It is clear that in Ramperti's view, operetta had lost its comic verve, the caricature effects of the variety show, the improvisation and naturalness of the performers that characterized French and Viennese operettas in Italy during the last quarter of the century. It had, to use an image widely popular at the time, reached its phase of decline, its silver age. Ramperti emphasizes the 'vulgarity' of operetta – in the original sense as the entertainment of 'common people' – with a heavily gendered comparison with a young licentious girl, dressed in rags and charming just because of her energy and joy:

> Daughter of whim and joy, since good old Offenbach has been her baptismal godfather, she [operetta] was just a light-hearted girl, shabby and carefree. Her skirt was made of rags; she used critical rebuke as leather for her soles. But as

soon as she gave in to a dance, without too much fear of revealing her legs, or as soon as she sang a little song, all *boulevardière*, smiling with her wide and sincere smile, nobody would dare reproach her for her undignified clothes, for the licentious innuendos. She did not know, at that time, of good and proper behaviour: two fast legs and two lively eyes were enough.

Golden-age operetta was not concerned, Ramperti argues, with morality and proper behaviour until it was transformed by the 'censors' of the bourgeoisie into a grand dame, clad in fake jewels, rich fabrics and the most fashionable dresses. The effect was devastating for the young girl, now 'unrecognizable'. That Ramperti was thinking about early French operetta is clear also from his next comparison, this time between operetta and the two '*gamins de Paris*' Friquet and Gavroche:

> Is it not true that we love Gavroche also because he is corrupt? And we love him just because he is Gavroche; that is, the child of the street, of sin and vice. But Friquet, raised in a palace, would not be Friquet anymore. Operetta, this Gavroche, this Friquet of the arts, educated by the censors, dressed by Caramba, ceased to be operetta. And so it dies, ostentatiously like a matron, wrapped in brocade like a *dogaressa*.

By wanting to appropriate, tame and 'moralize' operetta, the bourgeoisie was now depriving it of its freshness and replacing it by 'artistic dignity and human propriety' and the rich and luxurious costumes of one of the most influential men of theatre of the time whose vision changed the history of operetta in Italy, Luigi Sapelli, known as Caramba. Bourgeois values, sentimentality and lack of spontaneity were making operetta dangerously similar to opera, at this time in search of a new identity itself, and this meant the death or at least the decline of the genre.

Some critics, however, did not share Ramperti's fatalistic position. Giovanni Borelli, writing in *Teatro illustrato* in March 1907, just weeks before the premiere of *La vedova allegra*, welcomed the creation of the 'Compagnia Stabile d'operette' of Milan that would produce *La vedova* as the sign of the beginning of a new phase for musical theatre in Italy. 'La Scala', he argues, 'could not give us anything better than this', referring to the beauty of costumes and sets.[16] What Ramperti saw as the sign of the inevitable decline of operetta – its loss of peculiar characteristics and desire to assimilate elements from the high-opera tradition – was actually for Borelli a reflection of the increasing importance operetta was acquiring on the Italian musical theatrical scene. Among the elements operetta was borrowing from opera, in addition to magnificent costumes and sets, were also an increasing number of singers who were inexorably migrating 'from the lyric scene to the much disrespected operetta', 'a warm and much livelier place'.

And in what seems like a direct response to criticism on the lines of Ramperti's, Borelli argues that:

> Operetta should not be deprived of its natural function as amusing entertainment, but it is not true that it could not open the field to very legitimate expressions of art. Because [operetta] has its own style, its aims, its logic content, and its intellectual expression. To be sure, it can become the vehicle for musical satire with the wonderful elegance with which Lecocq and Offenbach, who founded it, sent it out into the world.

Despite their differences, Ramperti and Borelli agree on a fundamental point: the repertory of operetta needed to find a new path if it wanted to survive. 'One should rather wish that the repertory', argues Borelli, 'little by little, could be purified, renewing and aligning itself with a propriety that, in the genre, would not exclude art.' 'Neither Paris nor Vienna give us a viable author anymore. Originality, what is that? The simple sparkle of the composers of operetta is something of lost times', writes Ramperti, pointing to the anxiety that if Paris and Vienna could not offer anything new, operetta was destined to disappear from the Italian stage, thus assuming that Italians would not be able to fill the gap that the demise of French and Viennese operetta would leave. The two articles are emblematic of the two main critical stances around operetta that brewed in the intellectual circles of the late nineteenth century and came to the forefront at the beginning of the so-called 'silver age' of operetta. Both articles seem to point to a moment of transition and the need for a renewal for the genre. And a new generation of Italian composers was to take on the task.

Italian Operetta

Not everyone in the early twentieth century saw operetta as a dying genre and *La vedova allegra* as its swansong. Mascagni, writing in July 1918 about his future plans, reflected on the status of musical theatre in Italy and on the impact *La vedova allegra* had on the Italian musical scene:

> I have also had in my mind, for a couple of years, the idea of an operetta; because I have a feeling that in the tastes of our audience, the *merry widows* have remained fixed like a big nail and I fear that after the war Viennese operetta will return with the violence of an overflowing river to fill our theatres.[17]

The arrival of a more sensual, romantic, decadent and refined style of operetta towards the end of the nineteenth century, combined with increasingly sumptuous and sophisticated productions and a more established group of singers who specialized in the genre, posed a challenge to the world of opera in Italy, which was undergoing some major shifts in its post-Verdian phase. This opened a new path for the development of Italian operetta. Many opera composers of Mascagni's generation, including Puccini, Leoncavallo, Giordano and Mascagni himself, had to come to terms with the fact that operetta was no longer the 'Gavroche' of the Italian musical theatrical world. But most importantly, they had to come to terms with the fact that the worlds of opera and operetta were sharing more and more characteristics, also as an effect of many of the reforms of opera brought about by the popular *verismo* movement.[18]

One should only think about Puccini's *La rondine*, a work that premiered at the theatre of Monaco in 1917 and that divided Italian critics and audiences because of its perceived hybrid nature between opera and operetta, for its apparently light plot and a profusion of 'international' dance rhythms including waltz, foxtrot and polka.[19] Or, consider Ruggero Leoncavallo's *Zazà* (1900), 'a mix of opera and operetta', after which he wrote a number of other similarly experimental works between 1910 and 1919. Looking back at the model of Offenbach's mythological plots, Umberto Giordano wrote *Giove a Pompei* in 1921, and, after an early, unsuccessful attempt in 1885 with *Il re a Napoli*, in 1920 Mascagni wrote the operetta *Sì*, a more accomplished work on a libretto by Carlo Lombardo. By venturing – more or less convincingly and with more or less conviction – into the world of operetta, Italian composers were now recognizing it as a legitimate product of the Italian musical theatrical tradition.

To be sure, starting in the 1860s, translations of French works had already stimulated an early production of Italian operettas. These combined elements of the French model – frivolous and at times absurd plots, licentious innuendos, the integration of dance rhythms and numbers – with local elements, and particularly the use of dialects, a fair amount of *couleur locale*, sources inspired by Italian literature and elements of the *canzone popolare*, relying greatly on the acting and improvisatory skills of its interpreters. In addition to *opera buffa* and foreign operettas, therefore, Italian audiences could also enjoy works such as *El Granduca de Gerolstein* by Enrico Bernardi and Cletto Arrighi (1879), a parody of Offenbach's *La Grande-Duchesse de Gérolstein* in Milanese dialect, *Er Marchese der Grillo* (1889) by Giovanni Mascetti in Roman dialect, and *Funicolì Funicolà* (1921) by Arturo De Cecco in Neapolitan dialect, to mention only a few.

But it was not until the early twentieth century that Italian composers decided to engage with operetta on a more systematic basis. After 1910, companies of operetta proliferated around Italy and also began to export operettas in the Italian language abroad, especially to Latin America, where Italian immigration had already created a market. At this time the number of theatres and venues devoted mostly to operettas – particularly in Milan,

Turin, Rome, Naples and Palermo but reaching also smaller centres and provinces – increased and a few periodicals dealing exclusively with operetta were founded. Milanese publishing houses such as Ricordi, Suvini-Zerboni, Sonzogno and Lombardo and the Neapolitan Curci began to sense an appealing financial advantage in supporting the market for operettas. Giulio Ricordi himself – who had played such a fundamental role in the Italian operatic world of the previous years, publishing and promoting the music of Giuseppe Verdi, among others – tried his luck with the composition of an operetta, *La secchia rapita* (1910), under the pseudonym of Jules Burgneim.

Some of the most successful operettas performed in Italy between the 1910s and 1930s were not truly and completely Italian. At this time of increasing nationalistic and anti-Austrian feeling, many reputedly Italian works were artful adaptations of operettas in the German language, among which were many operettas by Lehár and Kálmán, made more palatable for the audience by disguising them as Italian. Carlo Lombardo, composer, librettist, publisher, impresario, producer but most importantly translator and author of adaptations, owed much of his fortunate and controversial career to his adaptations of such works, which at times were sent on to the Italian stages under his own name, with little or no effort to clearly establish their authorship. 'Lombardo's' *La Signorina del cinematografo* (1915) was an adaptation of an operetta by Carl Weinberger, and Bruno Granichstadten's *Majestät Mimi* became the quite successful *La Duchessa del Bal Tabarin* (1915) by Léon Bard, one of the pseudonyms used by Lombardo.[20]

Despite the persistence of Mitteleuropean works and Italian operettas that continued to use them as models, the years during and immediately following World War I saw also the production of arguably the most original and successful Italian operettas. Following upon the successes of *verismo* operas, these works showed an attempt to return to more realistic and sincere plots, still relying on the *couleur locale* that had characterized the first Italian operettas of the 1860s. Among them, the works of Giuseppe Pietri, particularly his *Addio giovinezza* (1915) and *Acqua cheta* (1920), were hailed as the heralds of the new-born genre of Italian operetta. Together with others such as *Il re di Chez Maxim* (1919) and *Scugnizza* (1922) by Lombardo and Mario Costa, and Virginio Ranzato and Lombardo's *Il paese dei campanelli* (1923), this strand of operetta 'forgets champagne, cocottes and viveurs, paillettes and glitter, and talks about seamstresses, students, youngsters full of life, strong and resilient mothers, fathers with a heart full of goodness' against the backdrop of small and picturesque Italian towns or cities such as Turin, in *Addio giovinezza*, or Naples, in *Scugnizza*, vividly painted through the use of Neapolitan melodies.[21] And, as 'paillettes and glitter' and 'cocottes and viveurs' are replaced by everyday men and women struggling with mundane reality and honest and simple feelings, the waltzes and csárdás leave room for the more fashionable rhythms of foxtrot, jazz and tango, but also for the melodies and art songs with folk inflections that gave this music a distinctively 'Italian' flavour for a nation in need of a new musical tradition and cultural identity.

The decline of Italian operetta coincided with the rise of the *rivista*, or revue, brought about by those extraordinary performers, in particular the tenors and soubrettes, who had been the main agents responsible for the continued popularity of operettas during the years immediately following World War I. Now able to negotiate more remunerative new positions, first in a growing light-entertainment industry and later on radio and television, many featured also in film versions of the most successful Italian operettas. If Italian audiences also kept a memory of many of these works, thanks to the adaptations that reached their home through the screens of their televisions, Italian critics and musicologists, such as Fausto Torrefranca, continued to dismiss operetta as *the* inferior form of musical theatre in Italy. The negative connotation of the term operetta became so predominant that during the 1930s and still today the expression '*da operetta*' is used figuratively to indicate a 'ridiculous institution, event or personage lacking credibility'.[22]

And yet, today this neglect seems utterly unjustified. Operetta played a particularly meaningful role in the Italian cultural arena at a juncture of profound social, political and cultural transformations for the nation, from the creation of a unified Italian state well into the inception of fascism. During these decades, which also encompassed very significant changes in the long-standing Italian operatic tradition, foreign as well as Italian operetta created a stimulating terrain for the articulation of critical discourses about music and national identity, in addition to offering broad strata of society welcome entertainment and an alternative to the increasingly codified operatic canon.

Notes

1. Bruno Traversetti, *L'operetta* (Milan: Mondadori, 1985), 122.
2. *Gazzetta musicale di Milano*, 29, no. 31 (2 August 1874), 252–3.
3. *Gazzetta musicale di Milano*, 30, no. 52 (27 December 1874), 425.
4. *Gazzetta musicale di Milano*, 29, no. 45 (8 November 1874), 366.
5. Carlotta Sorba, 'The Origins of the Entertainment Industry: The Operetta in Late Nineteenth-Century Italy'. *Journal of Modern Italian Studies*, 11, no.3 (2006): 282–302, at 295.
6. *Gazzetta musicale di Milano*, 29, no. 31 (2 August 1874), 252–3.
7. *Gazzetta musicale di Milano*, 27, no. 20 (19 May 1872), 171.
8. *Gazzetta musicale di Milano*, 29, no. 16 (19 April 1874), 124.
9. Both quotations are from *Gazzetta musicale di Milano*, 27, no. 3 (29 September 1872), 326.
10. *Gazzetta musicale di Milano*, 29, no. 16 (19 April 1874), 124.

11. Nietzsche to Heinrich Köselitz in Berlin (from Turin), 18 November 1888, www.nietzschesource.org/#eKGWB/BVN-1888,1148 (accessed 9 May 2019). Quoted in Sorba, 'The Origins', 293.

12. Emilio Sala, 'L'umorismo scapigliato e Rossini: "Ilbarbiere di siviglia" di Costartino Dall 'Argine (1868)', in Ilaria Narici, Emilio Sala, Emanuele senici and Ben Walton (eds.), *Gioachino Rossini, 1868–2018. La musica e il mondo* (Pesaro: Fondazione Rossini, 2018), 283-309.

13. *Gazzetta musicale di Milano*, 21, no. 12 (17 June 1866): 89–92, at 90.

14. *Gazzetta teatrale italiana*, 31, no. 11 (20 April 1909), 1.

15. All quotations are from Marco Ramperti, 'Da Offenbach a Caramba', *Gazzetta teatrale italiana*, 36, no. 17 (20 June 1907), 1, and 36, no. 18 (1 July 1907), 1.

16. All quotations are from Borelli's untitled article in *Il teatro illustrato* 39 (15–31 March 1907), unpaginated supplement.

17. Letter by Mascagni to Giovanni Orsini, 21 July 1918. Quoted in Mariella Busnelli, 'Sì, l'operetta di Pietro Mascagni', *Rassegna musicale Curci*, 41 (1988): 13–18, at 14.

18. See Andreas Giger, 'Verismo: Origin, Corruption, and Redemption of an Operatic Term', *Journal of the American Musicological Society*, 60 (2007): 271–315.

19. Alexandra Wilson, *The Puccini problem: Opera, Nationalism, and Modernity* (Cambridge: Cambridge University Press, 2007), 172–7.

20. See Roberto Piano, *Addio giovinezza: l'operetta a Torino* (Turin: Beppe Grande editore, 2002), 35.

21. Ernesto Oppicelli, *Operetta. Da Hervé al Musical Hall* (Genoa: Sagep Editrice, 1985), 186.

22. *Dizionario della lingua italiana Treccani*, www.treccani.it/vocabolario/operetta/ (accessed 25 Sept. 2017).

Recommended Reading

Bortolotto, Mario. 'Sul teatro d'operetta'. *Nuova rivista musicale italiana*, 3 (1971): 420–42.

Fiorentino, Waldimaro. *L'operetta italiana. Storia, analisi critica, aneddoti.* Bolzano: Catinaccio, 2006.

La Gioia, Diana. *I libretti italiani d'operetta nella Biblioteca Nazionale di Roma.* Florence: Olschki, 1979.

Niccolai, Michela. '"Oh fior di thé, t'amo credi a me!" Alcuni aspetti della ricezione del mito-Butterfly nella canzone e nell'operetta fino agli anni Trenta'. In Arthur Groos and Virgilio Bernardoni, eds., *Madama Butterfly: l'orientalismo di fine secolo, l'approccio pucciniano, la ricezione.* Florence: Leo Olschki, 2008, 375–91.

Niccolai, Michela. 'Portraits de femmes exotiques dans le café-chantant et l'opérette italiens (1910–1940 environ)'. In Michela Niccolai and Clair Rowden, eds., *Musical Theatre in Europe 1830–1945.* Turnhout: Brepols, 2017, 325–47.

Oppicelli, Ernesto. *Operetta. Da Hervé al Musical Hall.* Genoa: Sagep Editrice, 1985.

Piano, Roberto. *Addio giovinezza: l'operetta a Torino.* Turin: Beppe Grande editore, 2002.

Recupido, Giovanni. 'Un signore senza pace di Dino Rulli (1925): un esempio della ricezione del jazz nell'operetta italiana degli anni venti'. In Michela Niccolai and Clair Rowden, eds., *Musical Theatre in Europe 1830–1945.* Turnhout: Brepols, 2017, 311–24.

Sorba, Carlotta. 'The Origins of the Entertainment Industry: The Operetta in Late Nineteenth-Century Italy'. *Journal of Modern Italian Studies*, 11, no. 3 (2006): 282–302.

Traversetti, Bruno. *L'operetta.* Milan: Mondadori, 1985.

15 Operetta in Warsaw

ANASTASIA BELINA

Warsaw is not a city associated with the global success of operetta, and yet it was the place where operetta performances were not only popular but lucrative – they rivalled Vienna and Berlin with the quality of their productions and star-studded casts. Polish musicians, actors, and directors had direct links with European theatres, and Warsaw was close to such operetta centres as Vienna, Berlin and Budapest. Warsaw operetta divas were celebrities adored by the public and critics alike. Some of them died leaving astronomical fortunes and lasting memories and recordings, like Wiktoria Kawecka (1875–1929) and Lucyna Messal (1886–1953); some died tragically, like Kazimiera Niewiarowska (1890–1927), and some died in complete oblivion, like Józefina Bielska (1882–1964). The names of the most popular Polish singers, famous for performing operetta and often also opera, include Mieczysława Ćwiklińska (1879–1972); Elna Gistedt (1895–1982), the Swedish singer and film actress who was popular in Warsaw and St Petersburg; Helena Bogorska (1894–1920); Marcella Sembrich (1858–1935);[1] Olga Orleńska (1894–1956); Wincenty Rapacki-syn (1856–1943); Jósef Redo (1876–1942); Ludwik Sempoliński (1899–1981) and Władysław Szczawiński (1879–1951), to name but a few. This chapter will look at the most significant operetta theatre not only in Warsaw but arguably in the whole of Poland, Teatr Nowości, and some of the people who made it one of the city's biggest attractions.

Because so much of Warsaw was destroyed during and after World War II, including the Nowości building, it is difficult to find the pieces with which to complete the story of operetta's triumphant march in the Polish capital. So far, no full operetta score used for Warsaw performances has been found, although there are a large number of surviving publications of individual numbers from popular operettas, arranged for piano and voice, and booklets with libretti. Meant for home consumption, they show just how popular operettas and their stars were.

Fortunately, there are two publications by two Polish authors that paint a vivid picture of Warsaw theatres in the nineteenth and early twentieth centuries. These books tell the stories of famous divas, singers, directors and theatres and help us catch a glimpse of the glittering and sumptuous world of operetta in Warsaw.[2]

The history of operetta in Warsaw begins long before Léhar's *Die lustige Witwe* stormed global stages in 1906–7. Before World War I, operetta had no competition in Warsaw: it had publicity, stars, excellent productions, stunning stage sets and the latest lighting and stage equipment. Operetta audiences left the theatres whistling the catchy and memorable melodies, quickly making operetta a part of popular culture. French and home-grown operetta and farce could be seen in Warsaw's many theatres, both indoor and outdoor. Summer theatres were immensely popular with audiences and provided an excellent springboard for singers who later graced operetta stages not only in Poland but also abroad. Famous performers who started their careers there include Adolfina Zimajer (1852–1939), Rufin Morozowicz (1851–1931), Wanda Manowska (1855–1930), Kazimierz Kamiński (1865–1928) and many others.

One of the very first summer theatres in Warsaw, *Tivoli,* opened in 1868, and by 1876 there were already twenty in operation. *Alhambra* and *Eldorado* were the most popular; both had big stages, big auditoriums and areas of expensive seats that were protected from rain by canvas roofs. The biggest summer theatre was *Belle-Vue,* which could seat 2,100. To protect performances from the street noise and passing carts, the nearby streets were laid with straw mats, and some were even asphalted. Small tables were placed near the seats so that the audience could eat while watching, bringing the theatres even more income. In September 1874 alone, *Eldorado* had 27,000 visitors and *Alhambra* 19,000, which amounted to as many as the state theatre, Teatr Wielki, had in the entire season. By 1882 open-air theatres started to disappear, and, by the time the Nowości opened its doors in 1901, they were almost all gone (see Figure 15.1).[3]

The Nowości's inaugural performance on 5 January 1901 was attended by so many people that nearby streets were jammed with traffic. Its opening corresponded with the growth of Warsaw population, which in 1900 reached almost 700,000 and exceeded a million by World War I, resulting in increased demand for entertainment by the steadily expanding numbers of the bourgeoisie. The theatre was beautiful, it had electric lamps on the balcony, its auditorium could sit 1,300 people and its enormous stage was 13.5 metres deep and 30 metres wide, providing ample opportunity for the director's imagination to unfold. The Nowości had a buffet, special fittings for ladies' hats and comfortable seats. The first performance of selected numbers from well-known operettas was given by the biggest stars of Warsaw operetta, including Mieczysława Ćwiklińska, Wiktoria Kawecka, Jósef Redo and Rufin Morozowicz. The press compared Śliwiński to Napoleon, so beautifully did he arrange his own coronation as the emperor of Warsaw operetta.

Figure 15.1 Teatr Nowości

Until 1918, modern Poland did not exist: instead, its territory was divided between Russia, Prussia and Austria. From 1770 Warsaw was under Russian control, and its state theatres were governed by the Russian administrative body, the Warsaw Government Theatre Directorate

(Warszawskie Teatry Rządowe). It offered financial subsidies that enabled shows in Polish to be put on and new theatres to be built. It looked after companies that performed operettas, operas, ballets, dramas and comedies, and had five buildings under its jurisdiction, with the Nowości being the newest addition. The Nowości became very lucrative for the directorate; the prices of the seats were high: a box cost 14 roubles (a monthly wage of a working-class person), a seat in the first row cost 3.5 roubles, which was equal to the cost of maintaining a large family for three days. A gallery on a third level cost between 45 and 85 kopeks. A full house would have raised 1,000 roubles of earnings in one evening.[4] Even in the 1940s, when Warsaw was under German occupation, the prices of operetta were higher than those of opera or other performances (see Figure 15.2).

From the beginning of its existence, the Nowości's productions were without any competition, especially in terms of stage design and lighting.[5] Aleksander Poliński had a reputation as the most demanding and hard-to-please critic, but even he wrote after seeing Oscar Straus's *Smok i królewna* (Die lustigen Nibelungen) that the sets were 'rich, splendid and magnificent, and the lighting effects were the best that the theatre has ever seen so far, it was a performance that brought honour to costume and set designers, artists, and, above all, the director'.[6] The lighting was thought to be of a truly European standard. In Paul Lincke's *Lizystrata* (Lysistrata) given in 1909, there were not just a few but a whole series of new lighting and decorative effects.[7] An operetta director knew that its success did not depend only on the music or libretto and that the stage sets, lighting effects and careful directing were equally important. For additional effect, real horses, donkeys, dogs and even deer were used on the stage.[8]

Costumes were also carefully considered, and from the early 1910s operetta performances in the Nowości were famous for the splendid clothes worn by their stars. They were ordered together with the latest jewellery, lingerie, shoes and other items directly from shops, who thus were able to advertise their fashionable wares not only on the stage but also in operetta programmes. One could read about operetta gowns in the press, followed by what operetta divas wore as they travelled around the world; even the colour of their hair was not forgotten. Wiktoria Kawecka became the first diva who thus dictated women's fashions.[9]

The King of Diamonds

Without Ludwik Śliwiński (1857–1923), who was responsible for operetta productions in Warsaw from 1890 until 1915, the Nowości would literally

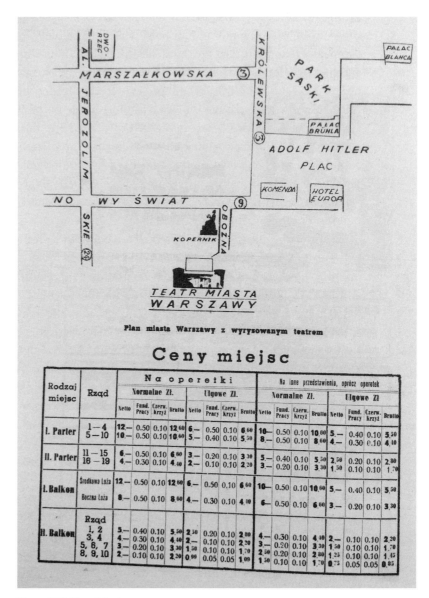

Figure 15.2 Nowości prices

not exist. For the first ten years of his leadership, operettas were performed in Mały and Nowy theatres, where they had to compete with performances of operas and ballets and other stage shows. Teatr Mały, particularly, was not very good for operetta performances: its capacity was 500, the seats were uncomfortable and the stage was too small.[10] Śliwiński set himself a goal to find a dedicated home for operetta in Warsaw where it could be performed all year around on its own terms. It took eleven years, 350,000 roubles and an investor who, to complete fundraising for the new theatre, found the missing 27,000 roubles somewhere in Russia.[11] Of course, the advantage of building a new theatre according to the last word on technology and design was immediately obvious when ecstatic reviews started to pour in. It also meant that operetta productions in Warsaw could successfully compete with those in Europe. The audiences in the Nowości could see all the new works of European operetta, many of which enjoyed enormous success, quickly reaching a hundred performances.

Śliwiński was quick to bring productions from Vienna and Berlin, adapting them for Polish audiences. In his *Encyclopedia on the Musical Theatre*, Kurt Gänzl often refers to Budapest as the first city to stage foreign-language productions outside Germany. There is no mention of Warsaw, but often it was the first city where German operettas were performed after Vienna. Such was the case with Lehár's *Die lustige Witwe* (Wesoła wdówka), *Der Graf von Luxemburg* (Hrabia Luxemburg), *Zigeunerliebe* (Miłość cygańska), *Gräfin Mariza* (Hrabina Marica) and Oscar Straus's *Ein Walzertraum* (Czar walca).

Śliwiński was an excellent organizer and director with extensive international networks, using them to promote the work of the theatre by always inviting important people from the industry to general rehearsals and performances. He also programmed operettas by Polish composers, including such works as Noskowski's *Don Kiszot* (Don Quixote), Duniecki's *Paziowie królowej Marysieńki* (Queen Marysia's Page, still performed in Poland), and Rapacki-syn's *Pajacyki* (Clowns) and *Chwila szczęścia* (A Moment of Happiness).[12]

Śliwiński was involved in every aspect of the staging: designs, costumes, lighting and stage directing. He also adapted operettas by translating them and writing new texts to suit Polish sensibilities. In fact, during his directorship, it was mainly Śliwiński, together with the two operetta singers and directors, Wincenty Rapacki-syn and Adolf Kitschman (1864–1917), who adapted operettas for Polish audiences. It is even more impressive, then, to learn that between 1910 and 1914 Śliwiński directed seventy-eight operettas.[13] He livened up operettas with current jokes and parodies, making critics wonder if some of his innuendos and double entendres transgressed the boundaries of propriety, as was the case with Gilbert's *Cnotliwa Zuzanna* (Die keusche Susanne).[14] In 1914, Poliński praised him for bringing *Die lustige Witwe* back to Warsaw in a sumptuous production and for refreshing its beautiful melodies 'with the aid of technology, extremely carefully and enchantingly presented and directed'.[15] One critic compared Śliwiński's production of Paul Lincke's operetta *Wenus w Warszawe* (Venus auf Erden) to the one he saw in Berlin six years earlier, stating that the Polish version was so great 'that the director from Berlin should visit us to learn from Ludwik how operettas should be produced.

I want to be fair, so I will admit that Berlin's version was impressive, but ours is amazing.'[16]

Śliwiński made the Nowości into a very much-loved institution in Warsaw, an integral part of life in the city and its popular culture. The building and the singers, as well as himself, were even immortalized on a set of playing cards. Only a few well-worn cards remain, on one of which Śliwiński can be seen as the King of Diamonds.[17]

The Queen of Diamonds

Of course, as important as the new theatre and its talented director were, they alone would not be enough to create operetta. An integral part of the recipe was the singers, who were also actors and dancers, and who, together with Śliwiński, put on dazzling shows that made them rich and famous.

Wiktoria Kawecka (1875–1929) was one of the most famous operetta performers in Warsaw. The daughter of an employee of the Warsaw Government Theatres, she made her debut on 14 February 1893 in Millöcker's *Student żebrak* (Der Bettelstudent). Five years later, she was an undisputed operetta prima donna in Warsaw.

Kawecka achieved fame beyond Poland as both operetta and opera singer and was in high demand as a guest artist in Russia, where she often performed in some of the most prestigious theatres. Her popularity in Russia came in handy in 1909, when she faced her first serious competition from Lucyna Messal, who took her crown as the Warsaw prima donna. Kawecka decided to remove herself from the scene rather than compete with her younger rival, spending almost ten years in St Petersburg, where she had little competition, performing leading operetta roles both in Polish and Russian in the famous Theatre Bouffe.[18] There was even a theatre built especially for her in St Petersburg, called Crystal Palace, where she sang her favourite roles.[19]

Kawecka was a gifted singer with excellent technical command. Critics raved about the colour, scale, range and power of her voice, together with her intricate phrasing and range of dynamic nuance, and a particular talent for the artistic whistle. Kawecka's most successful appearances in the Nowości include the roles in Lehár's *Wesoła wdówka* (1906), Jarno's *Krysia leśniczanka* (Die Försterchristel, 1909), Oscar Straus's *Czar walca* (Ein Walzertraum, 1909), Fall's *Królowa miliardów* (Die Dollarprinzessin, 1909), *Rozwódka* (Die geschiedene Frau, 1909), Sidney Jones's *Gejsza* (The Geisha, 1909), Lehár's *Cygańska miłość* (Zigeunerliebe, 1909) and Kálmán's *Manewry jesienne* (Tatárjárás, 1910). This is how Ludwik

Sempoliński described Wiktoria Kawecka at the height of her fame in 1909: 'Adored by the public, she was called the "nightingale of Warsaw". Beautiful, with sparkling eyes, with a beautiful voice and acting talent, she also became famous for her ability to whistle, with which she totally charmed the audience during her performances of *Wesoła wdówka* [Die lustige Witwe], premiered in Warsaw on 16 October 1906.'[20] Her voice was so famous that its strength was compared to that of Adelina Patti, and there were even rumours that after her death, American researchers bought her vocal cords in order to find out what made her voice so powerful.[21] Kawecka recorded for Syrena Records, and some still survive that feature her famous artistic whistle.[22]

Kawecka was also nicknamed 'the queen of diamonds' because of her passion for collecting diamonds, gifted to her by her many admirers. One of her many devotees was the confectioner Edmund Gwizdalski, who built her a new villa, *Versal* in Skolimow near Konstancin. It is not surprising that Kawecka managed to open her own theatre Vaudeville in 1921 and could easily afford her expensive hobby: playing roulette in Monte Carlo.

When she died in Warsaw during one of her performances, her fortune was valued at five million zloty (approximately 50 million zloty today, i.e. 10 million pounds or 15.5 million dollars).[23] Kawecka's grave is a spectacular monument, adorned with a statue which shows her just about ready to walk on to the stage. It was made by a famous Warsaw sculptor Bartołomiej Mazurek (1856–1937). Even one of the most celebrated operetta singers of all times, Richard Tauber, has only a modest grave stone in a London cemetery. Today, one of the streets in Warsaw carries her name.

The Tragic Diva (or *Ah, Those Panties*)

Kazimira Niewiarowska (1890–1927) was famous not only for her singing but also for her daring performances. She appeared topless, she sang with a live snake around her neck, and she danced a tango on a tray placed on the heads of eight male actors. She also starred in several films with titles as mischievous as her own stage antics: *Ah, te spodnie* (Ah, Those Panties, 1914) and *Kiedy kobieta zdradza meza* (When a Woman Betrays her Husband, 1924).

Already famous before World War I, after the outbreak of the war she left Poland and went to work in Russia, where alongside performing she also studied the art of acting pioneered by Nemirovich-Danchenko. The esteemed director even worked with her in his MKhAT (Moscow Art Theatre) studio on several operettas, including the role of Klarette in

Lecocq's *Córka pani Angot* (*La fille de Madame Angot*), an operetta given at least 200 times.[24]

With this valuable experience she returned to Warsaw in 1922, and immediately caused a sensation. Even Lucyna Messal, who reigned in the Nowości during her absence, for a while found herself in Niewiarowska's shadow. It is not difficult to see why: Niewiarowska brought with her from Russia a number of new approaches to her art, which consisted of considerable risk-taking and crossing the boundaries of what was acceptable on stage at that time. Witold Filler wrote that in one of the performances she smeared her body in various places (including the shoes) with phosphorescent liquid, so-called radian, which she ordered directly from the Folies-Bergère. Such tricks served her well, because they put a great deal of distance between her and the current Warsaw divas, Lucyna Messal and Elna Gistedt.[25]

In fact, Niewiarowska became known for designing her own stage costumes, creating outfits that showed off the best features of her figure or, indeed, finding ways to show even more flesh than the censors would allow. She called for a nationwide discussion about theatrical reforms, which included the 'striptease effect' – specially designed costumes that included see-through dresses made from pink and lilac gauze, adorned with forget-me-nots – and new, daring and sensational press advertisements, which she used on her own programmes, and in her own theatre.[26] Chic costumes and risky 'no-costumes' in clever and diverse advertisements helped Niewiarowska to conquer Warsaw.[27]

In 1923 she was even immortalized in the nude, in a painting by one of her contemporaries, the Polish artist Leonard Winterowski (1868–1927). The painting can be found in online gallery records under various titles: sometimes as Akt Aktorki Kazimiery Niewiarowskiej and sometimes as Niebieska wstążka (Blue Ribbon).[28] She freely used it on her programmes, causing a wave of excitement in the audiences, particularly the male faction, who opened them as they sat down to enjoy her performances.

In 1925 she founded her own Teatr Niewiarowska in Warsaw, where she appeared for a short while with Wiktoria Kawecka. Having played with metaphorical fire in her adventurous career, she was finally burned by real flames, dying from extensive burns caused by spilt alcohol, which she was using to clean her gown. Her death was even reported in *The New York Times*.[29]

The Nightingale of Warsaw
Lucyna Messal (1886–1953) started her career as a dancer, performing in 1904 in Johann Strauss's *Ach, ta wiosna* (Frühlingsstimmen). She found success as a singer in the role of Safia in Johann Strauss's *Baron*

cygański (Der Zigeunerbaron) on 24 March 1909 in the Nowości.[30] After that performance she was hailed as a new operetta prima donna of the Warsaw Government Theatres, and the two divas, Kawecka and Messal, performed together, with their first collaboration being Straus's *Czar walca* on 22 April 1909. Very soon, however, Messal took Kawecka's crown completely, forcing her to retreat from appearing in Poland for a decade. Messal became the legend of Polish operetta, adored by the audiences for her beauty and her voice. In her repertoire were more than fifty roles from such operettas as Oscar Straus's *Czar walca* and *Rozwódka* (both 1909), Kálmán's *Manewry jesienne* (1910) and *Bajadera* (1923); Lehár's *Hrabia Luxemburg*, *Cygańska miłość* (both 1910), *Wesoła wdówka* (1911), *Ewa* (1913), *Biały mazur* (1921), *Frasquita* (1924) and *Paganini* (1927); Gilbert's *Cnotliwa Zuzanna* (1911); and Granichstaedten's *Orłow* (1925).

Lucyna Messal, together with Józef Redo (1876–1942), introduced the tango for the first time in Poland on 28 October 1913, in Jacobi's *Targ na dziewczęta* (The Marriage Market). Redo was a popular Polish singer, who was nicknamed the 'king of tango', and a photograph of Messal and Redo in the tango embrace appeared on many operetta-related publications and postcards (see Figure 15.3). His phonogenic voice made him a very popular recording artist on Syrena records.[31]

Like many of her contemporaries, Messal also recorded for Syrena Records, and appeared in many films. The 1938 film *Szczęśliwa trzynastka* (Lucky Thirteen) is available on YouTube, where she can be seen in a cameo role as a pianist and singer called Wanda.[32] Messal on film provides the link to the past of Warsaw and its operetta stars.

Messal also left Poland at the outbreak of World War I, but unlike Niewiarowska and Kawecka, she came back to Warsaw as soon as it ended and was tumultuously welcomed back by the audiences. She resumed her role of the prima donna of the Nowości, combining it with extensive touring, which took her to the famous stages in Warsaw, Lublin, Lodz, St Petersburg, Moscow, Vienna and Budapest.

In 1929 she opened her own theatre, Operetta Lucina Messal, where she performed with Kazimiera Niewiarowska until Niewiarowska's tragic death. In the 1930s she was a popular guest artist in numerous cabarets and revues, including the *Happy Evening, Hollywood, Chameleon, Prague Eye* and *8.15*. During the German occupation, she opened her own bar in the centre of Warsaw, opposite the church were Chopin's heart is said to be kept. She outlived both Niewiarowska and Kawecka by a considerable number of years, cementing her reputation as one of the most prominent operetta singers in Warsaw and Russia.

Figure 15.3 Lucyna Messal and Józef Redo

Should These Instruments Be Allowed to Call Themselves Strings?

The Nowości had its own orchestra of thirty-three players, but it was a dull jewel in the otherwise glittering crown of Warsaw operetta, and many critics commented on its sorry and neglected state. In 1908, for example, the famous Poliński wrote after the premiere of Fall's *Księżniczca dolarów* (Die Dollarprinzessin) that 'instead of a harp, we heard hideous trembling sounds, coming out of such an old clavicembalo',[33] while another complained that it was a travesty to replace the harp with an instrument 'to which we cannot even give a name'.[34] In 1909 one reviewer called for the theatre to replace the instruments that do not have the right to call themselves strings.[35] These criticisms continued for almost ten years, and it is surprising that such an attentive, enterprising and dedicated director as Śliwiński did not improve the state of the orchestra. This could have been the result of the theatre directorate having little interest in offering financial support for the orchestra, since the theatre brought such good income anyway.

But while complaints about the orchestra rained from the critics, there was much praise about one particular person associated with the orchestra, the conductor Anda Kitschman (1895–1967). Also a composer, singer, actress, pianist and director, she was the first female Polish conductor to be educated in Vienna. Kitschman's father was the previously mentioned Adolf Kitschman, a stage actor, singer, director and author of many Polish adaptations of European operettas. Anda became a versatile musician who was equally respected for her performances of a wide array of music, both as a soloist, accompanist and singer and as a conductor. She was also well known for her cabaret songs, for which she wrote both music and texts that were witty and profound, and which she often performed herself. She translated and arranged operas and operettas and composed her own operettas.

Her strong personality and impeccable work ethic enabled her to hold her own in the field of conducting, where men dominated (and, indeed, still do). She worked alongside other conductors in the Nowości, who included Henryk Lasocki, Wacław Elszyk (as assistant) and Michał Zakrzewski. She was obviously respected for her work there and admired for her good sense of rhythm and ability to bring out the subtlest nuances in the music. Even the demanding Aleksandr Poliński wrote about her talent as a conductor while, together with his colleagues, often criticizing the conducting of her male colleagues.[36]

To Jest Ostatni Walc . . . Nowości's Final Years

When World War I started on 1 August 1914, it was a pre-season time for the theatres, and most of the actors were abroad on tour, including the theatre's brightest stars Messal, Kawecka, Niewiarowska, Szczawiński, Bielska and Ćwiklińska. Messal, Kawecka, and Niewiarowska all spent the war years in Russia, performing to the adoring audiences there. In Warsaw, theatre repertoires were altered as a result of the new political situation, and the plays became more serious, with more anti-German sentiment. One of the productions reflecting this new mood was the *Polenblut*, which had to be adapted to suit the demands of patriotic audiences. So, the director concealed its anti-Polish element and gave it some extra 'nationality'.

In these war years there were only three government theatres active, including the Nowości, and three private theatres: Bagatela, Polski and Wodewil. In July 1915 the Warsaw Government Theatre Directorate ceased to exist, and the Nowości became the property of the artists. Some think that 1917 was the year that brought one of the greatest successes to the Nowości, which also became its last: Kálmán's *Księżniczka czardasza* clocked up one hundred performances in one season. Widespread impoverishment, higher taxes and competition with other theatres which, perhaps, catered more to the patriotic mood of the nation, did not help the operetta at that time.[37]

In July 1921 the cast was disbanded, and the theatre was moved to another building, the former Marywil Street Theatre on 5, Bielańska Street, at that time under the management of the Capital Theatre Society. The era of stability was over, and between 1921 and 1932 Nowości changed management and names several times, being called Metropolitan Operetta Theatre, Messal-Niewiarowska Theatre and Orpheum. The troupe included new singers: Stanisław Gruszyński, Adam Bodosz, Waleria Markowska and Olga Orleńska. The directors who led the theatre during its final years included Władysław Szczawiński and Wasław Julicz. Finally, after numerous changes in management and name the theatre was closed in 1932.

Notes

1. She can be heard in the 1912 recording of the Waltz from The *Dollar Princess.*, www .youtube.com/watch?v=9aA3-621gPw (accessed 14 Sept. 2018).
2. Witold Filler, *Rendez-vous z Warszawską operetką operetką* [Rendez-vous with Warsaw operetta] (Warsaw: Państwowy Instytut Wydawniczy, 1961) and Ludwik Sempoliński, *Wielcy artyści małych scen* [Great artists of small stages] (Warsaw: Czytelnik, 1977).
3. Eugeniusz Szwankowski, *Teatry Warszawy w latach 1765–1918* [Warsaw theatres in 1765–1918] (Warszawa: Państwowe Wydawnictwo Naukowe, 1979), 141–5.
4. Filler, *Rendez-vous*, 90.
5. All reviewers praised Śliwiński's productions for beautiful stage sets, costumes and attention to detail. See, for example, reviews of Straus's *Cnotliwa Zuzanna* (Die Keuscher Susanne) by Felicjan Szopski in *Gazeta Warszawska*, 187 (1911): 3; Aleksander Poliński in *Kurier Warszawski*, 188 (1911): 6; and Czesław Jankowski in *Tygodnik Ilustrowany*, 29 (1911): 569.
6. Aleksander Poliński, 'A muzyki. "Smok i dziewczyna"', *Kurier Warszawski*, 192 (1906). This operetta was sometimes given under the title *Smok i dziewczyna.*
7. Anna Wypych-Gawrońska, *Warszawski teatr operowy i operetkowy w latach 1880–1915* [Warsaw opera and operetta theatre in 1880–1915] (Częstochowa: Wydawnistwo im. Stanisława Podobińskiego, 2011), 399.
8. Sempoliński, *Wielcy artyści małych scen*, 16 and 73.
9. Filler, *Rendez-vous*, 133.
10. Wypych-Gawrońska, *Warszawski teatr*, 412.
11. For an account of how the theatre was finally built and how the money was raised see Filler, *Rendez-vous*, 78–85.
12. Szwankowski, *Teatry Warszawy*, 135. See also Filler, *Rendez-vous*, 311.
13. Szwankowski, *Teatry Warszawy*, 138.

14. Poliński, *Kurier Warszawski*, 188 (1911): 6.

15. Poliński, *Kurier Warszawski*, 236, (1914): 3–4.

16. J. R. *Słowo*, 160 (1905), 2.

17. These cards are kept at the Museum Teatralne in Warsaw.

18. See Chapter 8, 'Operetta in Russia and the USSR'. Kawecka's voice can be heard in the 1911 recording, where she sings Tosti's *La Serenata* in Russian, www.youtube.com/watch?v=lIZfQKCOkNo (accessed 18 Sept. 2018).

19. Andrzej Chodkowski (ed.), *Encyklopedia muzyki*, 12 vols. (Warsaw: Wydawnictwo Naukowe PWN, 2001), Vol. 5, 430.

20. Sempoliński, *Wielcy artyści małych scen*, 16–17.

21. These rumours have not been verified. Quoted in Olga Grekova-Dashkovskaya, *Stariye mastera operetti* [Old masters of operetta] (Moscow: Iskusstvo, 1990), 95.

22. Russian-Records.com contains a list of surviving and available recordings by Polish artists, including Kawecka, Redo, Bielska and Rapacky-syn, www.russian-records.com /search.php?show_result=1&page=1 (accessed 16 Sept. 2018).

23. Museum Warszawy, https://muzeumwarszawy.pl/en/obiekt/postcard-featuring-the-portrait-of -diva-wiktoria-kawecka-1875-1929/ (accessed 16 Sept. 2018).

24. Filler, *Rendez-vous*, 234.

25. Filler, *Rendez-vous*, 230–2.

26. Ibid.

27. Ibid.

28. www.artnet.com/artists/leonard-winterowski/akt-aktorki-kazimiery-niewiarowskiej-kJrMzRbBilsMb6sYEC4lqg2 (accessed 16 Sept. 2018).

29. 'Mme. Niewiarowska Accidentally Set Fire to Her Clothing While in Sleeper', *The New York Times*, 1 July 1927.

30. Sempoliński, *Wielcy artyści małych scen*, 32.

31. His voice can be heard in the duet 'Usta milczą, dusza śpiewa' (Lippen schweigen) from Lehár's *Die lustige Witwe*, recorded in 1908 with Józefina Bielska, www.youtube.com/watch?v=w707XAFbVpI (accessed 15 Sept. 2018).

32. www.youtube.com/watch?v=eImQrHT_rRA (accessed 14 Sept. 2018).

33. Aleksander Poliński, 'Z muzyki', *Kurier Warszawski*, 89 (1908),8. See also Anna Wypych-Gawrońska, *Warszawski teatr operowy i operetkowy*, 391.

34. J. Rosenzweig, 'Teatr Nowości', *Szena I Sztuka*, 14 (1908), quoted in Anna Wypych-Gawrońska, *Warszawski teatr operowy i operetkowy w latach 1880-1915*. (Częstochowa: Wydawnistwo im. Stanisława Podobińskiego, 2011), 391.

35. J. Rosenzweig, 'Tydzień teatralno-muzyczny. Teatr Nowości', *Szena I Sztuka*, 23 (1909), quoted in Wypych-Gawrońska, *Warszawski teatr*, 391.

36. Aleksander Poliński, 'Teatr Nowości' *Kurier Warszawski*, 299 (1913). See also Felicjan Szopski, 'Teatr, muzyka i malarstwo. Z teatru Nowości', *Gazeta Warszawska*, 296 (1913). Both reviews are quoted in Wypych-Gawrońska, *Warszawski teatr*, 389.

37. Szwankowski, *Teatry Warszawy*, 165–6.

Recommended Reading

Filler, Witold. *Rendez-vous z Warszawską operetką / Rendez-vous with Warsaw operetta*. Warsaw: Państwowy Instytut Wydawniczy, 1961.

Sempoliński, Ludwik. *Wielcy artyści małych scen / Great artists of small stages*. Warsaw: Czytelnik, 1977.

Szwankowski, Eugeniusz. *Teatry Warszawy w latach 1765–1918 / Warsaw theatres in 1765–1918*. Warszawa: Państwowe Wydawnictwo Naukowe, 1979.

Wypych-Gawrońska, Anna. *Warszawski teatr operowy i operetkowy w latach 1880–1915 / Warsaw opera and operetta theatre in 1880–1915*. Częstochowa: Wydawnistwo im. Stanisława Podobińskiego, 2011.

16 British Operetta after Gilbert and Sullivan

DEREK B. SCOTT

George Edwardes, one of the most influential theatrical entrepreneurs in the decades before and after the turn of the twentieth century, twice detected a change of taste in the public's appetite for the musical stage. In the 1890s, he had noted a decline in enthusiasm for the type of comic opera associated with Gilbert and Sullivan. It was then that he commissioned and encouraged a fresh type of stage entertainment, which he called 'musical comedy'.[1] In the early twentieth century, he sensed another change in mood and took a chance with *The Merry Widow*, a modern operetta from Vienna that has come to be regarded as the foundation stone of the silver age of continental European operetta.

The musical comedies produced by Edwardes were in competition not only with the burlesques popular at the Gaiety Theatre, such as *Faust Up to Date*, but also with comic operas at the Savoy Theatre. This explains why a mixture of styles from the operatic to music hall is found in musical comedies, especially in early examples such as *In Town* (book and lyrics by Adrian Ross and James Tanner, music by F. Osmond Carr) and *A Gaiety Girl* (book and lyrics by Owen Hall, music by Sidney Jones). Gilbert and Sullivan's *Utopia Limited* opened at the Savoy the week before *A Gaiety Girl* in October 1893, following in the wake of successful runs at that theatre for Edward Solomon's *The Nautch Girl* (1891–2), and Sullivan and Sydney Grundy's *Haddon Hall* (1892–3). Edwardes's initial experiments with musical comedy took place at the Prince of Wales's Theatre, which had been home to a successful run of Alfred Cellier's *Dorothy*, an operetta that had had a disappointing premiere at the Gaiety in 1886, when Edwardes first took over management of that theatre. It had been a premature attempt by Edwardes to change the Gaiety audience's expectations.

In 1894, he had acquired sufficient confidence to produce *The Shop Girl* at the Gaiety Theatre, perhaps because *In Town* had transferred successfully there the year before. The book was by H. J. W. Dam, who claimed to have researched his subject in Whiteley's department store and the Army and Navy stores in order to capture 'the life of today'.[2] The music was by Ivan Caryll, with additional numbers by Lionel Monckton to lyrics by Adrian Ross. Caryll was born Félix Tilkin in Belgium and had studied at the Paris Conservatoire. Monckton's training was rather different; while a law student at the University of Oxford, he had acquired experience composing music for the university's dramatic society. *The Shop Girl* was a great success, running to 546 performances, and it established musical comedy as the most popular stage entertainment in the West End. 'Her Golden Hair Was Hanging Down Her Back', a risqué interpolated song by music-hall artist Felix McGlennon, became immensely popular. The variety elements present in musical comedy meant that a song reminiscent of the style of the music hall or American vaudeville did not jar as it would have done in a stage work more closely associated with comic opera or operetta.

The description 'musical play' was used for the first time in advertising *The Geisha* (Owen Hall and Sidney Jones) at Daly's Theatre in 1896. This label became common as a synonym for 'operetta' in the next decade and beyond. In a musical play, romance took precedence over comedy, and a higher standard of singing was expected. A lot of performers in musical comedy were actor-singers with little or no operatic vocal training or experience. The lead singers in *The Geisha* were Marie Tempest and Hayden Coffin, who were both up to the demands of its lyrical score. To a certain extent the interest in Japanese culture in this piece was genuine: Edwardes hired Arthur Diósy, the founder of London's Japanese Society, as a consultant,[3] and the choreographer was at pains to study dances at the Japanese exhibition village in London.[4] However, a British imperialist commitment to modernity and progress is present, for, even as it served up escapism and romance, it did so by means of the latest stage technology.

Sidney Jones made his international reputation with *The Geisha*. Statistics for numbers of performances on the German stage show that, of works composed between 1855 and 1900, it was second only to *Die Fledermaus* in popularity during the first two decades of the twentieth century.[5] It also enjoyed great success in France and the USA, and throughout the British Empire. Perhaps more unexpectedly, it was a hit in South America, Italy, Russia, Scandinavia and Spain.[6] Its character illustrates some of the typical differences between earlier operetta and musical comedy. Unlike *The Mikado* (1885), the foreign in *The Geisha* is a source of entertainment, rather than an allegoric means by which members of the audience recognize their own follies and prejudices. The satire of sentimentality is also more crudely handled in the song 'The Amorous Goldfish' from *The Geisha*, than in 'Tit-Willow' from *The Mikado*.

Another enormously successful show was Jones's *San Toy* (book by Edward Morton, lyrics by Adrian Ross and Harry Greenbank). It opened at Daly's in 1899, running for 768 performances, just ten short of the number *The Merry Widow* was to achieve there between 1907 and 1909.

In *San Toy*, Jones exchanged Japanese exoticism for Chinese. Two years later, Howard Talbot, who was born in New York but had moved to London as a child, mined Chinese exoticism to even greater commercial success in *A Chinese Honeymoon*, the first musical stage work to exceed 1,000 performances. It was at the Strand Theatre from early October 1901 until the middle of May 1904. At the Casino Theatre in New York, where it was produced in 1902, it ran to 364 performances, a number denoting an incontrovertible hit in that city. It was advertised as a musical play, but David Ewen calls it 'more of a vaudeville show than an operetta'.[7] That may be because it relied strongly on spectacle or because of songs such as 'Martha Spanks the Grand Pianner'.

The choice of the label 'musical play', 'musical comedy' or 'operetta', is often motivated by marketing decisions, but there is a general expectation that a theatre work described as an operetta will contain more than tuneful songs and that ensembles and concerted finales will engage with the dramatic action so as to create an integrated musical stage work. The presence of such features makes it easy to categorize Ivan Caryll's *The Duchess of Dantzic* (1903) as an operetta. Caryll returned to musical comedy, however, and, after moving to New York, was to take pleasure at the sight of audiences flocking to see the Broadway production of his *The Pink Lady* in 1911.

A Chinese Honeymoon was one of the prolonged theatrical successes of turn-of-the-century London that did not spring from the Edwardes stable. Two others were Gustave Kerker's American operetta *The Belle of New York* (1897), produced in London in 1898, and Leslie Stuart's *Florodora* (1899). In a rare error of judgement, Edwardes had turned down the opportunity to buy the rights to Kerker's operetta at a cheap price after it managed only sixty-four performances at New York's Casino Theatre.[8] Unexpectedly, it ran for 693 performances at the Shaftesbury Theatre. Stuart's *Florodora* was an enormous hit on Broadway in 1900 and spent eight years on the road touring American cities.[9] The opening words of the sextet, 'Tell me, pretty maiden, are there any more at home like you?', are still widely known, even if the tune is only vaguely remembered. The song 'The Shade of the Palm', which begins with the words 'Oh My Dolores, Queen of the Eastern Sea', is referenced in the Sirens chapter of James Joyce's *Ulysses*. Three songs in *Florodora* were by Paul Rubens, who was to enjoy considerable success with *Miss Hook of Holland* in London in 1907 (it was also produced in New York that year).

The appetite for musical comedy in the West End of the 1890s and 1900s made Edward German's operettas seem outdated in style. The reasons for this are not difficult to find and may be put down to his concern for moral and musical propriety.[10] In terms of content, this translates as an eradication of anything too saucy in the book or lyrics and an avoidance of music-hall idioms in the music. Musical comedies were less inhibited about occasional lapses into vulgarity if the strength of the comedy provided justification. German was given the task of completing the unfinished score of Sullivan's *The Emerald Isle*, which was performed at the Savoy Theatre in the spring of 1901 and had a respectable run of 195 performances. Basil Hood had written the libretto of *The Emerald Isle*, a mythical historical romance set in Ireland, and he also provided the libretto for German's operetta of the following year, *Merrie England*. It was another historical romance, this time set in the Elizabethan period. Its run of 119 performances at the Savoy was enough to bring the composer to public attention, and it became popular with amateur operatic societies. Indeed, it was assumed by some that Sullivan's mantle had fallen on German's shoulders.[11] In 1946, it was produced at the Princes Theatre, London, with a revised libretto by Edward Knoblock, and enjoyed a highly successful run of 367 performances.

German had slightly less success with *A Princess of Kensington* (1903) and *Tom Jones* (1907), but both had more than 100 performances. At this time, musical comedy was still going strong, and, in 1907, *Tom Jones* had to compete not only with the likes of *Miss Hook of Holland* and Caryll and Monckton's *The Girls of Gothenburg* but also with Lehár's *The Merry Widow*. In 1909, German's musical version of W. S. Gilbert's play *The Wicked World* (1873) was given as *Fallen Fairies* at the Savoy but proved something of disappointment, closing after fifty performances. Liza Lehman worked with musical comedy librettist Owen Hall (real name, Jimmy Davis) on her operetta *Sergeant Brue* (lyrics by J. Hickory Wood), which met with considerable success at the Strand Theatre in 1904. In fact, it transferred from there to the Prince of Wales Theatre and back again as it progressed to an unanticipated run of 243 performances.

It was common for musical comedy to involve composer collaborations, and Lionel Monckton and Howard Talbot created together one of the most enduring musical comedies in *The Arcadians* (1909), which had a book by Mark Ambient and Alexander Thompson, and lyrics by Arthur Wimperis. Monckton and Talbot composed musical numbers separately, although the latter was probably responsible for all of the orchestration. The West End production was by actor-manager Robert Courtneidge, and on Broadway it was presented by Charles Frohman. It was Monckton and Talbot's finest joint achievement, praised by critics and public alike, and became one of the few works of this period to be revived with any regularity in the second half of the century. It is by no means easy in this instance to decide whether the category of 'musical comedy' or 'operetta' suits it best.

Among other triumphs for Monckton were *A Country Girl*, composed with Rubens (1902), and *The Quaker Girl* (1910). They both make much of the friction between the country and town (London in the former and Paris in the latter). *Our Miss Gibbs*, composed with Caryll (1909), is somewhat different, because its department-store heroine hails from Yorkshire's largest city, Leeds. The title character, who was played by Yorkshire-born Gertie Millar, has a no-nonsense attitude in contrast to the sophisticated Londoner, and that is particularly evident when she sings her song 'In Yorkshire', for which Monckton supplied the lyrics and Caryll composed the music.

> The girls up in London are all very well,
> But they just want to come down to Leeds for a spell.
> Their manners are better than ours are, perhaps,
> But still they don't know how to manage the chaps.
> They'll say if a fellow should squeeze them too tight.
> 'Sir, you insult me, good night!'
> But we never waste words in Yorkshire,
> Yorkshire, Yorkshire!
> If a young fellow is taking you out,
> And you don't like the nonsense he's talking about,
> You up with your hand and you give him a clout –
> That's what we do up in Yorkshire!

Just before World War I, operetta began to face a challenge from revue, which made use of a general theme to give loose cohesion to a varied bill of comic sketches, songs and dances. It was growing increasingly popular after *Hullo, Ragtime* (1912) and *Hullo, Tango* (1913). The most celebrated of the wartime revues in London was *The Bing Boys Are Here* with music by American composer Nat D. Ayer (1916). Operetta productions declined because so many necessitated the purchase of English rights from theatrical agents in Berlin, but there were two operetta-like entertainments that broke box-office records: *Chu Chin Chow* (book and lyrics by Oscar Asche, music by Frederick Norton), which opened at His Majesty's in 1916 and ran for 2,238 performances, and *The Maid of the Mountains* (book by Frederick Lonsdale, lyrics by Harry Graham and music by Harold Fraser-Simson), which opened at Daly's in 1917 and ran for 1353 performances. Both were examples of theatrical escapism, the first to a fantasy Orient and the second to the mountains of Italy. José Collins became forever associated with Teresa, the title role of *The Maid of the Mountains*. Her singing ability was an advantage in music that had, in places, clearly been influenced by the operettas from the German stage heard in the previous decade. Compare the melody of 'Love Will Find a Way' with the famous waltz from *The Merry Widow* (Examples 16.1 and 16.2).

Example 16.1 'Lippen schweigen' from *Die lustige Witwe*

Example 16.2 'Love Will Find a Way' from *The Maid of the Mountains*

Collins's success as Teresa meant she became a highly paid star, and in 1920, when she undertook the role of Dolores in Fraser-Simson's *A Southern Maid*, her salary rose from £50 to £300 a week (an equivalent of around £11,840 in 2018).[12]

In the 1920s, operettas such as Montague Phillips's *The Rebel Maid* (1921), with its much-loved song 'The Fishermen of England', and Fraser-Simson's *The Street Singer* (1924) held the stage.[13] There is a tendency, however, to see the twin triumphs in 1925 of Vincent Youmans's *No, No, Nanette* at the Palace Theatre, and Rudolf Friml's *Rose-Marie* at Drury Lane, as marking the beginning of Broadway conquering all. In fact, Thomas Dunhill, Walter Leigh and Alfred Reynolds each composed a well-received operetta in the early 1930s (*Tantivy Towers, The Pride of the Regiment* and *Derby Day*, respectively).

Noël Coward, who had already built a reputation in revue, established himself as a British operetta composer when Charles B. Cochran presented *Bitter Sweet* to huge success at His Majesty's Theatre in 1929, with American Peggy Wood making her London debut as Sari Linden. The orchestration of Coward's operetta was by J. A. de Orellana, an experienced West End musical director who had obliged in a similar capacity for Monckton and Rubens.[14] *Bitter Sweet* began playing simultaneously in New York from November, and films were made of the operetta in 1933 and 1940. *Conversation Piece* followed at His Majesty's in 1934 (and also in New York that year). It was set in nineteenth-century Brighton and raised issues of social class. It starred Yvonne Printemps as Melanie, and her hit song was 'I'll Follow My Secret Heart'. In *Operette*, which opened at His Majesty's in 1938, Coward created a role for Fritzi Massary, one of the most famous stars of the German musical stage, who, being Jewish, had fled to London to avoid Nazi persecution. Its best-known song is 'The Stately Homes of England'. Coward continued to be productive: his musical romance *Pacific 1860* was given at Drury Lane in 1946, and his musical play *After the Ball* (based on Oscar Wilde's *Lady Windermere's Fan*) opened at the Globe in 1954.

Mark Steyn names Noël Coward as 'the most famous British theatrical composer in America' before Andrew Lloyd Webber arrived on the scene.[15] However, it was the Welsh composer Ivor Novello who did most to keep English operetta alive in the late 1930s and the decade after. He was born in Cardiff in 1898 as David Ivor Davies and changed his name to Ivor Novello, using the middle name of his mother (who had been named after the celebrated soprano Clara Novello). His mother was a highly regarded singing teacher, and George Edwardes often sent performers to be coached by her at the Salle Erard during her visits to London. Novello began writing songs while a scholar and choir boy at Magdalen College School, Oxford.[16] He developed a love of opera and theatre during visits to London as a young man and, in 1913, moved into an apartment rented by his mother at the top of the Strand Theatre in the Aldwych. It was to be his London home for the rest of his life.[17]

In 1914, he achieved fame as the composer of 'Keep the Home Fires Burning', to lyrics by Lena Guilbert Ford, and his first commissioned musical play was *Theodore and Co.*, given at the Gaiety in 1916, with additional music by Jerome Kern. In 1921, he composed a hit comic song, 'And Her Mother Came Too' (lyrics by Dion Titheradge) for the revue *A to Z*. In this song, the restaurant that once functioned as an escape for Danilo in *The Merry Widow* no longer offers any refuge for the vexed lover.

> We dine at Maxim's
> And her mother comes too!

Novello became a silent film actor. He was asked by the renowned American film director D. W. Griffith to appear in *The White Rose* (1923) and was chosen by Alfred Hitchcock to star in *The Lodger* (1926).[18] He was also an actor in, and writer of, spoken drama. Lily Elsie, the star of *The Merry Widow* whom he adored,[19] performed with him in his play *The Truth Game* (1928) at the Globe, one of several dramas he authored. When, in 1934, *The Three Sisters* was a surprise flop at Drury Lane, despite lyrics by Oscar Hammerstein and music by Jerome Kern, it opened up an opportunity for Novello. He had not composed a musical score for several years, having been occupied with films and plays. Now, he embarked on *Glamorous Night*, the first of his works that can be called an operetta. He wrote the leading female role for the versatile American star Mary Ellis, who had played the title role of *Rose-Marie* on Broadway, but who now lived in London with her English husband. He asked Christopher Hassall to write the lyrics, and it was the beginning of a long-term partnership. To direct the operetta, he chose Viennese producer Leontine Sagan, who had worked for the acclaimed Austrian theatre director Max Reinhardt. Despite the hot summer of 1935, *Glamorous Night* attracted large audiences and did much to restore Drury Lane's status as a premier theatre for operettas and musical plays. The plot had a sad ending, however, and so did the production. The manager had booked performers for a Christmas pantomime well in advance, and the operetta had to be terminated to make way for it.

At £25,000, the production expenses of *Glamorous Night* were large, and the running costs meant only a small profit was made, even though it ran for 243 performances.[20] This may explain why the board of Drury Lane rejected Novello's next operetta *Careless Rapture*. Drury Lane has a large stage and, in keeping with the audience's appetite for spectacle, *Glamorous Night* had an expensive scene in which an ocean liner sank; ominously, the new work contained an earthquake. Novello was catering to the audience's appetite for romance and spectacle, but the last stage earthquake was in Monckton and Talbot's *The Mousmé* at the Shaftesbury in 1911, and that production made a loss of £20,000.[21]

The pieces chosen instead of *Careless Rapture* turned out to be disappointments, and this put Novello in a position to dictate his own terms: he was prepared to finance 75 per cent of the costs of production if Drury Lane would cover the remaining 25 per cent. The consequence was that he was now working as composer, writer, actor and manager. It seemed he could do anything except sing, this ability having deserted him in his sixteenth year.[22] He circumvented the problem by playing roles in which he accompanied another singer at the piano. *Careless Rapture* was a huge success, and the board offered no objection to housing the next Novello operetta, *Crest of the Wave*, even if they noticed it, too, was strong on spectacle and included a train crash.

With a run of 205 performances, *Crest of the Wave* fell into the category of success, but not at the magnitude hoped for. That was to be achieved, after a bumpy start, with the next offering by Novello and Hassall, *The Dancing Years*. It opened in March 1939, but all London theatres were ordered to close on 3 September, the day the British and French declared war on Germany. A decision was taken to produce it again in March 1942 at the Adelphi Theatre, and it became the surprise hit of the war years, running there until July 1944. By then it had notched up a total of 1,158 performances.

Arc de Triomphe of 1943 was intended to be more operatic in character, and, indeed, contained within it a one-act operetta, *Joan of Arc*. It was produced at the Phoenix Theatre, running for 222 performances. Novello could play no part in it, because he was appearing in *The Dancing Years*. As it happened, he had to quit his role in the latter for other reasons. He was found guilty of a breach of the wartime regulations governing the use of petrol and private cars and was sentenced to two months' imprisonment. The case was complex, and his term was reduced on appeal to one month.[23] Novello's successes continued unabated after the war: *Perchance to Dream*, which opened at the London Hippodrome in 1945, ran for over a thousand performances, and *King's Rhapsody* of 1949 notched up 842 performances.

Novello commented on the difference between his working methods and those of Coward: 'even his lightest comedies have been written with most meticulous care … I work the other way. If a thing does not come out at once, quite spontaneously, I scrap it.'[24] Yet, Coward, like Novello, could work at speed: despite having other obligations, writing and composing the whole of *Bitter Sweet* took him around six months, and, in his first autobiography, he tells of composing its hit song 'I'll See You Again' in a taxi during a twenty-minute traffic jam.[25] He and Novello had much else in common: they were both actor-managers, playwrights, author-composers and both gay. There was gossip in the theatre world about Novello's sexual orientation, but his relationships with men seem to have had no negative effects career-wise, save for a suspicion that his harsh sentence for breach of traffic regulations may have owed something to a judge who had a 'marked dislike for the acting profession and for gay men in particular'.[26]

Novello had many male friends and in their company was relaxed enough to refer to *The Dancing Years* as *The Prancing Queers*.[27] His affectionate partnership with Hassall continued after the latter's marriage.[28] Hassall supplied the lyrics to every Novello operetta from *Glamorous Night* on, with two exceptions. One was *Perchance to Dream*, which has lyrics by Novello himself, because Hassall was serving in the army at that time. The other was Novello's final stage work, *Gay's the Word*, which had lyrics by Alan Melville. It starred Cicely Courtneidge as Gay, an ex-stage performer who had set up a drama school. It opened on 16 February 1951 and was described as 'quintessentially English' by the *New Statesman*.[29] *Gay's the Word* burlesques his earlier work in places, taking a shot at his Ruritanian operettas *Glamorous Night* and *King's Rhapsody*.[30]

> Ruritania!
> The former delights
> Of Glamorous Nights
> No longer constitute a raving mania.

Ruritania in *Glamorous Night* is Krasnia, and in *King's Rhapsody* it is Murania. Frederick Lonsdale had popularized Ruritanian settings in his librettos for *King of Cadonia* of 1908 (lyrics by Adrian Ross, music by Sidney Jones), and *The Balkan Princess* of 1910 (lyrics by Arthur Wimperis, music by Paul Rubens). Novello admitted to Lonsdale that the Ruritanian exoticism of the former had influenced *King's Rhapsody*.[31] Old-fashioned as such settings now were, the press coverage of the premiere indicated a widespread conviction that Novello had challenged the dominance of the American musical in London.[32] On 6 March 1951, however, aged fifty-eight, Novello suffered a fatal heart attack, a few hours after he had been performing in *King's Rhapsody* at the Palace Theatre.

Statistics showing performance runs, outstanding as they often are, cannot be regarded as a reliable gauge of Novello's success. *The Dancing Years*, for example, came to a premature end twice because of bombing raids, and he took off *Perchance to Dream* while it was still filling the theatre, simply because he had other plans to fulfil. In the case of his Drury Lane operettas, it must be borne in mind that this theatre was twice the size of many other West End theatres. Furthermore, London performance statistics do not take account of the many productions elsewhere. In the late 1940s, Novello's operettas were being performed by touring companies, repertory theatres and amateur societies all over the UK. Yet none of them made it to Broadway although some of his plays had been successful there and in Hollywood. Only *Glamorous* Night and *The Dancing Years* were given productions in the USA, and both were one-week outdoor performances given by St Louis Municipal Opera (in 1936 and 1947).[33]

Perhaps, his biggest triumphs in London came at an awkward time, during and immediately after World War II.

Novello preferred to label his operettas 'musical plays' or 'musical romances', but, as noted earlier, labels were often chosen for marketing reasons. He relied on others to orchestrate his music: the musical director at Drury Lane, Charles Prentice, obliged in that capacity for *Glamorous Night*, and, later, Harry Dacres was a trusted orchestrator. Novello's style was influenced by Viennese music and Hungarian-Gipsy music but also carried qualities associated with British drawing-room ballads, as can be detected in 'Keep the Home Fires Burning', 'Rose of England' (from *Crest of the Wave*) and 'We'll Gather Lilacs' (from *Perchance to Dream*). There is, too, a flavour of music hall in a song such as 'Winnie, Get Off the Colonel's Knee' from *Careless Rapture*, and the enduring influence on Novello of British musical comedy is recognizable in 'Primrose' from *The Dancing Years*. Novello claimed that, as a young man, Lehár was his guide.[34] Thus, it is a matter of some irony that Novello composed the last 'Viennese' operetta to be given in London before World War II: *The Dancing Years*. The Jewish protagonist was played by Novello himself. The idea of the persecuted composer came to him after a friend related to him what he had seen happening in Vienna following the Nazi occupation of the city.[35] *The Dancing Years* contained a controversial scene of Nazi officers arresting Rudi. There is a letter in the Lord Chamberlain's Plays collection in the British Library, which shows that hostility to the Third Reich was not unanimous in Britain, even in March 1939. The writer complains about the anti-Nazi scene: 'It undoubtedly pleased a certain section of the audience and was wildly applauded, but it jarred others and some of the people booed.'[36]

The last figure to receive attention in this chapter is Vivian Ellis, who began as a composer for revues, but had a resounding success with the musical comedy *Mister Cinders* (1929), co-composed with Richard Myers. Ellis describes his stage works *Big Ben* (1946), *Bless the Bride* (1947) and *Tough at the Top* (1949) as 'light operas', but explains that this was not a label that would draw an audience, and so the term 'musical show' was chosen.[37] Despite that precaution, the first and third of these were modest successes only. Ellis was not an imitator of Coward or Novello: he sometimes looks back stylistically to Edwardian musical comedy and Paul Rubens in particular, but often spices up his music with elements of a syncopated style reminiscent of Jerome Kern. Sometimes, a French character can be detected, indicating Ellis's regard for André Messager and Reynaldo Hahn.[38] In composing *Bless the Bride*, he claims to have often turned to the score of *Carina* by Julia Woolf, his maternal grandmother, which had been performed at the Opera Comique, London, in 1888.[39]

Whereas Novello wrote music to which Hassall added lyrics, Ellis worked on all of his three 'light operas' with A[lan]P[atrick] Herbert, who preferred writing the words first.[40] Although A. P. Herbert – as he was usually known – has been praised as 'one of Britain's cleverest, wittiest wordsmiths',[41] he has also been criticized for lyrics that fall 'too frequently into the same dreary ABAB pattern, alternating feminine and masculine rhymes: 'doing/done/brewing/sun', and so on', leading Ellis to compose 'predictable tumpty-tumpty music'.[42] Ellis asserts, on the contrary, that his settings were, in fact, 'no compliant tumpty-tumpty music' and that he 'opened up the words for the music'.[43] Ellis was not normally a fast worker, explaining that the simplest composition was the result of hours of work spent 'altering, erasing, and eradicating any signs of effort'.[44]

Novello apart, *Bless the Bride*, with its 886 performances at the Adelphi, seems to mark the end of British operetta as a popular West End genre. Shortly after it opened, Rodgers and Hammerstein's *Oklahoma!* was produced in London, and the massive success of the latter heralded a new era of dominance of the West End by Broadway musicals. Few home-grown products could withstand this incursion, but there were two notable triumphs in 1954: Sandy Wilson's *The Boy Friend* at Wyndham's Theatre (1,740 performances) and Julian Slade's *Salad Days* at the Vaudeville Theatre (2,289 performances).

Afterword

It might easily be argued that British, American and German operetta of the early twentieth century became absorbed into the modern Broadway musical. Less persuasively, perhaps, twentieth-century ballad operas, such as Ethel Smyth's *The Boatswain's Mate* (1916) and Vaughan Williams's *Hugh the Drover* (1924), might be seen as precursors of the modern musical that relies on existing songs, such as *Mama Mia!* Most difficult of all, however, is to decide what befell comic opera. When this term is taken to be synonymous with 'light opera' or 'operetta', a case can also be made for its having been absorbed into the modern musical. Problems arise when 'comic opera' is intended to suggest a kinship with the high-art status of operas such as Mozart's *Marriage of Figaro* or Verdi's *Falstaff*. Vaughan Williams must have had this kind of distinction between art and entertainment in mind when he labelled *Sir John in Love* a comic opera, but *The Poisoned Kiss*, which he called a 'romantic extravaganza', has been described as an 'uncertain cross between operetta and musical comedy'.[45] High-status comic opera does not appear to have survived into the second half of the century with any degree of strength, despite the success of Benjamin Britten's *Albert Herring* in 1947, and Stravinsky's *The Rake's Progress* in 1951. Coincidentally, each of those years saw the premieres of two acclaimed productions in the West End that could be labelled operettas: Ellis's *Bless the Bride* and Novello's *Gay's the Word*. After this, the descriptions 'comic opera' or 'operetta' for new stage works became a rarity.

Notes

1. John Hollingshead, manager of the Gaiety Theatre until 1886, credits Edwardes with the invention of musical comedy in '*Good Old Gaiety*': *An Historiette and Remembrance* (London: Gaiety Theatre Company, 1903), 72.
2. Sketch, 28 Nov. 1894, quoted in Peter Bailey, 'Naughty but Nice: Musical Comedy and the Rhetoric of the Girl, 1892–1914', in Michael R. Booth and Joel H. Kaplan (eds.), *The Edwardian Theatre: Essays on Performance and the Stage* (Cambridge: Cambridge University Press, 1996), 36–60, at 41.
3. Alan Hyman, *The Gaiety Years* (London: Cassell, 1975), 80.
4. Len Platt, *Musical Comedy on the West End Stage, 1890–1939* (Basingstoke: Palgrave Macmillan, 2004), 66.
5. Otto Keller, *Die Operette in ihrer Geschichtlichen Entwicklung: Musik, Libretto, Darstellung* (Leipzig: Stein Verlag, 1926), 420.
6. See Platt, *Musical Comedy*, 38.
7. David Ewen, *The Book of European Light Opera* (New York: Holt, Rinehart and Winston, 1962), 50.
8. Ursula Bloom, *Curtain Call for the Guv'nor: A Biography of George Edwardes* (London: Hutchinson, 1954), 150.
9. Ewen, *European Light Opera*, 100. *Florodora*, its music and its British and American premieres are discussed in Andrew Lamb, *Leslie Stuart: The Man Who Composed Florodora* (London: Routledge, 2002), 82–111.
10. A lack of concern for moral propriety may explain why Frederic Austin's arrangement of John Gay's *The Beggar's Opera*, which opened at the Lyric, Hammersmith, in 1920, enjoyed resounding success (1,463 performances), despite being an eighteenth-century piece.
11. Landon Ronald, 'The Revival of Comic Opera in England', Supplement to *Play Pictorial*, 34, no. 205 (Sept. 1919): 1–2, at 1.
12. José Collins, *The Maid of the Mountains: Her Story* (London: Hutchinson, 1932), 124, 164. Value comparison taken from average real earnings index on Measuring Worth website, http://measuringworth.com/calculators/ppoweruk/ (accessed 24 Nov. 2017).
13. *The Rebel Maid* had a book by Alexander M. Thompson and lyrics by Gerald Dalton; *The Street Singer* had a book by Freddy Lonsdale and lyrics by Percy Greenbank.
14. His 'brilliant orchestration' is praised by James Agate, *Immoment Toys: A Survey of Light Entertainment on the London Stage, 1920–1943* (London: Jonathan Cape, 1945), 69.
15. Mark Steyn, *Broadway Babies Say Goodnight: Musicals Then and Now* (London: Faber, 1997), 169.
16. W. J. MacQueen-Pope, *Ivor: The Story of an Achievement* (London: W. H. Allen, 1951), 49–51.
17. Ibid., 76–7.
18. See Sandy Wilson, *Ivor* (London: Michael Joseph, 1975), 62–5, 75–6.
19. See Peter Noble, *Ivor Novello: Man of the Theatre* (London: Falcon Press, 1951), 43. During holidays as a schoolboy, he saw *The Merry Widow* twenty-seven times.
20. MacQueen-Pope, *Ivor*, 351.
21. Ernest Short, *Sixty Years of Theatre* (London: Eyre & Spottiswoode, 1951), 167.
22. James Harding, *Ivor Novello* (London: W. H. Allen, 1987), 9.
23. MacQueen-Pope discusses it at length in *Ivor*, 410–30.
24. Noble, Ivor Novello, 111.
25. Noël Coward, *Present Indicative* (London: Heinemann, 1937), 348. Coward told Charles Castle that if all went well he could write a play in a few days. Castle, *Noël* (London: W. H. Allen, 1972), 234.

26. Paul Webb, *Ivor Novello: Portrait of a Star* (London: Haus Publishing, rev. ed. 2005), 164.
27. Webb, *Ivor Novello*, 145.
28. Harding, *Ivor Novello*, 142–3.
29. *New Statesman*, 3 Mar. 1951, 246. Quoted in J. P. Wearing, *The London Stage, 1950–1959* (Lanham, MD: Rowman & Littlefield, 2nd ed. 2013), 165.
30. Ruritania was the fictional kingdom of Anthony Hope's novel *The Prisoner of Zenda* (1894) but became the general name for any imaginary central European country.
31. Richard Traubner, *Operetta: A Theatrical History* (New York: Routledge, 2003), 207. It also had an impact on the young Noël Coward; see his autobiography, *Present Indicative*, 20.
32. Enthusiastic press notices are excerpted in Noble, *Ivor Novello*, 259–60.
33. Richard C. Norton, 'Coward and Novello' (2007), http://operetta-research-center.org/coward-novello/ (accessed 26 Apr. 2019).
34. W. MacQueen-Pope and D. L. Murray, *Fortune's Favourite: The Life and Times of Franz Lehár* (London: Hutchinson, 1953), 125.
35. Noble, *Ivor Novello*, 227–8.
36. Cited in Len Platt, 'West End Musical Theatre and the Representation of Germany', in Len Platt, Tobias Becker and David Linton (eds.), *Popular Musical Theatre in London and Berlin, 1890–1939* (Cambridge: Cambridge University Press, 2014), 224–41, at 238.
37. Vivian Ellis, *I'm on a See-Saw* (London: Michael Joseph, 1953), 220.
38. Ibid., 51. Messager's *Véronique* had been revived in London in 1915, and his English operetta, *Monsieur Beaucaire* (book by Frederick Lonsdale, lyrics by Adrian Ross), was well received in 1919. The best-known example of Ellis's French style is 'Ma Belle Marguerite' from *Bless the Bride*.
39. Ellis, *I'm on a See-Saw*, 15.
40. Ibid., 220.
41. Traubner, *Operetta*, 354.
42. Steyn, *Broadway Babies Say*, 168.
43. Ellis, *I'm on a See-Saw*, 229. He illustrates with reference to 'I Was Never Kissed Before', 'Ma Belle Marguerite' and 'This Is My Lovely Day', which all became hits.
44. Ibid., 129.
45. Michael Kennedy, 'The Poisoned Kiss', *Grove Music Online*, www.oxfordmusiconline.com/public/book/omo_gmo (accessed 26 Apr. 2019).

Recommended Reading

Coward, Noël. *Present Indicative*. London: Heinemann, 1937.
Ellis, Vivian. *I'm on a See-Saw: An Autobiography*. London: Michael Joseph, 1953.
Everett, William A., ed. *The Cambridge Companion to the Musical*. Cambridge: Cambridge University Press, 2008.
Ewen, David. *The Book of European Light Opera*. New York: Holt, Rinehart and Winston, 1962.
Harding, James. *Ivor Novello*. London: W. H. Allen, 1987.
Hyman, Alan. *The Gaiety Years*. London: Cassell, 1975.
Lamb, Andrew. *Leslie Stuart: The Man Who Composed Florodora*. London: Routledge, 2002.
MacQueen-Pope, Walter. J. *Ivor: The Story of an Achievement*. London: W. H. Allen, 1951.
Niccolai, Michela and Clair Rowden, eds. *Musical Theatre in Europe 1830–1945*. Turnhout: Brepols, 2017.
Noble, Peter. *Ivor Novello: Man of the Theatre*. London: Falcon Press, 1951.
Norton, Richard C., 'Coward & Novello'. Operetta Research Center Amsterdam. http://operetta-research-center.org/coward-novello/ (accessed 9 May 2019).

Platt, Len. *Musical Comedy on the West End Stage, 1890–1939*. Basingstoke: Palgrave Macmillan, 2004.

Platt, Len, Tobias Becker and David Linton, eds. *Popular Musical Theatre in London and Berlin, 1890–1939*. Cambridge: Cambridge University Press, 2014.

Short, Ernest. *Sixty Years of Theatre*. London: Eyre & Spottiswoode, 1951.

Snelson, John. 'The Waltzing Years: British Operetta 1907–1939'. In Michela Niccolai and Clair Rowden, eds. *Musical Theatre in Europe 1830–1945*. Turnhout: Brepols, 2017. 241–66.

Webb, Paul. *Ivor Novello: A Portrait of a Star* [1999]. London: Haus Publishing, rev. ed. 2005.

17 Operetta During the Nazi Regime

MATTHIAS KAUFFMANN

'Operetta is dead! Long live the operetta!' This is how Hans Herbert Pudor, a Nazi director for operetta at the theatre of Breslau, cheered in an essay of 1937. He was convinced by the efficiency of the purges in the repertoire that occurred after 1933, making it clear with lofty words: 'Dead is the operetta that dangled insubstantially on a string of a revue-plots, for the purpose only of a magnificent setting, paired with the exhibition of more or less titillating female amenities.' In general, Pudor fought against the modern type of revue-operetta, with its glamour and eroticism, and generally rejected it as 'non-German'. But significantly, he was not able to point to an alternative for the future of the genre: on the contrary, in his essay he criticized two central strategies that defined new operettas in the Third Reich, when he declared both as failed: new chauvinistic operettas and works that 'crank out operetta with rural folk motifs'.[1] However, this leads to an aporia: Pudor knows what he does not tolerate on operetta stages – but he does not know what he should tolerate instead.

Today two questions remain: what was operetta in the Third Reich really made of, and was the genre really as dead as claimed? An investigation into operetta between 1933 and 1945 must adopt three different approaches: first, the Nazi 'fight' against a genre widely condemned for ideological reasons; second, the Nazi aim to create a new 'German operetta' to replace an ostracized repertoire; and third, how theatre practice really reacted to political orders.

In fact, the Nazi political censorship of operetta should not be underestimated: nearly the entire genre was condemned as non-German for both artistic and ideological reasons. Mainly it was simply the regime's blind racism that classified the genre's tradition as Jewish: nearly every artist was accused of being a Jew, whereas not everyone saw himself or herself as Jewish by religion or culture. This culminated in the use of the term 'degeneracy', which led to Nazi purges in the repertoire. Significantly, it was not possible to justify the accusation of degeneracy by examining the operettas themselves; instead, it had to be motivated by invectives against single artists. A list of banned works dated 1 September 1935 exemplifies this. It was signed by Hans Hinkel as Director of the Reich Culture Chamber – but even if it was directed against certain 'musical works', it remained merely an amateurish brainstorming exercise around the names of suspicious composers, who were supposed to be Jewish.[2] It was not possible to defame their work by reference to technical quality.

Another prime aspect of the Nazi fight was against the dazzling aesthetics of the modern revue-operettas of the twenties: modern show concepts were condemned as an artistic reminiscence of the detested Weimar Republic – and its commercial style was declared as characteristic of Jewish business behaviour. Certainly, this verdict stands against the very nature of operetta itself: the aesthetics of popular musical theatre are cosmopolitan, dealing with the questions of its time by reflecting the mentality of the audience. The quest for financial success has always been part of the background of every new piece, and so the Nazi counterattack had to question the genre itself.

A law dated 22 September 1933 established the so-called Reich Chamber of Culture, with its several chambers designed to embrace the entirety of cultural life in Germany. Every artist had to be legalized by being registered in his specific chamber. Thus, the system became a perfidious instrument for dejudaization, because not being registered in a chamber resulted in an occupational ban. A little later, the 'Theatre Law' from 15 May 1934 empowered Joseph Goebbels as the Reich Minister of Popular Enlightenment and Propaganda to fully control the schedules of plays: now the minister was able to order or to hinder play performances by law. It was realized in practice by the Reich Drama Adviser Rainer Schlösser (1899–1945) who, with his staff of the Reich Dramaturgical Bureau (which was integrated into the Propaganda Ministry), promulgated a system of censorship in the theatre business. Nevertheless, their claim that they would renew the operetta schedule immediately was not easy to realize: traditional operettas remained indispensable for the commercial situation of the theatres – and their repertoire could not be easily changed. This led to the paradoxical situation in which, after 1933, so-called non-German operettas remained on stage until 1935. From that year on, the Reich Dramaturgical Bureau intensified the restrictions on Jewish operettas – but, even then, Schlösser and his staff took care not to provoke a crisis concerning the economic basis of the genre.

This led to a system of pragmatism and double moral standards: because there were not very many Aryan composers left, it became necessary to idealize the genre's tradition, mainly the Viennese operetta of Johann Strauss Jr, Carl Millöcker, Franz von Suppé and Carl Zeller. They were declared to be the incarnation of typical German artists – until it was discovered in 1938, that Johann Strauss, whose name was used to replace Jacques Offenbach as the founder of operetta in Nazi theatre history, had to be declared an 'eighth-Jew'. It was Goebbels himself who decided to 'forbid to make that public. Because firstly this is not proven and, secondly, I am not in the mood to excavate the entire German cultural heritage.'[3] So, this fatal detail was erased in the Viennese archives as well as in the related parish register.

It was much easier to erase non-German librettists: the Reich Music Editing Office (Reichsstelle für Musikbearbeitungen), established on 1 May 1940 under the lead of Heinz Drewes (1903–80) and Hans Joachim Moser (1889–1967), took charge of changing plots and details in librettos, as demanded by daily politics. Many operettas were meant to be saved for the market after having their non-German style excised. However, in many cases it sufficed simply to keep quiet about the Jewish texts of popular works – such as those of Franz Lehár, a composer widely known for being the Führer's favourite. Hiding the names of undesirable collaborators became an easy trick.

Such was the case with Fritz Löhner-Beda, who was vilified for being a Zionist but, on the other hand, created wonderful, indispensable verses such as those for *Das Land des Lächelns* (The Land of Smiles) of 1929. This operetta was given in the Vienna State Opera on 30 April 1940, on the occasion of Lehár's seventieth birthday, with Hitler in the audience. Löhner-Beda and his colleague Ludwig Herzer were not mentioned on the playbill; in fact, Herzer was already in exile, while Löhner was arrested and sent to a concentration camp, still hoping that Lehár could save him. He was murdered in Auschwitz, probably on 4 December 1942.

Many important artists had to suffer: Léon Jessel for example, the composer of the smash hit operetta *Schwarzwaldmädel* (The Black Forest Girl) of 1917, was declared Jewish, although he saw himself as a German nationalist – and even sympathized with the Nazi regime. He died after being tortured by the Gestapo on 4 January 1942. Some artists succeeded in finding exile just in time: Paul Abraham, Emmerich Kálmán, Leo Ascher, Robert Gilbert, Bruno Granichstaedten, Robert Katscher and Oscar Straus, for example. Ralph Benatzky and Robert Stolz left Germany by choice. Other important operetta experts tried to hold out: Edmund Eysler, for example, survived in a hiding place in Vienna; the librettists Béla Jenbach, Victor Léon and Julius Wilhelm attempted the same but died before 1945.

In the meantime, 'German' artists used the opportunity to fill the gap: many of them did that for both economical and ideological reasons. The problem was that they had no clue how to define an original German operetta in a way that would not be bound to the old standards, which were widely banned for being Jewish. Nazi cultural politics knew exactly what to stand against but did not how to define alternatives. There was not a single hint on how to freshen up the genre in an official Nazi way. Going back to the polemics of Hans Herbert Pudor at the very beginning of this chapter,

two central ways can be seen of how to conceive a new German operetta
after 1933. On the one hand, there was an urge to use heroic and patriotic
subjects and, on the other, an inclination to deal with homebound, often
rural subjects, which came close to the Nazi 'blood-and-soil' ideology. It
has to be pointed out that those concepts were usually motivated by an
attitude of 'self-ideologization': composers and librettists worked strategi-
cally to succeed – or even to survive – under the new political conditions
after 1933.

The first way was taken exemplarily by the Austrian composer Heinrich
Strecker (1893–1981), who succeeded with his new operetta *Ännchen von
Tharau* (1933), which reached over 4,000 performances by 1973. After the
war, Strecker declared himself a non-political artist – but that is imprecise,
in view of his activities from 1934 on as a cultural leader of the initially
forbidden Austrian National Socialist German Workers' Party (NSDAP),
which even led to his imprisonment in May 1936. *Ännchen von Tharau*,
created with the librettist Hans Spirk (1897–1966), must be rated as
a highly ideological attempt to, in his own words, 'awaken the old,
German musical comedy'.[4] This leads to an operetta paradigm inspired
by the genre's nineteenth-century tradition but now enriched with typical
'German' slogans as the publisher claimed: 'German emotional life, mili-
tant attitude and fidelity between friends pervade the piece in ever-new
variations.'[5]

The plot is a very romantic, free interpretation of how the old folk song
Ännchen of Tharau by the German poet Simon Dach might have been
invented. In the operetta, Dach and his best friend Johannes Portatius are
in love with the same young woman. In the end, Dach will subdue his
feelings because he appreciates 'fidelity between friends is higher than
love'.[6] Johannes Portatius in turn tries to forget Ännchen by joining the
army – like Sandor Barinkay in Strauss's *Der Zigeunerbaron* (The Gypsy
Baron). In the time that follows, Portatius succeeds in becoming
a distinguished commander – and finally wins Ännchen's heart, of course –
while Simon Dach attains a professorship that suddenly cures him of his
lovesickness. Before that, however, the operetta takes place in a military
camp. There, patriotic and heroic scenes are drawn, reminiscent of
Friedrich Schiller's *Wallenstein* trilogy or Heinrich von Kleist's *Prinz
Friedrich von Homburg* (The Prince of Homburg). Of course, this is
contrasted with the comical situations necessary in operetta: it is the
comical character Schnerzlein, an incompetent Saxon soldier, who provokes absurd situations. All the more, Johannes and his very own 'devil
squadron' appear as a soldier's ideal, which also came close to Nazi
requirements. But this does not make Strecker's operetta an innovative
piece at all: this kind of military romanticism was part of the genre's

tradition since the aforementioned *Gypsy Baron* and reveals nothing but the fact that operetta is always adapted to its time: it does not create politics but reacts to them by dealing with varying established dramaturgical standards. Yet, that was not how to define a brand-new Nazi 'German operetta'; so, instead, Strecker merely picked up some very old standards and used them to please the regime.

In fact, the open ideologization of operetta subjects by dealing with everyday politics was taken up by artists who wanted to succeed in the regime even by adopting its ideological beliefs. Librettist Hermann Hermecke (1892–1961), who claimed to have developed a new kind of Nazi operetta, exemplifies the strategy of combining artistic and political ambitions with strong commercial interests. Today, Hermecke is primarily known for his collaboration with the composer Nico Dostal. Together they developed pieces like *Monika* (1937) or *Die ungarische Hochzeit* (The Hungarian Wedding) of 1939. Those special pieces remained in the genre's tradition without dealing with daily politics; in fact, they celebrated escapism on stage and, of course, were used to fill the gap that opened up because of the Nazi purges: *Monika* could easily replace Jessel's *Black Forest Girl* just as *The Hungarian Wedding* replaced Kálmán's *Gräfin Mariza* (Countess Mariza). What is more, Hermecke was proud of his collaboration with the composer Arno Vetterling (1903–63) because both were proud members of the Nazi party. Together they wanted to show that 'operetta that apparently only serves for entertainment, could be culturally effective in its best sense': 'If operetta were to be banned totally from the repertoire, people would lose an efficient instrument for an extensive cultural influence on the entire nation – apart from the economic consequences.'[7] Hermann Hermecke's and Arno Vetterling's operetta *Die Dorothee*, developed in 1936 and published by the publishing house of the NSDAP, Eher Nachf., serves as a striking example of how to serve the regime by conceiving a new piece dealing with everyday politics.

The plot is set in Transylvania and was meant to show the battle between brave German immigrants living there under hard conditions, longing for their state, and the Romanian villains who act against them. There is Dorothee Werner, who owns a little farm in Transylvania, but becomes indebted to a cruel Romanian farmer called Radu Milescu, who appears as a drastic 'non-German' incarnation of chauvinism and sexism. His counterpart is a young, elegant and – of course – German hussar, called Klaus Engelberg, who arrives to teach Dorothee about thrift and patriotism. But the young lady does not accept Klaus's lessons in 'speaking German to her'![8] Dressed as a simple maidservant, she tries to demonstrate her autonomous rural ability to work – and provokes a romantic disaster when Klaus falls in love with her. A dispute occurs during the finale of

Act 2. For a short time, the intrigues of the Romanians seem to work, until even the church elder of the village warns Dorothy: 'Your farm is German! It has to remain German!'[9] But, naturally, the operetta comes to a happy German ending: Klaus and Dorothee succeed against the Romanians – not least because of the intrigues of the comical character, a patriotic Saxon called Bemmrich, who served under Lt Engelberg and finally helps to trick the Romanians.

The staging of this operetta demonstrates the art, adornment and traditions of Germans in Transylvania. That is why Act 2 is set during a rural celebration, featuring Transylvanian wine as well as old folk songs and, finally, an original Transylvanian cudgel-dance, performed by the farmers. Unsurprisingly, Hermecke claimed the originality of those elements: costumes and dances were fixed in a detailed production book, because as 'old cultural assets they have to be rehearsed without a slight deviation'.[10]

Dorothee was premiered on 18 April 1936 in Fürth, and during the season 1936–7 it really succeeded on stage, becoming the fourth most important operetta of the year, with around 603 performances.[11] Yet it has to be said that this success ran short and was restricted to the provinces.

Hermecke, himself, wished to see his work realized in the metropolis, but he failed: even if the publisher thanked him 'for supporting our arduous fight for appropriate works in German operetta literature',[12] the Reich Dramaturgy Department came to the conclusion, 'for fundamental reasons, it sadly is not possible to give you an explicit certificate for the operetta *Dorothee* that could be used for advertising purposes'.[13]

Internally, operettas had not been rated as the perfect vehicle to promote daily politics. So the musical consultant of the leadership of the Volksbund for Germans Abroad voted against *Dorothee* because 'given the present seriousness of the actual situation of the Germans abroad, it does not seem to be advisable to campaign for an operetta'.[14] In the end, the work was suspected of plagiarism. It was Rainer Schlösser who came to the conclusion that 'Hermecke's *Dorothee* has indeed a very extraordinary similarity in its plot to *Dichter und Bauer* (*Poet and Farmer*) by Gustaf Quedenfeldt and Eugen Rex. This is admitted by all those involved.'[15] Thus, the self-declared ideological innovation of Hermecke and Vetterling that was meant to be a very German operetta was nothing but a counterfeit.

In general, the German audience did not favour heroic, chauvinistic or even rural subjects after 1933. Those pieces may have succeeded in the so-called provinces, but Nazi politics did not have the power to change common tastes in popular musical theatre. In fact, audiences were used to the dazzling standards of the Roaring Twenties, and the audience of the capitals – Berlin and Munich – did not suddenly abandon their taste for erotic dance displays in favour of a liking for Hermecke's original cudgel-dances. Operetta, serving as an indicator of public taste of the time, may exemplify that there was a gap between official ideology, given by the potentates, and the wishes of a still powerful audience that was able to preserve – or even endanger – theatres through its spending power. That's what politics had to react to: Joseph Goebbels did not have the power to force stage successes. In fact, the audiences had to be seduced by the regime.

Besides, potentates themselves had been quite bourgeois admirers of operettas – and they also preferred the non-German erotic revue style for cheering up their private life. It should be pointed out that the leading operetta playhouses of the Reich did not promote new operettas that tried to support the regime with open politics. Another strategy was chosen: the audience of the metropolis was confronted with a mock liberality; the regime appeared to openly tolerate modern shows with outlandish glamour. In Berlin, it was Heinz Hentschke (1895–1970), who ran the famous Metropol-Theater as the most prestigious venue for new operettas between 1934 and 1944.[16] And in Munich it was Fritz Fischer (1898–1985), who established the aesthetics for the Gärtnerplatz Theatre, which opposed every theoretical claim for German operetta. Fischer almost succeeded in both satisfying the audience and enchanting Adolf Hitler, who greatly admired these shows, even though (or because?) they were made up of elements that had originally been banned for being Jewish across the entire Reich.

'He let artists dance nude for the Gauleiter': such was the headline of an epitaph published in 1985 for Fritz Fischer, who had been director of Munich's Gärtnerplatz Theatre between 1938 and 1944. In fact, Fischer's artistic style seemed to be diametrically opposed to the ordered aesthetic in Nazi Germany: 'Outrageously for this time, he let nude stars climb out of giant champagne glasses'[17] – as in his staging of Strauss's *Die Fledermaus* on New Year's Eve 1939. Fischer's work took a tendency in Nazi theatre practice to an extreme: he created a dazzling counter-world to the cruelty of everyday life between 1933 and 1945. This illustrates the contradictions between official cultural politics, as dictated by the rulers, and the ordinary standards of theatre practice with its well-tried formulas for success, which took inspiration from American revue standards and maintained the established routines of the 'Roaring Twenties'. It can also be shown that this kind of double moral standard was important for the Nazi claim that they influenced the mood of the Nazi *Volksgemeinschaft*, and that was much more important for Goebbels and his staff than openly dealing with everyday politics on operetta stages.

Fritz Fischer, born on 16 July 1898 in Backnang, studied acting, ballet and singing before he had his first successes between 1923 and 1928 as manager of the German Theatre in Milwaukee. There he was introduced to American revues – at least by studying the legendary shows of Florenz Ziegfeld Jr. He used to claim that Ziegfeld once stuck a red carnation in his, Fischer's, buttonhole, thus declaring him his successor.[18] He returned to Germany in 1928 and earned his first successes with his decidedly transatlantic art of staging. After 1933 it was the Munich Gauleiter Arthur Wagner who was attracted by Fischer's so-called 'Speed-speed-revue' *1002 Nights* that had been developed for the famous Scala in Berlin and also had an acclaimed guest performance in Munich. After seeing the show in 1937, Wagner tried to hire Fischer for the Gärtnerplatz Theatre, which had just been punished for its alleged lack of quality. In 1937, the private theatre had been nationalized on Hitler's demand and reopened with a brand-new production of *Die Fledermaus*, known to be the Führer's favourite piece.

Nevertheless, the new staging of Carl Ehrhart-Hardt embarrassed Hitler, who left the opening night during the interval. Now Wagner needed a quick success and tried a new beginning with Fischer, who became director of the Gärtnerplatz Theatre from 1 May 1938. It was a risk whether or not Hitler, whose conservative taste for operettas was well known, would accept Fischer's new style, but the new production of *The Merry Widow* in 1938 pleased both Hitler and Goebbels: The propaganda minister wrote in his diary that the 'set is awesome and tasteful ... The performance itself has an adorable peppiness. We are all very enthused.'[19] Fischer frequently loved to tell people that Hitler soon declared the new revue standard as 'the only way to do operetta today'.[20] But this way stood against every claim for a traditional 'German operetta', such as Hermecke had attempted with his *Dorothee*.

Fischer chose a completely different way: usually, for no significant reason, he split the original operettas into thirty-three scenes, something that was to become his trademark. Those scenes were altered significantly, and the structure of the original plots was not strictly followed. A single musical number could be defined as a single scene or even an interpolated sketch lasting only a few seconds. So, Fischer's stagings became almost post-dramatic revues, full of attachments and even circus elements. In 1939, for instance, *Die Fledermaus* was 'arranged in 33 bouquets' (*Sträusse!*): the first scene was set in heaven, where Fischer's superstar Johannes Heesters, dressed as an immortal Johann Strauss, conducted a heavenly orchestra, playing the famous overture. Fischer did not hesitate to give that orchestra a very jazzy sound – a touch, that was usually heavily criticized for being 'non-German' in Nazi cultural politics. In the end, the show culminated in a 'musical prison' that became more or less a bunch of revue scenes, featuring artists like the famous Munich comedian Karl Valentin, who created the role of Frosch by improvising entertaining numbers. This was all completely against every pronouncement about German operetta – but the audience loved it! The show became a smash hit in the entire town; all performances were sold out, and spectators queued for hours to get in.

It is clear that Fischer served as an important underling for a regime that ordered distraction during the war. On the other hand, his success was condemned by line-toeing Nazis: it was a Munich music professor and idealistic member of the NSDAP called Gottfried Rüdinger (1886–1946) who wrote an exemplary pamphlet to the Reich Music Chamber, condemning what he saw in 1940: 'The whole thing looks like a Jewish warehouse which offers a few tempting items alongside worthless and gaudy goods.' What confused Rüdinger the most were the erotic aesthetics of Fischer's staging: 'I could speak and write seriously about the tradition of "beauty dances" in recent years, but it will suffice to hint at the battle that the party and its press fought, before and after the Nazis came to power, against this unwholesome practice that damages the German nation's natural sense of morality.'[21] Indeed, Fischer supported nudity and even burlesque elements on stage: he became popular for displaying nude women and men in his artistic as well as his infamous private life. Sex served as a spectacular effect that was much more attractive to the German audiences than propagandist plays about military successes or the rural life of orthodox German patriots. So, Fischer helped the regime to narcotize the *Volksgemeinschaft*, and, after the war, it was easy for him to continue his career because his style did not look like Nazi propaganda. He produced his thirty-three-pieced shows in German theatres long into the seventies.

Popular theatre has to be regarded as a mediation of the mentality of the people who pay for it. That is why operetta may give a glimpse into everyday culture, even under a dictatorship. Fischer's success, therefore, is not as paradoxical as it may seem: it typifies the contrast between official ideology and ordinary life praxis in the Third Reich. Nevertheless, modern revue-operettas served as a corrupting gift – working to enchant and manipulate the mood of a *Volksgemeinschaft* that had to be managed every day. Propaganda minister Goebbels knew that; he literally had to 'buy' the acceptance of the *Volksgemeinschaft* by offering apparent continuity of the glitter of the 'Roaring Twenties' on operetta stages.

During the war, this brilliance served as distraction and relaxation. That is why established formulas, originally condemned as 'non-German', survived on stage after 1933; they were necessary because neither a single ideologist nor Nazi artist had any clue about how to develop a new kind of Nazi operetta. It may be impossible for a functional genre to become a victim of time – because it just embodies its time. The operettas of National Socialism, however, may illustrate two things: first, the difference between theoretical politics and the daily culture in Nazi Germany; and, second, the striking impotence of the regime's cultural politics – and political artists – to develop something new.

An old and well-known anti-Semitic accusation levelled at 'Jewish' artists is that they are unable to develop original art by themselves but, instead, are parasites who steal the inspiration of others. It is symptomatic of National Socialism that this old allegation had to be inverted to define operetta between 1933 and 1945: it was the Nazis who behaved as cultural parasites when they banned the so-called 'Jewish' operetta tradition, because they filled the gap with replacements full of stolen ideas.

The Nazi essayist Hans Herbert Pudor, whose words opened this essay, serves as an example of the absurdity of operetta in the Third Reich: Pudor claimed that the genre should present original, 'modern words, thoughts and rhythms' after 1933.[22] Yet he had no clear vision about how to do this. Pudor dared to proclaim the 'death of the genre', but he did not know anything about its possible resurrection. It demonstrates the rift that National Socialism created in the development of the genre: the Nazis actually did not have the power to kill the genre, but they let it die.

Notes

1. Hans Herbert Pudor, 'Die Operette ist tot! – Es lebe die Operette!', *Schlesische Monatshefte*, 12 (1937): 472f.
2. Cf. Matthias Kauffmann, *Operette im 'Dritten Reich': Musikalisches Unterhaltungstheater zwischen 1933 und 1945* (Neumünster: Von Bockel 2017), 393.
3. 'Diary of 5 June 1938' in Joseph Goebbels, *Die Tagebücher von Joseph Goebbels*, Part I, Vol. 5, ed. Elke Fröhlich (Munich: K. G. Saur 1993–2008), 334.
4. Raimar Wieser and Peter Ziegler, *'Liebes Wien, Du Stadt der Lieder'. Heinrich Strecker und seine Zeit* (Vienna/Munich: Amalthea 1997), 196.
5. Wiener Boheme Verlag GmbH to Otto Laubinger on 23 January 1934. In the German Federal Archives, R55/20.199, 84f.
6. Bruno Hardt-Warden and Hans Spirk/Heinrich Strecker, *Ännchen von Tharau. Singspiel in drei Akten. Studier- und Soufflierbuch* (Vienna: Strecker 1933), 213.
7. Hermann Hermecke, 'Operette – ein Kulturfaktor', *Freiburger Theaterblätter*, 19 (1935): 152.
8. Hermann Hermecke and Arno Vetterling, *Die Dorothee. Operette in drei Akten* (Berlin: Eher Nachf. 1935), unnumbered.
9. Ibid., 69.
10. Ibid., 89.
11. Wilhelm Altmann, 'Operettenstatistik 1936/37', *Allgemeine Musikzeitung*, 44 (1936): 641f.
12. Eher Nachf. to Schlösser on 11 June 1936. In the German Federal Archives, R55/20.228, 388.
13. Schlösser to Eher Nachf. on 8 June 1936. In the German Federal Archives, R55/20.228, 390.
14. Musical consultant Reimesch to Schlösser on 27 January 1936. In the German Federal Archives, R55/ 20.228, 369.

15. Schlösser to Quedenfeldt on 10 October 12936. In the German Federal Archives, R55/ 20.228, 398.
16. Matthias Kauffmann, 'Operetta and Propaganda in the Third Reich: Cultural Politics and the Metropol-Theater' in Len Platt, David Linton and Tobias Becker (eds.), *Popular Musical Theatre in London and Berlin, 1890–1939* (Cambridge: Cambridge University Press, 2014), 258–73.
17. N. N., 'Er ließ Nackte vorm Gauleiter tanzen . . .' in *Tz*, 11 February 1985. Press cutting archive, Munich Town Archive.
18. Hans Martin Schäfer, 'Sein Kennzeichen: Blume am Revers', *Münchner Merkur*, 20 July 1978. Press cuttings archive, Munich Town Archive.
19. 'Diary of 22 February 1939' in Goebbels, *Die Tagebücher*, Part I, Vol. 6, 264f.
20. Fritz Fischer, *Berichte, die Fritz Fischer in seinem Leben gegeben hat vom 8. August bis zum 19. August 1970 in Oberstdorf* (Self-published, 1970). Private archive, Stefan Frey, 60.
21. Rüdinger on 21 February 1940, in the Bavarian Public Record Office, SpkA K417, Fischer, Fritz, 16 July 1898, unnumbered.
22. Pudor, 'Die Operette ist tot!', 473.

Recommended Reading

Dompke, Christoph. *Unterhaltungsmusik und NS-Verfolgung*. Neumünster: Von Bockel 2011.

Drewniak, Bogusław. *Das Theater im NS-Staat. Szenarium deutscher Zeitgeschichte 1933–1945*. Düsseldorf: Droste 1983.

Grünberg, Ingrid. '"Wer sich die Welt mit einem Donnerschlag erobern will . . ." Zur Situation und Funktion der deutschsprachigen Operette in den Jahren 1933–1945'. In Hanns-Werner Heister and Hans-Günter Klein, eds., *Musik und Musikpolitik im faschistischen Deutschland*. Frankfurt a. M.: Fischer 1984. 227–42.

Haken, Boris von. *Der 'Reichsdramaturg'. Rainer Schlösser und die Musiktheater-Politik in der NS-Zeit*. Neumünster: Von Bockel 2007.

Hüpping, Stefan. *Rainer Schlösser (1899–1945). Der 'Reichsdramaturg'*. Bielefeld: Aisthesis 2012.

Kauffmann, Matthias. *Operette im 'Dritten Reich'. Musikalisches Unterhaltungstheater zwischen 1933 und 1945*. Neumünster: Von Bockel, 2017.

Kieser, Klaus. *Das Gärtnerplatztheater in München 1932–1944. Zur Operette im Nationalsozialismus*. Frankfurt am Main: Lang, 1991.

Odenwald, Florian. *Der nazistische Kampf gegen das 'Undeutsche' in Theater und Film 1920–1945*. Munich: Utz, 2006.

Rischbieter, Henning, ed. *Theater im 'Dritten Reich': Theaterpolitik, Spielplanstruktur, NS-Dramatik*. Seelze-Velber: Kallmeyer, 2000.

Schaller, Wolfgang, ed. *Operette unterm Hakenkreuz. Zwischen hoffähiger Kunst und 'Entartung'*. Beiträge einer Tagung der Staatsoperette Dresden. Berlin: Metropol, 2007.

18 Operetta Films

DEREK B. SCOTT

At the beginning of the chapter, I should distinguish between two meanings in which the label 'operetta films' is used: one refers to film adaptations of stage works and the other to operettas specially created for the medium of film. To avoid confusion, whenever I refer to a screen operetta, it will be the latter I have in mind. Most of this chapter will, however, be concerned with film versions of stage operettas. For reasons of space, I am concentrating on American, British and German films. It would be unpardonable not to mention *Trois valses* (1938), the film of the French version of Oscar Straus's *Die drei Wälzer*, starring Yvonne Printemps and Pierre Fresnay. Yet, even in this case, I must add that its director, Ludwig Berger, had many years of experience in the German film industry and had previously enjoyed much acclaim for his silent film of an earlier Straus operetta, *Ein Walzertraum*, in 1925.

Berlin and Hollywood were not dissimilar in their approach to musical films. There had been links between the industries of both countries even before the Nazis drove many German-Jewish film directors to seek employment in the USA. As in the UK and USA, German films were, at first, short music-hall or vaudeville attractions. In the early days of motion pictures, it was common to regard the medium of film as second best to the stage. However, in the 1920s, the case for the independent artistic status of film was already being made. Cultural historian Egon Friedell argued that film had areas of activity and effects that were subject to its own generic laws (*eigentümliche Gattungsgesetze*); moreover, he believed it was the art form that represented contemporary times most clearly and completely.[1] This chapter offers an overview of operetta films, and reveals how star singers, such as Richard Tauber, responded to the dictates of film, which sometimes ran counter to stage performance practice.

Even before the advent of sound, there were film adaptations of operetta. Metro-Goldwyn-Mayer's (MGM) first film of Franz Lehár's *The Merry Widow*, which appeared in 1925, was silent. It was directed by Erich von Stroheim, who departed considerably from the operetta and devised what would now be called a 'backstory' of the widow as an American ex-vaudeville performer who arrives in the small kingdom of Monteblanco and goes to Paris later. Lehár's music was arranged by

William Axt and David Mendoza. The film has some erotic content, showing scantily clothed dancers at Maxim's restaurant and featuring a love scene on a bed in a *chambre séparée* with half-naked blindfolded musicians playing in an alcove. John Gilbert is Danilo, and Mae Murray the widow. There was, of course, music to be heard while the silent film was being shown; larger cinemas had orchestras, and scores were specially put together to accompany films. It was exciting, no doubt, to watch such films to the accompaniment of musical excerpts but not so thrilling as in the 1930s, when audiences flocked to cinemas to both see and hear screen stars. Films of that decade also offer valuable historical insight now into vocal practice and performance technique. In addition, they contribute important knowledge to our understanding of adaptation. The absence of singing in silent film versions of operetta did affect the way operetta was later adapted for the screen. There was always a tendency to have more dialogue than music, and there was often a desire to locate musical numbers in a context where they might plausibly have occurred. The music, when it was heard, however, often differed to some degree from that in the stage work because it was usually rearranged by a composer specifically employed for the making of the film.

The Jazz Singer (1927), starring Al Jolson, is frequently cited as the first 'talkie' or sound film,[2] but it remained silent in large parts, and the accolade of the first musical film with continuous sound goes to MGM's *Broadway Melody* of 1929, directed by Wesley Ruggles. The first German film with sound throughout was *Der blaue Engel* (1930), directed by Josef von Sternberg, and starring Emil Jannings and Marlene Dietrich. The first screen operetta was *Zwei Herzen im Dreivierteltakt* (1930) directed by Géza von Bolváry. The screenplay was by Walter Reisch and Franz Schulz, and the music by Robert Stolz. Apart from setting a trend for title songs, it relied too much on older models to be influential, even though they were given a modern polish. Perhaps that is why, although it began life on screen, it was soon adapted for the stage, as *Der verlorene Walzer* (1933).

In September 1930, the major German film company Universum-Film, better known as Ufa, released another film that had sound throughout, a screen operetta directed by Wilhelm Thiele called *Die Drei von der Tankstelle*.[3] Although the title, 'The Three from the Filling Station', might seem unexciting, it proved to be Ufa's most commercially successful film of the 1930s. The days of the Weimar Republic are often associated with an outpouring of unruly behaviour and hedonism preceding the establishment of the authoritarian Third Reich in 1933. However, this film offers more than dance, song and frivolity. The humour is infectious, and the three best friends who are rivals for the hand of the wilful young woman (played by Lilian Harvey) finally resolve their differences amicably.

It is the end of the film that is most surprising because it reveals that Bertolt Brecht was not alone in his ideas about breaking frame in dramatic representations nor in his desire to remind audiences of the mechanics of construction of representational forms. After the apparent happy conclusion, the stars of the film step through theatre curtains and react with sudden surprise, as if seeing the 'real' audience in the cinema staring at them. They wonder why no one has gone home because the show is over. Then they realize that the audience wants a proper operetta finale and will only then be satisfied that the film has ended. In the later twentieth century, this kind of self-referentiality and exposure of the means by which a narrative code, dramatic meaning and illusion are constructed would be termed 'postmodernism'.

Not everyone was ready to applaud operetta films, however. Siegfried Kracauer argued that analysing German films of 1918–33 reveals 'deep psychological dispositions' that 'influenced the course of events during that time'.[4] He accused most operetta films of the early 1930s of romanticizing the past and representing an enchanted Vienna with gentle archdukes, tender flirtations, baroque decors, Biedermeier rooms and customers drinking and singing in suburban garden restaurants. Psychologically, he claimed, it had the effect of suggesting such people presented no threat.[5] He recognized that *Die Drei von der Tankstelle* did not fit this mould, but it was still to be mistrusted because of its escapism: it was a 'playful daydream' that shifted 'the operetta paradise from its traditional locales to the open road'.[6] Instead of perceiving the innovative way in which music and sound is used in this film, he complained that the score was eccentric and full of whims, that it interfered with 'the half-rational plot', and he gave the example of a waltz that invites the workers who are clearing out the friends' unpaid furniture 'to transform themselves into dancers'. Even the clever use of the sound of the heroine's car horn – an imaginative example of turning noise into a leitmotiv – does nothing but attract his scorn.[7]

Ufa was created in 1917, and although it was to absorb other companies, it did not enjoy any kind of monopoly. Nonetheless, it was the only serious European challenge to Hollywood, and Ufa's international success lay firmly in operettas and comedies. Versions were often shot in three languages: German, English, and French, *Die Drei von der Tankstelle* being an example. The music to that film was by Werner R. Heymann, who was also the composer for Ufa's *Der Kongreß tanzt*, released in 1931. Once more, the star was Lilian Harvey, who had been born in London to a German father and English mother. On the strength of the acclaim he had received for his revue operettas at the Großes Schauspielhaus, Berlin, Erik Charell was engaged as director, and he immediately established himself as one of the most skilful directors of operetta on film, making use of Carl Hoffman's unusually flexible camera movement to demonstrate how camera mobility and sound film could work together. The lengthy scene in which Lillian Harvey travels through the wood by carriage and is greeted by singing onlookers caused a sensation and was much imitated.[8] This film also had the services of the influential set designer Walter Röhrig, who had created the expressionist sets for Robert Wiene's *Das Cabinet des Dr Caligari* (1920). Being of Jewish descent, Charell's career in Germany came to an end in 1933; it was, however, resumed after World War II.

Three original screen operettas were released in 1931: *Die Privatsekretärin*, with music by Paul Abraham; *Ronny*, with music by Emmerich Kálmán; and *Die große Attraktion*, with music by Franz Lehár. Lehár was to compose another two screen operettas during the Weimar years (as well as seeing film adaptations made of three of his stage operettas: *Das Land des Lächelns*, *Friederike* and *Der Zarewitsch*). Abraham had first made a name for himself with music for film in 1929. In the later film of his operetta *Die Blume von Hawaii* (1933), spectators were given sight of what was an unattainable destination in the Depression years. For people who could not afford to travel anywhere, it must have been exciting to see palm trees, the sea hitting the rocks and so forth brought to life on screen. A halfway house between stage operetta and screen operetta was *Die 3-Groschen Oper* (1931), directed by G. W. Pabst, with Theo Mackeben as musical director. It omitted a lot of Kurt Weill's music, but it was common for German films of the 1930s to include four or five numbers only. Lotte Lenya played Jenny, Carola Nehr was Polly and Macheath was a non-singing role played by Rudolf Förster. In Pabst's film, there is non-mimetic delivery of songs by characters, most strikingly 'Seeräuber Jenny' sung by Lenya. Her blank expression operates as a mask, and its effect is to force a critical position on to the viewer, something Brecht constantly strove for in his epic theatre. At the same time, the film credits make clear that the screenplay is a free adaptation of Brecht, and not his stage play. In the film, for instance, there is a burglary at the large London department store Selfridges, absent from the original play.

Film was a hugely popular medium in Weimar Germany, and cinema numbers grew in this period from 2,000 to 5,000.[9] It was a similar story in Britain: by February 1930, there were 1,000 cinemas wired for sound, and at the end of 1934 over a thousand cinemas had a capacity of between 1,000 and 2,000 seats, although cinema numbers themselves exceeded 2,000 only in the mid-1930s.[10] German films lost a lot of talented people as a consequence of Nazi 'racial purity' laws (*Rassenreinheit Gesetze*). Richard Traubner cites the publication of lists in the 1930s that were designed to reveal how strong the Jewish influence was on German cinema:

one list claimed 45 per cent of film composers and 48 per cent of film directors had a Jewish background.[11]

From 1933 on, Jewish artists began to be omitted from film credits. The Ufa film of *Die Csárdásfürstin*, directed by Georg Jacoby, was a huge box-office success in 1934 but made no reference to its Jewish composer Emmerich Kálmán or its Jewish librettists Leo Stein and Béla Jenbach. Hans-Otto Borgmann is credited for the musical adaptation, and Jacoby, along with Hans Zerlett and B. E. Lüthge, for the script (Figure 18.1). However, the star was Marta Eggerth, whose mother was Jewish. It was soon found necessary to replace Jewish singers. Fritzi Massary was associated with recent leading stage roles in *Eine Frau, die weiß, was sie will* and *Der letzte Walzer* but did not appear in the films of those operettas. The next step was to remove 'Jewish music' and rewrite 'Jewish lyrics', as happened in Carl Lamac's film of *Im weißen Rössl* (1935).[12] Finally, persecution of Jews increased to the extent that even a famous singer such as Eggerth had to flee Austria for New York in 1938 (the year of the *Anschluss*).

Die Csardasfürstin

Nach der gleichnamigen Operette

mit

Marta Eggerth, Hans Söhnker, Paul Hörbiger Paul Kemp, Ida Wüst

Drehbuch: Hans Zerlett, B. E. Lüthge, Georg Jacoby
Bild: Karl Hoffmann / Bau: Robert Herlth, Walter Röhrig
Ton: Dr. Carlheinz Becker / Schnitt: Herbert Fredersdorf / Aufnahmeleitung: Eduard Kubat
Musikalische Bearbeitung: Hans-Otto Borgmann

Herstellungsgruppe: Max Pfeiffer
Spielleitung: Georg Jacoby

Darsteller

Sylva Varescu	Marta Eggerth
Edwin, Prinz Weylersheim	Hans Söhnker
Graf Boni Kancsianu	Paul Kemp
Feri von Kerekes	Paul Hörbiger
Komtesse Stasi von Planitz	Inge List
Fürstin Weylersheim	Ida Wüst
Fürst Weylersheim	Friedrich Ulmer
Der Kommandeur	Hans Junkermann
Der Manager	Edwin Jürgensen
Der Zigeunerprima	Andor Heltai

Weiter wirken mit: Ilse Fürstenberg, Marina von Dittmar, Charlott Daudert, Hedi und Margot Höpfner, Karin Lüsebrink, Liselotte Heßler, Olga Engl, Josef Karma, Tomy Bonsch, Sauter-Sarto, Carl Walther-Meyer und Meyer-Falkow

Aufgenommen auf Klangfilm - Gerät   /   Afifa - Tonkopie

Ufaton-Film im Ufaleih

Figure 18.1 Film cast of *Die Csárdásfürstin*. *Illustrierte Film-kurier*, Vol. 16, 1934

In Georg Jacoby's remake of *Die Csárdásfürstin* (1951), his wife Marika Rökk played Sylva Varescu, and Johannes Heesters was Edwin von Weylerheim. Both singers were admired by Hitler and suspected of being Nazi sympathizers. However, when secret intelligence documents were declassified in February 2017, there was a surprising revelation about Rökk: they revealed that she had been, in fact, a Soviet agent.[13]

During the early 1930s, it is interesting to see the impact on performers when they move from a theatre stage to a film studio and are faced with a camera instead of a live audience. There are some significant differences between theatre and film: in the theatre, the whole space of the action is seen, but the spectator's position and angle of vision is fixed. Béla Balázs observes that, in film, four new devices take over: a scene can be broken into several shots, the spectator can be given a close-up, the angle of vision can be changed and montage can be used.[14] In film, the camera does the focussing. Moreover, there is a need to consider the editing of shots, for example, the speed of change from one to another. There was a range of conventional shot positions in the 1930s, the most common being the long shot, the mid-shot (often used for two actors in the same scene) and the close-up (head and shoulders). The relationship of the performer to the camera was important. If the performer sang to camera, it emphasized the performance act, breaking with naturalistic illusion. There were many differences between working to camera and working with a live audience. In a theatre, a performer could turn unexpectedly to a section of the audience in any part of the auditorium. Film-makers liked to edit shots; they did not like a performer suddenly deciding which camera to speak to.

In many cases, screen adaptations of operetta were far from being filmed versions of the original stage production: the music of more than one operetta might be included, and the dialogue and narrative might change. About thirty British films made in the 1930s leaned heavily on operetta from the German-language stage, and the fondness for this genre may have been partly motivated by the thought that there was a possibility of good returns from the European box office. British International Pictures' (BIP) *Blossom Time* of 1934 was a notable success, and even Alfred Hitchcock tried his hand that year with *Waltzes from Vienna*, an adaptation of *Walzer aus Wien* (which had music of the Strauss family arranged by Erich Korngold and Julius Bittner).

Blossom Time cost BIP much more than its other films, owing largely to the expensive sets and crowd scenes.[15] It was an adaptation of Schubert melodies by G. H. Clutsam and was a screen operetta that differed from his earlier Schubert operetta *Lilac Time*, which was based on Berté's *Das Dreimäderlhaus*. To add to the confusion, it differed also from Romberg's Broadway adaptation of the latter as *Blossom Time*, which is why the film was given the title *April Blossoms* in the USA. The director, Paul Stein, was Viennese but had worked for five years in Hollywood.[16] The cast included the Austrian tenor Richard Tauber, hero of many a Franz Lehár operetta, and the most famous star to work for BIP at that time. *Blossom Time* was a triumph commercially as well as being well received by the critics and encouraged BIP to follow up with *My Song Goes Round the World*, another film starring a famous tenor, this time Josef Schmidt. The coloratura soprano Gitta Alpár, who had started her career with Budapest State Opera and then joined Berlin State Opera, can be heard in *I Give My Heart* (Wardour Films, 1935), which was based on *The Dubarry* (Theo Mackeben's adaptation of Carl Millöcker's *Gräfin Dubarry*). She fled the Nazis in 1933, first to Austria, then to the UK and USA because of her Jewish heritage.

Famous singers of the stage were not always quick to adapt to the medium of film. An examination of the scene in *Blossom Time* in which Tauber accompanies himself on piano singing 'Once There Lived a Lady Fair', reveals that his mimic and gestural signs are in accord with operatic performance practice, and contrast with the naturalistic code adopted by the members of the drawing-room audience in the film. His gestures are theatrical, whereas theirs are economical. *Variety* remarked backhandedly of his acting in this film that it was 'surprisingly good – for a world-famous tenor'.[17] Jane Baxter, cast in the role of Vicki Wimpassinger, the object of Schubert's affection, was a glamorous film star of the 1930s and was careful to adopt the restrained mimetic code of cinema (having already appeared in several films). Tauber is first and foremost a celebrated singer. Shots are intercut showing details of dramatic significance, such as the emotional impact his performance is having on his audience. We gauge their reactions from the use of montage, which presents us with a sequence of different shots from which we interpret what is going on and build a picture of the whole (an idea of the space of the room, for instance). In one sense Tauber's audience 'stands in' for us, the viewers of the film, since we have no presence in a film equivalent to that which we enjoy in a theatre.

British and American operetta films, when compared to German films of the same era, add to our insight into performance style and technique, dramaturgical practice, musical priorities and cultural values. British and Dominions Film Corporation released a film in 1933 of Noël Coward's *Bitter Sweet*, starring Anna Neagle and Fernand Gravey. Another film of this operetta was released by MGM in colour in 1940, starring Jeanette MacDonald and Nelson Eddy. Coward described the second film as 'dreadful' and claimed it prevented him from ever being able to revive *Bitter Sweet* (adding, with his customary humour, that it was a pity, because he had been 'saving it up as an investment').[18] *Mister Cinders*

(1934), with music by Vivian Ellis (from his stage musical), was produced by BIP shortly after *Blossom Time*, but it is noticeable how much more smoothly the musical numbers are integrated into the film, and, under Frederic Zelnik's direction, how at ease the singers now appear in front of the camera. A film version of Ivor Novello's spectacular Drury Lane operetta *Glamorous Night* (1937) was directed by Brian Desmond Hurst at Elstree Studios and featured two Americans in the leading roles, singing star Mary Ellis and matinee idol Otto Kruger. Its popularity encouraged Associate British Pictures to plan films of Novello's next operettas, but a financial crisis hit British films in 1938, and war broke out the next year.[19] It was not until 1950 that the company released a film of *The Dancing Years*, directed by Harold French and produced in colour. Dennis Price played Rudi, Gisele Preville was Maria, and Patricia Dainton was Grete. The success of the film rivalled that of the acclaimed theatre production.

In the USA, German director Ernst Lubitsch, whose family was Ashkenazi Jewish, was making his mark in musical films, the first being *The Love Parade* (Paramount, 1929), with Jeanette MacDonald and Maurice Chevalier. They also starred in his film *One Hour with You* (1932, music by Oscar Straus). In *The Merry Widow* (MGM, 1934), Chevalier played Danilo, and MacDonald was Sonia (Hanna). The screen play was by Ernest Vajda and Samson Raphaelson. The name of the Ruritanian country was changed to Marshovia, and fresh lyrics were provided by Lorenz Hart (uncredited), with some additional lyrics by Gus Kahn. The musical adaptation was by Herbert Stothart, aided by orchestrators Paul Marquardt, Charles Maxwell and Leonid Raab. Herbert Stothart was a composer, arranger and musical director for MGM in the 1930s. He had plenty of Broadway experience and had worked with Vincent Youmans and Rudolf Friml before his involvement in an early sound film adaptation, released in June 1930, of *Golden Dawn*, a Broadway operetta composed by Kálmán to an English text. A month earlier that year, another early MGM sound film had been released, based on a loose adaptation of a Lehár operetta (*Zigeunerliebe*); it was *The Rogue Song*, directed by Lionel Barrymore and Hal Roach (uncredited). It starred Catherine Dale Owen, Lawrence Tibbett and, perhaps unexpectedly, Stan Laurel and Oliver Hardy.

As the Depression began to lift in the USA in 1934, Hollywood producers took renewed interested in Broadway and sponsored many plays there. At the end of the 1935–6 season, however, Hollywood producers (such as MGM, who had backed productions by Max Gordon and Sam H. Harris) took umbrage at the provisions in a new contract made between play producers and the new Dramatists' Guild-League of New York Theatre. It divided the money paid for rights to a play into 60 per cent for the author and 40 per cent for the producer, and even if a film producer had financed the play, the film rights were still to be offered in the open market.[20] There was an inevitable reduction in interest from Hollywood. Perhaps, at this point, it would be helpful to draw upon Vivian Ellis's neat distinction between a film producer (such as Samuel Goldwyn in Hollywood or Erich Pommer in Berlin) and a film director: the producer assembles the picture, and the director shoots the picture.[21]

Lubitsch's *Merry Widow* had won many admirers but was not a huge box-office success, and that prompted MGM to seek a change of partner for MacDonald. Nelson Eddy was soon found.[22] MacDonald and Eddy were first brought together in *Naughty Marietta* (1935; based on Victor Herbert's operetta), which was followed by *Rose-Marie* (Friml, 1936). Their third film together, and their biggest success, was *Maytime* (Romberg, 1937), directed by Robert Z. Leonard. Their film partnership continued until 1942.

The Austrian film director Arthur Maria Rabenalt commented on the various advantages possessed by screen adaptations over the stage originals: complicated intrigues could be edited in a way that made them more credible, awkward scene changes could become lither, and characters could be made more convincing by making certain dramatic situations more visible.[23] Another way of removing stage rigidity in screen adaptations was to reduce the quantity of music and be flexible about the sequence of an operetta's musical numbers. In films, means were usually found to moderate the affront to realism when characters suddenly feel a compulsion to sing.

Three short examples can be given to illustrate some of the variety in the practice of adapting from stage to screen. In the film *The Smiling Lieutenant* (1931), based on Oscar Straus's *Ein Walzertraum* (1907) and directed by Lubitsch, the adaptation is designed to help the American audience recognize itself in the imported operetta, which had placed much emphasis on the charms of Vienna. In the Viennese stage version, in order to help a foreign princess to win the affections of the Austrian lieutenant, Franzi (the vivacious leader of a women's orchestra) has to teach her about what makes Viennese women so attractive: it is their lively temperament. She also encourages the princess to cater for the lieutenant's delight in other Viennese pleasures, such as food. In the film, Franzi proffers advice of a rather different character: she plays the piano and sings a ragtime song: 'Jazz up your lingerie'. The next time we see the princess on screen, she is playing syncopated music at the piano with a cigarette dangling from her lips. It is clear that her behaviour now resonates with the bold, emancipated American city woman of the 1920s (the original operetta belongs to 1907).

Sometimes adaptations could entail complete reworking. In the film of *The Chocolate Soldier* (1941), the adapter faced a difficult challenge. Bernard Shaw had given permission (with a high degree of scorn) for the original German libretto to be based on his play *Arms and the Man*. However, he now refused to allow his work to be used in a film unless he was paid a substantial sum. MGM refused and, instead, went ahead, retaining Straus's music but commissioning a new screenplay from Leonard Lee and Keith Winter based on Ferenc Molnár's *The Guardsman*.

In *Maytime*, there was an opposite state of affairs. The Broadway stage version of *Wie einst im Mai* in 1917 had jettisoned Walter Kollo's music, and Rida Johnson Young had adapted the libretto by Rudolf Bernauer, Rudolf Schanzer and Willy Bredschneider for a fresh score by Sigmund Romberg. In the film version, much of Romberg's score was itself discarded, and replaced by interpolated numbers. *Maytime* was a film triumph, however, and revealed that audiences enjoyed a tear-jerker as much as a song and dance show. Unfortunately, it appeared in 1937, the year in which Hollywood lost its interest in adapting stage entertainments because of the new contractual conditions. Perhaps that was why so little use was made of the Romberg score and why the musical director, Herbert Stothart, chose to include public-domain music that did not require payment of copyright fees.

In Germany and Austria, the 1950s and early 1960s witnessed the halcyon days of *Heimat* films (homeland films). These films became a celebration of forests, mountains and dirndls. They had a nostalgic appeal in their emphasis on wholesome and supposedly traditional values lived by honest folk overcoming adversity in idyllic rural locations. The *Heimat* film is often confused with the *Bergfilm* (mountain film), but the latter had a simpler plot, usually involving an accident and rescue. Remakes in colour of old films were popular in the 1950s. The taste for the *Heimat* film was initiated by *Schwarzwaldmädel* (The Black Forest Girl) of 1950, directed by Hans Deppe, which was the first German colour film to be released after World War II. Remarkably, it was the fourth time a film had been made of this operetta. The script was by Bobby Lüthge, who kept the same characters and plot but moved the period of action to the present – although that did not preclude the wearing of traditional Black Forest costumes. The scenery is of serene landscapes unspoiled by war. The conciliatory mood of the film made it enormously appealing, and it engendered a succession of *Heimat* films.

The influence of the 1950 *Schwarzwaldmädel* is felt in the 1952 film of *Im weißen Rössl*, despite Charell's contribution to the screenplay. Jazzy songs are gone. The intervention of the Emperor Franz Josef is no longer an ironic twist on the crisis-resolving power of the *deus ex machina* but is, instead, presented seriously. It was a marker of what was to come: in the 1960 film directed by Werner Jacobs, all traces of the frivolity, mischief, camp and caricature of Charell's original revue operetta – the features that lent it a tone of social critique – had vanished. Although its re-orchestrated score now reveals its age, it remains the most popular version of *Im weißen Rössl*, largely because of the presence of Peter Alexander, who sang in popular films, then operetta adaptations and, later, became a TV presenter.

Die Försterchristl (*Christel the Forest Ranger*) first filmed in 1926, had been remade in 1931, and was remade in black and white in 1952 and in colour in 1962. The 1952 *Die Försterchristl*, which starred Hannerl Matz and was directed by Arthur Rabenalt, was admired for having the romantic comedy touch associated with Lubitsch. The operetta, with music by Georg Jarno, was set just after the 1848 revolution in Austria and Hungary. Eighteen minutes into the 1962 version of *Die Försterchristel* [sic], there is a surprising interpolated number. It is British composer Ronald Binge's *Elizabethan Serenade*, arranged for a chorus, who greet the arrival of the Kaiser and Countess Elisabeth. It had been a hit tune in Germany in the early 1950s. Oskar Sima plays Leisinger in both *Försterchristl* (1952) and *Försterchristel* (1962). These two films have many scenes in common; it is almost as if the film company Carlton simply wished to remake it in colour so as to do justice to the Austrian landscapes.

There were, all the same, non-homeland films made during this period, one of which was of Oscar Straus's operetta *Der letzte Walzer* (1953), directed by Rabenalt. The screen adaptation is by Curt J. Braun, but Julius Brammer and Alfred Grünwald remain credited for the libretto. There is also interpolated music, and Robert Gilbert and Fritz Rotter are credited for the lyrics to the songs of the interludes, the music of which one assumes is by Straus. The composer is shown conducting the Bavarian Symphony Orchestra at the beginning of the film, while the credits roll, although the musical director for the film was Bruno Uher.

Operetta had a final flowering on television, and one of the pioneers of TV operetta was Kurt Wilhelm, who was fond of big production numbers. Television production was often a hybrid of stage and screen practice. Studio sets resembled stage sets, but the changing camera angles are indebted to film.[24] The German television company Beta, founded in 1959, became interested in operettas in the 1960s and was able to produce them with a budget beyond the affordability of Zweites Deutsches Fernsehen (ZDF) and Österreichischer Rundfunk (ORF; Austria).

Notes

1. Egon Friedell, 'Kunst und Kino' [c.1912] in *Wozu das Theater? Essays, Satiren Humoresken* (Munich: Deutsche Taschenbuch Verlag, 1969), 87–95, at 91 and 95.
2. Jolson's co-star was Mary McAvoy, and the director was Alan Crosland. It was a Warner Brothers production.
3. It starred Willy Fritsch and Lilian Harvey and was directed by Wilhelm Thiele. The writers were Franz Schulz and Paul Frank, and the music was composed by Werner R. Heymann; the Comedian Harmonists were among the performers.
4. Siegfried Kracauer, *From Caligari to Hitler: A Psychological History of the German Film* (Princeton, NJ: Princeton University Press, 1947), v.
5. Ibid., 141.
6. Ibid., 207.
7. Ibid.
8. Ibid., 208.
9. Joseph Garncarz and Thomas Elsaesser, 'Weimar Cinema' in Thomas Elsaesser with Michael Wedel (eds.), *The BFI Companion to German Cinema* (London: BFI Publishing, 1999), 247–8, at 247.
10. Linda Wood, *British Films 1927–1939* (London: British Film Institute, 1986), 19, 119–20.
11. Richard Traubner, 'Der deutsche Operettenfilm vor und nach 1933' in Wolfgang Schaller (ed.), *Operette unterm Hakenkreuz: Zwischen hoffähiger Kunst und 'Entartung'* (Berlin: Metropol Verlag, 2007), 147–69, at 163. Regrettably, no source is given.
12. Bruno Granichstaedten's music to the song 'Zuschau'n kann i net' was omitted, and Robert Gilbert's lyrics altered, but Ralph Benatzky's music remained intact, although his music was later banned because he was (wrongly) assumed to be a Jewish composer.
13. Kate Connolly, 'Hitler's favourite actor was Soviet spy', *The Guardian*, 21 Feb. 2017, 14.
14. Béla Balázs, *Theory of Film*, trans. Edith Bone (London: Dobson, 1952; originally published as *Filmkultúra*, Budapest: Szikra kiadás, 1948).
15. Rachel Low, *The History of the British Film 1929–1939: Film Making in 1930s Britain* (London: George Allen and Unwin, 1985), 123.
16. Roy Ames, *A Critical History of the British Cinema* (London: Secker and Warburg, 1978), 85.
17. 'Blossom Time', *Variety*, 24 July 1934, 14.
18. Charles Castle, *Noël* (London: W.H. Allen, 1972), 106.
19. Peter Noble, *Ivor Novello* (London: Falcon Press, 1951), 191.
20. Burns Mantle (ed.), *The Best Plays of 1935–36* (New York: Dodd, Mead, 1936), 4.
21. Vivian Ellis, *I'm on a See-Saw* (London: Michael Joseph, 1953), 128.
22. Amy Henderson and Dwight Blocker Bowers, *Red, Hot & Blue: A Smithsonian Salute to the American Musical* (Washington: Smithsonian Institution Press, 1996), 124.
23. Arthur Maria Rabenalt, *Der Operetten-Bildband: Bühne, Film, Fernsehen* (Hildesheim: Olms Presse, 1980), 33.
24. Rabenalt, *Der Operetten-Bildband*, 47.

Films Referenced

Bitter Sweet (1933), dir. Herbert Wilcox. British and Dominions Film Corporation. (*British Classics Collection*, 2015).

Bitter Sweet (1940), dir. W. S. Van Dyke. MGM. *Archive Collection.* (Warner, 2011).

Blossom Time (1934), dir. Paul Stein. BIP. *British Film Musicals of the 1930s*, Vol 2, disc 1 (Network, 2014).

Die Blume von Hawai (1933), dir. Géza von Cziffra. Arion-Film.

Das Cabinet des Dr Caligari (1920), dir. Robert Wiene. Decla-Bioscop. *Masters of Cinema.* (Eureka Entertainment, 2014).

The Chocolate Soldier (1941), dir. Roy Del Ruth. MGM. *Archive Collection.* (Warner, 2012).

Die Csárdásfürstin (1934), dir. Georg Jacoby. Ufa. *Die grossen Klassiker.* (Ufa, 2000).

Die Csárdásfürstin (1951), dir. Georg Jacoby. Deutsche Styria Film. (Kinowelt, 2009).

The Dancing Years (1950), dir. Harold French. Associate British Pictures. *The British Film.* (Network, 2015).

Die 3-Groschen Oper (1931), dir. G. W. Pabst. Tobis Filmkunst. *Klassiker Edition.* (Ufa, 2008).

Die Drei von der Tankstelle (1930), dir. Wilhelm Thiele. Ufa. *Klassiker Edition.* (Ufa, 2009).

Friederike (1932), dir. Fritz Friedmann-Frederich. Indra-Film Rolf Raffé.

Die Försterchristl (1952), dir. Arthur Rabenalt. Carlton Film. (Filmjuwelen, 2013).

Die Försterchristel (1962), dir. Franz Gottlieb. Carlton Film. (Filmjuwelen, 2013).

Glamorous Night (1937), dir. Brian Desmond Hurst. Associated British Picture Corporation. *British Film Musicals of the 1930s*, Vol. 5, disc 2 (Network, 2016).

Golden Dawn (1930), dir. Ray Enright. Warner Bros and the Vitaphone Corporation. *Archive Collection.* (Warner, 2009).

Die große Attraktion (1931), dir. Max Reichmann. Münchner Lichtspielkunst (Emelka).

I Give My Heart (1935), dir. Marcel Varnay. Wardour Films. *British Film Musicals of the 1930s*, Vol. 6, disc 2 (Network, 2016).

Im weißen Rössl (1935), dir. Carl Lamac. Hade-Film. (Filmjuwelen, 2014).

Im weißen Rössl (1952), dir. Willi Forst. Carlton Film. (Kinowelt, 2004).

Im weißen Rössl (1960), dir. Werner Jacobs. Carlton Film. (Filmjuwelen, 2016).

The Jazz Singer (1927), dir. Alan Crosland. Warner Bros. (Warner Home Video, 2013).

Der Kongreß tanzt (1931), dir. Erik Charell. Ufa. *Klassiker Edition.* (Ufa, 2009).

Das Land des Lächelns (1930), dir. Max Reichman. Richard Tauber Tonfilm-Produktion.

Der letzte Walzer (1953), dir. Arthur Maria Rabenalt. Carlton Film and Eichberg-Film. (Filmjuwelen, 2013).

The Love Parade, (1929), dir. Ernst Lubitsch. Paramount Pictures. *Comedias Musicales, Ernst Lubitsch*, Vol. 1 (Regia Films, 2010).

Maytime (1937), dir. Robert Z. Leonard. MGM. *Archive Collection.* (Warner, 2012).

The Merry Widow (1925), dir. Erich von Stroheim. MGM. *Archive Collection.* (Warner, 2011).

The Merry Widow (1934), dir Ernst Lubitsch. MGM. *Archive Collection.* (Warner, 2013).

Mister Cinders (1934), dir. Frederic Zelnik. BIP. *British Film Musicals of the 1930s*, Vol. 2, disc 2 (Network, 2014).

My Song Goes Round the World (1934), dir. Richard Oswald. BIP. *British Film Musicals of the 1930s*, Vol. 3, disc 2 (Network, 2014).

Naughty Marietta (1935), dir. Robert Z. Leonard. MGM. *Archive Collection.* (Warner, 2011).

One Hour with You (1932), dir. Ernst Lubitsch. Paramount Pictures. *Comedias Musicales, Ernst Lubitsch*, Vol. 2 (Regia Films, 2010).

Die Privatsekretärin (1931), dir. Wilhelm Thiele. Greenbaum Film.

The Rogue Song (1930), dir. Lionel Barrymore and Hal Roach. MGM. Excerpt on YouTube, www.youtube.com/watch?v=qBff3jwIZrU (accessed 10 May 2019).

Ronny (1931), dir. Reinhold Schünzel. Ufa.

Rose-Marie (1936), dir. W. S. Van Dyke. MGM. *Archive Collection.* (Warner, 2015).

Schwarzwaldmädel (1950), dir. Hans Deppe. Berolina. (Filmjuwelen, 2013).

The Smiling Lieutenant (1931), dir. Ernst Lubitsch. Paramount Pictures. *Comedias Musicales, Ernst Lubitsch*, Vol. 2 (Regia Films, 2010).

Trois valses (1938), dir. Ludwig Berger. SOFROR.

Waltzes from Vienna (1934), dir. Alfred Hitchcock. Gaumont British Picture Corporation. (Universal Classics, 2012).

Ein Walzertraum (1925), dir. Ludwig Berger. Ufa.

Der Zarewitsch (1933), dir. Victor Janson. Prima-Tonfilm.

Zwei Herzen im Dreivierteltakt (1930), dir. Géza von Bolváry. Super-Film.

19 Australian Director Barrie Kosky on the Subversiveness of a Predominantly Jewish Genre: An Interview by Ulrich Lenz

BARRIE KOSKY AND ULRICH LENZ

UL: Is there an operetta tradition in Australia?

BK: Well, there was. On the one hand, Australia is one of the youngest countries in the world and, on the other, one of the oldest. There is no kind of music theatre tradition in the indigenous culture of Australia. Very soon after the English invasion, the British started to do theatre and opera, and English operetta played a big role. They played a lot of Gilbert and Sullivan but also a lot of Australian or English versions of Offenbach. My hometown, Melbourne, which towards the end of the nineteenth century was one of the largest colonial cities in the world, had a huge tradition of pantomime and revue. I think it all ended in the 1950s because other things took over. With the birth of television, Australian comedy went in that direction, and the opera houses weren't particularly interested in doing operetta. You got occasionally a very bad *Fledermaus* or a really shocking *Merry Widow*. In fact, I saw Joan Sutherland in *The Merry Widow*, and, I must say, it was not one of her greatest nights. Which means that when I grew up there was no performance tradition any more. A Kálmán here, a Lehár there. But that's it.

UL: And when did you first become acquainted with this genre?

BK: It was through my grandmother, because my opera and music education was taken over by my Hungarian grandmother who came to Australia in 1935 and brought with her her entire central European baggage. She was a great Wagner fan and Bartók fan but also a great Emmerich Kálmán fan. She liked operetta very much, as most Hungarians do. She liked Lehár, but it was really the Kálmán operetta that she adored. I was given Kálmán as part of my musical education, but it was mixed in with Bartók and Wagner, Janáček and Mozart. Quite a good mixture, I think! I was maybe twelve or thirteen years old when I listened for the first time to my grandma's records of *Gräfin Mariza* and *Die Csárdásfürstin*. And I instantly adored it; I was absolutely obsessed by it! It did something to me. I think even then as a teenager I loved its kind of schizophrenia. This perfect combination of the Vienna music, the Budapest music and the Jewish music, and this mixture of pain, melancholy, joy, lust for life and unfulfilled desire fascinated me. Kálmán drips with this fantastic desire; his music is completely marinated in it. I think also that I identified the music with my grandmother. It was like the music of her soul. She was born in Budapest to an upper-middle-class Hungarian family. She went to the opera in Budapest nearly every week, and every month the whole family went to Vienna to go to the Staatsoper. She was this Vienna–Budapest assimilated Jew, who then suddenly found herself in exile. I picked up all that through her love for this music, and I also picked up her desire and her melancholy.

UL: Why do so many young people of today obviously dislike operetta, thinking that it's just fusty and boring?

BK: For a number of reasons: operetta needs the same radical investigation of authenticity that baroque music started to have thirty years ago. Take the interpretations of Bach and Handel from conductors like Klemperer or Furtwängler, or Cavalli performances conducted by Raymond Leppard in Glyndebourne: in their way they are fabulous, but today we know that something is not right. This radical reworking of the entire baroque tradition in the last thirty years with original instruments in combination with rediscovering the way it was sung has brought so many new sounds to musicians as well as to audiences. Operetta hasn't quite had this revolution, though it needs to! Unfortunately, the way operetta has been performed and recorded since 1945 has been so terrible that people have really forgotten the 'original' sound, even though unlike the baroque music there weren't 200 years in between but less than thirty years. If you listen to the very early Offenbach recordings from the 1920s and 1930s or these wonderful René Leibowitz recordings, there's a quality in the way they sing and play Offenbach which I believe is much closer to the way it was done in Offenbach's time. There's a rawness and lightness; it's not sung so perfectly. Up until before the war there was a clear separation between operetta and opera singers because operetta was a genre, a '*Fach*' (subject) of its own, one that operetta stars like Gitta Alpár, Fritzi Massary or Richard Tauber were very proud of being part of. They were bigger stars than most of the opera stars in terms of their fame. Then after the war many opera singers wanted to have a holiday in the land of operetta, people like Nicolai Gedda, Anneliese

Rothenberger, Elisabeth Schwarzkopf. They and other operetta singers in the 1940s, 1950s and 1960s, recorded all these operettas by
Lehár, Kálmán and Abraham. And it's atrocious what happened
because the orchestrations were either rewritten or simplified; the
jazz was taken out, the sex and the erotic and also the hard-edge
Jewish elements of a lot of pieces were excised. It started in the Nazi
time and went on into the 1950s. Suddenly, operetta went from being
a subversive art form – which it always was, in Offenbach's time as
well as in Johann Strauss's time or later in the Berlin operetta – to
being the most harmless and sexless art form. Everything that was
subversive, erotic, ironic and contemporary became harmless, nostalgic and aryanized! It was bad enough that the Nazis killed most of the
composers and librettists of operetta; the double hit came in that they
then aryanized the music that was left. Listen to all the post-war
Kálmán, Abraham, Lehár or Straus recordings. They are almost
unbearable to listen to. They are heavy, they are over-sung, there is
no irony, no lightness, no erotic! Originally, it was never done like
this. The roles were not written for people who sing Wagner, Verdi or
Puccini. The result of all this is that two generations were brought up
with the idea that operetta is something that grandma listened to,
something that doesn't work anymore, some sort of harmless nostalgia. It couldn't be further from the truth.

UL: But why was post-war musical theatre unable to go back to the way it
had been before the war?

BK: It's complicated. After the war, there was a certain degree of guilt
associated with what was essentially a Jewish art form. It was a fact
that there were no Jewish performers left to sing or play it. The majority
of the successful operetta stars of the German speaking world were
Jews. Most of the composers, librettists and performers were also
Jewish, and in Berlin all the producers were. There were also talented
non-Jews, but in the end it was essentially a Jewish art form. And all
these composers, librettists, performers and producers went into exile
or to their death. So, suddenly, you were just left with these dots on the
page. And it affected the whole world, not only Germany. When the
composers or performers went into exile, they didn't have a chance to
build up what they had had before. Emmerich Kálmán, Paul Abraham
or Kurt Weill didn't have real long-term success in America. So, this
mixture of exile and death, guilt and misunderstanding and misinter-
pretation of what the pieces are, all combined to bring in these dreadful
recordings and performances. They took this most subversive branch of

the tree of European music theatre and muted it, desexualized it, de-Jewished, de-jazzed and de-ironized it. And what they left was not just a pale reflection but an absolute destruction.

UL: When did this kind of misunderstanding change?

BK: Let's say there has been something in the air in the last ten years. Various institutions around the world started to look more closely at the material. And the audience started to have an interest in it, too. I don't subscribe to the idea that we link our time today with 'the dance on the volcano' of the 1920s and 1930s. That sounds interesting but is not the truth. That's not the reason why people like the pieces. We're not even in a renaissance yet; we're only at the very beginning of it. We need to be able to say that in their genre, Offenbach, Lehár, Kálmán or Abraham are as good and as important as Verdi, Puccini or Wagner. I hope it will become this courageous one day. Anyway, it's a good time to be involved in operetta. If we had had this discussion twenty years ago, it would have been a completely different discussion.

UL: Does it reach a bigger part of the audience? Or just a small minority?

BK: I can only talk about Berlin. You cannot say that we have a small audience because we have had phenomenal success with these Berlin jazz operettas in the last seven years, which means that there are hundreds and thousands of people of all ages who come to our performances. What has happened is that it's suddenly seen as being legitimate. We have legitimized it in saying: 'These scores and these stories are actually fantastic! And this is the way to perform it!' Though our way is, of course, not the only way. There are a hundred ways to do it.

UL: What are the ingredients of a good operetta?

BK: First, it needs a fabulous score. There are operettas that have great stories and fantastic characters, but when you hear the music you are disappointed. It must have a great score otherwise it's never going to work in the theatre. The second thing is that it has to work on a number of different levels. From the very beginning of the rehearsals for every single operetta production, I keep on saying to the performers that they must do two things: with the left eye you must be deadly serious; treat your characters seriously; treat the situation seriously. With the right eye you must be completely objective and outside the action and winking to the audience saying, 'Isn't this fantastic? Isn't this ridiculous? Isn't life a joke?' So you have to have this combination of 'objective–subjective', of 'serious but ironic', of 'I am treating the situation and characters very seriously, but I'm also laughing at the whole ridiculousness of life.' That's a very hard combination for a performer to achieve. But this sort of schizophrenia has to be part of the performing technique of operetta. And the third thing you need is characters, scenes and situations that can reveal performers' virtuosity in the mixture of singing, dancing, speaking and acting. All these pieces are written for virtuosic performers.

In addition to these qualities is the fact that, though it can be fun, there still has to be something which is being investigated. The Offenbach operettas, for example, are a mixture of politics and Dada – actually Dada was invented by Offenbach. But there is an incredible level of meaning in his emancipated female characters on stage. In the spoken theatre or in the opera of the nineteenth century, women were mainly victims; they died of disease or were killed. Only on the operetta stage appeared emancipated self-confident characters like Helena or the Grand Duchess of Gerolstein.

The Berlin jazz operetta of Abraham delivers another form of subversion: you get the whole spectrum of sexual experience plus the subversion of the Weimar Republic. In Abraham's *Ball in Savoy*, for example, there is a song about Lady Stern and Mr Brown dancing together, which means nothing else other than a New York Jewish lady and a New York African American man dancing jazz together. For us today it seems to be just a delightful song, but in fact in Abraham's time it was a shockingly subversive idea for the audience.

While Offenbach was satirizing the structure of the French political system of his time, Abraham was exploring gender politics, playing with cross-dressing, gender fluidity etc. This is also the case in the operettas by Oscar Straus. Look, for example, at his *Eine Frau, die weiß was sie will* – it's outrageous what the female leading role is talking about – or Madeleine de Faublas in Abraham's *Ball im Savoy*. Or Madeleine de Faublas in Abraham's *Ball im Savoy*. No spoken theatre character and no opera characters spoke like that at this time. The audience came because they wanted exactly that. So, just as in Offenbach's time in the nineteenth century, in Berlin at the beginning of the twentieth century – though the situation was different in Vienna – and certainly also in Budapest, the operetta became this meeting place of subversiveness that actually came from the cabaret, which in Paris and Berlin was very important. Chanson, variété, vaudeville, plus the classical music tradition all mixed together to form this new style of music theatre.

We have to be very clear in the German-speaking world: if the Nazis hadn't come in 1933 and the Jews had been left to stay and these composers had been able to go on with what they had been doing before, goodness knows what masterpieces we would have received. We know that Paul Abraham in *Ball in Savoy* was moving towards through-composed operettas, which means he was moving towards something much more operatic. We know that Kurt Weill was interested in bringing more jazz into his operas. We have *Mahagonny,* but imagine what the next one would have been! The history of German music would have been very different if the German-speaking operetta composers had stayed in Germany. I am sure they would have had a huge influence on the musical landscape. But we can only hypothesize about that.

UL: How can we transfer to our own times the many references of these pieces to the period in which they were created?

BK: I hate the idea of rewriting the dialogues. If the dialogues aren't good enough, then don't do the piece. The dialogues of Offenbach's major pieces are fantastic. The same applies to the texts of Paul Abraham or Oscar Straus. They don't need to be rewritten. Just find a way to perform them. You have to play with another level in the contemporary world to find the double irony in these pieces.

UL: Is operetta queer itself, or is this more part of the mise-en-scène?

BK: Consciously and unconsciously there is an incredible queerness to operetta. We have to go right back to the Greeks, to Aristophanes. Look at *Lysistrata, The Wasps* or *The Birds*! This is where it's coming from. This is the sort of mother of it all. The idea was that you could have Antigone and Medea and the house of Atreus; you could have blood and violence; you could have the murder of children, fathers and mothers and terrible wars – but at the same time you could also have these bacchanalian pieces with big penises and people making fart jokes and women going on strike telling their husbands that they won't have sex any more until they stop the war. The ancient Greeks got it all right! They had the two masks, the mask of comedy and the mask of tragedy. And they knew that human life is made up of both. Just tragedy or just comedy is not going to work. And they treated both parts very seriously. And remember, there were only male actors. So, they played with cross-dressing. In the very inception of comedy in Western theatre there was already a queerness, a playing with sexuality. Jump then to Shakespeare and his comedies, and you find also cross-dressing: thirteen-, fourteen-year-old boys playing women as well as young men. Of course, music theatre is different, but the combination of sexuality, cross-dressing and irony has been a very important part of queer culture for hundreds and hundreds of years. You can call it queer, you can call it camp. I would call it campy queer.

We don't know what it was like to look at Hortense Schneider, who premiered Offenbach's most important female roles like Helena, Boulotte, the Grand Duchess of Gerolstein or La Périchole. You just read the reports and you realize she wasn't a traditionally beautiful woman. She was a very Rubenesque woman in kinky costumes. She was a voluptuous, erotic woman with a very low voice who improvised and constantly played with her sexuality. It must have been amazing. I'm sure at least half of the theatres were full of gay men and gay women. When you go to Emmerich Kálmán and particularly Paul Abraham and the Berlin period of Oscar Straus, you're dealing with a very savvy queerness, though most of the men who wrote these pieces were not homosexual. But there is an awareness that is absolutely connected to queer culture. It's not enough to say there are fabulous costumes, there are dance routines, therefore it's camp and queer. I hate these clichés. That's not why the pieces are camp and queer. Look at the text! Look at the gender playing! Look at the idea of sexuality! Look at the idea of who marries whom! Most of the operettas' marriage scenes are a disaster. Marriage is a disaster in *La belle Hélène* as well as in *Orphée aux enfers*. Offenbach takes the greatest sacrifice story of all time – Orpheus' beloved wife dies, and he risks all and goes into the underworld as a living man to wrench her out of Hades – and subverts that right at the beginning by showing that this marriage is a complete catastrophe. As I said, all this was not happening in the spoken theatre or in the opera. Then in pieces of the Weimar Republic like *Ball in Savoy*, there's a whole layer of bisexuality. That just reflected the Weimar Republic. Berlin was the sex capital of the world. It was Berlin where the Magnus Hirschfeld Institute was founded and where the first Museum of Sexuality opened. So, it makes sense to me that, while in the city of Freud, Vienna, all of this was suppressed, in Berlin it was the absolute opposite: it exploded through jazz. Jazz was the dynamite that exploded the harmlessness of the Viennese operetta.

UL: Is it this what so many younger people now find attractive in operetta?

BK: People say that the Komische Oper Berlin has made operetta groovy and funky. That's nice. But we are not the only people presenting these operettas. We found our way to do them by serving the original score.

You can't just do it with ten instruments. You need a big orchestra like they had when it was performed for the first time, with fabulous brass and percussion sections. It must be a wild sound coming out of the orchestra pit. You must perform them in scale. In the Berlin operettas of the Weimar Republic, there were sometimes performances with three or four hundred people on stage. We now can't do even that. You must create a world which fluctuates between subversiveness and outrageousness. People must feel that this is a place where anything is possible. You must then find the arrangers and musical directors who understand the pieces and their music. And the most important thing is to find the performers who can do it. Because, from Offenbach's time up until 1933, the composers wrote their pieces for particular performers. They weren't just planning to write a 'masterpiece' in their attic for two years. No! It was the fabulous Hortense Schneider who needed a new show, or Fritzi Massary or Richard Tauber. So, let's sit down and write something for these genius performers. And the public came, first of all, because of the performers. They wanted to see the new operetta with Rosy Barsony and Oskar Dénes. They wanted to see the next 'Tauber operetta'. It was an amazingly contemporary art form. We don't have this anymore. My job as director and intendant is to find the contemporary equivalents of those performers who these pieces were written for. And you won't find them among most opera singers.

UL: Given all that, the writing of new operettas seems to have come to an end though. Is it definitely finished, or do you think that the new fascination for operetta one day will bring about new operettas?

BK: That's a question difficult to answer. For sure as an intendant I can't curate it. It has to come from the artists. I don't want to go to a composer saying, 'Would you be interested in writing an operetta?' This is not how it should work. The artists have to be creating it. Because you can't go from writing no operetta to suddenly writing an operetta for the Komische Oper Berlin with 1,200 people in the auditorium and a hundred people on stage. It just doesn't work like that. So where will it come from? I get people sending me operetta ideas, but they are just nostalgic reworkings of what has already been done. I'm ready for the hip-hop composer or the jazz composer to say to me, 'This is my idea for a new piece, Barrie!'

It's not just the music. You have to have an understanding of the genre. The history of operetta is a history which goes back to Aristophanes through Shakespeare, through commedia dell'arte, through Singspiel, into *opéra comique* and further beyond. It's like architecture: you can't design an abstract building without knowing 2,000 years of architecture. So, you can't suddenly write an operetta without knowing what the history of the operetta has been.

Let me go back to this idea that – with exceptions – it's a predominantly Jewish art form. Offenbach's father was a Klezmer musician and a cantor in the synagogue. Offenbach sang as a boy in the synagogue choir in Paris. A German Jew, exiled, teenager, living in Paris. You couldn't get a Frenchman doing what he did. From the very beginning of the nineteenth century, Jewish exile and assimilation or non-assimilation was absolutely in the DNA of operetta. When you look at Emmerich Kálmán, Oscar Straus, Paul Abraham and Kurt Weill and their librettists like Fritz Löhner-Beda and Alfred Grünwald, ingenious writers, you wonder why Jewish artists were so connected to and attracted by this genre. It seems to be clear for me: because operetta itself is in a way about assimilation, irony and disconnectedness. No wonder these Hungarian, Austrian and German Jews felt completely at home in this genre. Also, most of the great American music theatre composers like George Gershwin, Irving Berlin, Rodgers and Hammerstein, Frederick Loewe, Stephen Sondheim – they all were Jews. So is that the core of the problem? Did it all die in 1933? Or did it have a new invention on Broadway with Jewish American composers of musicals? I'd like to be optimistic and say, 'Yes, of course, it's going to have a future.' But if you get me on a non-optimistic day, I'd say, that it all finished in 1933. However, my job here at the Komische Oper Berlin is to ensure that even though these Jewish composers and librettists died without being able to enjoy their success, we can still honour them by listening to their music. Because their pieces are still alive through their music. And that's a burning missionary zeal I have. I'm very proud of what we do in the Komische Oper Berlin. It's great to do *Moses und Aron*; it's great to do *Die Soldaten*; it's great to do *Pelléas et Mélisande*. But the thing that I'm most proud of is that hundreds of thousands of people over the last six years have heard Berlin operetta music that they have never heard before. All these people have heard operetta played and per-formed in a way that is truer, I think, to the composers' intentions than what we have had in the last hundred years.

Select Bibliography

Agate, James. *Immoment Toys: A Survey of Light Entertainment on the London Stage, 1920–1943*. London: Jonathan Cape, 1945.

Ainger, Michael. *Gilbert and Sullivan: A Dual Biography*. Oxford; New York: Oxford University Press, 2002.

Allinson, Mark, *Germany and Austria Since 1814*. Abingdon, UK and New York, Routledge, 2014.

Ames, Roy. *A Critical History of the British Cinema*. London: Secker and Warburg, 1978.

Anderson, James. *The Complete Dictionary of Opera and Operetta*. New York, NY: Wings, 1993.

Anker, Öyvind. *Fullstendig registrant over forestellinger, forfattare, oversettere og komponister. Sesongregister / The Repertoire of Christiania Theatre 1827–1899*. Oslo: Gyldendal Norsk Forlag, 1956.

Anon., '"The Merry Widow" Making a Million', *The New York Times*, 22 Dec. 1907.

Arnbom, Marie-Theres, Kevin Clarke and Thomas Trabitsch, eds. *Die Welt der Operette. Glamour, Stars und Showbusiness*. Vienna: Brandstätter, 2011.

Asenjo Barbieri, Francisco. *La Zarzuela*. Madrid: Ducazcal, 1864.

Bailey, Peter. 'Naughty but Nice: Musical Comedy and the Rhetoric of the Girl, 1892–1914'. In Booth and Kaplan, eds., *The Edwardian Theatre*, 36–60.

Balázs, Béla. *Theory of Film*. Trans. Edith Bone. London: Dobson, 1952. (Originally published as *Filmkultúra*, Budapest: Szikra kiadás, 1948.)

Baranello, Micaela. 'The Operetta Empire: Popular Viennese Music Theater and Austrian Identity, 1900–1930'. PhD dissertation. Princeton University, 2014.

Bartmuss. Hartmut. *Hugo Hirsch: 'Wer wird denn weinen ...'* Berlin: Hentrich & Hentrich, 2012.

Bartoš, František, ed. *Bedřich Smetana: Letters and Reminiscences*. Trans. Daphne Rusbridge. Prague: Artia, 1955.

Bartoš, Josef. *Prozatimní divadlo a jeho opera / The Provisional Theatre and Its Opera*. Prague, 1938.

Becker, Tobias. 'Die Anfänge der Schlagerindustrie: Intermedialität und wirtschaftliche Verflechtung vor dem Ersten Weltkrieg'. *Lied und Populäre Kultur*, 58 (2013): 11–40.

Becker, Tobias. *Inszenierte Moderne. Populäres Theater in Berlin und London, 1880–1930*. Munich: De Gruyter Oldenbourg 2014.

Bellman, Jonathan. *The Style Hongrois in the Music of Western Europe*. Boston: Northeastern University Press, 1993.

Bisztray, George. 'Hungary, 1810–1838'. In Laurence Senelick, ed., *National Theatre in Northern and Eastern Europe, 1746–1900*. Cambridge: Cambridge University Press, 1991.

Bloom, Ursula. *Curtain Call for the Guv'nor: A Biography of George Edwardes*. London: Hutchinson, 1954.

Bond, Jessie. *The Life and Reminiscences of Jessie Bond, the Old Savoyard*. Edited by Ethel MacGeorge. London: John Lane The Bodley Head, 1930.

Booth, Michael R. and Joel H. Kaplan, eds. *The Edwardian Theatre: Essays on Performance and the Stage*. Cambridge: Cambridge University Press, 1996.

Bordman, Gerald. *American Operetta: From H.M.S. Pinafore to Sweeney Todd*. New York: Oxford University Press, 1981.

Bordman, Gerald Martin and Richard Norton. *American Musical Theatre: A Chronicle*. New York: Oxford University Press, 4th ed. 2011 (orig. pub. 1978).

Bortolotto, Mario. 'Sul teatro d'operetta'. *Nuova rivista musicale italiana*, 3 (1971): 420–42.

Bozó, Péter. 'Operetta in Hungary, 1859–1960', Magyar zene a 20. században, MTA BTK ZTI, 2014. http://real.mtak.hu/13117/1/bozo_operetta_in_hungary.pdf (accessed 27 Nov. 2017).

Bradley, Ian C. *Oh Joy! Oh Rapture! The Enduring Phenomenon of Gilbert and Sullivan*. Oxford; New York: Oxford University Press, 2005.

Bradley, Ian, ed. *The Complete Annotated Gilbert and Sullivan*. New York: Oxford University Press, new ed. 2016 (orig. pub. 1996).

Brandl-Risi, Bettina, Ulrich Lenz, Clemens Risi and Rainer Simon, eds. *Kunst der Oberfläche: Operette zwischen Bravour und Banalität*. Leipzig: Henschel, 2015.

Burchell, Samuel C. *Upstart Empire: Paris During the Brilliant Years of Louis Napoleon*. London: MacDonald, 1971.

Burton, Nigel. 'Sullivan Reassessed: See How the Fates'. *The Musical Times*, 141, no. 1873 (Winter 2000): 15–22.

Casares Rodicio, Emilio, ed. *Diccionario de la Zarzuela*. 2 vols. Madrid: ICCMU, 2002–3.

Casares Rodicio, Emilio. *Francisco Asenjo Barbieri. Vol. 1: El hombre y el creador*. Madrid: ICCMU, 1994.

Castle, Charles. *Noël*. London: W.H. Allen, 1972.

Chodkowski, Andrzej, ed. *Encyklopedia muzyki*. 12 vols. Warsaw: Wydawnictwo Naukowe PWN, 2001.

Clarke, Kevin, ed. *Glitter and be Gay: Die authentische Operette und ihre schwulen Verehrer*. Hamburg: Männerschwarm Verlag, 2007.

Collins, José. *The Maid of the Mountains: Her Story*. London: Hutchinson, 1932.

Coward, Noël. *Present Indicative*. London: Heinemann, 1937.

Crittenden, Camille. *Johann Strauss and Vienna: Operetta and the Politics of Popular Culture*. Cambridge: Cambridge University Press, 2000.

Crowther, Andrew. *Gilbert of Gilbert & Sullivan: His Life and Character*. Stroud: History Press, 2011.

Csáky, Moritz. *Ideologie der Operette und Wiener Moderne: Ein kulturhistorischer Essay*. Vienna: Böhlau, 1996.

Czerný, František and Ljuba Klosová, eds. *Dějiny Českého divadla*. Vol. 3 / *The History of Czech Theatre*. Prague: Academia nakladatelství Československé akademie věd, 1977.

Davis, Tracy C. and Peter Holland, eds. *The Performing Century. Nineteenth-Century Theatre History*. Basingstoke: Palgrave Macmillan, 2007.

D'Cruze, Shani. 'Dainty Little Fairies: Women, Gender and the Savoy Operas'. *Women's History Review*, 9, no. 2 (2000): 345–68.

Decker, Todd. *Show Boat: Performing Race in an American Musical*. New York: Oxford University Press, 2013.

Deer, Joe, and Rocco Dal Vera. 'Unit 16.2: Gilbert and Sullivan Operetta'. In *Acting in Musical Theatre: A Comprehensive Course*. London; New York: Routledge, 2008. 320–8.

Dompke, Christoph. *Unterhaltungsmusik und NS-Verfolgung*. Neumünster: Von Bockel 2011.

Drewniak, Bogusław. *Das Theater im NS-Staat. Szenarium deutscher Zeitgeschichte 1933–1945*. Düsseldorf: Droste 1983.

Drone, Jeanette Marie. *Index to Opera, Operetta and Musical Comedy Synopses in Collections and Periodicals*. Metuchen, NJ: Scarecrow Press, 1978.

Eden, David. *Gilbert & Sullivan: The Creative Conflict*. Cranbury: Fairleigh Dickinson University Press, 1986.

Eden, David and Meinhard Saremba, eds. *The Cambridge Companion to Gilbert and Sullivan*. Cambridge: Cambridge University Press, 2009.

Ehrmann-Herfort, Sabine. 'Operette'. In Albrecht Riethmuller, ed., *Handwörterbuch der musikalischen Terminologie*, Vol. 4. Stuttgart: Steiner Verlag, 2001, 505–24.

Ellis, Vivian. *I'm on a See-Saw: An Autobiography*. London: Michael Joseph, 1953.

Everett, William A. ed. *The Cambridge Companion to the Musical*. Cambridge: Cambridge University Press, 2008.

Ewen, David. *The Book of European Light Opera*. New York: Holt, Rinehart and Winston, 1962.

Faris, Alexander. *Jacques Offenbach*. London: Faber & Faber, 1980.

Fenby, Jonathan. *France: A Modern History from the Revolution to the War with Terror*. New York: St. Martin's Press, 2015.

Feurzeig, Lisa. 'Can Creative Interpretation Keep Operetta Alive? Kaìlmaìn's *Die Herzogin von Chicago* at the Vienna *Volksoper* in 2004'. *Studia Musicologica*, 57, no. 3–4 (2016): 441–70.

Filler, Witold. *Rendez-vous z Warszawską operetką / Rendez-Vous with Warsaw Operetta*. Warsaw, Państwowy Instytut Wydawniczy, 1961.

Fink, Robert. 'Rhythm and Text Setting in *The Mikado*'. *19th-Century Music*, 14 (1990): 31–47.

Fiorentino, Waldimaro. *L'operetta italiana. Storia, analisi critica, aneddoti*. Bolzano, Catinaccio, 2006.

Forser, Tomas and Sven Åke Heed, eds. *Ny svensk teaterhistoria. Vol. 2: 1800-talets teater*. Stockholm: Gidlunds förlag, 2007.

Forser, Tomas and Sven Åke Heed, eds. *Ny svensk teaterhistoria. Vol. 3: 1900-talets teater*. Stockholm: Gidlunds förlag, 2007.

Frame, Murray. 'The Early Reception of Operetta in Russian, 1860s-1870s'. *European History Quarterly*, 42, no. 1 (2012): 29–49.

Freifeld, Alice. *Nationalism and the Crowd in Liberal Hungary, 1848–1914*. Washington, DC: Woodrow Wilson Center Press, 2000.

Frey, Stefan. *Was sagt ihr zu diesem Erfolg: Franz Lehár und die Unterhaltungsmusik des 20. Jahrhunderts.* Frankfurt: Insel, 1999.

Frey, Stefan. '*Laughter Under Tears*': *Emmerich Kálmán. An Operetta Biography.* Culver City: Operetta Foundation, 2014.

Fritzsche, Peter. *Reading Berlin 1900.* Cambridge, MA: Harvard University Press, 1996.

Frolova-Walker, Marina and Jonathan Walker. *Music and Soviet Power 1917–1932.* Woodbridge: The Boydell Press, 2012.

Gammond, Peter. *Offenbach: His Life and Times.* London: Omnibus Press, 1980.

Gänzl, Kurt. *The Encyclopedia of the Musical Theatre.* 2 vols. Oxford: Blackwell Reference, 1994.

Gänzl, Kurt and Andrew Lamb, *Gänzl's Book of the Musical Theatre.* London: The Bodley Head,1988.

Gluck, Mary. *The Invisible Jewish Budapest: Metropolitan Culture at the Fin de Siècle.* Madison, WI: University of Wisconsin Press, 2016.

Goodman, Andrew. *Gilbert and Sullivan at Law.* Rutherford; London: Fairleigh Dickinson University Press; Associated University Presses, 1983.

Goron, Michael. *Gilbert and Sullivan's 'Respectable Capers': Class, Respectability and the Savoy Operas 1877–1909.* Palgrave Studies in British Musical Theatre. London: Palgrave Macmillan, 2016.

Green, Stanley. *Encyclopedia of the Musical Theatre.* New York: Dodd, Mead, 1976.

Grosch, Nils, ed. *Aspekte des modernen Musiktheaters in der Weimarer Republik.* Münster: Waxmann, 2004.

Grun, Bernard. *Prince of Vienna: The Life, the Times and the Melodies of Oscar Straus.* London: W. H. Allen, 1955.

Grun, Bernard. *Die leichte Muse: Kulturgeschichte der Operette.* Munich: Langen Müller Verlag, 1961.

Grünberg, Ingrid. '"Wer sich die Welt mit einem Donnerschlag erobern will . . ." Zur Situation und Funktion der deutschsprachigen Operette in den Jahren 1933–1945'. In Hanns-Werner Heister and Hans-Günter Klein, eds., *Musik und Musikpolitik im faschistischen Deutschland.* Frankfurt a. M.: Fischer, 1984, 227–42.

Haken, Boris von. *Der 'Reichsdramaturg': Rainer Schlösser und die Musiktheater-Politik in der NS-Zeit.* Neumünster: Von Bockel, 2007.

Hanák, Péter. *The Garden and the Workshop: Essays on the Cultural History of Vienna and Budapest.* Princeton, NJ: Princeton University Press, 1998.

Harding, James. *Folies de Paris: The Rise and Fall of French Operetta.* London: Chappell, 1979.

Harding, James. *Jacques Offenbach: A Biography.* London: John Calder, 1980.

Harding, James. *Ivor Novello.* London: W. H. Allen, 1987.

Harewood, Earl of, and Anthony Peattie, eds. *The New Kobbé's Opera Book.* London: Ebury Press, 1997.

Harris, S. Jose. *Private Lives, Public Spirit: A Social History of Britain 1870–1914.* Oxford: Oxford University Press, 1993.

Heed, Sven Åke. 'Operett och musikal'. In Tomas Forser and Sven Åke Heed, eds., *Ny svensk teaterhistoria. 3. 1900-talets teater.* Stockholm: Gidlunds förlag. 2007, 258–84.

Henderson, Amy, and Dwight Blocker Bowers. *Red, Hot & Blue: A Smithsonian Salute to the American Musical*. Washington: Smithsonian Institution Press, 1996.

Hirn, Sven. *Operett i Finland 1860–1918*. Svenska Litteratursällskapet i Finland. Helsinki: SLS, 1992.

Hollingshead, John. *'Good Old Gaiety': An Historiette and Remembrance*. London: The Gaiety Theatre Company, 1903.

Hollingshead, John. 'Theatres'. In Walter Besant, ed., *London in the Nineteenth Century*. London: Adam and Charles Black, 1909.

Hooker, Lynn M. 'Turks, Hungarians, and Gypsies: Exoticism and Auto-exoticism in Opera and Operetta'. *Hungarian Studies*, 27, no. 2 (2013): 291–311.

Horne, Alistair. *The Seven Ages of Paris*. New York: Alfred A. Knopf, 2002.

Hughes, Gervase. *The Music of Arthur Sullivan*. London: Macmillan, 1960.

Hughes, Gervase. *Composers of Operetta*. London: Macmillan,1962.

Hüpping, Stefan. *Rainer Schlösser (1899–1945): Der 'Reichsdramaturg'*. Bielefeld: Aisthesis 2012.

Hussey, Andrew. *Paris: The Secret History*. New York: Bloomsbury, 2006.

Hyman, Alan. *The Gaiety Years*. London: Cassell, 1975.

Hyman, Alan. *Sullivan and His Satellites: A Study of English Operettas, 1860–1914*. London: Chappell, 1978.

Iberni, Luis G. *Ruperto Chapí*. Madrid: ICCMU, 1995.

Imre, Zoltàn. 'Operetta Beyond Borders: The Different Versions of *Die Csárdásfürstin* in Europe and the United States (1915–1921)'. *Studies in Musical Theatre*, 7, no. 2 (2013): 175–205.

Jansen, Wolfgang. *Glanzrevuen der Zwanziger Jahre*. Berlin: Hentrich, 1987.

Jarchow, Ute. *Analysen zur Berliner Operette: Die Operetten Walter Kollos (1878–1940) im Kontext der Entwicklung der Berliner Operette*. Munich: AVM, 2013.

Jassa Haro, Ignacio. 'Con un vals en la maleta: viaje y aclimatación de la opereta europea en España'. In Emilio Casares Rodicio, ed., *Cuadernos de Música Iberoamericana*. Vol. 20. Madrid: ICCMU, 2010.

Jelavich, Peter. *Berlin Cabaret*. Cambridge, MA: Harvard University Press, 1993.

Jones, Colin. *Paris: The Biography of a City*. New York: Viking 2004.

Karl, Viola. *Eduard Künneke (1885–1953): Komponistenportrait und Werkverzeichnis*. Berlin: Ries & Erler, 1995.

Katz, Pamela. *The Partnership: Brecht, Weill, Three Women, and Germany on the Brink*. New York: Doubleday, 2015.

Kauffmann, Matthias. 'Operetta and Propaganda in the Third Reich: Cultural Politics and the Metropol-Theater'. In Platt, Linton and Becker, eds., *Popular Musical Theatre in London and Berlin*, 258–73.

Kauffmann, Matthias. *Operette im 'Dritten Reich'. Musikalisches Unterhaltungstheater zwischen 1933 und 1945*. Neumünster: Von Bockel, 2017.

Keller, Otto. *Die Operette in ihrer Geschichtlichen Entwicklung: Musik, Libretto, Darstellung*. Leipzig: Stein Verlag, 1926.

Kennedy, Michael. 'The Poisoned Kiss'. In *Grove Music Online*. https://doi.org/10.1093/gmo/9781561592630.article.O008802 (accessed 10 May 2019).

Kenrick, John. *Musical Theatre: A History*. New York: Bloomsbury, 2017.

Kertzer, Jon. 'Life Plus Ninety-Nine Years: W. S. Gilbert and the Fantasy of Justice'. *Mosaic: An Interdisciplinary Critical Journal*, 36, no. 2 (2003): 1–18.

Kieser, Klaus. *Das Gärtnerplatztheater in München 1932–1944. Zur Operette im Nationalsozialismus*. Frankfurt am Main: Lang, 1991.

Kirkland, Stephane. *Paris Reborn: Napoleon III, Baron Haussmann, and the Quest to Build a Modern City*. New York: St. Martin's Press, 2013.

Klotz, Volker. *Operette: Porträt und Handbuch einer unerhörten Kunst*. Kassel: Bärenreiter, rev. ed. 2004 (orig. pub. Munich: Piper, 1991).

Knapp, Raymond. *The American Musical and the Formation of National Identity*. Princeton, NJ: Princeton University Press, 2005.

Knapp, Raymond. *The American Musical and the Performance of Personal Identity*. Princeton, NJ: Princeton University Press, 2006.

Knapp, Raymond. '"How great thy charm, thy sway how excellent!": Tracing Gilbert and Sullivan's Legacy in the American Musical'. In Eden and Saremba, *The Cambridge Companion to Gilbert and Sullivan*, 201–15.

Knapp, Raymond. *Haydn, Musical Camp, and the Long Shadow of German Idealism*. Durham, NC: Duke University Press, 2018.

Komisarjevsky, Theodore. *Myself and the Theatre*. London: William Heinemann Limited, 1929.

Kracauer, Siegfried. *Jacques Offenbach and the Paris of His Time*. Trans. Gwenda David and Eric Mosbacher. New York: Zone Books, 2002 (orig. pub. London: Constable, 1937).

Krasner, Orly Leah. 'Birth Pangs, Growing Pains and Sibling Rivalry: Musical Theatre in New York, 1900–1920'. In Everett, ed., *The Cambridge Companion to the Musical*, 29–46.

Kuykendall, James Brooks. 'Motives and Methods in Sullivan's Allusions'. In Everett, ed., *The Cambridge Companion to Gilbert and Sullivan*, 122–35.

Kvam, Kela, Janne Risum and Jytte Wiingaard, eds. *Dansk teaterhistorie*. 2 vols. Copenhagen: Gyldendal, 1992–3.

La Gioia, Diana. *I libretti italiani d'operetta nella Biblioteca Nazionale di Roma*. Florence: Olschki, 1979.

Lagerroth, Ulla-Britta and Ingeborg Nordin Hennel, eds. *Ny svensk teaterhistoria. Vol. 2: 1800-talets teater*. Stockholm: Gidlunds förlag, 2007.

Lamb, Andrew. *150 Years of Popular Musical Theatre*. New Haven, CT: Yale University Press, 2000.

Lamb, Andrew. 'Operetta, §5: The Modern Scene'. In Stanley Sadie, ed., *The New Grove Dictionary of Music and Musicians*. Vol. 18. London: Macmillan, 2nd ed. 2001, 497–8.

Lamb, Andrew. *Leslie Stuart: The Man Who Composed Florodora*. London: Routledge, 2002.

Lamb, Andrew and Webber, Christopher. 'De Madrid a Londres: Pablo Luna's English Operetta, The First Kiss', 2016. www.academia.edu/26447008 (accessed 10 May 2019).

Lange, Kerstin. *Tango in Paris und Berlin: Eine transnationale Geschichte der Metropolenkultur um 1900*. Göttingen: Vandenhoeck & Ruprecht, 2015.

Lareau, Alan. *Victor Hollaender: Revue meines Lebens: Erinnerungen an einen Berliner Unterhaltungskomponisten um 1900*. Berlin: Hentrich & Hentrich, 2014.

Laskaris, Nikolaos I. *Historia tou neohellenikou theatrou / History of Modern Greek Theatre*. Vol. 1. Athens: M. Vassiliou, 1938–9.

Letellier, Robert Ignatius. *Opéra-Comique. A Sourcebook*. Newcastle upon Tyne: Cambridge Scholars Publishing, 2010.

Letellier, Robert Ignatius. *Operetta: A Sourcebook*. 2 vols. Newcastle upon Tyne: Cambridge Scholars Publishing, 2015.

Linhardt, Marion. *Residenzstadt und Metropole: Zu einer kulturellen Topographie des Wiener Unterhaltungstheaters (1858–1918)*. Berlin: De Gruyter, 2012 (orig. pub. Tübingen: Niemeyer, 2006).

Linke, Norbert. *Johann Strauß (Sohn) in Selbstzeugnissen und Bilddokumenten*. Reinbek bei Hamburg: Rowohlt, 1982.

Low, Rachel. *The History of the British Film 1929–1939: Film Making in 1930s Britain*. London: George Allen and Unwin, 1985.

Lubbock, Mark. *The Complete Book of Light Opera*. With an American section by David Ewen. London: Putnam, 1962.

MacQueen-Pope, Walter J. and David L. Murray, *Fortune's Favourite: The Life and Times of Franz Lehár*. London: Hutchinson, 1953.

MacQueen-Pope, Walter J. *Ivor: The Story of an Achievement*. London: W. H. Allen, 1951.

McConachie, Bruce. *Melodramatic formations. American theatre and society, 1820–1870*. Studies in Theatre, History and Culture. Iowa City: University of Iowa Press, 1992.

McKay, Frederic Edward. '"Merry Widow" Wins an Instant Success', *The Evening Mail*, New York, 22 October 1907.

McMillin, Scott. *The Musical as Drama*. Princeton: Princeton University Press, 2006.

Mejías García, Enrique. 'Cuestión de géneros: la zarzuela española frente al desafío historiográfico'. In Tobias Brandenberger, ed., *Dimensiones y desafíos de la zarzuela*. Münster: LIT Verlag, 2014.

Minor, Ryan. 'Operetta Dramaturgies Today? On Barrie Kosky's Ball im Savoy'. In Brandl-Risi, Risi and Simon, eds., *Kunst der Oberfläche*, 208–10.

Morat, Daniel, Tobias Becker, Kerstin Lange, Johanna Niedbalski, Anne Gnausch and Paul Nolte. *Weltstadtvergnügen: Berlin 1880–1930*. Göttingen: Vandenhoeck & Ruprecht, 2016.

Nemes, Peter. *The Once and Future Budapest*. DeKalb, IL: Northern Illinois University Press, 2005.

Newark, Cormac and William Weber, eds. *The Oxford Handbook of the Operatic Canon*. New York: Oxford University Press, forthcoming.

Niccolai, Michela. '"Oh fior di thé, t'amo credi a me!" Alcuni aspetti della ricezione del mito-*Butterfly* nella canzone e nell'operetta fino agli anni Trenta'. In Arthur Groos and Virgilio Bernardoni, eds., *Madama Butterfly: l'orientalismo di fine secolo, l'approccio pucciniano, la ricezione*. Florence: Leo Olschki, 2008, 375–91.

Niccolai, Michela and Clair Rowden, eds. *Musical Theatre in Europe 1830–1945*. Turnhout: Brepols, 2017.

Niska, Adolf. *Mitt livs mazurka med Thalia. Äventyr i olika länder.* Stockholm: Albert Bonniers Förlag, 1931.

Noble, Peter. *Ivor Novello: Man of the Theatre.* London: Falcon Press, 1951.

Norton, Richard C., *A Chronology of American Musical Theater.* 3 vols. New York: Oxford University Press, 2002.

Norton, Richard C., 'Coward & Novello'. Operetta Research Center Amsterdam. http://operetta-research-center.org/coward-novello/ (accessed 9 May 2019).

Odenwald, Florian. *Der nazistische Kampf gegen das 'Undeutsche' in Theater und Film 1920–1945.* Munich: Utz, 2006.

Oost, Regina B. *Gilbert and Sullivan: Class and the Savoy Tradition, 1875–1896.* Farnham; Burlington: Ashgate, 2009.

Oppicelli, Ernesto. *Operetta. Da Hervé al Musical Hall.* Genoa: Sagep Editrice, 1985.

Oster, Louis. *Guide raisonné et déraisonnable de l'opérette et de la comédie musicale.* Paris: Fayard, 2008.

Otte, Marline. *Jewish Identities in German Popular Entertainment, 1890–1933.* Cambridge: Cambridge University Press, 2006.

Paavolainen, Pentti. 'Two Operas or One – or None. Crucial Moments in the Competition of Operatic Audiences in Helsinki in the 1870s'. In Anne Sivuoja, Owe Ander, Ulla-Britta Broman-Kananen and Jens Hesselager, eds., *Opera on the Move in the Nordic Countries during the Long 19th Century.* Docmus Research Publications 4. Helsinki: Sibelius-Academy, 2012.

Piano, Roberto. *Addio giovinezza: l'operetta a Torino.* Turin: Beppe Grande editore, 2002.

Pitts, Stephanie E. 'Champions and Aficionados: Amateur and Listener Experiences of the Savoy Operas in Performance'. In D. Eden and M. Saremba, eds., *The Cambridge Companion to Gilbert and Sullivan.* Cambridge: Cambridge University Press, 190–200.

Platt, Len. 'West End Musical Theatre and the Representation of Germany'. In Platt, Becker and Linton, eds., *Popular Musical Theatre in London and Berlin,* 224–41.

Platt, Len. *Musical Comedy on the West End Stage, 1890–1939.* Basingstoke: Palgrave Macmillan, 2004.

Platt, Len, Tobias Becker and David Linton, eds. *Popular Musical Theatre in London and Berlin, 1890–1939.* Cambridge: Cambridge University Press, 2014.

Prokopovych, Markian. 'Celebrating Hungary? Johann Strauss's Der Zigeunerbaron and the Press in Fin-de-Siècle Vienna and Budapest'. *Austrian Studies,* 25 (2017): 118–35.

Prokopovych, Markian. *In the Public Eye: The Public Opera House, the Audience and the Press, 1884–1919 .* Vienna: Böhlau, 2014.

Qvamme, Børre. *Opera og operette i Kristiania.* Oslo: Solum Forlag, 2004.

Rappaport, Erika D. *Shopping for Pleasure: Women in the Making of London's West End.* Princeton, NJ: Princeton University Press, 2000.

Raptis, Michalis A. *Epitomi historia tou Hellinikou Melodramatos kai tis Ethnikis Lyrikis Skinis 1888–1988 / A Concise History of Greek Melodrama and Greek National Opera.* Athens: Ktimatiki Trapeza, 1989.

Raymond, Jack, *Show Music on Record from the 1890s to the 1980s.* New York: Frederick Ungar Publishing, 1982.

Rischbieter, Henning, ed. *Theater im 'Dritten Reich': Theaterpolitik, Spielplanstruktur, NS-Dramatik*. Seelze-Velber: Kallmeyer, 2000.

Romsics, Ignác. *Hungary in the Twentieth Century*. Budapest: Corvina/Osiris, 1999.

Roser, Hans-Dieter. *Franz von Suppé: Werk und Leben, Neue Musikportraits III*. Vienna: Steinbauer, 2007.

Schaller, Wolfgang, ed. *Operette unterm Hakenkreuz. Zwischen hoffähiger Kunst und 'Entartung'*. Beiträge einer Tagung der Staatsoperette Dresden. Berlin: Metropol, 2007.

Schneidereit, Otto. *Operette A–Z: Ein Streifzug durch die Welt der Operette und des Musicals*. Berlin: Henschelverlag, 1975.

Schweitzer, Marlis. *Transatlantic Broadway: The Infrastructural Politics of Global Performance*. Philadelphia: University of Pennsylvania Press, 2009.

Schweitzer, Marlis. *When Broadway was the Runway: Theatre, Fashion, and American Culture*. Philadelphia: University of Pennsylvania Press, 2009.

Scott, Derek B. *German Operetta on Broadway and in the West End, 1900–1940*. Cambridge: Cambridge University Press, 2019.

Scott, William Herbert. *Edward German*. London: Cecil Palmer, 1932.

Sebestyén, György. *Paul Ábrahám: Aus dem Leben eines Operettenkomponisten*. Vienna: Verlag der Österreichischen Staatsdruckerei, 1987.

Sempoliński, Ludwik. *Wielcy artyści małych scen / Great artists of small stages*. Warsaw: Czytelnik, 1977.

Short, Ernest. *Sixty Years of Theatre*. London: Eyre & Spottiswoode, 1951.

Šípek, Karel. *Vzpomínky na Prozatímní / Reminiscences of the Provisional (Theatre)*. Prague, 1918.

Smaczny, Jan. *Daily Repertoire of the Provisional Theatre in Prague, Chronological List*. Prague: Miscellanea Muscologica, 1994.

Snelson, John. *Andrew Lloyd Webber*. New Haven: Yale University Press, 2004.

Sontag, Susan. 'Notes on Camp' [1964]. In *Against Interpretation [and Other Essays]*. New York: Dell, 1966, 275–92.

Sorba, Carlotta. 'The Origins of the Entertainment Industry: The Operetta in Late Nineteenth-Century Italy'. *Journal of Modern Italian Studies*, 11, no. 3 (2006): 282–302.

Stempel, Larry. *Showtime: A History of the Broadway Musical Theater*. New York: W. W. Norton, 2010.

Steyn, Mark. *Broadway Babies Say Goodnight: Musicals Then and Now*. London: Faber, 1997.

Stites, Richard. *Russian Popular Culture: Entertainment and Society since 1900*. Cambridge: Cambridge University Press, 1992.

Szwankowski, Eugeniusz. *Teatry Warszawy w latach 1765–1918 / Warsaw theatres in 1765–1918)*. Warsaw: Państwowe Wydawnictwo Naukowe, 1979.

Taylor, Timothy D. *Beyond Exoticism: Western Music and the World*. Durham, NC: Duke University Press, 2007.

Thomas, Gavin. 'The Sullivan Paradox. A Fresh Look at Sullivan's Achievements: And Failures'. *The Musical Times*, 133, no. 1791 (May 1992): 222–4.

Traubner, Richard. *Operetta: A Theatrical History*. New York: Routledge, rev. ed. 2003 (orig. pub. Garden City, NY: Doubleday, 1983).

Traversetti, Bruno. *L'operetta*. Milan: Mondadori, 1985.

Tsakasianos, Ioannis. *Theatrika erga. Apo to komeidyllio sto melodrama / Theatre Plays. From Comic Idyll to Music Theatre 1876–1898*, ed. Georgia Kokla-Papadatou. Zante: Public Historical Library of Zante, 2008.

Tyrrell, John. *Czech Opera*. Cambridge: Cambridge University Press, 1988.

Versteeg, Margot. *De Fusiladores y Morcilleros (El discurso cómico del género chico, 1870–1910)*. Amsterdam: Rodopi, 2000.

Wagner, Heinz. *Das große Operettenbuch: 120 Komponisten und 430 Werke*. Berlin: Parthas-Verl., 1997.

Wearing, J. P. *The London Stage 1890–1959: A Calendar of Productions, Performers, and Personnel*. 14 vols. Lanham, MD: Rowman and Littlefield, 2nd ed. 2013.

Webb, Paul. *Ivor Novello: A Portrait of a Star* [1999]. London: Haus Publishing, rev. ed. 2005.

Webber, Christopher, ed. *zarzuela.net*. www.zarzuela.net/, 1997–2017.

Webber, Christopher. 'The alcalde, the negro and "la bribona": "género ínfimo" zarzuela, 1900–1910'. In Max Doppelbauer and Kathrin Sartingen, eds., *De la zarzuela al cine. Los medios de comunicación populares y su traducción de la voz marginal*. Munich: Martin Meidenbauer, 2009, 63–76.

Webber, Christopher. *The Zarzuela Companion*. Lanham, MD: Scarecrow Press, 2002.

Williams, Carolyn. 'Comic Opera: English Society in Gilbert and Sullivan'. In Robert Gordon and Olaf Jubin, eds., *The Oxford Handbook of the British Musical*. Oxford Handbooks. New York: Oxford University Press, 2016, 91–116.

Williams, Carolyn. *Gilbert and Sullivan: Gender, Genre, Parody. Gender and Culture*. New York: Columbia University Press, 2011.

Wilson, Sandy. *Ivor*. London: Michael Joseph, 1975.

Wood, Linda. *British Films 1927–1939*. London: British Film Institute, 1986.

Wypych-Gawrońska, Anna. *Warszawski teatr operetowy i operetkowy w latach 1880–1915 / Warsaw opera and operetta theatre in 1880–1915*. Częstochowa: Wydawnictwo im. Stanisława Podobińskiego, 2011

Xepapadakou, Avra. 'Idolatry and Sacrilege: Offenbach's Operetta in Nineteenth-century Athens'. *Studies in Musical Theatre*, 8, no. 2 (2014), 129–41.

Xepapadakou, Avra and Alexandros Charkiolakis. *Interspersed by Musical Entertainment: Music in Greek Salons of the Nineteenth Century*, Athens: Hellenic Music Centre, 2017.

Xepapadakou, Avra. 'European Itinerart Opera and Operetta Companies Touring in the Near and Middle East'. In Reinhard Strohm, ed., *The Music Road, Coherence and Diversity in Music from the Mediterranean to India*. Oxford: Oxford University Press, 2019, 316–31.

Yates, W. E. *Theatre in Vienna: A Critical History, 1776–1995*. Cambridge: Cambridge University Press, 1996.

Young, Clinton D. *Music Theater and Popular Nationalism in Spain, 1880–1930*. Baton Rouge: Louisiana State University Press, 2016.

Index

[305]